THE
DREAM
REVISITED

THE
DREAM
REVISITED

*Contemporary Debates About Housing,
Segregation, and Opportunity in the
Twenty-First Century*

EDITED BY
INGRID GOULD ELLEN
AND JUSTIN PETER STEIL

Columbia University Press
New York

Columbia University Press
Publishers Since 1893
New York   Chichester, West Sussex
cup.columbia.edu

Library of Congress Cataloging-in-Publication Data
Names: Ellen, Ingrid Gould, 1965- editor. | Steil, Justin, editor.
Title: The dream revisited : contemporary debates about housing segregation and
opportunity in the twenty-first century / edited by Ingrid Ellen and Justin Peter Steil.
Description: New York : Columbia University Press, [2019]
Identifiers: LCCN 2018035787| ISBN 9780231183628 (hardback) |
    ISBN 9780231183635 (pbk.) | ISBN 9780231545044 (e-book.)
Subjects: LCSH: Discrimination in housing—United States. | African
    Americans—Housing. | Minorities—Housing—United States. |
    Segregation—United States.
Classification: LCC HD7288.76.U5 D74 2019 | DDC 363.5/10973—dc23 LC record
available at https://lccn.loc.gov/2018035787

Cover design: Milenda Nan Ok Lee
Cover photo: dbimages / © Alamy

CONTENTS

PART III: CONSEQUENCES OF SEGREGATION

ACKNOWLEDGMENTS

We have many people to thank for helping us to produce this book and the "slow-debate" blog from which it draws. First, and foremost, we could not have produced this book without the more than 100 contributors who were willing to share their insights about segregation and to engage in reasoned debates with their colleagues. But many others whose names do not appear on the contributor list deserve thanks too. Vicki Been, Shannon Moriarty, Jessica Yager, and other colleagues at New York University's Furman Center helped to envision the original Dream Revisited project and to shape it along the way. The Open Society Foundation provided essential support that allowed us to create the original Furman Center blog. The project initially gained momentum through the contributions of several scholars in residence at NYU in 2013–2014, including Roger Andersson, Leah Boustan, Camille Charles, Charles Clotfelter, Jennifer Hochschild, Jerry Kang, Desmond King, Christopher McCrudden, Mary Pattillo, Robert Sampson, and Patrick Sharkey. Many research assistants at NYU and MIT patiently helped us to check citations and to copy edit, including Haleigh Collins, Reed Jordan, Nick Kelly, Ronnie Seeley, and Obiamake Ude. The students who took the Dream Revisited seminar at MIT that was centered on the debates inspired us to complete the book, asking candid and incisive questions that informed the substance of our introductory chapters. Finally, the anonymous reviewers and the editorial team at Columbia University Press offered critical feedback that helped us translate the prior work into this book.

THE
DREAM
REVISITED

INTRODUCTION

Segregation is the separation or setting apart of one group of people from others. This volume focuses on the separation or setting apart of people on the basis of race or income in places of residence in the United States. Residential clustering by race, ethnicity, or income need not be inherently troubling if it is not a product of force, coercion, or constrained choices. People may affirmatively choose to live among those who share experiences, languages, collective histories, or cultural references. And individuals in the contemporary United States surely have some agency as to where they choose to live.

So why do we care about residential or educational segregation in the United States today? From the perspective of some sociologists and political philosophers, the separation of people spatially is one mechanism through which people are set apart socially, politically, and economically. It is a mechanism through which durable categories of inequality, such as race, are created and maintained.[1] From the perspective of some historians and advocates, contemporary racial segregation is the direct consequence of decades of white supremacist policies that continue to perpetuate racial inequality and require correction or reparation to create a truly multiracial democracy.[2]

This book takes as a starting point the belief that all people should be able to live with equal dignity and recognition of their humanity, and that part of the realization of the ideals of the United States is a continuing responsibility to advance equal access to opportunity for all individuals. Even with these basic principles as a starting point, there is still significant disagreement about the causes of contemporary residential segregation, the consequences of that segregation, and how we as individuals and as a nation should address it. Despite substantial research on these issues, it is not always clear what mechanisms perpetuate residential segregation and connect that segregation to inequality or what interventions can increase access to opportunity. Should the goal be more equal opportunities to choose among a full range of housing and neighborhood options? More racially integrated neighborhoods? Access to equal opportunities in neighborhoods that are predominantly nonwhite? Is the solution greater enforcement of existing fair housing regulations? The removal of local zoning and regulatory obstacles to more integrated communities? A more robust and better-designed housing voucher program? Greater investment in low-income communities of color? The book brings together scholars, policy makers, practitioners, and advocates with different perspectives on these questions in order to advance our knowledge of residential segregation and integration. Their debates show how much we can learn from engaging with perspectives with which we disagree. Such discussion is critical if we want to make progress in understanding why people live where they do, why that matters, and what constitutes the most appropriate and effective role for government action.

A Brief History of Segregation

Many societies historically have had some form of residential segregation to separate political, economic, or religious elites from everyone else, whether forbidden cities for emperors or temple complexes for priests. Through growing global trade and urbanization, districts for those marked as foreign because of their country of origin or religion became more prevalent in Europe in the 1400s and 1500s. One of the most famous of these was the district in Venice where Jewish residents were constrained to live. Indeed, the term "ghetto" that we are familiar with in the United States came from the name given to the district in Venice where Jewish residents were forced to withdraw at night.

In the process of subsequent colonial expansion, European powers developed and codified structures of systematic residential segregation by race in colonial cities such as Madras, Calcutta, and Hong Kong. The historian Carl Nightingale has unearthed the codification of these early formal segregation policies in maps and laws and has further identified the role that colonial powers played in the global spread of public policies requiring residential segregation by race.[3]

These systems of racial segregation arguably reached their apogee and had their most lasting impact in the United States. In the brief Reconstruction period after the Civil War, African Americans were elected in large numbers to local and national offices, from city councils to courts to the U.S. Senate.[4] But less than a decade after the Civil War ended, Southern resistance to black

equality led to the rise of the "Redeemers," the Ku Klux Klan, and other organizations leading campaigns of political terrorism to enforce white supremacy,
both through law and through violence. Jim Crow laws in the South restricted
by race the right to vote, to serve on juries, and to hold political office, and
they established *de jure* racial segregation in schools, public transportation,
and public accommodations. The Supreme Court approved of laws requiring
segregation in public accommodations in *Plessy v. Ferguson* (1896) and in public schools in *Berea v. Kentucky* (1908), among other cases.[5] Custom and law
similarly enshrined segregation in Northern neighborhoods, educational institutions, and labor markets. At the same time, explicit racial zoning ordinances
in the West targeted Asian Americans and Latinos, including alien land laws
designed to limit Asian property ownership.

In conjunction with the rise of Jim Crow laws, white mob violence against
integrated neighborhoods in the late 1890s and early 1900s drove African
Americans from their homes and businesses and helped create a newly segregated urban landscape, especially across the South and the Midwest.[6] Between
1910 and 1917, more than thirty cities passed zoning ordinances "to preserve
the public peace and promote the general welfare by . . . requiring . . . the use
of separate blocks for residences, places of abode and places of assembly by
white and colored people respectively" and to make it a crime "for any colored
person to move into or use as a residence" any building "on a block occupied
in whole or in part by white persons."[7] Legal restrictions were accompanied by
continuing violence. The "Red Summer" of 1919 witnessed white mobs attack-
ing African American neighborhoods and crowds in cities across nearly twenty
states, from Arkansas to Texas, Alabama to New York, Connecticut to Tennes-
see, and Maryland to Nebraska.[8] In the 1920s, prosperous black communities
were burned to the ground by white mobs in Tulsa, Oklahoma and Rosewood,
Florida, among other locations.[9] Recent analyses using complete census man-
uscript files to derive a measure of segregation based on the racial similarity of
next-door neighbors have found that urban areas in the South were the most
segregated in the country at the beginning of the twentieth century and that
segregation only increased in subsequent decades.[10] One factor contributing
to increasing segregation during this period was a national increase in racial
sorting at the household level.[11]

At the same time, real estate developers such as Edward Bouton, director of
the Roland Park Company in Baltimore, and J. C. Nichols, of the J. C. Nichols
Company in Kansas City, were working with landscape architects Frederick
Law Olmsted, Jr. and John Charles Olmsted to popularize suburban living in
planned communities.[12] A crucial attraction of these new suburban developments was reliance on detailed deed restrictions governing the use and occupancy of properties. Beginning in 1913, in Baltimore's Guilford neighborhood,
those covenants included explicit prohibitions on residence by nonwhites.[13]

After the National Association for the Advancement of Colored People (NAACP) challenged explicit racial zoning provisions and the Supreme Court found these municipal laws unconstitutional in *Buchanan v. Warley* (1917), efforts to mandate segregation shifted to the promotion of private racially restrictive covenants by real estate developers and private neighborhood improvement associations.[14] These legally binding agreements attached to the property deed took many forms, but generally required future owners to sell the property only to white buyers. With the support of the National Association of Real Estate Boards and the National Conference on City Planning, these racially restrictive covenants spread quickly across the country, from Baltimore to Kansas City, Chicago, Los Angeles, and hundreds of other cities in between.[15] By 1924, the National Association of Real Estate Boards had revised its code of ethics to prohibit realtors from "introducing into a neighborhood a character of property or occupancy, members of any race or nationality, or any individual whose presence will clearly be detrimental to property values in that neighborhood."[16]

To encourage mortgage lending and home building during the Great Depression, Congress created the Federal Housing Administration in 1934 to insure mortgages and encourage long-term loans with high loan-to-value ratios and fixed monthly payments. The Federal Housing Administration created an Underwriting Manual that encouraged "proper zoning and deed restrictions" as protection against adverse influences that undermine "desirable neighborhood character."[17] It stated that the "more important among the adverse influential factors are the ingress of undesirable racial or nationality groups" and assigned more favorable ratings to those properties and neighborhoods with restrictive covenants.[18] It further encouraged the use of a model restrictive covenant, which provided that "no persons of any race other than [race to be inserted] shall use or occupy any building or any lot, except that this covenant shall not prevent occupancy by domestic servants of a different race domiciled with an owner or tenant." Subsequent versions of the Underwriting Manual continued these provisions encouraging racially restrictive covenants, encouraged "barriers" to prevent "the infiltration of . . . inharmonious racial groups," and included a warning against homes in neighborhoods where public schools included "an incompatible racial element."[19]

Beginning in 1935, the federal Home Owners Loan Corporation created "Residential Security Maps" that color-coded neighborhoods of major cities according to its perception of their security for mortgage lending. Neighborhoods whose residents were primarily nonwhite or who came from multiple racial or ethnic backgrounds were generally colored red, indicating that lending was discouraged, leading to the term "redlining" to describe practices of limiting or denying financial services to residents because of the racial and ethnic composition of the neighborhood. These Federal Housing Administration provisions and Home Owners Loan Corporation maps encouraged private discrimination by lenders, brokers, sellers, and landlords and meant that residents of predominantly nonwhite or racially integrated neighborhoods would have to pay significantly more for mortgage financing, if they could obtain it at all.[20] Between 1880 and 1940, levels of segregation increased dramatically in all areas of the United States.[21] The likelihood that an African American household had a non–African American neighbor dropped by more than 15 percentage points over the first half of the century.[22] After multiple legal challenges led by the NAACP, the Supreme Court in *Shelley v. Kraemer* (1948) held the private racially restrictive covenants that had spread through the first half of the twentieth century to be unenforceable by the courts. Even without legally enforceable restrictive covenants, however, the Federal Housing Administration, the Veterans' Administration, and the majority of the banking industry continued to discriminate by race in the provision of mortgage insurance and mortgage loans at least into the mid-1960s. This discrimination meant that the loan programs that facilitated widespread suburbanization after World War II effectively locked most black households out of the opportunity to move to new developments and continued to limit their ability to accumulate home equity.[23] By purchasing homes with government-guaranteed mortgages in all-white postwar suburbs, white Americans "came to accept as natural the conflation of whiteness and property ownership with upward social mobility," creating a new collective identity based on issues of property, taxation, and segregation.[24]

With public investment in suburban infrastructure and private investment in suburban land came growing disinvestment from inner cities in the postwar period. Congress passed the Housing Acts of 1949 and 1954 to address urban decline with national urban renewal programs. Urban renewal made federal funds available to municipalities to acquire land, clear it, and prepare it for redevelopment. The program was frequently used to raze poor, predominantly African American neighborhoods that were seen as "blighted" or as encroaching on central business districts or elite institutions. Those displaced residents were frequently moved to public housing developments or other land away from business centers, further dispossessing black households and contributing to segregation.[25]

The civil rights movement challenged public policies and private practices contributing to segregation throughout the twentieth century, from municipal segregation ordinances to racially restrictive covenants to redlining. As we have seen, the NAACP succeeded in invalidating segregation ordinances in *Buchanan v. Warley* (1917) and racially restrictive covenants in *Shelley v. Kraemer* (1948). In 1953, NAACP attorney Thurgood Marshall argued before the Supreme Court, on behalf of black elementary school students denied access to integrated schools, that "if segregation thus necessarily imports inequality, it makes no great difference whether we say that the Negro is wronged because he is segregated, or that he is wronged because he received unequal treatment."[26] In its subsequent decision in *Brown v. Board of Education* (1954), the Court held that "[s]eparate educational facilities are inherently unequal" and that segregation in public education deprived black students of their right to equal protection of the laws guaranteed by the Fourteenth Amendment.[27] The *Brown* decision continues to be a touchstone in the struggle for racial justice and equality today. Efforts to enforce the ruling were met with hostility and violence, however, and racial discrimination in housing by lenders, brokers, landlords, and other private actors continued to be legally permissible. After the passage of the Voting Rights Act in 1965, Martin Luther King, Jr. and the Southern Christian Leadership Conference in January 1966 announced the start of a collaboration with the Coordinating Council of Community Organizations on the Chicago Freedom Campaign to "eradicate a vicious system" of housing discrimination and residential segregation "which seeks to further colonize thousands of Negroes within a slum environment."[28]

Success at passing fair housing legislation was elusive, however, at the state and especially the federal level. At the state level, fair housing legislation, to the extent it was passed at all, lagged behind fair employment and public accommodation laws.[29] At the federal level, President Lyndon Johnson pushed for a federal fair housing bill in 1966 and 1967, but it was roundly defeated both times. One of the bill's sponsors, Senator Walter Mondale, recalled, "A lot of civil rights was about making the South behave and taking the teeth from George Wallace," but the proposed fair housing law "came right to the neighborhoods across the country. This was civil rights getting personal."[30]

Urban uprisings across the country in 1967 and previous years led President Johnson to convene a commission to study these "civil disorders." The Kerner Commission's report, released in February 1968, described the nation as "moving toward two societies, one black, one white—separate and unequal."[31] The report recommended, among other prescriptions, that the federal government "enact a comprehensive and enforceable open housing law to cover the sale or rental of all housing" and that it "reorient federal housing programs to place more low and moderate income housing outside of ghetto areas."[32] Whether the highly publicized report would actually lead to legislative change was unclear.

Then, on April 4, 1968, Martin Luther King, Jr. was assassinated, and the threat of racial conflict seemed to consume the country. One week after King's assassination, Congress finally passed the Fair Housing Act, prohibiting discrimination on the basis of race, religion, national origin, or sex, in the sale, rental, or financing of a home. The Fair Housing Act was later amended in 1988 to prohibit discrimination on the basis of disability or family status.

The Fair Housing Act also instructed the Department of Housing and Urban Development (HUD) to ensure that its funds were used "affirmatively to further" fair housing. President Richard Nixon's first appointee as HUD Secretary, George Romney, sought to fulfill that mandate by denying HUD funds to municipalities that continued to discriminate and that used zoning to exclude nonwhite residents, in order to remove what he called the "high-income white noose" surrounding predominantly black urban communities.[33] President Nixon instructed his aides simply to "stop this" and eventually forced Romney from the Cabinet.[34]

The causes of continuing segregation by race and increasing segregation by income today are more complex than they were fifty or a hundred years ago. In the 1976 General Social Survey, nearly two out of every three white respondents nationwide favored a hypothetical local law allowing homeowners to discriminate on the basis of race when selling their home.[35] By 2016, that share had fallen dramatically, but still included more than one out of every seven white respondents.[36] Most agree that the history of institutional racism continues to play some role in shaping today's residential patterns, but households today have significantly more freedom to choose what metropolitan areas and neighborhoods they live in than they did a half-century ago. Indeed, as the twentieth century advanced, white departures from integrated neighborhoods and white flight in response to black arrivals increased as a factor contributing to segregation.[37] The causes of continued segregation continue to be analyzed, updated, and debated, as discussions in this book will show.

One significant factor contributing to segregation today is the fragmented political boundaries of municipalities within most metropolitan areas. The United States has a dramatically fragmented structure of local government, with more than ninety thousand local governments and an average of more than one hundred municipalities per metropolitan area.[38] The economist Charles Tiebout has suggested that this proliferation of local governments is efficient in that it allows residents to sort into municipalities by selecting the one that best meets their preferred set of amenities and their desire (or ability) to pay for those amenities through taxes.[39] But these municipal governments are also invested with significant power, especially over local land use. They frequently use this power to restrict the type and number of housing units within their borders, leading local government boundaries to serve often as boundaries between different socioeconomic or racial groups.[40]

Any simple dichotomy of poor black cities and affluent white suburbs, however, can no longer capture the reality of segregation in metropolitan regions in the United States, if it ever did.[41] Metropolitan areas are now home to an increasingly multiethnic population as well as a significant minority middle class, spread across a range of urban and suburban communities. Public concern about segregation in recent years has focused less on suburban exclusion than on urban gentrification and the changing racial and income composition of many central-city neighborhoods. Despite the transformation of our population and our geographies, residential segregation based on race nevertheless continues to characterize both our schools and our living environments.

Whatever the causes, the architecture of metropolitan segregation has proven durable. A particularly vivid example of this durability is how rapidly the residential patterns of the growing Latino population have become part of the structure of spatial stratification long experienced by African Americans.[42] The structures established over generations to maintain segregation by race have also arguably contributed to exacerbating segregation by income, which has increased over the past three decades in both neighborhoods and schools.[43] There is growing evidence that, contrary to the cherished U.S. ideal of social mobility, disparities in wealth are ever more difficult to overcome. There is also evidence that aspects of our metropolitan areas, including segregation by race and by income, play a significant role in transmitting inequality from one generation to the next.

As the history above suggests, residential segregation has also been the subject of intense political debate and policy conflict. The effects of the Fair Housing Act, while significant, have long been limited by lack of funding for investigation and enforcement.[44] Perhaps the most far-reaching tool of the Fair Housing Act is its requirement that all executive departments and agencies administer their programs relating to housing and urban development "in a manner affirmatively to further the purposes" of the Fair Housing Act.[45] After President Nixon forced George Romney from HUD, this provision was largely ignored by both Democratic and Republican administrations until the Obama administration issued a new federal rule in 2015 clarifying what it meant for recipients of HUD funding to further fair housing. Indeed, the end of the Obama administration witnessed several major developments in fair housing policy, including the finalization of rules implementing the Fair Housing Act's discriminatory-effects standard,[46] defining affirmatively furthering fair housing,[47] and establishing Small Area Fair Market Rents for the Housing Choice Voucher Program.[48] Additionally, private litigation filed against Westchester County (New York) for defrauding the federal government by falsely certifying its compliance with the Fair Housing Act led to a landmark settlement with the Department of Justice, and the Supreme Court in *Texas Department of Housing and Community Affairs v. The Inclusive Communities Project* (2015) upheld the viability of disparate impact claims under the Fair Housing Act.[49]

Many of these fair housing policy developments were heavily criticized by conservative commentators, particularly the Affirmatively Furthering Fair Housing Rule, which then presidential candidate Ben Carson condemned as "government-engineered attempts to legislate racial equality" and described as "social engineering" akin to historical "failed socialist experiments."[50] Donald

Trump was elected in 2016, pledging to roll back Obama-era policies, and he appointed Ben Carson as Secretary of HUD. Under Carson's leadership, HUD suspended the Small Area Fair Market Rent Rule in 2017 and the Affirmatively Furthering Fair Housing Rule in 2018.[51] Fair housing advocates challenged both suspensions in court; at the time of this writing, the Small Area Fair Market Rent Rule had been reinstated and the litigation regarding the Affirmatively Furthering Fair Housing Rule was pending. The election of Donald Trump and these policy developments took place after many of the debates that follow were written, but the policy issues underlying them remain relevant and timely even as the context continues to change.

How Segregated Are We?

In 1966, Martin Luther King, Jr. moved into a run-down apartment in Chicago's Lawndale neighborhood to draw attention to pervasive residential segregation and its national reach. Leading marches into two all-white Chicago neighborhoods to call for open access to housing, King was jeered and taunted by thousands of white residents. Rocks, bottles, and firecrackers rained down on the marchers, and King was knocked to his knees after being struck in the head with a stone. He said, "I have seen many demonstrations in the South, but I have never seen anything so hostile and so hateful as I've seen here today."[52]

While the open hostility to integration has subsided since then, residential segregation stubbornly persists. Even fifty years after the passage of the Fair Housing Act, metropolitan areas continue to be highly segregated along racial lines. Figure 0.1 uses the dissimilarity index to measure segregation over time. The most common measure of racial segregation, the dissimilarity index captures the degree to which two different groups are distributed differently across the neighborhoods within a city. The index ranges from 0 to 100, with 100 indicating complete segregation and 0 describing a world in which every neighborhood has exactly the same composition as the city as a whole. As figure 0.1 shows, black-white segregation has consistently declined since 1980, but by 2010 it remained high in most cities and extremely high in many of them.[53] Further, as figure 0.1 shows, we have not seen the same decline in segregation for other racial groups. White-Latino segregation has shown only a slight drop, and only in the most recent decade, and white-Asian segregation has been fairly constant since 1980. If we try to capture segregation by using the isolation index, which measures the degree to which members of a racial group live among other members of their same group, we find that segregation has actually increased over time for Latinos and Asians. So while some observers have declared the "end of segregation," the data suggest otherwise.[54]

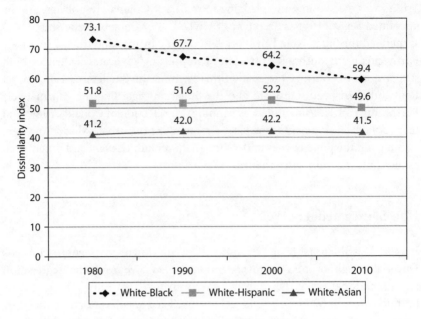

Figure 0.1 Mean metropolitan-area levels of dissimilarity

Source: U.S. 2010, using data from decennial censuses.

Meanwhile, economic segregation appears to have grown significantly between 1970 and 2010 as income inequality increased. Measuring income segregation is far more challenging than measuring segregation by race, but the indices again try to capture the degree to which people with different income levels live in different sets of neighborhoods. Using several different measures, Bischoff and Reardon show that the growth in income segregation was particularly pronounced during the 1980s and the 2000s.[55] These trends were driven by an increase both in the concentration of poverty and in the concentration of affluence. According to Iceland and Hernandez, for example, the percentage of poor people living in neighborhoods where at least 40 percent of the population is poor rose from 12.7 percent to 16.4 percent during the 1980s, dropped to 11.4 percent in 2000, and rose again to 14.1 percent by 2014.[56]

While economic segregation overall rose in the first decade and a half of the twenty-first century, a modest countertrend was also taking place in some central-city neighborhoods. Gentrification may not be as widespread as some headlines would lead you to believe, but many cities did see an increase in the share of white, college-educated, and higher-income households choosing to live in central and relatively low-income urban neighborhoods.[57] At least in the short run, such residential moves hold out the promise of both economic and racial integration.

Why Do We Care?

Much of this book is dedicated to debating how much we should care about the persistence of racial segregation. Many people do not view segregation as inherently troubling. Cities in the United States, however, are not just segregated, but also unequal, in part because of residential segregation. Segregation has resulted in large disparities in the resources and services available in the neighborhoods in which different groups live and widely divergent neighborhood experiences of poverty and educational attainment.

Table 1 compares the population characteristics of the average neighborhood lived in by people of different races in U.S. metropolitan areas. In 2010, the typical white metropolitan resident found herself in a neighborhood with a poverty rate of 10.5 percent, while the typical Latino and typical black resident lived in neighborhoods with poverty rates 8 and 10 percentage points higher. We also see large black-white and Latino-white gaps in the percentage of neighbors with college degrees and a black-white gap in the percentage of neighbors who are employed. The pattern differs for Asian Americans, who live in neighborhoods quite similar to those of whites. These gaps persist after controlling for poverty, and importantly, they are significantly larger in more segregated metropolitan areas, suggesting that segregation steers different racial groups into very different social and economic environments.[58]

These same disparities extend to neighborhood services and conditions. In terms of schools, the average white person in 2010 lived in a census tract where the nearest elementary school within the district ranked at the 58th percentile of proficiency scores in the metropolitan area. In contrast, the average black person lived in a tract linked to an elementary school scoring at only the 37th percentile, creating a 21-percentage-point racial gap in proficiency ranking. The white-Latino gap is only a bit smaller, at 16 percentage points, while the

Table 1 Average neighborhood characteristics by race

	Share of neighborhood residents (2010)		Neighborhood's percentile rank	
	In poverty	College graduates	Proficiency test scores at nearest school (2008)	Violent crime (2000)
White	10.5%	32.9%	58	37
Black	20.3%	22.3%	37	66
Hispanic	18.5%	21.0%	42	58
Asian	11.5%	38.2%	57	43

Source: Jorge De la Roca, Ingrid Gould Ellen, and Katherine M. O'Regan, "Race and Neighborhoods in the Twenty-First Century: What Does Segregation Mean Today?," *Regional Science and Urban Economics* 47 (July 2014): 138–151, https://doi.org/10.1016/j.regsciurbeco.2013.09.006.

white-Asian gap is only 2 percentage points. Once again, these gaps are more pronounced in more segregated metropolitan areas. The same pattern holds when looking at exposure to violent crime. Indeed, De la Roca, Ellen, and O'Regan report that the average poor white person lived in a less violent neighborhood than the average *nonpoor* black person.[59]

In sum, residential segregation is not creating 'separate but equal' communities. It is creating separate and *unequal* ones. Growing evidence demonstrates that these unequal neighborhood conditions matter in shaping the long-run outcomes of children.[60] Research suggests that residence in segregated metropolitan areas undermines the health, employment, and educational outcomes of both blacks and Latinos.[61] As some of the discussions in this book illustrate, though, there continues to be some debate about exactly how much segregation contributes to (rather than reflects) racial disparities, and even more debate about why.

The creation of separate and unequal neighborhoods that have both short- and long-term impacts on individual access to opportunity is perhaps the most glaring reason to be concerned about segregation and a reason to advocate for integration. However, segregation might still be troubling even if it were to create separate but equal communities, as it might continue to feed, or at least sustain, racial divisions. As some of the contributors to this book argue, segregation might also undermine overall social welfare by inhibiting interaction, the flow of information, and economic mobility.[62]

What Is Integration?

If segregation is the problem, then integration would seem to be the answer. We titled this book, and the blog on which it is based, *The Dream Revisited*, deliberately referencing Martin Luther King, Jr.'s stirring 1963 "I Have a Dream" speech. But not everyone shares Dr. King's dream of integration, and even those who do may not agree about what it entails. Racial and economic integration are terms that are used widely but rarely defined precisely. If you asked ten people what integration means to them, you would probably get ten different answers. One fundamental question is whether integration is about process or outcomes. Defined as a process, integration could be described as a world in which all residents choose their neighborhoods freely and without regard to race. Alternatively, it could be described as world in which all residents choose their neighborhoods freely, valuing our differences and affirmatively choosing to live in communities with residents diverse by race, ethnicity, class, occupation, political beliefs, or other characteristics. For many, integration requires neither color blindness nor assimilation.[63]

Most people seem to define (or at least operationalize) integration, though, as being about outcomes rather than process. Researchers, for example, typically label a neighborhood as racially integrated if it houses a threshold number or share of residents of different races.[64] There is less consensus about which groups must be present, in what proportions, and for how long. For instance, South and Crowder define neighborhoods as integrated if they are between 10 and 90 percent black.[65] Ellen, Horn, and O'Regan, by contrast, define integrated neighborhoods to be those in which at least 20 percent of residents are non-Hispanic white and at least 20 percent are black, Hispanic, or Asian.[66] They require the presence of whites because whites continue to be the dominant group in the United States and because whites continue to have the highest rates of residential isolation and have historically excluded or avoided other groups. In this conception, neighborhoods shared by Latinos, Asians, and African Americans, but without whites, may be highly diverse but not integrated.

Researchers diverge in their choices of what share of residents of different groups must be present in an integrated neighborhood. Some anchor the proportions to the racial composition of the larger metropolitan area;[67] others anchor it to the racial composition of the country as a whole.[68] Still others view neighborhoods to be integrated only if different racial groups are present in relatively equal numbers.[69] There is also the question of how long neighborhoods must remain racially diverse in order to be meaningfully integrated, and how to tell whether or for how long they will remain diverse. Bader and Warkentien question whether neighborhoods that are in transition (however slowly) from all white to all black should be considered meaningfully integrated.[70] Finally, there is the question of scale, which we will say more about later. Should we be aiming for integration at the level of a municipality, a neighborhood, a block, or an individual building? Integration tends to describe the characteristics of an individual neighborhood (in contrast to segregation, which describes the distribution of the population across neighborhoods within a city). But there is little clarity about how to define neighborhoods, and people living on the very same block or in the same building may have different views about the boundaries of their community depending on their mobility patterns.

These definitions reflect only demographic composition. But many view integration as more than just sharing the boundaries of neighborhood, or more than the absence of segregation. Borrowing again from the words of Martin Luther King, Jr.:

> We do not have to look very far to see the pernicious effects of a desegregated society that is not integrated. It leads to "physical proximity without spiritual affinity." It gives us a society where men are physically desegregated and spiritually segregated, where elbows are together and hearts are apart. It gives us spatial togetherness and spiritual apartness. It leaves us with a stagnant equality of sameness rather than a constructive equality of oneness.[71]

From this perspective, a neighborhood is not integrated if all of its poor residents live in public housing and have little day-to-day contact with their affluent neighbors who live in luxury condominiums. An integrated neighborhood is instead one in which residents attend the same schools, use the same public spaces, ride the same buses, and interact on relatively equal footing. For Harvey Molotch, true integration should involve unconstrained and "nonantagonistic" social interaction.[72] For Elizabeth Anderson, true integration should involve "cooperation, ease, welcome, trust, affiliation, and intimacy."[73]

Unfortunately, measuring meaningful social interaction on a large scale is challenging (if not impossible), and researchers have thus tended to rely instead on measures of demographic composition to capture integration or segregation. And most researchers have tended to focus on analyzing the overall segregation levels in different cities rather than the extent of integration in individual neighborhoods.

Outline of the Book

This book is unique in its format and content. The heart of the book is a series of twenty-five debates about issues related to segregation, authored by a diverse set of scholars and practitioners. The debates originated as a blog, with contributions written between 2014 and 2017. In each case, we asked someone to write an initial essay on a topic, and then we invited three people to respond. The first five discussions offer broad perspectives on integration. They consider whether integration is necessary to achieve economic and racial equality, offer a set of comparative perspectives that take us outside the United States, debate the nature and significance of segregation by income, explore the significance of the suburbanization of poverty, and discuss the meaning of segregation in schools.

The second set of discussions debates the various factors that contribute to racial segregation, from discrimination to income differences, racial preferences, and public policies. The third set of discussions considers the consequences of segregation, focusing again on segregation by race. The fourth debates the merits of different policy responses. More of the policy responses address economic segregation, in part because racial segregation is far more troubling when it is accompanied by income segregation, but also because the political and legal landscape make race-conscious policies far more challenging to implement. Each of the four groups of discussions is preceded by an introductory chapter that outlines the key debates and themes in that area.

In the discussions that follow, readers may note inconsistency in the capitalization of "black" and "white." Race is a social construction and therefore a construction of language as well. Many style guides, such as the *Associated Press Stylebook*, call for writing "white" and "black" in all lower case letters. Yet there have been ongoing struggles to capitalize "Black" as a form of recognition of the

African diaspora. Lori L. Tharps, for instance, has made the compelling case for why she "refuse[s] to remain in the lower case" and have her "culture . . . reduced to a color."[74] As Tharps points out, W. E. B. Du Bois fought nearly a century ago to have the "n" in Negro capitalized, and when the *New York Times* ultimately agreed, in 1930, the editorial board wrote, "In our 'style book' 'Negro' is now added to the list of words to be capitalized. It is not merely a typographical change; it is an act of recognition of racial self-respect for those who have been for generations in 'the lower case.' "[75]

If "Black" is capitalized, should "white" then also be capitalized? Some style guides, such as that of the *Columbia Journalism Review*, accept the capitalization of both words arguing that for the sake of both consistency and equality, if one of the terms is capitalized the other should be as well.[76] But the writer Touré explains that he chooses to capitalize "Black" and write "white" in lowercase because he believes " 'Black' constitutes a group, an ethnicity equivalent to African-American, Negro, or, in terms of a sense of ethnic cohesion, Irish, Polish, or Chinese" but that whiteness does not merit the same treatment.[77] Touré notes that "[m]ost American whites think of themselves as Italian-American or Jewish or otherwise relating to other past connections that Blacks cannot make because of the familial and national disruptions of slavery." Because "Black speaks to an unknown familial/national past it deserves capitalization" but not white.[78] In short, the decisions about capitalization of white and black are individual ones, laden with meaning, about which many disagree. To respect each author's choice, we printed each discussion with the capitalization that the author chose.

Notes

1. Charles Tilly, *Durable Inequality* (Berkeley: University of California Press, 1999); Patrick Sharkey, *Stuck in Place: Urban Neighborhoods and the End of Progress Toward Racial Equality* (Chicago: University of Chicago Press, 2013); Elizabeth Anderson, *The Imperative of Integration* (Princeton, NJ: Princeton University Press, 2013); Iris Marion Young, *Inclusion and Democracy* (Oxford: Oxford University Press, 2002).
2. Richard Rothstein, *The Color of Law: A Forgotten History of How Our Government Segregated America* (New York: Liveright, 2017); Ta-Nehisi Coates, "The Case for Reparations," *Atlantic*, June 2014, https://www.theatlantic.com/magazine/archive/2014/06/the-case-for-reparations/361631/.
3. Carl H. Nightingale, *Segregation: A Global History of Divided Cities* (Chicago: University of Chicago Press, 2012).
4. William Edward Burghardt DuBois, *Black Reconstruction in America, 1860–1880* (New York: Free Press, 1998); Eric Foner, *Reconstruction: America's Unfinished Revolution* (New York: HarperCollins, 1989).
5. Plessy v. Ferguson, 163 U.S. 537, 544 (1896), which determined that the Fourteenth Amendment "could not have been intended to abolish distinctions based upon color, or

to enforce social, as distinguished from political, equality, or a commingling of the two races upon terms unsatisfactory to either"; Berea Coll. v. Commonwealth of Kentucky, 211 U.S. 45, 58 (1908), which upheld a state law prohibiting the education of black and white students by the same institution.

6. Thomas W. Hanchett, *Sorting Out the New South City: Race, Class, and Urban Development in Charlotte, 1875–1975* (Chapel Hill: University of North Carolina Press, 1998); C. Vann Woodward, *The Strange Career of Jim Crow*, Commemorative edition (Oxford: Oxford University Press, 2001).

7. Baltimore City Council, *Ordinances and Resolutions of the Mayor and City Council of Baltimore Passed at the Annual Session, 1910–11* (Baltimore, 1911), 379.

8. Cameron McWhirter, *Red Summer: The Summer of 1919 and the Awakening of Black America* (New York: St. Martin's Griffin, 2012); David F. Krugler, *1919, The Year of Racial Violence: How African Americans Fought Back* (New York: Cambridge University Press, 2014).

9. Elliot Jaspin, *Buried in the Bitter Waters: The Hidden History of Racial Cleansing in America* (New York: Basic Books, 2007).

10. Trevon Logan and John Parman, "The National Rise in Residential Segregation," *Journal of Economic History* 77, no. 1 (2017): 127–170.

11. Logan and Parman, "The National Rise in Residential Segregation."

12. Andrew Wiese, *Places of Their Own: African American Suburbanization in the Twentieth Century* (Chicago: University of Chicago Press, 1987).

13. Paige Glotzer, "Exclusion in Arcadia: How Suburban Developers Circulated Ideas About Discrimination, 1890–1950," *Journal of Urban History* 41, no. 3 (2015): 479–494, https://doi.org/10.1177/0096144214566964.

14. Richard Brooks and Carol M. Rose, *Saving the Neighborhood: Racially Restrictive Covenants, Law, and Social Norms* (Cambridge, MA: Harvard University Press, 2013).

15. Glotzer, "Exclusion in Arcadia."

16. Glotzer, "Exclusion in Arcadia."

17. Federal Housing Administration, *Underwriting Manual: Underwriting and Valuation Procedure Under Title II of the National Housing Act* (Washington, DC, 1934).

18. Federal Housing Administration, *Underwriting Manual* (1934).

19. Federal Housing Administration, *Underwriting Manual: Underwriting and Valuation Procedure Under Title II of the National Housing Act with Revisions to April 1, 1936* (Washington, DC, 1936), http://wbhsi.net/~wendyplotkin/DeedsWeb/fha36.html.

20. Kenneth T. Jackson, *Crabgrass Frontier: The Suburbanization of the United States* (New York: Oxford University Press, 1987); Amy E. Hillier, "Redlining and the Home Owners' Loan Corporation," *Journal of Urban History* 29, no. 4 (2003): 394–420, https://doi.org/10.1177/0096144203029004002; Jennifer S. Light, "Nationality and Neighborhood Risk at the Origins of FHA Underwriting," *Journal of Urban History* 36, no. 5 (2010): 634–671, https://doi.org/10.1177/0096144210365677.

21. Logan and Parman, "The National Rise in Residential Segregation."

22. Logan and Parman, "The National Rise in Residential Segregation."

23. Melvin L. Oliver and Thomas M. Shapiro, *Black Wealth, White Wealth: A New Perspective on Racial Inequality* (New York: Routledge, 2006); Ira Katznelson, *When Affirmative Action Was White: An Untold History of Racial Inequality in Twentieth-Century America* (New York: Norton, 2005).

24. Robert O. Self, *American Babylon: Race and the Struggle for Postwar Oakland* (Princeton, NJ: Princeton University Press, 2005).

25. Thomas J. Sugrue, *The Origins of the Urban Crisis: Race and Inequality in Postwar Detroit* (Princeton, NJ: Princeton University Press, 2005).
26. Thurgood Marshall, "Dismantling Segregation: Brown v. Board of Education," in *Ripples of Hope: Great American Civil Rights Speeches*, ed. Josh Gottheimer (New York: Basic Civitas Books, 2003), 207–209, at 208.
27. Brown v. Bd. of Ed. of Topeka, Shawnee Cty., Kan., 347 U.S. 483, 495 (1954), supplemented sub nom. Brown v. Bd. of Educ. of Topeka, Kan., 349 U.S. 294 (1955).
28. Martin Luther King, Jr., "Chicago Campaign (1966)," accessed November 4, 2017, http://kingencyclopedia.stanford.edu/encyclopedia/encyclopedia/enc_chicago_campaign/.
29. William J. Collins, "The Political Economy of State Fair Housing Laws Before 1968," *Social Science History* 30, no. 1 (April 2006): 15–49, https://doi.org/10.1017/S0145553200013377.
30. Nikole Hannah-Jones, "Living Apart: How the Government Betrayed a Landmark Civil Rights Law," ProPublica, June 25, 2015, https://www.propublica.org/article/living-apart-how-the-government-betrayed-a-landmark-civil-rights-law.
31. The National Advisory Commission on Civil Disorders, *Report*, 1968, 1.
32. The National Advisory Commission on Civil Disorders, 2 *Report*, 8.
33. Hannah-Jones, "Living Apart."
34. Hannah-Jones, "Living Apart."
35. Tom Smith et al., "General Social Surveys, 1972–2016 [machine-Readable Data File]," *NORC at the University of Chicago*, 2017.
36. Smith et al., "General Social Surveys."
37. Leah Boustan, *Competition in the Promised Land: Black Migrants in Northern Cities and Labor Markets* (Princeton, NJ: Princeton University Press, 2016); Allison Shertzer and Randall P. Walsh, "Racial Sorting and the Emergence of Segregation in American Cities," National Bureau of Economic Research Working Paper No. 22077, March 2016, rev. June 2017, http://www.nber.org/papers/w22077; Ingrid Gould Ellen, *Sharing America's Neighborhoods* (Cambridge, MA: Harvard University Press, 2000).
38. Richard Briffault, "Our Localism: Part I—The Structure of Local Government Law," *Columbia Law Review* 90, no. 1 (1990): 1–115, https://doi.org/10.2307/1122837.
39. Charles M. Tiebout, "A Pure Theory of Local Expenditures," *Journal of Political Economy* 64, no. 5 (1956): 416–424.
40. Briffault, "Our Localism"; Gerald E. Frug, *City Making: Building Communities Without Building Walls* (Princeton, NJ: Princeton University Press, 1999); Lee Anne Fennell, *The Unbounded Home: Property Values Beyond Property Lines* (New Haven, CT: Yale University Press, 2009).
41. Wiese, *Places of Their Own*.
42. Marta Tienda and Norma Fuentes, "Hispanics in Metropolitan America: New Realities and Old Debates," *Annual Review of Sociology* 40, no. 1 (2014): 499–520, https://doi.org/10.1146/annurev-soc-071913-043315; Justin Steil, Jorge De la Roca, and Ingrid Gould Ellen, "Desvinculado y Desigual: Is Segregation Harmful to Latinos?," *Annals of the American Academy of Political and Social Science* 660, no. 1 (2015): 57–76, https://doi.org/10.1177/0002716215576092.
43. Kendra Bischoff and Sean F. Reardon, "Residential Segregation by Income, 1970–2009," in *Diversity and Disparities: America Enters a New Century*, ed. John R. Logan (New York: Russell Sage Foundation, 2014), 208–233; Ann Owens, Sean F. Reardon, and Christopher Jencks, "Income Segregation Between Schools and School Districts," *American Educational Research Journal* 53, no. 4 (2016): 1159–1197, https://doi.org/10.3102/0002831216652722.

44. Michael H. Schill and Samantha Friedman, "The Fair Housing Amendments Act of 1988: The First Decade," *Cityscape* 4, no. 3 (1999): 57–78; Mara Sidney, "Fair Housing and Affordable Housing Advocacy: Reconciling the Dual Agenda," in *The Geography of Opportunity: Race and Housing Choice in Metropolitan America*, ed. Xavier de Souza Briggs (Washington, DC: Brookings Institution Press, 2005).

45. 42 U.S.C. § 3608(d); 42 U.S.C. § 3608(e)(5).

46. *Federal Register* 78, no. 32 (February 15, 2013): 11460.

47. *Federal Register* 80, no. 136 (July 16, 2015): 42357.

48. *Federal Register* 81, no. 221 (November 16, 2016): 80567.

49. U.S. ex rel. Anti-Discrimination Center v. Westchester County, 2009 WL 455269 (S.D.N.Y. Feb. 24, 2009); 135 S.Ct. 2507 (2015).

50. Ben S. Carson, "Experimenting with Failed Socialism Again," *Washington Times*, July 23, 2015, https://www.washingtontimes.com/news/2015/jul/23/ben-carson-obamas-housing -rules-try-to-accomplish-/.

51. *Federal Register* 82, no. 237 (December 12, 2017): 58439; *Federal Register* 83, no. 4 (January 5, 2018): 683.

52. King, "Chicago Campaign (1966)."

53. Jorge De la Roca, Ingrid Gould Ellen, and Katherine M. O'Regan, "Race and Neighborhoods in the Twenty-First Century: What Does Segregation Mean Today?," *Regional Science and Urban Economics* 47 (July 2014): 138–151, https://doi.org/10.1016/j .regsciurbeco.2013.09.006.

54. Jacob Vigdor and Edward L. Glaeser, "The End of the Segregated Century: Racial Separation in America's Neighborhoods, 1890–2010," Manhattan Institute, January 22, 2012, https://www.manhattan-institute.org/html/end-segregated-century-racial-separation -americas-neighborhoods-1890-2010-5848.html.

55. Bischoff and Reardon, "Residential Segregation by Income."

56. John Iceland and Erik Hernandez, "Understanding Trends in Concentrated Poverty: 1980–2014," *Social Science Research* 62 (2017): 75–95, https://doi.org/10.1016/j.ssresearch .2016.09.001.

57. Nathaniel Baum-Snow and Daniel Hartley, "Causes and Consequences of Central Neighborhood Change, 1970–2010," May 16, 2016, https://www.philadelphiafed.org/- /media/community-development/events/2016/research-symposium-on-gentrification /pdfs/panel1_nathanielbaumsnow-paper.pdf?la=en; Lena Edlun, Cecilia Machado, and Maria Sviatschi, "Bright Minds, Big Rent: Gentrification and the Rising Returns to Skill," National Bureau of Economic Research Working Paper No. 21729, November 2015, rev. January 2016, http://www.nber.org/papers/w21729; Ingrid Gould Ellen and Lei Ding, "Advancing Our Understanding of Gentrification," *Cityscape* 18, no. 3 (2016), https://www.huduser.gov/portal/periodicals/cityscpe/vol18num3/guest.pdf; Jackelyn Hwang and Jeffrey Lin, "What Have We Learned About the Causes of Recent Gentrification?," *Cityscape: A Journal of Policy Development and Research* 18, no. 3 (2016): 9–26.

58. De la Roca, Ellen, and O'Regan, "Race and Neighborhoods."

59. De la Roca, Ellen, and O'Regan, "Race and Neighborhoods."

60. Raj Chetty, Nathaniel Hendren, and Lawrence Katz, "The Effects of Exposure to Better Neighborhoods on Children: New Evidence from the Moving to Opportunity Project," *American Economic Review* 106, no. 4 (2016): 855–902.

61. David M. Cutler and Edward L. Glaeser, "Are Ghettos Good or Bad?," *Quarterly Journal of Economics* 112, no. 3 (1997): 827–872; Ingrid Gould Ellen, *Sharing America's Neighborhoods: The Prospects for Stable Racial Integration* (Cambridge, MA: Harvard University Press, 2000); Ingrid Gould Ellen, Justin P. Steil, and Jorge De la Roca, "The Significance

of Segregation in the Twenty-First Century," *City & Community* 15, no. 1 (March 2016): 8–13, https://doi.org/10.1111/cico.12146.

62. Raj Chetty et al., "Where Is the Land of Opportunity: The Geography of Intergenerational Mobility in the United States," *Quarterly Journal of Economics* 129, no. 4 (2014): 1553–1623.

63. Anderson, *The Imperative of Integration*.

64. Ellen, *Sharing America's Neighborhoods*.

65. Scott J. South and Kyle D. Crowder, "Housing Discrimination and Residential Mobility: Impacts for Blacks and Whites," *Population Research and Policy Review* 17, no. 4 (August 1998): 369–387, https://doi.org/10.1023/A:1005917328257.

66. Ingrid Gould Ellen, Keren Horn, and Katherine O'Regan, "Pathways to Integration: Examining Changes in the Prevalence of Racially Integrated Neighborhoods," *Cityscape* 14, no. 3 (2012): 33–53.

67. Philip Nyden, Michael Maly, and John Lukehart, "The Emergence of Stable Racially and Ethnically Diverse Urban Communities: A Case Study of Nine U.S. Cities," *Housing Policy Debate* 8, no. 2 (1997): 491–534, https://doi.org/10.1080/10511482.1997.9521262.

68. Ellen, *Sharing America's Neighborhoods*.

69. Barrett A. Lee and Peter B. Wood, "Is Neighborhood Racial Succession Place-Specific?," *Demography* 28, no. 1 (February 1991): 21–40, https://doi.org/10.2307/2061334.

70. Michael D. M. Bader and Siri Warkentien, "The Fragmented Evolution of Racial Integration Since the Civil Rights Movement," *Sociological Science* 3, no. 8 (2016): 135–166, https://doi.org/10.15195/v3.a8.

71. Martin Luther King, Jr., *A Testament of Hope: The Essential Writings and Speeches of Martin Luther King, Jr.*, ed. James M. Washington (New York: HarperCollins, 1991).

72. Harvey L. Molotch, *Managed Integration: Dilemmas of Doing Good in the City* (Berkeley: University of California Press, 1973).

73. Anderson, *The Imperative of Integration*, 116.

74. Lori L. Tharps, "I Refuse to Remain in the Lower Case," *My American Melting Pot* (blog), June 2, 2014, https://myamericanmeltingpot.com/2014/06/02/i-refuse-to-remain-in-the-lower-case/.

75. Tharps, "I Refuse to Remain in the Lower Case."

76. Merrill Perlman, "Black and white: why capitalization matters," Columbia Journalism Review, June 23, 2015, https://www.cjr.org/analysis/language_corner_1.php.

77. Touré, *Who's Afraid of Post-Blackness?: What It Means to Be Black Now.* (New York: Simon and Schuster, 2011), viii.

78. Touré, viii.

PART I

THE MEANING OF SEGREGATION

Introduction

The five discussions that follow lead us to ask what the shorthand term "segregation" means in different contexts, and why segregation continues to matter in the United States and internationally. Segregation in the United States generally refers to the separation of racial or ethnic groups in places of residence or in schools. This implicit focus on race to the exclusion of class is somewhat surprising given significant levels of residential and educational segregation by income, extensive municipal fragmentation by class, and tax structures that contribute to dramatic neighborhood-based inequalities in access to public goods. Indeed, increasing residential segregation by income in the United States is creating a growing spatial concentration of both the poor and the affluent, as well as declines in the share of households living in mixed-income neighborhoods. Perhaps the lack of popular focus on income segregation should not come as a surprise given the idea that opportunity in the United States is, or at least should be, available to all, regardless of where they start on the economic ladder. But the widening of economic inequality in recent decades has driven an increase in income segregation that appears to be making socioeconomic mobility ever more elusive.[1]

A focus on segregation is frequently understood to imply that the appropriate solution is integration. But the concept of integration itself is complicated. James Baldwin, in *The Fire Next Time* (1963), famously asked, "Do I really want to be integrated into a burning house?"[2] And Harry Belafonte (2011) describes Martin

Luther King, Jr. expressing concerns shortly before his assassination about integrating into a dominant ideology insufficiently concerned about the poor and disenfranchised.[3] Several of the authors here debate the extent to which integration should be seen as a solution to the inequalities that segregation generates and what assumptions often accompany a focus on racial integration.

Several tensions run through the discussions, including who is harmed by segregation, whether we should be concerned about the concentration of advantage or only disadvantage, the effectiveness of focusing on race as compared to class, and the degree to which integration should be a goal in and of itself. One source of widespread agreement is the intertwining of residential and educational segregation and the need for policy responses to consider both housing and schools simultaneously.

Who Is Harmed?

Several of the discussions in this section ask the extent to which segregation harms us all or only harms those who are already disadvantaged. There is widespread agreement that those who are already disadvantaged are further harmed by segregation, as Richard Rothstein, Richard Kahlenberg, Roger Andersson, and others review. But the effects of segregation on society more broadly is debated. Reaching back to the *Brown v. Board of Education* decision, Sherrilyn Ifill notes that the Supreme Court even then ignored the argument made by Kenneth Clark that "school segregation twisted the personality development of white as well as Negro children." Ifill and James Ryan argue that a focus on integration is important in part because segregation harms society more broadly and because greater diversity in schools and neighborhoods can improve the school performance, psychological well-being, and civic engagement of all students.

Where Should the Focus Be?

Related to this question, the discussions ask whether we should be concerned only about the concentration of disadvantage or also the concentration of advantage. Sean Reardon and Kendra Bischoff argue that we should care about the concentration of affluence, in addition to the concentration of poverty, because of the effects that concentrated affluence can have on our democracy and our social institutions. Patrick Sharkey implies that the residential isolation of whites is problematic because it allows whites to hoard opportunities for themselves and undermines equality of opportunity. Michael Lens, by contrast, argues that given limited resources, until there is more direct evidence of the negative effects of affluent segregation, solutions for concentrated poverty should be prioritized.

How Do Approaches Based on Race and Class Compare?

Nationwide, average levels of residential segregation by race have been decreasing slowly over the past four decades, while segregation by income has been increasing. Several contributors discuss the effectiveness and wisdom of socioeconomically targeted strategies for addressing racial segregation and associated inequality. For instance, Andersson points out that policies encouraging a mix of low- and middle-income households have been found to have positive neighborhood and individual effects in Sweden, whereas those focusing on avoiding ethnic clustering have had less impact. Rothstein chronicles the long history of public policies in the United States creating and perpetuating disadvantage for nonwhite groups and then argues that substituting class for race in attempting to address that inequality will not work because race and poverty, though correlated, are different both in degree and in spatial distribution. Glenn Harris explains how building a racial-equity frame for policy evaluation will actually reduce economic inequality as well as racial inequality. Alan Berube points out that reductions in racial segregation are not always accompanied by reductions in economic segregation and that, while levels of residential segregation by race in suburban areas have declined over the past several decades, the concentration of poverty in suburbs has risen.

Is Integration the Goal?

The initial discussion debates the extent to which integration should be a goal in itself or whether integration is better considered one strategy for achieving racial or economic equity, and the remaining discussions in this section pick up on this theme as well. Mary Pattillo argues that a focus on integration "stigmatizes Black people and Black space and valorizes Whiteness." Andersson, however, points out that even programs designed to invest in particular neighborhoods without promoting integration can similarly "further stigmatize the targeted area" and often "turn out either to displace problems somewhere else or to be simply ineffective." What, then, to do? Ifill contends that racial integration has value as a goal in itself and promises benefits for all that do not rest on stigmatizing blackness—namely, the promise of a truly equal, inclusive, multiracial society characterized by greater cross-racial understanding and civic engagement, as well as a more equitable allocation of public services. Rothstein argues that racial integration is essentially a constitutional imperative, to redress centuries of public policy enforcing an apartheid state. Others, such as Sharkey, argue that regardless of the value placed on integration as a goal, segregation reproduces inequality and integrative moves are therefore at least one worthwhile path toward greater racial equality. Charles Clotfelter and Kahlenberg similarly posit that socioeconomic integration of schools is important as a step to create enduring benefits for all students. Scott Allard, however, points out that sometimes integration into suburban neighborhoods may actually make crucial supports, such as emergency financial assistance, employment services, and affordable housing programs, harder to access for lower-income households coming from cities where there is a greater density of supportive institutions.

The Discussions in Part I

Why Integration?

Drawing on her own experience of a school-desegregation busing program, Mary Pattillo argues that promoting integration as the solution to improving the lives of individuals who are poor or black further stigmatizes poverty or blackness and valorizes wealth or whiteness as "both the symbol of opportunity and the measuring stick for equality." The substance of equality, Pattillo writes, requires more than just the "co-location of Black and White bodies" but real, tangible, material equality in things like school performance, air quality, parks, and other goods. Noting that whites are the most segregated of all racial and ethnic groups in the United States, Sherrilyn Ifill replies that integration has two crucial benefits that do not involve stigma: first, white students who learn in integrated classrooms benefit significantly in increased civic engagement and heightened awareness of the treatment of others; and second, integration may be the surest path to an equitable distribution of public investment and public services for all households, regardless of race. Rucker Johnson looks to the narrowing of the black-white achievement gap in the decades after the *Brown v. Board of Education* decision and argues that well-crafted policies can make a difference, and that we need a variety of simultaneous strategies, such as school desegregation and school finance reform, to advance equal access to educational opportunity. Patrick Sharkey argues that racial integration is an important social goal because residential segregation is a central mechanism in the production of racial inequality and allows whites to hoard resources and opportunities that should be equally accessible to all.

Comparative Perspectives on Segregation

The second discussion in this section brings a comparative perspective, examining similarities and differences between segregation in the United States and

Europe. Roger Andersson begins by pointing out that, compared to Europe, in the United States socioeconomic disparities are wider, poverty deeper, intergenerational mobility lower, crime rates higher, and the degree of segregation by both race and class greater, making residential segregation an especially salient issue. He also notes that structures of local government and taxation in the United States exacerbate neighborhood inequality, in contrast to Europe where redistributive taxation policies and social services mitigate the consequences of spatial segregation. Chris McCrudden notes that the scholarship on antidiscrimination laws focusing on race and segregation in the United States have not often taken a comparative perspective, thus cutting off legal responses to segregation from innovations in Europe. Dolores Acevedo-Garcia takes a comparative approach within the United States, highlighting how rapidly the residential patterns of the growing U.S. Latino population have become part of the structure of spatial stratification long experienced by African Americans, and how the consequences of segregation may differ for first-generation immigrants compared to subsequent generations. Glenn Harris takes another approach to the domestic comparative perspective, emphasizing that a structural perspective on institutional racism is essential to understanding class in the United States and to passing legislation that improves access to opportunity for all low-income residents.

Neighborhood Income Segregation

The third discussion analyzes the increase in residential segregation by income and debates the relative significance of the increasing isolation of the affluent and the poor. Sean Reardon and Kendra Bischoff present data on the growing share of families that live in neighborhoods characterized by either concentrated wealth or concentrated poverty and find that families in the top 10 percent of the income distribution are more segregated from others than are families in the bottom 10 percent. Reardon and Bischoff argue that this concentration of the wealthy deserves more attention than it has received because it means that the community investments of higher-income households are less likely to spill over to benefit others and that their isolation may erode their support for redistributive social programs. Lee Fennell asks whether greater dispersion of the affluent is necessary or sufficient to counter these potential negative effects. The answer, she suggests, depends in part on whether the negative effects of income segregation derive from wealth, which could itself be redistributed, or from other characteristics, such as social networks, which can only be shared in person. Paul Jargowsky agrees that we should be concerned about the concentration of affluence, but primarily because it helps to explain why poverty has become more concentrated and because it makes addressing the concentration of poverty more difficult. Michael Lens goes further to argue that the real focus should remain firmly on concentrated poverty, because substantial evidence demonstrates the limited opportunities faced by those living in high-poverty neighborhoods.

Suburban Poverty and Segregation

Long-standing perceptions of affluent white suburbs and impoverished central cities do not reflect the reality of residential segregation by race or class today. Indeed, people of color accounted for the majority of suburban growth in the past decade. But as Alan Berube describes, although suburbs have diversified racially, they have also experienced increases in poverty rates and a growing concentration of poverty over the past decade. He notes that in some cases we are seeing a shift of economic disadvantage from central cities to smaller municipalities with relatively few resources to address it—localities that are already farther from jobs and have limited public budgets. Scott Allard concurs, noting that much of the assistance provided to low-income households comes through community organizations that may be more numerous, more experienced, and better resourced in central cities than suburban areas. Drawing on his experience as executive director at Arch City Defenders, Thomas Harvey describes how the fragmented municipal structure associated with the suburbanization of poverty not only reinforces segregation but contributes to discriminatory policing in order to balance municipal budgets, wreaking havoc on the lives of poor suburban residents in the process. Georgette Phillips similarly calls for more research on how the jurisdictional boundaries that have played historic roles in racial segregation are now contributing to the concentration of suburban poverty.

Economic Segregation in Schools

The final discussion examines economic segregation in schools, the relationship between residential and educational segregation, and the role that policy can play in attenuating both. Using the example of North Carolina school districts to focus on the intersection of racial and economic segregation in schools, Charles Clotfelter finds that policies focused on the economic integration of schools can have substantial effects on levels of both economic and racial segregation. Richard Kahlenberg presents substantial evidence of the positive impact of economically integrated schools on student performance, and suggests that peer effects from classmates and parental involvement may play particularly important roles. Richard Rothstein describes how nationwide residential racial segregation today is a product of explicitly segregated government policies and argues that a focus on socioeconomic integration of schools or residences alone will not be enough to address persistent racial disparities in neighborhood contexts. James Ryan explores the significance of the shift from the dominant conversation in K–12 education about the harms of segregation to the dominant conversation in higher education about the benefits of diversity. Ryan argues that a focus on the benefits to every student of attending a racially and economically diverse elementary, middle, and high school could have a more meaningful impact on public policy than a narrow focus on the harms of segregation.

Notes

1. Facundo Alvaredo, Anthony B. Atkinson, Thomas Piketty, and Emmanuel Saez, "The Top 1 Percent in International and Historical Perspective," *Journal of Economic Perspectives* 27, no. 3 (2013): 3–20; David H. Autor, Lawrence F. Katz, and Melissa S. Kearney, "Trends in U.S. Wage Inequality: Revising the Revisionists," *Review of Economics and Statistics* 90, no. 2 (May 2008): 300–323; Sean F. Reardon, and Kendra Bischoff, "Income Inequality and Income Segregation," *American Journal of Sociology* 116, no. 4 (January 2011): 1092–1153; Raj Chetty, Nathaniel Hendren, Patrick Kline, and Emmanuel Saez, "Where Is the Land of Opportunity? The Geography of Intergenerational Mobility in the United States," *Quarterly Journal of Economics* 129, no. 4 (November 2014): 1553–1623.
2. James Baldwin, *The Fire Next Time* (New York: Dial, 1963).
3. Harry Belafonte, *My Song: A Memoir* (New York: Knopf, 2011).

WHY INTEGRATION?

The Problem of Integration

by Mary Pattillo

> *Between me and the other world there is ever an unasked question. . . .*
> *They approach me in a half-hesitant sort of way, eye me curiously or*
> *compassionately, and then, instead of saying directly, How does it feel to*
> *be a problem? they say, I know an excellent colored man in my town; or,*
> *I fought at Mechanicsville; or, Do not these Southern outrages make your*
> *blood boil? At these I smile, or am interested, or reduce the boiling to a*
> *simmer, as the occasion may require. To the real question, How does it feel*
> *to be a problem? I answer seldom a word.*

—W. E. B. DuBois, *The Souls of Black Folk*

Nothing can match the poetry and potency of these words by the scholar and
activist W. E. B. DuBois. I invoke them in this debate about integration in the
twenty-first century because they demand that we interrogate the ideological
and normative assumptions that motivate integration rhetoric and politics. In
this essay, I use personal reflections to argue that calls for integration rest on the
unstated "problem" of Blackness, making it a problematic principle upon which
to build equality.

I must begin by stating that I am by no means against integration. I am Black and work in a diverse and integrated university where Whites are the majority. I love my job. My comments are not to promote racial separatism, nor to argue that people of the same "race"—and we must always signal just how time- and place-specific "race" is—"naturally" want to be around each other. Moreover, I surely do not mean to denigrate the courage and martyrdom of generations of activists who made and make my integrated life possible.

Instead, my point is simply to identify the following conundrum of integration politics: promoting integration as the means to improve the lives of Blacks stigmatizes Black people and Black spaces and valorizes Whiteness as both the symbol of opportunity and the measuring stick for equality. In turn, such stigmatization of Blacks and Black spaces is precisely what foils efforts toward integration. After all, why would anyone else want to live around or interact with a group that is discouraged from being around itself?

This argument can be extended to include other non-Whites in the U.S. context (recognizing all of the relevant historical, geopolitical, and economic contingencies) as well as to include the issue of economic integration. Poverty is a highly stigmatized condition. Working to get poor people away from other poor people, and around nonpoor people, reaffirms the stigma of poverty and affirms the decisions of nonpoor people to move "up and out." (The comparison is not perfect for a number of reasons, including the fact that poverty is less fixed than racial identity, although the latter is less fixed than we often assume.)[1]

My perspective on this topic was likely shaped by a less-than-perfect experiment in integration. I was part of Milwaukee's desegregation busing program.[2] I lived in Milwaukee but attended high school in the adjacent suburb of White-fish Bay. In 1980, around the time I started high school, Whitefish Bay was .003 percent Black; today it is 1.9 percent Black. The high school had no Black students who were not a part of the busing program. All of us Black students arrived at school together in the mornings and went home together in the afternoons. It was not conducive to joining activities or sports, although some of us made it work. We hung around together in the hallways and at the snack bar for lunch while our White classmates went home or drove to area fast food joints. It was desegregation without integration.

What did I learn from this experience? The research of economist Rucker Johnson suggests that my fellow Black "Blue Dukes" (Whitefish Bay's mascot) and I probably learned a whole lot more than our peers who attended Milwaukee's predominately Black public schools, and the extra learning likely boosted our success in life.[3] But what else did I learn? I learned that Black schools were bad schools. I learned that Whites in Whitefish Bay only begrudgingly allowed us into their school. I learned that White students enjoyed a massive new field house and a swimming pool and a student theater. And, as an illustration of just how disconnected I was from high school, what I did not learn (or remember) was the high school mascot, which I had to google for this piece!

I wonder what my White peers learned. Did they learn that not even Black students wanted to attend the schools in Milwaukee? Did they learn to avoid Milwaukee even more as a result? Did they learn that Black students needed to be saved from the bad Black schools in their neighborhoods? Did they pity us? Resent us? Enjoy us? Fear us? Did they secretly want to ask: "How does it feel to be a problem?"

It is from this experience that I approach the question of integration as a strategy to promote opportunity and equality. Instead of providing hard and concrete opportunities or equality that would make Black (or poor) people's lives better, integration dwells on and is motivated by the relatively problematic nature of Black people and Black spaces and posits proximity to Whiteness as the solution, or the most likely way to get to a solution. Is there no such thing as happiness or material well-being or good health without White people?[4]

I don't want to go too far down that road because I am not a racial separatist. Moreover, I do not deny or devalue the wonderful human fulfillment that can come from interacting across differences. My point is only that integration is a strategy to achieve equality, not the substance of equality itself. As a strategy, it is flawed by assumptions that have the inherent potential to backfire and undermine the effort.

Of course, I am not the first person to highlight the stigma of Blackness (or of non-Whiteness or of poverty) and the celebration of Whiteness as central to integration logics. My use of the term *stigma* comes in part from economist Glenn Loury (who builds on sociologist Erving Goffman). In his book, *The Anatomy of Racial Inequality*, Loury argues that "'Race' is all about embodied social signification," and chattel slavery and other practices create and maintain a range of "negative social meanings associated with blackness."[5] Legal scholar Derrick Bell similarly argues that "American racism . . . is the dominant interpretive framework for rendering bodies intelligible."[6] On the valorization of Whiteness, and specifically on integration, Bell continues, "the integration ethic centralizes whiteness. White bodies are represented as somehow exuding an intrinsic value that percolates into the 'hearts and minds' of black children."[7] There are several other sources I could cite, but instead let me conclude with the following, and see what comes.

"I answer seldom a word," DuBois commented about the always lurking question "How does it feel to be a problem?" He would not dignify the question with a response. The problem—the lack of fairness, opportunity, justice, equality, and recognition of shared humanity—did not and does not reside within the bodies (or souls) of Black people, but rather within the fabric— the political, economic, and social institutions—of American society (which is itself constituted under the logics of imperialism, colonialism, and capitalism, but that's for another day). Therefore, the material and spiritual solutions cannot be realized through the colocation of Black and White bodies alone, but must include the real stuff of equality: wages that support a family, and income maintenance in the absence of work; schools that compensate for inequalities in family resources; policing that does not always have its finger on the trigger; and parks and music and health-care centers and clean air and good food whose distribution is not driven by the stigma of Blackness, of non-Whiteness, or of poverty . . . until and in pursuit of the day that such stigma is no longer.

Focus on the Costs of Segregation for All

by Sherrilyn Ifill

Does the pursuit of integration stigmatize black people? Does it, as Mary Pattillo suggests, "posit proximity to Whiteness as a solution" to the problems of urban, poor black people? This a tough question, one that must be confronted if we are to understand how and why segregation plays such an important role in reproducing poverty and educational inequality sixty years after the Supreme Court's landmark embrace of integration in *Brown v. Board of Education*.

Like Pattillo, I too experienced firsthand the policies that school districts implemented in an effort to live up to the promise of *Brown*. My family moved into our home in the early 1960s, in a neighborhood turned entirely African American after white families fled South Jamaica, Queens, for the further, whiter reaches of Long Island. The twelve of us—my nine siblings and two parents—proudly moved into our three-bedroom, one-bathroom home, convinced, despite crushing financial troubles, that we were "middle class." I was bused to school far from home beginning in kindergarten. Although my high school was closer to home, it still required a long bus ride and then a nearly mile-long walk. The student population was a veritable United Nations. About 40 percent of the students were African American, 40 percent were white, and the other 20 percent were Latino and foreign-born students—children of diplomats from Indonesia, Malaysia, and other Asian countries, who lived in nearby neighborhoods. Unlike Pattillo, I recall a richly integrated life of school activities. My sister and I participated in all the annual school musicals—from *Brigadoon* to *Lil Abner*—fully integrated productions with alternative casting and interracial romantic leads. For the two years I edited the yearbook, most of the yearbook staff was white. Our senior class president was African American. African American students seemed to thrive at our high school, and racial tension seemed to be at a minimum.

Still without question, school was the only part of our lives that was racially integrated. When we left school for the day, we abruptly returned to our segregated lives. And while African American students may have prospered at our school, our segregated communities did not. Precious few economic investments were made in our communities. One fallout of integration was the loss of population during the weekday to support local stores and businesses. From 8 a.m. to 4 p.m., our neighborhood became a ghost town, with parents at jobs in other parts of the city and most children bused to schools in white neighborhoods. The closure of schools in our African American neighborhood meant the loss of an African American resident teacher class in our neighborhood as a resource, and as patrons of local businesses. As a result, family-owned stores struggled but failed to stay in business, lacking the foot traffic of customers during the week and of course without the inherited capital and well-resourced social networks of white small-business owners in other parts of the city. Moreover, redlining and other discriminatory policies by the federal government, banks, and mortgage companies deprived aspiring neighborhood entrepreneurs of credit and starved the community of commercial investment. Without small businesses and the jobs they produced in our community or other opportunities beyond it, drug dealing and petty crime became a growing source of employment for young adults.

Over the next thirty years, we made some progress, but ongoing racial discrimination continued to deprive our community of opportunity. Worse, economic stagnation drove housing prices down. Then the 2008 housing crisis dealt the final blow. Like hundreds of other families, the modest homes that our parents had so proudly acquired and invested in were siphoned off by predatory and regressive economic forces. The combined processes of disinvestment, exploitation, and neglect were made easier and more complete because of how segregated our community was. In truth, many of the children of integration left for college without looking back, as I did. When we finished college there were few employment opportunities in which we could use our education in our old neighborhood. Most of us left for good. Working class children who didn't attend college took advantage of existing opportunities for municipal and union work. But the community suffered from the loss of the more economically secure and upwardly mobile members of our neighborhood. By the late 1980s, the integration experiment had ended. White flight was nearly complete by 2000, leaving a neighborhood integrated by a mix of immigrants from Asia and Africa. Even if white families had remained, decisions by federal courts in the late 1990s had shut down even voluntary integration programs that were available to me and my generation.

At my thirtieth high school reunion a few years ago, it was encouraging to see the results of our integrated educational experience. We had thrived. We were teachers, retired police and corrections officers, preachers, nurses, social workers and lawyers. African American and white former classmates danced and laughed, but sat on opposite sides of the room.

The harms experienced by the children of families who remain trapped in high-poverty, hypersegregated neighborhoods have been starkly documented in recent research by Patrick Sharkey and others.[8] Indeed, there is mounting evidence that exposure to violence in very poor communities is akin to missing an entire year of school. A recent Century Foundation report found that if you take children who live in public housing and randomly assign them to economically integrated schools, you can reduce the achievement gap. For poor students who finished elementary school in economically integrated schools, the achievement gap was cut in half for math and by one-third for reading.[9]

And what about white students and communities—the most segregated of all racial and ethnic groups? Focusing on the benefits and burdens of integration and segregation for African Americans and other racial minorities concedes Pattillo's critique without challenging its premise. The truth is we are only considering a portion of the available information to gauge integration's value. We must also assess whether whites benefit from integration.

Consider the findings of Dr. Kenneth Clark who, along with his wife Dr. Mamie Clark, conducted the famous "doll tests" that laid the foundation for the Clarks' findings that segregation damaged the self-esteem of African American students. The Clarks' findings were noted by Chief Justice Earl Warren in *Brown* for the proposition that segregation may confer upon African American students "a feeling of inferiority . . . that may affect their hearts and minds in a way unlikely ever to be undone."[10] But as Nat Hentoff noted in "The Integrationist"— his essay about the impressive and ambitious work of the Clarks—"Clark was somewhat disappointed that the Court, in citing his research, had ignored two other points he had made: that racism was as profoundly American as the Declaration of Independence, and that school segregation twisted the personality development of white as well as Negro children."[11] In essence, the potentially negative effect of segregation on white students, and thus conversely the benefits of integration to white students, was jettisoned early on as a foundation to support the project of integration. I suggest that we return to that course of study now.

I propose that integration may have two critically important benefits, neither of which rests on stigmatizing "blackness" as a problem to be solved. The first, as stated above, is recognizing how school integration benefits white students. Consistent with the Clarks' early work, more recent research by Gary Orfield and others has shown that whites who attend integrated schools and learn in integrated classrooms exhibit more cross-racial understanding.[12] Students who attend integrated schools also demonstrate an increased sense of civic engagement and are better able to realize the existence of discrimination and its effect on other students. This heightened sensitivity to the treatment of others helps students make decisions not based on stereotypes. The work of Linda Tropp and Thomas Pettigrew also finds that interactions between different groups reduce conflict and prejudice.[13] Thus the benefits for whites, and for our society as a whole, must be a part of the conversation.

Second, we should also recognize the pragmatic reality that housing integration may be the most foolproof way to ensure the equitable allocation of public services and development dollars for black children and families. More than seven decades after *Brown*, the quality of a school remains largely dependent on its students' race and socioeconomic status. Because the problems in our nation's schools are integrally affected by race and class, we won't solve our education crisis without solutions that are race- and class-conscious. Housing and neighborhood economic development are key elements driving class mobility for all Americans. Schools cannot perform in isolation; they need healthy communities with adequate housing, jobs, safe streets, and political institutions that are inclusive. In most inner cities, we have failed on every one of those essential requirements. School funding based on property taxes has ensured that poor school districts will be underresourced.[14] We must and should shore up the economic stability of African American communities. But integration can also help ensure that African American families and children receive their fair share of public dollars and support. We needn't embrace only one response to address our failures. But we must address with renewed vigor those failures that threaten to unravel any sense of overarching community or mutual respect and that, in the long run, could undermine our nation's survival as a democracy.

In Search of Integration: Beyond Black and White

by Rucker C. Johnson

As we commemorate the fiftieth anniversary of one of the singular high points of the civil rights movement—the March on Washington—it is important to recall that its educational goal was the desegregation of all school districts. Despite the march and the resulting policy changes, today as a nation we sit in a backslidden condition. America's schools are more segregated now than they were in the early 1970s.

Often the words *desegregation* and *integration* are used interchangeably, as if they were one and the same. Conflating the two is erroneous, indicating a failure to understand the process MLK envisioned—"to change behavior, not only laws." Desegregation alone was not enough. Along the highway of justice, desegregation was to be an immediate point of origination; the final destination was equal opportunity for all. Integration was to be the map guiding the hearts and minds to a paradigm shift that would take us beyond legalistic compliance with desegregation into the spirit of the democratic dream of integration and inclusion. *Brown* was intended not only to promote equitable access to school quality, but also to alter the attitudes and socialization of all children—beginning at the youngest ages. Beyond the removal of the legal and social prohibitions of segregation, beyond law enforcement agencies and the courts, desegregation was a necessary but not sufficient condition that represented the partial down payment, the layaway plan, toward the final goals of equal educational opportunity and inclusion.

Outmoded and unjust laws are not the only barriers to change. While the rollout of civil rights laws washed away segregated public facilities, it could not wash away the greatest barriers to true equality: fear, prejudice, and irrationality. Efforts to achieve either desegregation or integration singularly have proven elusive because the two are inseparable. King anticipated this when he said, "Desegregation is enforceable . . . integration is not," because it requires changes in attitudes. The response—white and middle-class flight, segregated classes within desegregated schools, lower expectations for students of color, disparate disciplinary measures, and racist attitudes—certainly short-circuited the efforts to move beyond desegregation to integrated communities. Too often policy makers have settled for superficial fixes to the complexities of integration. As a result, we are fifty years down the path but, in many respects, virtually no closer to the destination.

Because of the persistent patterns of segregation, many view segregation as inevitable. Spoiler alert: not so, and history is our witness that policy choices play a key role. Metropolitan areas are hypersegregated because of the legacy of historic patterns of racial discrimination in mortgage lending, the geography of public housing units, racially motivated city planning and zoning policy, highway construction, and gentrified development strategies that price poor families out of their existing neighborhoods, to name a few of these policies. Such unfairness creates greater inequities and exacerbates existing poverty. It is unconscionable that in 1968, when MLK died, the black child poverty rate was 35 percent, and it is the same rate today. Poverty, like segregation, is man-made, and thus can be unmade by man.

Focusing again on desegregation: at first glance, the initial effort toward school desegregation may appear to have been about merely placing people as pawns, mixing up the social Rubik's cube, or constructing a color compound for success. Placing brown bodies next to white bodies does not osmotically improve the life trajectory of blacks, nor does it infuse blacks' wealth holdings or resources with that of whites. Though the cultural mosaic of diversity is a positive outcome of integration, for the proponents of *Brown*, diversity per se was not the steam propelling the train down the "long road to freedom." More than anything, for many in the black community, the goal was to galvanize and redistribute school resources to ensure a quality education in every district, for every child, from every neighborhood, of any race, ethnicity, and class. *Brown* insisted that America acknowledge and make reparations for the existing inequities that left one people a step behind in education, and therefore earnings, and therefore health, wealth, and so forth.

I am hopeful, yet I question how the goal of providing high-quality educational opportunities can be successfully achieved and sustained for children of all racial, ethnic, and income groups without addressing housing policies that shape residential segregation patterns along these lines. Segregation too often leaves poor and minority schools with lower-quality facilities, larger class sizes, and less effective teachers, which leads to poor academic outcomes and diminished later-life success. Moreover, unjust systems of inequality can shackle children to the poverty cycle and keep them from discovering their true potential. For example, school finance systems that rely primarily on the local property tax base generate significant differences in per-pupil spending, which is intensified by wealthy parents' capacity to enhance and enrich existing resources.[15] School desegregation and school finance reform have in common the goal of promoting equal access to educational opportunity. One strategy focuses on redistributing schoolchildren, the other on redistributing money, targeted toward poor and minority children. Pursuing strategies to promote integration and championing ones that ensure equal educational opportunity should not be conceived as an "either/or" proposition, but a "both-and" one.

Even if America had ever achieved separate and equal, that equilibrium could not be maintained in perpetuity. As long as one people has lesser, and fewer resources and opportunities than another, the socioeconomic imbalance will again emerge. Less fortunate communities would again be found contending with single parenthood, high crime rates, non-college-educated parents, a low property tax base, and more, while trying to simply gain an education. *Brown* was to position these underserved communities so they could eventually have an educated mass that could not only advocate for their children with confidence but could also advocate for the principles from which all children could benefit.

As we look for solutions to address the achievement gap, I am reminded of the story of the person searching for a lost key under a lamppost—not because the key was lost under the lamppost but because under the lamppost is where the light is. Perhaps we are looking in the wrong places, or perhaps we have incorrectly assumed that there is only one place to look. The search for a single key is misguided, for in reality there are multiple keys that collectively open the doors of success and close the doors to opportunity gaps. Whether we choose desegregation, school finance reform, or charter schools, all offer an answer, but none is the single and complete answer to addressing inequality.

The black-white achievement gap narrowed substantially in the 1970s and '80s and has been stagnant since then. We can learn from our previous success. Desegregation and improved access to quality (reductions in class size, increases in school spending) were key contributors to closing the gaps back then.

For blacks a generation ago, school desegregation significantly increased both educational and occupational attainments, enhanced college quality and adult earnings, reduced the probability of incarceration, and improved adult health status; desegregation had no effects on whites across each of these outcomes. The mechanisms through which school desegregation led to beneficial adult attainment outcomes for blacks included improvement in access to school resources, as reflected in reductions in class size and increases in per-pupil spending.[16] Also at that time, the federal government began to invest in early childhood education. Case in point: those very investments set me, and people like me, on a path to experience and achieve things beyond what my parents attained. These approaches work and will work again, if we invest in them.

Unfortunately, some of the gains of the 1970s and '80s eroded as both whites and middle-class blacks left the cities, and urban school systems became in some ways as socioeconomically and racially segregated as they were at the time of the *Brown* decision. The combination of racial segregation and concentrated poverty can be toxic without addressing both the school and nonschool educational needs of our most disadvantaged children. Such toxicity is further exacerbated in the heat of any economic crisis when we seem more drawn to the loss of financial capital than the need for human and health capital investments. We ought not leave such jaded footprints on children's early-life experiences.

Today, segregation may not be as conspicuous as it was thirty to forty years ago. Contemporary segregation takes on more nuanced forms, but the consequences are no less pernicious. We have desegregated schools, yet segregated classrooms. The quality of curricular content between districts differs substantially (e.g., access to early childhood education programs, gifted and talented programs, AP offerings, tracking beginning at young ages). There are larger between-district than within-district differences, and interdistrict metrowide desegregation plans have been ruled unconstitutional, limiting the efficacy of that policy lever. A new legal environment, beginning in the early 1990s, diminished desegregation standards and resulted in the release of hundreds of districts from their court-mandated desegregation orders, which led to a resegregation of schools. Since then, more than half of all school districts that were once under court order have now been released.

Furthermore, contemporary segregation and its effects on racial inequality have taken an even more negative turn with regard to criminal justice policy, and the early antecedents can be seen in elevated minority school suspension rates. Profound changes in sentencing policy since the 1980s have been fueled, in part, by the politics of fear—perceptions of neighborhood safety colored by race. To underscore how much this has changed things, we would have to release four out of five people from behind bars in order to return to the rates of incarceration of the 1970s.[17] In today's schools, these fears are evident in the assumptions and judgments that teachers make about black boys, in particular, and underscore that ultimately without parent advocacy and agency, institutions will foster and sustain disparate outcomes. Regardless of our dogged intentions, true integration has escaped our grasp, and American apartheid haunts us over and over again. The more we slam the hammer of justice on the head of segregation, the more it evades us and rears its nefarious head in a different place and a different guise.

These negative outcomes are recorded in history, but there are some promising models of successful modern-day interventions that provide a blueprint for us to follow. The Harlem Children's Zone is noteworthy for its comprehensive, full-scale initiatives that seek to improve children's educational opportunities with wraparound services from birth to college and beyond, by providing family support and programs in preschool academics, media, technology, fitness, and nutrition, as well as college and career preparation. Another meritorious enterprise is the mixed-housing income intervention of Montgomery County, Maryland, which demonstrates that achievement among poor black children increases with integration, attendance at middle-class schools, and increased compensatory education funding for disadvantaged children.[18] These policies have promise to break the vicious cycle of poor school performance leading to poverty, and poverty leading to poor school performance, and constitute reform models for other cities to follow.

Consider that, within the next ten years, the majority of children in our country will be minorities. The era of integration that existed during the civil rights movement is not the same as the world we now inherit: the black-white dichotomy is an old paradigm. We have shifted from communities that are black and white to ones that are multiethnic in a globally competitive, twenty-first-century knowledge economy. The global community requires multicultural competencies. No matter where our children live and work in the future, their neighborhood will be part of a multicultural and global community; our failure will be in not adequately preparing them for that new reality.

Our diversity as a country has always been a jewel, but far too often not treasured as such. Strategies to further the goals of racial, ethnic, and economic integration in schools have faded from mainstream policy agendas. While we have better data and better research on what works, we do not expend sufficient effort collecting data to track the extent of school segregation by race and economic status, which in my view reflects a diminished policy priority. In the past, we counted the percentage of students who were black versus white. If we balanced the percentages, we thought we were done—we did what the court said. We now need to collect data and conduct research that offers a different and clearer picture of where we see evidence of success, where disparate outcomes persist, how the combination of factors (education, early childhood, health, jobs, wages, family support structures) matters, and which levers to push. We cannot afford to ignore, or merely put a bandage on, the low achievement of minority children in racially isolated inner cities. Apathy is often the enemy of progressive action that confronts inequity and injustice.

How can we best marshal our collective voice and actions to confront these challenges? We must renew our commitment to challenge discrimination and segregation in whatever form it takes, engage our passions in serving youth, fulfill our purpose in life, and learn from others who have fulfilled theirs. King and Nelson Mandela are our best models of the duality of being both an agitator and a healer for justice. In following their example, we must have the courage to initiate uncomfortable conversations about race and inequality. We must fear the cost of inaction more than the cost of action.

Making Our Assumptions About Integration Explicit

by Patrick Sharkey

The idea that residential integration is a desirable goal is shared widely. But the underlying assumptions about why it is desirable are often left unstated. When the rationale for integration is left implicit, there is the potential to reify unstated assumptions about the depravity or deficiencies of segregated groups and the virtues of the dominant group. Mary Pattillo's contribution provides a powerful argument about the pernicious nature of such unstated assumptions.

Despite this danger, there are valid and important reasons to believe that integration is an important goal worth pursuing through public policy. How, then, can we negotiate this tension between the dangerous assumptions lying just beneath the surface of the integration debate, and the practical benefits of integration?

I argue that we should start by making explicit the rationale for residential integration. By being explicit about why integration might be thought of as a desirable goal, we allow all of our unstated assumptions to rise to the surface and be subjected to critique. In doing so, we can clarify what social outcomes are advanced by confronting residential segregation, and what mechanisms are most appropriate for reaching those outcomes. Here I will consider three possible reasons why integration might be viewed as desirable, although I acknowledge that there are others I am not considering. I will focus on residential integration by race, but a parallel (though not identical) argument could be made about residential integration by ethnicity or economic status.

A first reason for pursuing racial integration focuses on the importance of interpersonal contact and interactions that cross racial and ethnic lines. There are many possible assumptions underlying this rationale for integration, including all of the following: (1) residential integration expands intergroup contact; (2) contact with whites is beneficial for the life chances of black Americans;

(3) contact with black Americans is beneficial for the life chances of whites; (4) contact between groups is beneficial for society as a whole by enhancing trust, breaking down racial stereotypes, etc.

I believe that most of these assumptions can be questioned, if not altogether rejected, on both empirical and normative grounds. Most available evidence shows that integration through housing policy does not generate meaningful interaction across racial or class lines.[19] Although the literature is complex, I have seen little persuasive evidence for the hypothesis that neighborhood integration enhances social trust or reduces racial prejudice.[20] And Patillo's essay provides a compelling argument about the dangerous assumption that living near whites is inherently beneficial, or that living among other black Americans is inherently harmful.

A second rationale for racial integration is based on the assumption that segregation is driven largely by racial discrimination in the housing and lending markets. The dual goals of reducing housing discrimination and promoting integration have been linked together since the passage of the Fair Housing Act of 1968, and some advocates for fair housing continue to portray them as one and the same. The best experimental evidence tells us very clearly that racial and ethnic discrimination is present in urban housing markets.[21] However, I read the results of the most recent housing discrimination study as evidence indicating that blatant racial discrimination is unlikely to be an important contributing factor to racial segregation.[22] Informal discrimination and hostility remain significant barriers to housing opportunity for black families, yet are very difficult to address through existing fair housing policy. Reducing discrimination in housing and lending markets is an important goal in its own right; however, my sense is that doing so would not reduce racial segregation substantially.

As is probably clear, I am skeptical of these first two rationales for racial integration. I don't think housing policy has been shown to be effective in generating interracial contact, nor do I think that contact and interaction are particularly important goals to pursue through public policy. Reducing discrimination is an extremely important goal for the advancement of social justice, but it is distinct from the goal of racial integration. I am doubtful that reducing discrimination in the housing market would have a substantial effect on levels of racial segregation.

Still, I believe that racial integration is an important social goal, for a third reason. Residential segregation provides a mechanism for the reproduction of racial inequality. Living in predominantly black neighborhoods affects the life chances of black Americans not because of any character deficiencies of black people, not because of the absence of contact with whites, but because black neighborhoods have been the object of sustained disinvestment and punitive social policy since the emergence of racially segregated urban communities in the early part of the twentieth century.[23] Residential segregation has been used consistently over time as a means of distributing and hoarding resources and opportunities among white Americans and restricting resources and opportunities available to black Americans. Racially segregated communities provide one of several mechanisms through which racial inequality is made durable.[24]

Making explicit the rationale for racial integration enables us to have a clearer discussion about the outcomes we hope to achieve through integration. It is then possible to consider the range of mechanisms that may be most effective in reaching those outcomes. In my view, confronting racial segregation should be seen as one way to weaken a core mechanism by which racial inequality is maintained and reproduced in America. However, it is not the only way, and one could make a strong case that it is not the most effective way. In my recent book, I argue for a greater focus on sustained investments in nonwhite, low-income communities.[25] I agree with Pattillo in thinking that this type of durable investment represents "the real stuff of equality."

Notes

1. Aliya Saperstein and Andrew M. Penner, "Racial Fluidity and Inequality in the United States," *American Journal of Sociology* 118, no. 3 (November 2012): 676–727.
2. For information on this program, see Michael Bonds, Marie G. Sandy, and Raquel L. Farmer-Hinton, "The Rise and Fall of a Voluntary Public School Integration Transportation Program: A Case Study of Milwaukee's 220 Program," *Education and Urban Society* 47, no. 6 (September 2015): 623–645; Emily Van Dunk and Anneliese Dickman, *School Choice and the Question of Accountability: The Milwaukee Experience* (New Haven, CT: Yale University Press, 2003); John F. Witte and Christopher A. Thorn, "Who Chooses? Voucher and Interdistrict Choice Programs in Milwaukee," *American Journal of Education* 104 (1996): 186–217.
3. Rucker C. Johnson, "TED Talk: Desegregation & (Un)Equal Opportunity," TEDx Conference, Miami University, September 2012.
4. For more on this point, see Mary Pattillo, "Investing in Poor Black Neighborhoods 'As Is,' " in *Public Housing and the Legacy of Segregation*, ed. Margery Austin Turner, Susan J. Popkin, and Lynette Rawlings (Washington, D.C.: Urban Institute Press, 2009), 31–46.
5. Glenn C. Loury, *The Anatomy of Racial Inequality* (Cambridge, MA: Harvard University Press, 2003), 58, 74.
6. Derrick A. Bell, "Derrick A. Bell (dissenting)," in *What Brown v. Board of Education Should Have Said: The Nation's Top Legal Experts Rewrite America's Landmark Civil Rights Decision*, ed. Jack M. Balkin (New York: New York University Press, 2001), 185–200, at 190.
7. Bell, "Derrick A. Bell (dissenting)," 192.
8. Patrick Sharkey, *Stuck in Place: Urban Neighborhoods and the End of Progress Toward Racial Equality* (Chicago: University of Chicago Press, 2013).
9. Heather Schwartz, "Housing Policy Is School Policy: Economically Integrative Housing Promotes Academic Success in Montgomery County, Maryland," in *The Future of School Integration*, ed. Richard Kahlenberg (New York: Century Foundation, 2012).

10. Brown v. Board of Education of Topeka, No. 483 (U.S. 1954).
11. Nat Hentoff, *The Nat Hentoff Reader* (Cambridge, MA: Da Capo Press, 2001), 165–166.
12. Gary Orfield, Erica Frankenberg, and Liliana M. Garces, "Statement of American Social Scientists of Research on School Desegregation to the US Supreme Court in *Parents v. Seattle School District* and *Meredith v. Jefferson County*," *Urban Review* 40, no. 1 (2008): 96–136.
13. Thomas F. Pettigrew and Linda R. Tropp, *When Groups Meet: The Dynamics of Intergroup Contact* (London: Psychology Press, 2013).
14. San Antonio Independent School District v. Rodriguez (U.S. 1973).
15. Kirabo Jackson and Rucker C. Johnson, "Long-Term Impacts of School Finance Reform," UC-Berkeley Working Paper, 2014, http://socrates.berkeley.edu/~ruckerj/abstract _LRschoolfinancereform.pdf.
16. Rucker C. Johnson, "Long-Run Impacts of School Desegregation and School Quality on Adult Attainments," National Bureau of Economic Research Working Paper No. 16664, January 2011, http://www.nber.org/papers/w16664.
17. Michelle Alexander, *The New Jim Crow: Mass Incarceration in the Age of Colorblindness* (New York: New Press, 2010).
18. Schwartz, "Housing Policy Is School Policy."
19. Laura Tach's ethnographic account of a mixed-income housing development in Boston provides one particularly interesting portrayal of social dynamics when populations mix. Laura M. Tach, "More Than Bricks and Mortar: Neighborhood Frames, Social Processes, and the Mixed-Income Redevelopment of a Public Housing Project," *City & Community* 8, no. 3 (2009): 269–299.
20. Although it can be interpreted in multiple ways, Robert Putnam's research based in the United States provides the best-known refutation of the idea that community diversity leads to social trust. Robert D. Putnam, "E Pluribus Unum: Diversity and Community in the Twenty-First Century—The 2006 Johan Skytte Prize Lecture," *Scandinavian Political Studies* 30, no. 2 (June 2007): 137–174, https://doi.org/10.1111/j.1467-9477.2007.00176.x. See also Lee Sigelman et al., "Making Contact? Black-White Social Interaction in an Urban Setting," *American Journal of Sociology* 101, no. 5 (1996): 1306–1332.
21. "Exposing Housing Discrimination," Urban Institute, February 21, 2015, http://www .urban.org/features/exposing-housing-discrimination.
22. Fred Freiberg, "PRRAC—Housing," 2013, http://www.prrac.org/full_text.php?text_id =1459&item_id=14508&newsletter_id=131&header=Housing&kc=1.
23. Douglas S. Massey and Nancy A. Denton, *American Apartheid: Segregation and the Making of the Underclass* (Cambridge, MA: Harvard University Press, 1993).
24. Douglas S. Massey, *Categorically Unequal: The American Stratification System* (New York: Russell Sage Foundation, 2007).
25. Sharkey, *Stuck in Place*, 347.

DISCUSSION 2

COMPARATIVE PERSPECTIVES ON SEGREGATION

Reflection on Segregation and Integration: A Swedish Perspective

by Roger Andersson

In 2000, the Berkeley geography professor Allan Pred published his book *Even in Sweden: Racisms, Racialized Spaces, and the Popular Geographical Imagination* (2000). The title alluded to Gunnar Myrdal's *The American Dilemma* (1944) and underscored that even a country renowned for social cohesion and progressive social policies was plagued by racially biased behaviors and faced increasing problems integrating new immigrants. Like Gunnar Myrdal writing about the United States, Pred provided somewhat of an outsider's perspective on what was going on in Sweden. If anything, his prescient book is even more relevant now than it was nearly two decades ago.

After a year in the United States, I have also have reflected on how similar and how different the United States and Sweden are, and how difficult the challenges of racial and ethnic integration are in both contexts. The wider contextual differences are of course profound and span many dimensions: history, geography, constitutionalism, party politics, and welfare regime. Let me briefly touch upon some current issues.

In contrast to social science research in the United States, attention to race and ethnicity until relatively recently played a marginal role in European segregation studies. This difference was likely due to a stronger emphasis on social class and a relative absence of immigrants in Europe. Today, however, the proportion of foreign-born residents in some European countries is equal to or greater than that of the United States. What is still a key difference, of course, is the legacy of slavery and what this means for all aspects of American life and politics.

Not only have European scholars started to study racial/ethnic segregation patterns and processes, but the conceptual frame for doing so has more or less been imported from the United States (from the Chicago school of urban sociology to later works by William Julius Wilson, Douglas Massey and Nancy Denton, and many more). For U.S. scholars interested in comparisons, there is a growing European body of literature addressing issues such as spatial mismatch, selective migration and neighborhood dynamics, white flight and avoidance, discrimination in housing and work, and contextual (school and neighborhood) effects. The availability of register-based longitudinal data provides richer data in many European countries than in the United States to address a range of research questions related to neighborhood and school segregation.

Many European countries have recognized that segregation in the form of concentrated disadvantage needs to be addressed by targeted political efforts. A large number of countries have launched area-based urban programs with the aims of improving housing stocks and infrastructure, encouraging local employment opportunities, combating crime, and putting extra resources into schools and cultural facilities. As far as I know, no European country has embarked on a route similar to the Moving to Opportunity (MTO) program as a means of combating negative effects of concentrated poverty (by moving individuals from one place to another). MTO of course has some merits, but it strikes many Europeans as a defensive and individualistic way of handling structural problems. Instead of launching long-term structural reforms to make society less socioeconomically and racially polarized, it boils down to a policy of assisting some individuals to escape poor contextual conditions.

Unfortunately, area-based programs also face severe constraints as countersegregation measures. They point at particular places—neighborhoods providing homes for often socially marginalized people—as being problematic, instead of highlighting the whole segregated city or metropolitan region as the problem. Area-based programs often turn out either to displace problems somewhere else or to be simply ineffective, sometimes even further stigmatizing the targeted area. As I see it, they are sometimes necessary but need to be launched in a framework of wider structural reforms.[1]

In countries like Sweden, social/public housing has often been used as a tool either to provide housing for both the middle and working classes or to offer affordable housing in mixed-tenure developments. This has been very successful, and shows that income mix in neighborhoods is not an unachievable illusion but rather a matter of political will. However, recent developments in

Sweden show that such mixed neighborhoods can rapidly become less mixed if the role of public housing changes.[2] Finding effective measures and planning practices to avoid poverty concentrations in neighborhoods is a challenge everywhere, and it requires stronger market regulations and institutional reforms. Although neither seems likely in the short term, it is important for social researchers to keep emphasizing the importance of such a normative planning ambition if we would like to secure less conflict and more equal social opportunities in the decades ahead. Patrick Sharkey is right (see discussion 1) in emphasizing that we should have a sound research-based rationale for mixing strategies; however, I do think that housing policy has a role to play in achieving greater socioeconomic equality (though maybe not in relation to racial mix). What we've found in Sweden is that mixing low- and middle-income households has positive neighborhood and individual impacts but that focusing on avoiding ethnic clustering makes less sense from an economic-integration perspective, at least if ethnic concentration does not covary strongly with employment rates.[3]

In the aftermath of the recent financial crisis in Europe, we have witnessed the rise of populist, right-wing, nationalistic, and anti-immigrant parties, which are increasingly affecting the daily life of racial, ethnic, and/or religious minorities. Most observers agree that the loss of job opportunities for less educated people following deindustrialization, along with a sustained period of increasing income disparities, provides fertile ground for antidemocratic developments. The same processes have taken place in the United States, but the majority-vote system, maybe along with a very long history of immigration, probably makes it more difficult for such sentiments to make a political breakthrough. Nevertheless, I would argue that because socioeconomic disparities are greater in the United States, the poverty of the poor is deeper, segregation along class and race dimensions more profound, crime rates higher, and the opportunities for intergenerational upward mobility even more limited than in Europe (where the cost of higher education is generally much lower), economic and ethnic/racial segregation are still an even bigger challenge in the United States.

Let me finally discuss one aspect of the institutional setup for dealing with the challenges facing all who believe a reduced level of socioeconomic and racial/ethnic segregation is a good thing. In his book on Detroit, George Galster illustrates how a lack of regional political and planning coordination can ruin a city.[4] Yes, Detroit has a particular history tied to capital in the form of the motor industry, and yes, it has experienced severe class and racial conflicts. It is, however, astonishing to someone coming from a country where all municipalities are guaranteed a similar per-capita tax base, that people (predominantly whites) can abandon a particular jurisdiction and avoid paying for the externalities of their behavior. This situation seems fairly similar across the United States, posing a severe threat to the ability to build social cohesion and provide reasonably equal opportunities. In Sweden, municipalities are financially strong; they have the right to decide on local income tax levels (normally around 21 percent plus around 11 percent in county income tax), but are also compensated by the central state if their inhabitants collectively earn little income. Tax equalization measures have been in place since the early 1900s. In 2014, all municipalities disposed of at least 115 percent (yes, 115) of the national average income tax base. In addition, there is a type of "Robin Hood tax" that distributes tax money among municipalities, calculated according to demographic composition and population change, employment rate, social deprivation, and to some extent geographical features (climate, population density). Together, these resource-allocation mechanisms make sure that social services like schools, day care, care for the elderly, public transportation, water and sewage services, etc., can be provided relatively equally across jurisdictions, which reduces incentives for households to relocate to avoid "problems." The system does not put an end to segregation dynamics, but it does mitigate segregation and reduces its negative consequences.

The concept of metropolitan planning was launched in the United States toward the end of the nineteenth century, in response to rapid urbanization.[5] Some metropolitan planning still does take place—particularly with respect to transportation systems—but it does not and never did include housing or tax redistribution. Political fragmentation of metropolitan regions is a notorious problem everywhere, constraining efforts to desegregate communities, but in the absence of efficient reallocation of resources from rich to poor localities, the United States faces bigger problems in countering segregation than many other developed countries. I have learned during this year in the United States that if anything sounds like a progressive political idea, it will probably be ruled unconstitutional. But maybe I'm wrong, and the "real stuff of equality" (as Patillo in this collection says) can begin to materialize sooner rather than later.

Reflections on a Comparative Perspective Within the United States

by Dolores Acevedo-Garcia

Roger Andersson's reflection on segregation in the United States and Sweden reminds us of the importance of examining segregation using a comparative perspective, which can help us understand the relative importance of different factors that contribute to segregation, as well as the types of policies that seem to reduce it or mitigate its effects. Andersson's call to undertake comparative studies can be applied to examining differences between countries but also differences between racial/ethnic groups within countries. He suggests that while in Sweden racial residential segregation is relatively recent and due to increasing immigration, in the United States segregation has been shaped by the African American experience. While this general point is valid, today's segregation in the United States also reflects the experience of the Latino population—the largest racial/ethnic minority group—and its rapid growth fueled by immigration in the past five decades. I am aware of and have done research on the nuanced differences between black and Latino segregation. Yet, what I find most striking is the "efficiency" of the U.S. spatial stratification system in building such segregated patterns for Latinos over a few decades. Andersson has rightly identified some of the key elements of this stratification system, including high municipal governance fragmentation and very limited cross-jurisdictional housing and school systems.

Research on segregation in the United States continues to focus largely on the African American experience, while research on Latinos more commonly uses the immigrant-assimilation paradigm. This may be a helpful distinction, and one would hope that eventually Latinos will emulate previous immigrant groups and integrate spatially and otherwise. However, today more than two-thirds of the Latino population is second or later generation—that is, born in the United States—and multiple indicators suggest limited residential integration.

Because of current demographic trends in the United States, we should examine and try to undo patterns of segregation not only among blacks but also among other groups, especially Latinos. There is, of course, a wealth of research on U.S. immigrants, and some researchers routinely calculate indices for all the main U.S. racial/ethnic groups.[6] However, when it comes to housing-policy research or just policy debate, Latinos are often missing. When I attend housing-policy (research) conferences, I am often struck by the limited discussion of Latino housing issues. Housing problems—from affordability to crowding to segregation—disproportionately affect Latinos and blacks. However, possibly due to eligibility restrictions for immigrants and/or limited outreach and cultural competency, Latinos are underrepresented in housing programs. For example, the Housing Choice Voucher program serves approximately 34 percent of income-eligible renter black households with children, but only 6 percent of similar Latino households and 10 percent of similar white households.[7] Latinos are also underrepresented in public housing and project-based housing vouchers. Thus, paradoxically, and in sharp contrast with our demographic reality—close to 25 percent of U.S. children are Latino—Latinos may not be seen as a major housing-policy constituency. This may help explain why housing-policy (research) discussions often center on black/white issues.

Another reason why Latino segregation may not be a main focus of policy discussions is that Latinos are not as highly residentially segregated as blacks. However, they are highly segregated, and the patterns we observe are not promising. For example, school segregation is now higher for Latino children than for black children, and the trend is that their segregation will continue to increase.[8] Residential segregation of black and Latino children declined modestly from 2000 to 2010. However, segregation of Latino children increased in many small- to medium-size metro areas in the South and Midwest, which are experiencing some of the fastest Latino growth.[9]

Residential and school segregation are associated with vast differences in neighborhood and school environments. Here, too, the trend is that Latino children's neighborhood and school environments are not as bad as but fairly similar to those of black children. According to the Child Opportunity Index—an index that our project diversitydatakids.org has developed in collaboration with the Kirwan Institute for the Study of Race and Ethnicity—across the one hundred largest metropolitan areas, 32 percent of Latino and 40 percent of black children are concentrated in the lowest-opportunity neighborhoods in their metro area, compared to only 12 percent of Asian children and 9 percent of white children. Similarly, today the majority of Latino (and black) children in large metro areas attend a school in which the majority of the students are low-income.[10]

While the pattern seems to be one of convergence, the effects of segregation may be different for Latinos than for blacks. In public health, several studies suggest that first-generation Latino immigrants seem to be resilient to concentrated neighborhood disadvantage, possibly due to beneficial effects of ethnic enclaves or to health selectivity. However, segregation has negative effects on second-generation Latino immigrants, who now constitute the majority of the Latino population.[11] Andersson makes the point that it would be helpful to know the benefits of income mixing in housing and notes that in Sweden income mixing, but not racial mixing (e.g., avoiding ethnic clustering), has been found to have positive effects. I worry that his point ignores that although ethnic enclaves may be beneficial, or at least not detrimental, for first-generation immigrants, this may not be true for the second generation. In the United States, the evidence indicates that segregation is not beneficial for second- or later-generation immigrants, for whom segregation is a sign of downward assimilation.

Also, it is important to make a clear distinction between our knowledge of the effects of mixed-income housing and the stark reality of extremely unequal distributions of neighborhood opportunity by race/ethnicity. It is true that at least from a health perspective, the research evidence that mixed-income housing improves health outcomes is mixed.[12] Yet, as discussed earlier, there are extreme racial/ethnic inequities in children's neighborhood environments. Can we really wait to have strong research evidence on mixed-income housing to state, as a normative planning ambition (borrowing Andersson's terms), that children's neighborhood and school environments should not be so strongly predicted by their race/ethnicity?

Reflections on Race and Equity: A Structural Perspective

by Glenn Harris

Sixty years after the seminal Supreme Court decision in *Brown v. Board of Education*, school integration in the United States has stalled, and in many places, reversed. While the U.S. population has become increasingly racially diverse, black and Latino students today are largely isolated in poorly resourced schools and neighborhoods. Race remains a key indicator for all social and economic outcomes for success in American life. As Ta-Nehesi Coates recently wrote in the *Atlantic*, "The concentration of poverty has been paired with a concentration of melanin. The resulting conflagration has been devastating."[13]

Roger Andersson's thought-provoking contribution notes the similarities and distinctions in racial segregation in Europe and the United States. As Andersson notes, many European countries have a history of economic sharing, at least among their citizenry, and a history of utilizing government mechanisms to address persistent inequities.

One of the primary differences between the United States and European nations is that in the United States, class and race are almost synonymous. The taking of Native lands, slavery, and Jim Crow segregation built and maintained U.S. wealth along racial lines. Moreover, New Deal policies that created the middle class continued this legacy of racial inequity. This history intertwines American notions of race and class and lays a foundation for manipulating poor and working-class white people against the interests they should share with people of color.

From school busing in the 1960s to the election of Donald Trump in 2016, race remains a political wedge in the United States. We need ways of talking about race that not only cut through fearmongering and race wedge politics, but also are transformative in nature, allowing us to develop into healthy and whole communities. Given the reality of race and its historic, cultural, and institutional impact, we not only need progressive economic policy development, but must also reimagine the roles and practices of community and government in addressing inequity. To achieve this, we must start with a clear understanding of the meaning of racism in America and the ways that race is hard-baked into our institutions. We must move beyond defining racism as individual acts of bigotry. An institutional and structural approach to racism names our history and its cumulative impacts, and provides policy solutions that cut across multiple institutions.

This is the approach that we took during my tenure as the manager of the city of Seattle's Race and Social Justice Initiative (RSJI). We developed a common language and understanding of race and inequity across city departments that proved essential in helping to move new policies and practices. As a way to gauge progress, RSJI surveys city employees every two years to assess their understanding of race. In 2012, nearly five thousand city employees participated. More than four thousand employees (86 percent) stated that it is valuable to examine the impact of race in their work, and 70 percent said they could identify examples of institutional racism.

Building a strong racial-equity frame helped the city pass legislation to eliminate criminal background checks (in many instances a needless impediment to employment, disproportionately affecting communities of color), ensure paid sick time, and establish a fifteen-dollar minimum wage. While raising the minimum wage benefits all low-wage workers, using a racial-equity analysis to consider additional consequences, such as the impact on small immigrant and refugee businesses or access to social safety net programs, helps to mitigate unintended outcomes that disproportionately affect communities of color. Naming race allows for a more meaningful discussion of class. Uncovering our history of policy decisions that created racial disparities, whether they intended to or not, helps to debunk the "makers and takers" myth—a myth that denies our shared contributions and needs—and allows us to envision the possibility of an equitable future.

RSJI recognizes that government has played a historic role in creating racial inequity, and has a role in undoing it. Put simply, racial inequities stem from systemic, avoidable, and unjust policies and practices. Racial equity requires transforming organizational culture, policies, and decision making to reflect the needs and strengths of all communities.

Andersson notes the limitations of creating greater access in high-opportunity neighborhoods, by building more low-income housing as a way to advance racial equity. Indeed, lasting equity demands race-conscious policy and investments that strengthen low-income neighborhoods and communities of color. For example, the city of Seattle is adding specific language on race and equity to its Comprehensive Growth Management plan, naming the need for growth that benefits all. Providing community and government with language and policy opportunities is critical to addressing the injuries of racial segregation. As was the case sixty years ago, separate is inherently unequal.

Defining real inclusion is the first step to addressing segregation in the United States. Like RSJI, the Center for Social Inclusion (CSI) takes a structural approach to addressing racial equity. For too long, race has been a polarizing issue in America, but it doesn't have to be. We partner with community organizations to understand the social and political realities on the ground, and we support the leadership and organizing of communities of color to push the right policies forward. We also support productive conversations about race by crafting research-tested messages that counter the race wedge and build support for policies that help us all.

We must listen to our communities and change the culture of the institutions that represent them. From transportation to food equity and beyond, we can craft public policies that change the structural arrangements that produce racial disparities. We must recognize, as a growing body of research shows, that policies that explicitly address the needs of communities of color will build a healthier society that improves the well-being of us all.

Why Not Compare?

by Christopher McCrudden

Roger Andersson makes a powerful case for the insights gained from taking a comparative approach to tackling racial and ethnic segregation, pointing to the benefits of an outsider's perspective in making the ignored more visible, and the impossible much more plausible. Yet the reality is that this type of comparative perspective is the exception rather than the rule. Why do American racial and ethnic equality scholars and practitioners not use comparative approaches more frequently?

Andersson, indirectly, suggests several reasons: that U.S. scholars may (wrongly) think that there is no equivalent scholarship to engage with elsewhere, or that the ideological preferences are so significantly different as to make the suggestion that policy from one jurisdiction might lead to policy change in another seem quixotic. But I am interested more in thinking aloud about the line near the end of Andersson's essay: "I have learned," he writes, "that if anything sounds like a progressive political idea, it will probably be ruled unconstitutional." A rhetorical flourish, perhaps, but it does raise an interesting question.

Here is the puzzle: There seems to be a considerable degree of pessimism about the future of U.S. law as a progressive force and its ability to address the deep-seated inequalities, particularly racial inequalities, in this society. With some notable exceptions, however, there seems to be very little sense that it is worthwhile looking beyond the United States for ways forward.

Two caveats seem appropriate at this point. The first is that my discussion of American legal insularity in addressing inequality and continuing segregation is directed primarily at the central problem of American race-discrimination law, rather than in other areas involving race such as immigration policy, in which comparative approaches are more common. The second caveat is that some "newer" areas of American equality law, such as sexual orientation, have drawn on more comparative thinking than "older" areas. But the issue of race still so dominates the discussion of American law dealing with inequality as to make it appropriate to treat it as the central case.

The main explanation put forward for insularity in this context is geopolitical: that it is a characteristic of the global hegemon in any period of history not to look outward, except to teach and influence. Another explanation may lie in the scale of the United States itself, and the range of experiences to be found here: why look outside, given the range of differences inside the country? Race-equality law insularity may also simply reflect American legal insularity more generally. The absence of comparative approaches in American antidiscrimination law is just an example of a general phenomenon of insularity in American law, both in practice and in the academy. Though possibly partially convincing, these explanations do not account for the continuing insularity in race-equality law even as other areas of antidiscrimination law engage somewhat more with international developments.

I want to distinguish here the absence of comparison by scholars and academics from the absence of comparison by practitioners, including policy makers, advocates, and judges. Merely assuming that scholars shouldn't use comparison because the courts won't is not enough of an answer. The second distinction I want to draw is between comparison for purposes of transplantation—to bring about change in U.S. law—and comparison for the purpose of better understanding the critical features of your own system. Comparison may be useful outside of the transplant model.

So, how do these distinctions help us explain the relative absence of comparison? First, history: In inventing the new system in the 1950s and 1960s, there were few, if any, external models on which to rely in the critical decades of the 1960s and 1970s, leading to a significant degree of self-reliance. Given its origins, therefore, it is hardly surprising that this approach has continued. Transplantation wasn't possible, so U.S. scholars and practitioners looked inward.

The violent backlash against this form of law and the significant changes that it brought about further encouraged an inward-looking stance, in which the main preoccupation was defending what had been achieved, rather than looking for new approaches from outside the United States. The current absence of comparisons seems significantly driven, also, by liberal scholars' ideological identification with the civil rights movement and an implicit understanding that their scholarship should serve the interests of progressive politics. Only where comparative work appears to serve those interests in the short term does it tend to appear, and in many cases it may not.

In most cases, a significant reason for American antidiscrimination law's domestic focus stems quite directly from contemporary judicial approaches to the Equal Protection Clause. Recent U.S. Supreme Court interpretations of equal protection provide a largely insurmountable structural barrier to the comparative project that Andersson refers to in the sentence quoted earlier. The United States is thought simply not to be able to do lots of things that are done elsewhere because the Constitution (as presently construed) does not let you.

Race-equality law scholars appear to consider that providing a very different legal approach or example from another country would have little persuasive impact on the current Supreme Court. Put another way, the reason why the bulk of race-equality law scholars do not look externally is that they are being pragmatic and see themselves as constrained by what seem to be plausible approaches for transplantation into U.S. courts.

Is the neglect of foreign antidiscrimination law desirable, from the viewpoint of either scholars or activists? I think not. Excluding comparative experience may end up excluding the kind of longer-term lateral thinking that might help address the problem. The paradox of adopting a comparative approach is that its principal utility may lie in helping us to understand our own system better: the questions it raises can be profoundly transgressive, as no doubt Andersson intended his comments to be in the American context. More, please!

Notes

1. Roger Andersson and Åsa Bråmå, "Selective Migration in Swedish Distressed Neighbourhoods: Can Area-Based Urban Policies Counteract Segregation Processes?" *Housing Studies* 19, no. 4 (July 2004): 517–539; Roger Andersson, Åsa Bråmå, and Emma Holmqvist, "Counteracting Segregation: Swedish Policies and Experiences," *Housing Studies* 25, no. 2 (March 2010), 237–256; Roger Andersson and Sako Musterd, "Area-Based Policies: A Critical Appraisal," *Tijdschrift Voor Economische En Sociale Geografie* 96, no. 4 (September 2005): 377–389; Roger Andersson, "'Breaking Segregation'— Rhetorical Construct or Effective Policy? The Case of the Metropolitan Development Initiative in Sweden," *Urban Studies* 43, no. 4 (April 2006): 787–799.
2. Roger Andersson and Lena Magnusson Turner, "Segregation, Gentrification, and Residualisation: From Public Housing to Market-Driven Housing Allocation in Inner City Stockholm," *International Journal of Housing Policy* 14, no. 1 (January 2014): 3–29.
3. George Galster, Roger Andersson, and Sako Musterd, "Are Males' Incomes Influenced by the Income Mix of Their Male Neighbors? Explorations Into Nonlinear and Threshold Effects in Stockholm," *Housing Studies* 30, no. 2 (February 2015): 315–343; Roger Andersson, Sako Musterd, and George Galster, "Neighbourhood Ethnic Composition and Employment Effects on Immigrant Incomes," *Journal of Ethnic and Migration Studies* 40, no. 5 (May 2014): 710–736; Sako Musterd, George Galster, and Roger Andersson, "Temporal Dimensions and Measurement of Neighbourhood Effects," *Environment and Planning A: Economy and Space* 44, no. 3 (March 2012): 605–627.
4. George Galster, *Driving Detroit: The Quest for Respect in the Motor City* (Philadelphia: University of Pennsylvania, 2014).
5. John Friedmann and Clyde Weaver, *Territory and Function: The Evolution of Regional Planning* (London: E. Arnold, 1979).
6. I thank Nancy McArdle for calculating these figures based on tabulations of the U.S. Department of Housing and Urban Development Public Use Microdata Sample (2012) and the Joint Center for Housing Studies of Harvard University tabulations of the U.S. Census Bureau American Housing Survey (2011).

7. David M. Cutler, Edward L. Glaeser, and Jacob L. Vigdor, "Is the Melting Pot Still Hot? Explaining the Resurgence of Immigrant Segregation," *Review of Economics and Statistics* 90, no. 3 (2008): 478–497.

8. Gary Orfield and Erica Frankenberg, "Brown at 60: Great Progress, a Long Retreat and an Uncertain Future," The Civil Rights Project, May 15, 2014, https://www.civilrightsproject .ucla.edu/research/k-12-education/integration-and-diversity/brown-at-60-great -progress-a-long-retreat-and-an-uncertain-future/Brown-at-60-051814.pdf.

9. Nancy McArdle, T. Osypuk, and E. Hardy, "Segregation Falls for Black Children in Most Metro Areas but Remains High; Fewer Metros Experience Declines for Latinos," Diversity Data Issue Brief, July 2011, http://diversitydata.org/Publications/Child_Segregation _Issue_Brief_July_2011.pdf.

10. Nancy McArdle, Theresa Osypuk, and Dolores Acevedo-García, "Segregation and Exposure to High-Poverty Schools in Large Metropolitan Areas, 2008–09," Diversity Data Special Report, September 2010, http://diversitydata.org/Publications/school_ segregation_report.pdf.

11. Theresa L. Osypuk, Lisa M. Bates, and Dolores Acevedo-Garcia, "Another Mexican Birthweight Paradox? The Role of Residential Enclaves and Neighborhood Poverty in the Birthweight of Mexican-Origin Infants," *Social Science & Medicine* 70, no. 4 (2010): 550–560.

12. Peter A. Bris et al., "Developing an Evidence-Based Guide to Community Preventive Services—Methods," *American Journal of Preventive Medicine* 18, no. 1 Suppl. (January 2000): 35–43.

13. Ta-Nehisi Coates, "The Case for Reparations," *Atlantic*, June 2014, https://www.theatlantic .com/magazine/archive/2014/06/the-case-for-reparations/361631/.

NEIGHBORHOOD INCOME SEGREGATION

No Neighborhood Is an Island

by Sean F. Reardon and Kendra Bischoff

In the past forty years, America has become increasingly residentially segregated by income. In 1970, two-thirds of families in large metropolitan areas lived in middle-class, mixed-income neighborhoods—neighborhoods where the median income was close to that of the region as a whole; today, only 42 percent of families live in such neighborhoods (figure 3.1). Mixed-income neighborhoods, and with them mixed-income schools and playgrounds, have been replaced by a rapidly growing number of neighborhoods that are either very poor or very affluent.

Economic segregation is the result of many factors, including inequality in family and household resources, differences in individual preferences, housing and land-use policies, and, in some cases, discrimination by landlords or real estate agents. Growing income and wealth inequality, in particular, have contributed significantly to the rapid increase in income segregation over the past four decades. The widening of the income distribution has exacerbated differences in families' ability to pay for housing, polarizing neighborhoods by income and slowly eliminating mixed-income communities.

One obvious negative consequence of economic segregation is that it concentrates poverty. In the absence of mixed-income neighborhoods, the poor can find housing only in poor neighborhoods. Moreover, in many large

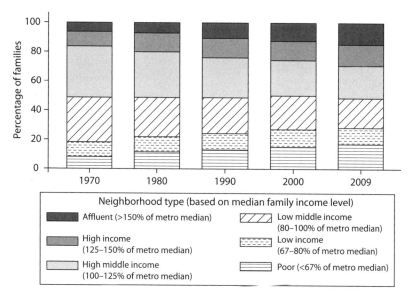

Figure 3.1 Percentage of families living in high-, middle-, and low-income neighborhoods in metropolitan areas with populations above 500,000, 1970–2009

metropolitan areas, poor neighborhoods cover very large areas: Chicago's South and West sides, South Central Los Angeles, North Philadelphia, central Detroit, or Brooklyn's East New York. In these places, poverty rates are extremely high, average educational attainment is low, and a host of social problems, such as street-level drug activity and school violence, are on display in the news and popular media. And these neighborhoods are no longer confined to urban areas; concentrated poverty in the suburbs has grown sharply as well. Such neighborhoods, home to those whom William Julius Wilson famously named "the truly disadvantaged," are hard places to raise children, with scarce opportunities for social mobility.[1] It is easy to think of neighborhoods like these as the primary "problem" that results from economic segregation.

But economic segregation concentrates not only poverty, but also affluence. The growth in the number of very poor neighborhoods in America over the past forty years has been mirrored by a concurrent increase in the number of very affluent neighborhoods. In 1970, only 7 percent of families in the Houston metropolitan area lived in affluent neighborhoods—those with median incomes more than 50 percent higher than the median for the area; in 2007, almost a quarter of families lived in such neighborhoods. Is this cause for concern? After all, such neighborhoods are generally considered highly desirable, places where many people would like to live, if they could afford to do so. Think of urban neighborhoods like Manhattan's Upper East Side, Chicago's

Gold Coast, and San Francisco's Pacific Heights; seceded municipalities within large cities, such as Highland Park (in Dallas) and Piedmont (in Oakland, California); or high-profile suburban communities within easy commuting distance of major cities, such as Scarsdale (New York) and Palo Alto (California). Although housing is very expensive in these places, and becoming increasingly so, many affluent families are willing to pay to gain access to protected school systems, robust public services, and high-quality retail establishments.

The growth of these communities—one in seven families now lives in such places, double the proportion in 1970—means that the affluent are increasingly isolated not only from the poor but also from the middle class. Indeed, the segregation of affluence is higher than the segregation of poverty: families in the top 10 percent of the income distribution are more isolated from families in the bottom 90 percent than are families in the bottom 10 percent from those in the top 90 percent. Moreover, affluent neighborhoods are increasingly geographically distant from poor and middle-class neighborhoods.

This aspect of economic segregation—the concentration of families with abundant resources in economically homogenous neighborhoods—deserves more attention. These patterns concentrate wealth, human and social capital, and political influence in places far from the poor, and increasingly far from the middle class as well. As a result, any self-interested investment the rich make in their own communities has little chance of "spilling over" to benefit middle- and low-income families. In addition, it is increasingly unlikely that high-income families will interact with middle- and low-income families, eroding some of the social empathy that might lead to support for broader public investment in social programs to help the poor and middle class. These processes pack a one-two punch that may do as much to harm the poor as does the concentration of poverty itself.

Why, given its potential consequences, do we not pay more attention to the isolation of the rich? Social scientists, journalists, and policy makers focus on poor neighborhoods in part because that is where the (visible) social problems are; in part because it is easier to study, report on, and intervene in poor places than in rich places; and in part because we routinely commit the outdated fallacy of assuming that concentrated social problems must have local causes. But neighborhoods are not islands. Poor neighborhoods may be shaped less by their residents than we think, and more by diffuse and often invisible decisions made by influential people living far away.

If this is true, we should be focusing our attention and public policy efforts as much on efforts to deconcentrate affluence as to deconcentrate poverty. This is not simple, of course, and we are not suggesting society should mandate where anyone lives. But we are suggesting that policy makers and citizens engage in serious discussions about the costs and consequences of what sociologist Robert Sampson has called, in a wry nod to Wilson's phrase, "the hypersegregation of the truly advantaged."[2]

Spread the Wealth, or Spread the Wealthy?

by Lee Fennell

In their essay, Sean Reardon and Kendra Bischoff provocatively suggest society should pay more attention to the residential isolation of the affluent. They posit that hypersegregation at the high end of the income scale allows the wealthiest families in metropolitan areas to hoard resources and power for themselves while cutting out the other 90 percent of the population. Their analysis also suggests that residential isolation itself, and the lack of incidental social contact it implies, works against any willingness of the well-off to share their bounty. If rich families were physically dispersed throughout the metropolitan area so that they shared neighborhoods, services, and amenities with other families, the argument runs, the affluent would have both a literal and empathic stake in the lot of the middle- and lower-income classes.

In this response, I want to raise three questions prompted by this analysis. First, is greater residential dispersion of the most affluent necessary to counter the effects Reardon and Bischoff identify? Second, is it sufficient to address those effects? And third, is it feasible?

Is Dispersion of Affluent Families Necessary?

As the title of this essay implies, we might first wonder whether countering the negative effects of high-end income segregation requires greater dispersion of the wealthy themselves, or simply greater dispersion of their wealth. That depends on whether the relevant aspects of their affluence come in spreadable form. Can the necessary resources be feasibly shifted to middle- and low-income families without bringing the wealthy themselves along for the ride? Here, it matters whether the affluent are thought to be husbanding within their enclaves (merely) money and political efficacy or also transmissible attributes, skills, contacts, and so on that can only be provided in person. The former might be addressed through political or fiscal changes, at least in theory. The latter would seem to depend on some form of social proximity, for which residential proximity might serve as an input.

Is Dispersion of Affluent Families Sufficient?

We might next wonder if a broader residential dispersion of affluent families would produce the hoped-for gains. This depends on what it is, exactly, that we hope the affluent will transmit to, and receive from, their neighbors. As an example (and perhaps metaphor), consider the recent controversy over a separate "poor door" for the subsidized residents of complexes that are otherwise occupied by affluent families.[3] The more we think that personal social contact is necessary to "spread the wealth," the more residential proximity might seem to matter—but the more contingent its success becomes on how residential proximity cashes out on the ground. The way in which the dispersed affluent would obtain services in economically integrated neighborhoods also matters. For instance, having many affluent families in a given school district may not necessarily translate into more support for the public schools, if those affluent families overwhelmingly opt for private schools.

Another facet of the "sufficiency" question goes to the different ways in which dispersal might occur. The astonishing visual symmetry between the growing hypersegregation of the top and bottom portions of the income spectrum revealed in Reardon and Bischoff's bar charts might lead us to think that reductions in hypersegregation at the top would be automatically matched by mirror-image reductions in hypersegregation at the bottom. But this does not seem inevitable. Suppose, for example, that the top 10 percent in income became far less residentially isolated from the next 40 percent, but that the entire top 50 percent remained wholly separate from the bottom 50 percent, and especially starkly divided from the lowest 10 percent. This might leave those at the lower end of the spectrum even worse off from a political perspective than the current state of affairs, in which 90 percent of the population shares the condition of being residentially separated from the top 10 percent.

Is Dispersion of Affluent Families Feasible?

Suppose we determine that there are real gains to be achieved by deconcentrating the highest-income families. Can it be done? Reardon and Bischoff say that no one should be forced to live in a particular place. But there are many other ways that law and policy can reconfigure the slate of residential alternatives. Existing residential choice sets have been heavily shaped by conscious governmental acts, from land use laws that control the location of different kinds of housing stock to financing mechanisms for schools and other services.[4] If well-off families must choose between a census tract filled with spacious single-family homes on large lots in an excellent school district, and a tract filled with low-rent apartment houses and run-down bungalows on tiny lots served by a failing public school, we should not be surprised if they overwhelmingly choose the former. If the affluent could find the same quality of home in a mixed-income area with access to good schools—a reality that law and policy could deliver—their pattern of choices might look very different.

Then again, they might not. Part of what people choose in selecting a home is a set of neighbors.[5] One's neighbors coproduce the neighborhood environment and other important local public goods—and people may resort to rough proxies like wealth in choosing them.[6] Another factor relates to home values: many affluent families may be happy to share neighborhoods with less well-off families but may fear that those to whom they will later need to sell their homes will feel differently.[7] These factors may call for nuanced interventions, from policies that help foster a "critical mass" of good neighborhood contributors to innovations that alter how the risk of changing home values is allocated.[8]

The questions I have posed are empirical ones and their answers are unclear. By shining a light on residential isolation at both ends of the income spectrum, Reardon and Bischoff have advanced our understanding of metropolitan income segregation and have laid the foundation for asking and answering these questions.

The Durable Architecture of Segregation

by Paul A. Jargowsky

Sean Reardon and Kendra Bischoff have done much to call attention to increasing economic segregation. They document that neighborhoods in the United States have become increasingly stratified at both extremes—concentrated poverty and concentrated affluence—with fewer neighborhoods that have a broad mix of households of different income levels. Should we be equally concerned with the concentration of the affluent as we are with the concentration of the poor? If so, why have social scientists mostly ignored the issue?[9] If not, why the asymmetry? Reardon and Bischoff rightly challenge us to address these questions.

Perhaps the scholarly focus on the spatial distribution of poverty rather than affluence can be attributed to the well-documented harms that are visited upon persons who are poor and who also live in high-poverty neighborhoods, harms that add insult to the injury of miserably low family income. The families and children subject to these conditions are among the nation's most vulnerable citizens. As such, they are naturally a primary concern of social scientists.

On the other hand, it is equally true that the affluent may be affected in various ways, positively or negatively, by the insularity of living in gated enclaves— whether in old money bastions or the sheetrock mansions of the new suburbs. Perhaps children who grow up in these environments absorb the message that they are destined for greatness and leadership and accomplish important things as a result. Or perhaps they become oblivious to the reality of the human condition and morph into pompous dullards reminiscent of Thurston Howell III, the marooned plutocrat from *Gilligan's Island*.

The harms or benefits that may accrue to residents of neighborhoods of concentrated affluence is certainly an appropriate subject of scientific study. All aspects of the human condition are legitimate topics of study for researchers. From a policy perspective, however, concerns about the affluent, who have the power and resources to choose where to live, pale in comparison to concerns about those whose meager resources relegate them to hostile and disadvantaged neighborhood environments. In that sense, it is tempting to respond to Reardon and Bischoff's argument with a weary shrug. Another angle hinted at by Reardon and Bischoff is that the affluent no longer co-reside with the middle-class, yet I am not aware of any research that suggests that the middle class suffers as a result. They do call attention to "opportunity hoarding," particularly in relation to schooling. But does it matter if the affluent do this through paying huge property taxes for superb public education in suburban enclaves or by paying copious tuition to private schools?

Having said all that, I think that there is more to Reardon and Bischoff's essay than a call to be concerned with the fact that concentration of affluence is a thing that is happening out there in the world, and therefore we should study it. We ought to be concerned about rich ghettoes, to abuse the word, not because the concentration of affluence is something that is a worrisome trend in itself, but because this trend is inextricably bound up in societal processes that create and sustain the concentration of poverty. They endorse this view obliquely when they say that poor neighborhoods "may be shaped less by their residents than we think, and more by diffuse and often invisible decisions made by influential people living far away."

To put the message more bluntly, I would say that we should be concerned about the concentration of affluence because it helps to explain why poverty has become more concentrated and also because it operates to make addressing the concentration of poverty more difficult. The process that creates economic segregation is driven by development decisions made by city governments, both urban and suburban, that bring about increasing economic segregation. Through such devices as exclusionary zoning, public subsidies for segregated developments, and tax abatements to spur gentrification, we are building a durable architecture of segregation. The housing stock so produced, which will live on for decades, virtually guarantees continued economic segregation and, given that minority groups have fewer resources, racial and ethnic segregation as well. Moreover, the pace of this new development is faster than that needed to accommodate metropolitan population growth, ensuring that inner cities and older suburbs experience population decline and high vacancy rates.

Thus, I am less concerned than Reardon and Bischoff with the concentration of affluence per se but more concerned with the profoundly misguided set of public policies that concentrates both poverty and affluence. And I entirely agree with them that the "secession of the successful," in Robert Reich's memorable phrase, makes it more difficult to generate the social empathy and political will needed to reverse our nation's retreat from the principle of equality of opportunity.[10]

Keep Concentrated Poverty at the Forefront

by Michael Lens

Sean Reardon and Kendra Bischoff call on us to pay more attention to the segregation of the affluent, which by the authors' measures has actually surpassed the segregation of the poor. While I agree that we should potentially be concerned about the increasing segregation of the affluent, there are also some fundamental reasons why concentrated poverty remains a greater concern.

While there is surely more that we can and should learn about the concentration of the affluent, there is no concrete evidence about negative societal impacts that stem from the concentration of the affluent. Reardon and Bischoff offer one plausible hypothesis—that segregated affluent people will be less likely to support policies that benefit poor or middle-class households. But even taking into account the outsized influence that the affluent have on American politics, do we know that spatial segregation limits political empathy? Without such evidence, we are left without a tangible effect from concentrated affluence.

On the other hand, we have substantial evidence demonstrating that people who live in high-poverty neighborhoods endure limited opportunities and negative outcomes. It makes intuitive sense that the disadvantaged suffer from being isolated from the advantaged. We cannot say the same about the highly advantaged. And these realities have clear policy implications: the people of Beverly Hills and Manhattan's Upper East Side are not suffering from a lack of public investment, unlike those in South LA and East New York.

The growing concentration of affluence does create the worrisome possibility that the affluent could hoard outsize amounts of the best public services and amenities even more so than is already the case. Yet children of middle-class parents in most metropolitan areas still go to high-performing public schools, and those families still live in safe neighborhoods. This is not typically the case for lower-income households. In research with Ingrid Ellen and Katherine O'Regan, we found that twice as many poor renter households lived in high-crime neighborhoods as the general population. Though the gap in income may be widening, the differences between the affluent and the middle class are not as stark in terms of exposure to neighborhood crime, low-achieving schools, and other neighborhood aspects as are the differences between the poor and the middle class. If we look at segregation not just of people but of the tangible benefits that a neighborhood offers its residents, then the poor are the outliers, not the affluent.

I agree with Reardon and Bischoff that "neighborhoods are not islands." Like the authors, I advocate for knowing more about the macroeconomic forces and metropolitan-level factors that can explain why economic segregation is occurring. There is a risk of dependent-variable overload, however, if we bring the concentration of the affluence to the fore in such research. The causes of the increased concentration of the affluent may well differ from the causes of the increased concentration of poverty. But in addressing those causes, it matters which types of segregation we care about the most. Until we see more evidence on the negative effects of affluent segregation, we should prioritize solutions for concentrated poverty.

Notes

1. William J. Wilson, *The Truly Disadvantaged: The Inner City, the Underclass, and Public Policy* (Chicago: University of Chicago Press, 1987).
2. Robert J. Sampson, "Division Street, U.S.A.," Opinionator, *New York Times*, October 26, 2013, https://opinionator.blogs.nytimes.com/2013/10/26/division-street-u-s-a/.
3. Laura Kusisto, "A 'Poor Door' on a Planned New York Apartment Tower with Affordable Housing Gets a Makeover," *Wall Street Journal*, August 28, 2014.
4. Although the focus here is on income segregation, the role of past governmental acts in producing and reinforcing patterns of racial segregation that continue to influence housing patterns today must also be emphasized. See, for example, Adam Gordon, "The Creation of Homeownership: How New Deal Changes in Banking Regulation Simultaneously Made Homeownership Accessible to Whites and Out of Reach for Blacks," *Yale Law Journal* 115, no. 1 (October 2005): 186–226; or Richard Rothstein, *The Color of Law: A Forgotten History of How Our Government Segregated America* (New York: Liveright, 2017).
5. Thomas C. Schelling, "Dynamic Models of Segregation," *Journal of Mathematical Sociology* 1, no. 2 (July 1971): 143–186, at 145 ("To choose a neighborhood is to choose neighbors.").
6. Robert M. Schwab and Wallace E. Oates, "Community Composition and the Provision of Local Public Goods: A Normative Analysis," *Journal of Public Economics* 44, no. 2 (March 1991): 217–237; Lee Anne Fennell, "Beyond Exit and Voice: User Participation in the Production of Local Public Goods," 80 *Tex. L. Rev.* 1 (2001).
7. For analysis of the role of homeowner risk aversion with respect to home values, see William A. Fischel, *The Homevoter Hypothesis: How Home Values Influence Local Government Taxation, School Finance, and Land-Use Policies* (Cambridge, MA: Harvard University Press, 2005).
8. For discussion and citations to literature relating to these and other possibilities, see Lee Anne Fennell, *The Unbounded Home: Property Values Beyond Property Lines* (New Haven, CT: Yale University Press, 2009).

9. A notable exception is Doug Massey, who has repeatedly examined the concentration of the affluent. See, for example, Douglas S. Massey, "The Age of Extremes: Concentrated Affluence and Poverty in the Twenty-First Century," *Demography* 33, no. 4 (1996): 395–412; Douglas S. Massey, Mary J. Fischer, William T. Dickens, and Frank Levy, "The Geography of Inequality in the United States, 1950–2000 [with Comments]," *Brookings-Wharton Papers on Urban Affairs*, 2003, 1–40.

10. Robert Reich, "The Secession of the Successful," *New York Times Magazine*, January 20, 1991.

SUBURBAN POVERTY AND SEGREGATION

Segregation, Suburbs, and the Future of Fair Housing

by Alan Berube

Racial segregation persists in America, but most researchers agree that it has declined over the long term. Edward Glaeser and Jacob Vigdor find that black/nonblack segregation has decreased steadily since 1970. Research points to a variety of factors that may account for that decline, several of which reflect changes in American suburbs.[1]

Increasing Nonwhite Population

Because racial segregation is often measured with respect to differences in the locations of white and nonwhite populations, one result of a rapid increase in the nation's nonwhite population is increasing neighborhood contact between whites and other groups. John Iceland and Barrett Lee show that the share of U.S. population that is non-Hispanic white dropped from 80 percent in 1980 to 64 percent in 2010. Over that same period, the share of all places in the United States that are at least 90 percent white declined dramatically, from two-thirds to a little more than one-third.[2]

Increasing Suburbanization of Nonwhite Population

As the nonwhite population has increased, people of color have also suburban-ized in greater numbers. My Brookings colleague William Frey notes that by 2010, a majority of metropolitan residents in each of the nation's three major racial/ethnic minority groups—blacks, Asians, and Latinos—lived in suburbs. People of color now represent a combined 35 percent of the suburban popula-tion in major metropolitan areas, and accounted for 91 percent of total subur-ban population growth from 2000 to 2010.[3]

Greater Integration in Suburbs

As people of color have suburbanized in greater numbers, they have accessed communities where levels of racial separation are lower than those character-izing many urban neighborhoods. John Logan finds that in 2010, the average black suburban resident lived in a neighborhood where 45 percent of residents were white, compared to only 26 percent for the average black city resident. Similar, though slightly smaller, segregation disparities exist between Latino residents of suburbs and cities.[4]

Movement Toward Less Segregated Regions of the Country

Most changes in segregation are happening within metropolitan areas, but Glae-ser and Vigdor point out that shifts across metropolitan areas account for about one-fifth of the decline in segregation between blacks and other groups since 1970. Over the past forty years, people of color have tended to move away from the most segregated areas of the country—such as Baltimore, Chicago, Cleve-land, and Detroit—toward newer, more suburban metro areas such as Atlanta, Dallas, Houston, and Washington, D.C. that exhibit less racial separation.

Together, these trends indicate that suburbanization over the past few decades has coincided with, and helped contribute to, declines in racial segregation.

Yet suburbanization is not a social or economic panacea, as my colleague Elizabeth Kneebone and I have explored.[5] Indeed, two-thirds of the increase in poverty in major metro areas from 2000 to 2013 occurred in suburbs. Like declining racial segregation, this trend could be viewed as evidence that pol-icies to broaden low-income families' access to the suburbs (e.g., through fair housing, housing choice vouchers, and low-income housing tax credits) are achieving their goals.

Suburbs with high rates of poverty, particularly among people of color, do not enjoy access to the same kinds of opportunities as other suburbs. They tend to be located farther from jobs.[6] They have fewer transit connections. In many regions, they face significant fiscal stress, as Myron Orfield and colleagues have long documented.[7] These very real challenges are often complicated by local perceptions of the source of these social and economic changes that are out of step with reality and limit effective responses. Many local elected officials point to "new" populations as sources of rising poverty, even as many more longtime residents experience increasing hardship.

Evidence is mounting that while suburbs exhibit lower overall levels of poverty and racial segregation than large cities, these challenges may simply be reconcentrating in suburbia. In 2010–2014, 41 percent of poor suburban residents lived in a community where the poverty rate exceeded 20 percent, up from 31 percent in 2005–2009.[8] What's more, the economic recovery thus far seems to be reducing poverty somewhat in cities, while high rates persist in suburbs. The continued repopularization of cities may not lead to overall reductions in poverty, but instead shift concentrated economic disadvantage to places less equipped to confront it.

Notwithstanding the key role that suburbanization appears to have played in reducing racial segregation over the past few decades, these recent trends suggest that "moving out" provides no guarantee of "moving up." In that respect, efforts to expand residential mobility must take careful account of the community options afforded to low-income families, particularly in regions where affordable housing is undersupplied in high-opportunity suburbs. Likewise, policy attention should focus not only on reducing the prevalence of extremely poor neighborhoods (where poverty rates exceed 40 percent), which are still most likely to be found in cities, but also on stabilizing suburban communities with elevated and rising poverty rates. A vigorous push to regionalize the administration of housing subsidies and planning for affordable housing would help minimize the intersuburban fragmentation and competition that can often fuel racial and economic segregation in suburbia.[9]

The Changing Geography of Poverty Demands Changes to Safety Net Provision

by Scott W. Allard

As Alan Berube and the Brookings Metro Program have shown through their research, suburbs have experienced dramatic increases in poverty over the past several decades. Even though there is evidence that persons of color and those living in poverty in the suburbs may not experience the same levels of segregation as their counterparts in cities, many low-income suburban residents live isolated from jobs and programs of assistance.[10] Finding solutions to rising poverty in suburbs and cities, therefore, requires an understanding of when we might expect the safety net to be more (or less) responsive to poverty in metropolitan America.

First, contrary to much political rhetoric, federally funded and administered safety net programs can be incredibly responsive to rising need regardless of where it occurs. For example, the Earned Income Tax Credit and the Supplemental Nutrition Assistance Program have scaled to reach emerging need in suburban, as well as urban and rural, communities.[11] Not surprisingly, programs like the EITC and SNAP are among our most effective at reducing poverty.[12]

On the other hand, much of the other critical assistance we seek to provide to low-income populations—social services providing emergency assistance, employment services, housing, and behavioral-health services—are administered through local community-based organizations. Often this means that the safety net assistance needed to help someone find a better job, secure quality affordable housing, or feed her family are not provided to the same degree in suburbs as in cities.[13]

Why might suburban communities struggle to provide assistance to the poor? Whether real or imagined, local governments tend to operate as if there is a trade-off between supporting local social service programs for the poor and maintaining economic competitiveness. Many suburbs underprovide programs of assistance out of concern they will attract greater numbers of poor persons, which it is feared will dampen the local economic climate. Policies emerge, therefore, that prioritize economic development and residential exclusion over antipoverty assistance. Fragmentation of local governmental institutions matters as well. Suburban regions encompass dozens of county, school district, and municipal governance structures, each with its own set of responsibilities and priorities. The plurality of actors makes it difficult to coordinate activities across jurisdictions, even if funding and capacity are present. Although city government is complex, generally there are far fewer autonomous actors and agencies to engage. The fragmentation of local government in suburbs also makes it more difficult for low-income households and other underrepresented political groups to shape policy agendas than may be the case in cities.

There are no quick fixes for these obstacles to safety-net provision. Urban poverty rates rest at historic levels despite increases in suburban poverty. Reallocating funds from cities to suburbs, therefore, is not a viable strategy. Current proposals to block-grant and cut funding to federal safety-net programs, promised to give local places more discretion, will only make it harder for communities to deliver assistance to those in need. Private giving to human service charities has not kept pace with rising need in recent decades, which means that many urban and suburban communities simply do not provide adequate support to local nonprofit organizations serving the poor. The complex web of suburban government has emerged over decades and is unlikely to change in the near term.

Given these daunting challenges, what can we do? For starters, greater federal funding of cash, in-kind, and social-service assistance is necessary to help tens of millions of families cope with job loss and reduced work earnings. With funding streams increasingly restricted to direct service spending, there is need for increased federal investment in local social-service administrative capacity in underserved suburban (and rural) communities. Another path may be to create collaborative "races to the top" in which the federal government incentivizes the creation of regional safety-net capacity. Without effort to enhance local suburban and metropolitan-wide human-service capacity, it is unlikely we will successfully reduce poverty in suburbs—a failure that will affect the future vitality of both suburbs and cities.

Debtors' Prisons and Discriminatory Policing: The New Tools of Racial Segregation

by Thomas B. Harvey

The experiences of ArchCity Defenders' clients reinforce a message that has echoed through generations: it is dangerous and a crime to be a poor, black person in a neighborhood that is, by design, majority white. No one knows this more acutely than a woman we'll refer to as Ms. C., a twenty-six-year-old African American mother who worked a minimum wage job at the Walmart in Maplewood, Missouri—a wealthy St. Louis suburb in which she could not afford to live. Her exemplary work ethic earned her a promotion and a raise and placed her on a fast track to becoming an assistant manager.

One evening, on her way to work the night shift at Walmart, Ms. C. was stopped by an officer who had on an earlier occasion ticketed her for having an unregistered vehicle. She had already parked and exited her car, but the officer ordered her back into her car. Ms. C. complied with his order, all the while desperately attempting to explain that she had her tags and proper insurance.

When Ms. C. tried to reach toward the tags to show them to the officer, he grabbed her left arm, dragged her out of the car, and slammed her against the vehicle. Ms. C. was arrested for unpaid traffic tickets and taken to the Richmond Heights jail. Ms. C. recalls the feeling of helplessness—she was "in their world now."

A $1,000 bond was set for Ms. C. Although she worked full-time at Walmart, the bond amount was nearly impossible to furnish. Ms. C. was only released after her husband and church pastor scraped together the $1,000 demanded for her release. But more than just losing the $1,000 that night, Ms. C. was fired from her job at Walmart for missing work the night she was arrested. For Ms. C., as for many other poor and black people, the steps she had taken toward economic stability were obliterated in a process that begins with alleged minor traffic violations and quickly transforms into a never-ending cycle of jail, debt, and humiliation.

For black residents of St. Louis like Ms. C., suburbanization has not marked the end of segregation, but rather the beginning of a new chapter in the region's history of profound racial division and oppression. Even after the civil rights victories of the 1960s, St. Louis remained highly segregated, and as of 2010, the city remained the ninth most segregated in the country. Municipal police, courts, and jails operate in concert to exacerbate black poverty and harass black people who dare to intrude into white neighborhoods.

As advocates for indigent defendants, ArchCity Defenders has observed the havoc St. Louis's fragmented municipal structure wreaks on the lives of our clients, and the way it reinforces historical patterns of segregation. Until this highly localized, predatory, and discriminatory legal system is abolished, St. Louis will remain deeply divided.

St. Louis County is comprised of ninety-one municipalities, eighty-one of which have their own court systems and fifty-seven their own police force. This structure did not evolve by accident, but is, as E. Terrence Jones has observed, "fragmented by design."[14] Dating back to the Great Migration, white residents of the city have implemented a series of strategies to exclude the substantial black population of St. Louis from white neighborhoods. Local incorporation, like legally enforced segregation, restrictive covenants, and redlining, emerged as another "peculiar institution" that functioned to sustain and further entrench racial separation in St. Louis.[15] Between 1940 and 1960, the number of municipalities in St. Louis County exploded from thirty-five to ninety-five, in the face of other overtly discriminatory practices being ruled unconstitutional or prohibited by statute.[16]

Once incorporated, municipalities could independently enact zoning ordinances that preserved existing residential patterns and forestalled developments that would challenge the color and class of a neighborhood—by, for example, prohibiting multifamily housing and specifying minimum lot sizes. Black neighborhoods, by contrast, were generally underzoned and unincorporated, and often surrounded by commercial and industrial zones to geographically trap and segregate the black population.

But as black residents of St. Louis trickled into predominantly white suburbs following the civil rights victories of the 1960s, white residents fled those suburbs for the less accessible, whiter neighborhoods to the south and west of the city. For the municipalities to the north of St. Louis, the departure of the tax base, the subprime mortgage crisis, and the costs of sustaining municipal courts and police forces have resulted in financial crisis.

Suburbs like Ferguson responded by using police departments and municipal courts to collect money through traffic citations and enforcement of the municipal code. Thus, between 2010 and 2014, revenue from traffic tickets and fines increased by 50 percent and Ferguson collected approximated $10 million from its poorest citizens. To ensure that poor black residents paid the attendant exorbitant court costs and fees, Ferguson unconstitutionally and routinely jailed those who failed to pay, without inquiry into their financial means, forcing the city's poorest citizens to sacrifice money for food, diapers, clothing, and rent to pay off their penalties for minor offenses.[17]

In February 2015, ArchCity Defenders sued the city of Ferguson and its neighboring city, Jennings, for unlawfully jailing people who could not afford to pay minor tickets and court fees—essentially, for running modern-day debtors' prisons.[18] In August 2016, ArchCity Defenders simultaneously sued thirteen additional towns in North St. Louis for using one jail as a hub to operate another debtors' prison scheme.[19] The predatory practices of racial profiling, overpolicing, overticketing, arresting, and jailing people who cannot afford to pay minor tickets have persistently violated people's civil liberties and jeopardized their homes, vehicles, and jobs.

Elsewhere to the south and west, St. Louis's localized legal structure provides an apparatus for excluding black homeowners, commuters, and workers from white municipalities—people like Ms. C. In Ladue, which is more than 99 percent white, a black driver was 18.5 times more likely to be pulled over than a white driver, 2.4 times more likely to be searched, and nearly three times more likely to be arrested in 2014.[20] In May 2015, the city's former police chief described a conversation with the former mayor in which the mayor directed him to target black drivers so that "'those people' can see what happens to blacks and that we don't want them here."[21]

Even as black residents have moved into the suburbs, the region's fragmented governmental structure has perpetuated St. Louis's historical separation of white from black, wealth from poverty, and opportunity from joblessness. To the north of the city, black neighborhoods are economically oppressed by the municipal police forces and court systems that, from their inception, existed to exclude the families that now comprise their constituency. To the south and west of the city, municipal government actors engage in exclusionary practices that nurture white fears of racial integration. Without consolidating the municipal court system, St. Louis will remain deeply divided.

Delineating Race and Poverty

by Georgette Phillips

Alan Berube makes an interesting point that increased access to the suburbs, potentially through people-based subsidies such as housing vouchers, may have had the perverse effect of reconcentrating poverty from the city to certain suburbs. However, he dulls the edge of this argument by tying in evidence of decreased racial segregation. As he points out, decreasing suburban racial segregation may have more to do with the relative increase in nonwhite and Hispanic populations than with increased suburbanization of poor people. While race and poverty may be correlated, introducing evidence on decreasing racial stratification diffuses his more important point: certain suburbs are looking more like our cities in terms of poverty and economic segregation.

The idealized post–World War II suburb was sold as a peaceful enclave away from the grime and congestion of the city. Of course race-baiting played a role in the siren call of white flight, but poor people were limited to city housing no matter their race. I am certainly not ignoring the flagrant racial discrimination of mortgage lenders in establishing middle-class suburbs. But while the racial aspect was insidious, the more powerful aspect of suburbanization was employment decentralization, which produced a spatial discontinuity between poor people and jobs. Now, two generations later, poverty is increasingly spilling over city-suburban boundaries, and, just as Myron Orfield predicted, certain suburbs are looking more like their city neighbors than their suburban counterparts. The irony of this situation is that urban centers are experiencing a renaissance, with population increases and employers leaving the suburbs and returning to the urban core.[22]

As scholars, I suggest, we should focus more on researching the impact of jurisdictional boundaries on this concentration of suburban poverty. Berube makes a very good point when he considers that "efforts to expand residential mobility must take careful account of the community options afforded to low-income families." Those community options are severely limited by the reification of political boundaries that encourage exclusionary zoning. No amount of fair housing rules will counteract poverty concentration if zoning laws continue to erect barriers to low- and moderate-income housing. His call for regionalization is one that I, and others, made several decades ago but has yet to gain serious traction.[23]

I would also caution that we more clearly delineate the goals of our policy recommendations. Decreasing racial segregation and deconcentrating poverty are both admirable and worthy goals. However, we risk missing the mark in both if we continue to fuse the two.

Notes

1. Jacob L. Vigdor and Edward L. Glaeser, "The End of the Segregated Century: Racial Separation in America's Neighborhoods, 1890–2010," January 22, 2012, http://www.manhattan-institute.org/html/cr_66.htm.
2. Barrett A. Lee, John Iceland, and Gregory Sharp, "Racial and Ethnic Diversity Goes Local: Charting Change in American Communities Over Three Decades,"

Project US2010 Report, September 2012, https://s4.ad.brown.edu/Projects/Diversity/Data/Report/report08292012.pdf.

3. William H. Frey, "The Suburbs: Not Just for White People Anymore," *New Republic*, November 24, 2014, https://newrepublic.com/article/120372/white-suburbs-are-more-and-more-thing-past.

4. John R. Logan, "Separate and Unequal: The Neighborhood Gap for Blacks, Hispanics and Asians in Metropolitan America," *Project US2010 Report*, July 2011, https://s4.ad.brown.edu/Projects/Diversity/Data/Report/report0727.pdf.

5. Elizabeth Kneebone and Alan Berube, *Confronting Suburban Poverty in America* (Washington, DC: Brookings Institution Press, 2013).

6. Elizabeth Kneebone and Natalie Holmes, "The Growing Distance Between People and Jobs in Metropolitan America," March 24, 2015, https://www.brookings.edu/research/the-growing-distance-between-people-and-jobs-in-metropolitan-america/.

7. University of Minnesota Law School, "Metro," accessed August 8, 2017, https://www.law.umn.edu/institute-metropolitan-opportunity/metro.

8. Kneebone and Berube, *Confronting Suburban Poverty*.

9. Alan Berube and Natalie Holmes, "Affirmatively Furthering Fair Housing: Considerations for the New Geography of Poverty,", June 12, 2015, https://www.brookings.edu/opinions/affirmatively-furthering-fair-housing-considerations-for-the-new-geography-of-poverty/.

10. Scott W. Allard, *Places in Need: The Changing Geography of Poverty* (New York: Russell Sage Foundation Press, 2017).

11. Allard, *Places in Need*.

12. Arloc Sherman and Danilo Trisi, "Safety Net More Effective Against Poverty Than Previously Thought," Center on Budget and Policy Priorities, May 6, 2015, https://www.cbpp.org/research/poverty-and-inequality/safety-net-more-effective-against-poverty-than-previously-thought.

13. Allard, *Places in Need*; Scott W. Allard and Benjamin Roth, "Strained Suburbs: The Social Service Challenges of Rising Suburban Poverty," October 7, 2010, https://www.brookings.edu/research/strained-suburbs-the-social-service-challenges-of-rising-suburban-poverty/.

14. E. Terrence Jones, *Fragmented by Design* (St. Louis, MO: Palmerston & Reed, 2000).

15. Loïc Wacquant, "The New 'Peculiar Institution': On the Prison as Surrogate Ghetto," *Theoretical Criminology* 4, no. 3 (2000): 377–389.

16. *Shelley v. Kraemer*, 334 U.S. 1 (1948).

17. *Bearden v. Georgia*, 461 U.S. 660 (1983).

18. Trymaine Lee, "Ferguson Sued Over Alleged Modern-Day Debtors' Prison," MSNBC, February 9, 2015, updated July 21, 2015, http://www.msnbc.com/msnbc/Ferguson-sued-modern-day-debtors-prison; Monica Davey, "Ferguson One of Two Missouri Suburbs Sued Over Gantlet of Traffic Fines and Jail," *New York Times*, February 8, 2015, https://www.nytimes.com/2015/02/09/us/ferguson-one-of-2-missouri-suburbs-sued-over-gantlet-of-traffic-fines-and-jail.html.

19. Mariah Stewart and Ryan J. Reilly, "Groundbreaking Lawsuit Targets 'Extortionist' Cities Near Ferguson That Lock Poor People in Cages," *HuffPost*, August 9, 2016, http://www.huffingtonpost.com/entry/lawsuit-extortionist-ferguson-municipal-courts_us_57a8e636e4b06adc11f0f0c9.

20. ArchCity Defenders, "It's Not Just Ferguson: Missouri Supreme Court Should Consolidate the Municipal Court System," 2014, http://www.archcitydefenders.org/wp-content/uploads/2014/07/Its-Not-Just-Ferguson-Consolidate-the-Municipal-Courts.pdf.

21. KMOV.com Staff, "Former Ladue Police Chief Alleges He Was Ordered to Profile Black Motorists," May 4, 2015, http://www.kmov.com/story/28975097/former-ladue-police-chief-alleges-he-was-ordered-to-profile-black-motorists.

22. Nelson D. Schwartz, "Why Corporate America Is Leaving the Suburbs for the City," *New York Times*, August 1, 2016, https://www.nytimes.com/2016/08/02/business/economy/why-corporate-america-is-leaving-the-suburbs-for-the-city.html.

23. Georgette C. Poindexter, "Beyond the Urban-Suburban Dichotomy: A Discussion of Sub-Regional Poverty Concentration," *Buffalo Law Review* 46, no. 1 (2000): 67–82.

DISCUSSION 5

THE RELATIONSHIP BETWEEN RESIDENTIAL AND SCHOOL SEGREGATION

Economic Segregation in Schools

by Charles Clotfelter

In my professional experience, I have encountered two distinct meanings for the word "segregation." One refers to a legal regime or otherwise formalized system by which people in particular groups are kept apart or treated differently, as illustrated by the systems of state-enforced regulations under Jim Crow in the United States or under apartheid in South Africa. The second meaning is the one adopted by social scientists and other observers to refer to an empirical measure of separation or unevenness in distribution, typically across neighborhoods or schools. Sociologists such as Otis and Beverly Duncan and David James and Karl Taeuber developed and used various mathematically calculated indices to reflect segregation of this second sort.[1] In fact, creating a measure of segregation is a challenge that can be said to have launched a thousand articles. In this essay, I use the term "segregation" in this second sense.

To measure segregation in this sense, all you need is at least two groups of individuals, at least two sets of units containing individuals, one set nested within the other (such as schools within districts or census tracts within metropolitan areas), data on how these individuals are arrayed across these units, and a formula. Groupings of individuals that have been used by researchers include those differentiated by race, ethnicity, national origin, gender, age, religion, and housing tenure type. Unit designations can be geographical units such as census tracts, they can be schools, they can be places of employment, etc.

Although such measures can be devoid of value connotation, it is often assumed that less segregation is better than more. As Mary Pattillo's essay so eloquently argues, some of these implicit assumptions do not always stand up to close scrutiny. In contrast to racial segregation, it may be that economic segregation, which I have measured in schools, carries less of the misplaced normative baggage she addressed in her contribution. That is, education experts and social observers would be hard-pressed to come up with good things to say about economic segregation. Across schools, economic segregation almost inevitably means unequal access to the best teachers and other resources. In any case, empirical studies of segregation by economic status typically differentiate individuals or households according to a dichotomous indicator, such as poor versus nonpoor.

Since public schools typically draw their students from the surrounding neighborhoods and rarely enroll students from other jurisdictions, economic segregation in schools tends to reflect economic residential segregation. (Similarly, racial segregation in schools reflects residential segregation by race.) But the connection between residential and school patterns is not ironclad. Policy matters.

In work with Helen Ladd and Jacob Vigdor, I have applied one type of segregation index to two parallel groups of students in schools in North Carolina.[2] We divided students according to whether they were eligible to participate in the federal free lunch program, which requires a family income not too much higher than the income cutoff for poverty status. Our units of analysis for this study were counties and, within those, schools. (For this analysis, we paid no attention to districts within counties.) We used an index of segregation that, like the Dissimilarity Index, ranges from 1.0 for complete separation to 0 for perfectly balanced schools. We found that the statewide average rate of segregation between students eligible for free lunch and those not eligible increased between the 1994–95 school year and the 2010–11 school year. In Charlotte-Mecklenburg, a district that abandoned its previous policy of racial balance, the increase was about twice as fast as the statewide average. (As I note below, trends in racial segregation to some extent tend to mirror trends in economic segregation.) A contrasting policy was followed in Wake County, home of the state capital, Raleigh. Wake's practice was to rebalance schools periodically (necessitated by the constant growth in enrollments) with the objective of having no schools with more than 40 percent of students eligible to receive free or reduced-price lunches. As a result, economic segregation in Wake increased only modestly, slightly less than that for the state as a whole.

For comparison, we also tracked segregation by race and ethnic group. In 2010–11, average segregation between white and black students was higher than that between white and Hispanic students or that between black and Hispanic students, but all of these have increased over time. Comparisons across states using one measure related to segregation suggest that Southern states like North

Carolina, along with states in the West, have relatively less racial segregation than states in the highly balkanized Northeast and Midwest, where a plethora of jurisdictions makes any kind of segregation, racial or economic, much easier to sustain. Gary Orfield and colleagues report that the percentage of black students in schools that were 90–100 percent minority in 2009–10 ranged from 30 percent in the West and 33 percent in the South to 44 percent in the Midwest and 51 percent in the Northeast.[3] In addition, I would guess that economic segregation in K–12 schools has increased over time, during a period when income inequality has increased for the nation. This trend appears to be showing up in colleges as well. How these two things—income inequality and economic segregation in schools—are connected is a good topic for further research.

Attention to economic differences—and economic segregation—is growing. There are good reasons to pay attention. Economic disparities in education have implications for equity. They also have implications for the effective use of the nation's scarce resources if the economic return from investing resources in the education of low-income children is as great as or greater than the return from investing in the children of the affluent.

Why Economic School Segregation Matters

by Richard D. Kahlenberg

Charles Clotfelter has long been an astute observer of the problems associated with racial segregation in education, and now he properly turns himself to the next frontier: "economic school segregation." Concerns about economic segregation across schools have gained salience in recent years for three reasons. First, economic segregation across schools is rising, even as racial segregation (at least at the residential level) is seeing a modest decline. Second, the U.S. Supreme Court's 2007 decision in *Parents Involved in Community Schools v. Seattle School District No. 1* placed new limits on the ability of school districts to voluntarily employ race in student assignment but left the door wide open to integration interventions that consider socioeconomic status. Third, schools are under increasing pressure from the federal government to boost academic achievement of students, and research has long shown that to raise cognitive skills, it is even more important to avoid concentrations of poverty than concentrations of minority students per se. The congressionally authorized Coleman Report, for example, found back in 1966 that the "beneficial effect of a student body with a high proportion of white students comes not from racial composition per se but from the better educational background and higher educational aspirations that are, on the average, found among whites." More recent research confirms these findings.[4]

For all these reasons, districts are increasingly focusing their integration efforts on socioeconomic status. The number of districts pursuing socio-economic integration policies has increased from two in the early 1990s (La Crosse, Wisconsin and McKinney, Texas) to more than one hundred today—from Cambridge, Massachusetts to Wake County, North Carolina. These one hundred districts educate more than four million students.[5]

Why does socioeconomic school segregation matter? Clotfelter notes that school poverty concentrations are deeply troubling, in part because "economic segregation almost inevitably means unequal access to the best teachers and other resources." Teachers in middle-class schools are far more likely to be experienced and to have greater skills as measured by teacher test scores. They are more likely to be specifically trained to teach in their subject area, whereas teachers in high-poverty schools are more likely to teach "out of field" (i.e., an educator trained in physical education ends up teaching physics instead.)

But in addition to teachers, two other sets of school players—students and parents—help explain why economic segregation is detrimental. There is sub-stantial evidence involving "peer effects" to suggest that having middle-class and high-achieving classmates has a positive effect on student achievement. And being in schools with an actively involved group of parent volunteers is an advantage. In part because middle-class families are more likely to have flexible schedules and time to be involved in school affairs, they are four times as likely as low-income parents to be members of the PTA and twice as likely to volunteer in class, according to federal data from the 1988 National Educational Longitudinal Study and from the National Center for Education Statistics, respectively.[6]

All of this has a profound effect on student achievement. Middle-class schools are twenty-two times as likely to be high performing as high-poverty schools, according to research by Douglas Harris of Tulane University.[7] Like-wise, results from the National Assessment of Educational Progress shows that low-income fourth graders who have a chance to attend more affluent schools are two years ahead of low-income fourth graders in high-poverty schools in mathematics.[8]

And, carefully controlling for self-selection effects, a 2010 Century Founda-tion study conducted by Heather Schwartz of the RAND Corporation found that elementary students in Montgomery County, Maryland whose families were randomly assigned to public housing units throughout the county did far better in mathematics when they lived in lower-poverty neighborhoods and attended lower-poverty schools—even though the higher-poverty schools spent more per pupil.[9] The National Coalition for School Diversity has a series of reports that nicely summarizes the substantial body of evidence on the ben-efits of socioeconomic and racial integration.[10]

As Clotfelter notes, two large school districts in North Carolina have charted very different paths on diversity, as Charlotte-Mecklenburg allowed schools to resegregate by economic status and race and Wake County (Raleigh) sought to preserve economic school integration. Charlotte's nationally recognized pre-K program appears to have helped the district maintain strong academic achievement, though Wake County has achieved comparable results at substantially lower expense. These examples raise the profound question: what might be possible if we combined Charlotte's commitment to pre-K with Wake's commitment to socioeconomic integration?

Race Remains the American Dilemma

by Richard Rothstein

Charles Clotfelter describes two definitions of "segregation." I think it preferable to restrict the term to his first use, a "system of state-enforced regulations as under Jim Crow in the United States or under apartheid in South Africa." For statistics describing subpopulation concentrations, we should use terms like "dissimilarity" to avoid distraction from the important phenomenon of segregation itself.

Preserving this distinction makes it possible to have a conversation with millions of Americans who, following Chief Justice John Roberts and his conservative colleagues, won't call dissimilarity "segregation," instead labeling it racial "imbalance," or what is commonly termed "de facto segregation." Roberts himself avoids the de facto phrase, apparently considering it an oxymoron—if it is de facto, then it is not segregation.

In denying the Louisville and Seattle school districts a right to pursue explicit racial integration (in *Parents Involved in Community Schools v. Seattle School District No. 1* (2007)), Roberts wrote: "The distinction between segregation by state action and racial imbalance caused by other factors has been central to our jurisprudence. . . . 'Where [racial imbalance] is a product not of state action but of private choices, it does not have constitutional implications.'" Roberts went on to say that schools in the two cities were imbalanced because they are located in imbalanced neighborhoods; racial housing patterns in these cities might result from "societal discrimination," but remedying discrimination "not traceable to [government's] own actions" can never justify racial classifications of students.

The public, including scholars and liberal policy makers, has largely accepted Roberts's distinction between de jure segregation (by government action) and imbalance (statistical dissimilarity). But even if we accept the legitimacy of this distinction, the facts don't fit it the way Roberts supposes. What was unsettling about the *Parents Involved* opinions was not Roberts's view, entirely expected, but Justice Stephen Breyer's dissent which, while otherwise stirring and compelling, nonetheless accepted that segregation in Louisville and Seattle (and elsewhere) is indeed mostly de facto. Breyer's argument was that where de facto segregation exists, schools should be permitted to integrate even if they cannot constitutionally be compelled to do so.

But in fact, our schools in Louisville, Seattle, and elsewhere are racially imbalanced not because their neighborhoods are de facto imbalanced, but because those neighborhoods were segregated by government policy whose effects endure, structuring the residential opportunities of African Americans.

In some small cities, and in some racial border areas, some racial school integration can be accomplished by adjusting attendance zones, establishing magnet schools, or offering more parent-student choice. This is especially true—but only temporarily—where neighborhoods are in transition, either from gradual urban gentrification or in first-ring suburbs to which urban ghetto populations are being displaced. But generally, our most distressed ghettos are too far distant from truly middle-class communities for school integration to occur without racially explicit policies of residential desegregation.

Although Justice Breyer argued that racial integration should be permitted as a remedy even where schools are not legally segregated, his acceptance of the de facto notion lends unwitting support to policy makers hoping to avoid difficult (but necessary) discussions of race by advocating plans of socioeconomic rather than racial integration. They hope that this substitution of class for race can dissolve the perpetual "American dilemma" of a racial caste system, without arousing racist opposition.

But it won't work. Although race and poverty are correlated, they remain quite different, both in degree and in geographic distribution. As Paul Jargowsky shows, black poverty is more concentrated than white poverty: in 2011, 7 percent of poor whites lived in high-poverty neighborhoods, while a breathtaking 23 percent of poor blacks lived in such neighborhoods.[11] As Patrick Sharkey shows in his 2013 book, *Stuck in Place*, if African American parents themselves grew up in high-poverty neighborhoods, their children are likely to have the same debilitating experience, but if white parents grew up in high-poverty neighborhoods, their children are likely to escape that environment and live in middle-class neighborhoods.[12]

These differences are frequently obscured in education policy, to unfortunate effect. In most cases, the only socioeconomic data available to policy makers is whether students are eligible for free or reduced-price lunch. This category encompasses both poor and near-poor families with incomes up to 135 percent of the poverty line (and eligible for free lunches), and low-income working-class families with incomes up to 185 percent of the poverty line (and eligible for reduced-price lunches). In consequence, "lunch eligible" versus "noneligible" is not a good proxy for black versus white; it is not even a very good proxy for disadvantaged versus advantaged. If "free-lunch eligible" could be separated from "reduced-price eligible," it would be a closer proxy, but very few states or districts report separate data for free as distinct from reduced-price eligibility.

Analysts observe that lunch-eligible black children achieve at lower levels than lunch-eligible white children, and too often conclude that the black-white academic achievement gap cannot be driven by socioeconomic differences but must result from incompetent (or racist) teachers and school systems. The conclusion is unfounded. While some teachers and school systems are incompetent (in middle-class as well as in disadvantaged neighborhoods), poor black children are hobbled by much more serious poverty, and much more concentrated and multigenerational poverty, than poor whites. Even if all had highly qualified teachers, poor (free-lunch eligible) black children would have lower average performance than low-income (reduced-price eligible) white children because of the greater educationally relevant disadvantages with which typical free-lunch eligible children come to school.

For instance, low-income black children are more likely to be mobile, with unstable housing, than low-income whites; they are more likely to come from single-parent households, and their parents are likely to have lower educational attainment. As Jargowsky and Sharkey show, they are more likely than low-income whites to live in concentrated poverty in urban neighborhoods (and for multiple generations), and so are more likely to suffer from lead poisoning and asthma; they are more likely to be stressed (and have stressed parents) from environments where crime, drug dealing, and violence are prevalent; and they are less likely to have access to nutritious food, primary care physicians, and opportunities for safe physical activity. All these characteristics, and many more, make it more difficult to make educational progress, all other conditions (such as school quality) being equal.

We will not accomplish much reduction of the black-white educational achievement gap if we pretend it only reflects socioeconomic differences that are so grossly mismeasured by the free- and reduced-price lunch category.

There is a second unintended and unfortunate consequence of relying on lunch status for policy purposes. Pro-integration liberals have increasingly proposed balancing lunch-eligible and middle-class students in schools. Many hope to accomplish racial integration by this device, while avoiding both Supreme Court rejection and white families' racially motivated opposition. But the device will, in many cases, accomplish less racial integration than is being sought. Because lunch-eligible African American children are more likely to be poor or close to it, while lunch-eligible white children are more likely to be from working-class families with low incomes, some share of the effort expended to integrate by socioeconomic status will end up not integrating black with white students, but integrating white (including Hispanic) working-class students with white middle-class students. This is certainly a desirable goal, but not the same as racial integration.

To accomplish more, we will have to be race conscious. And before we can expect the public to consider this, we must first discredit the widely accepted notion that residential racial imbalance is de facto, or as the late Justice Potter Stewart once reflected, the result of "unknown and perhaps unknowable factors such as in-migration, birth rates, economic changes, or cumulative acts of private racial fears."[13]

In truth, nationwide metropolitan residential racial segregation today results largely from the ongoing effects of racially explicit government policies, quite similar to Jim Crow in the U.S. South and apartheid in South Africa. These government policies, although no longer explicit, had and continue to have enduring effects. Policies of de jure residential segregation (within Chief Justice Roberts's meaning—intentional and racially explicit) have been well documented but largely forgotten, including by many contemporary advocates of racial equality. It is urgent that we refamiliarize ourselves with this history because if we become aware of how African American ghettos were government created and sustained, we will conclude that residential integration is constitutionally mandated—opinions of Chief Justice Roberts and Justice Breyer notwithstanding. With that conclusion, we may be more willing to challenge the conventional wisdom that racially explicit remediation is to be avoided, and less willing to seek socioeconomic proxies to avoid speaking about race.

Here are some ways that government created de jure segregation:

From its New Deal inception, and especially during and after World War II, federally funded public housing was explicitly racially segregated, by both federal and local governments. Not only in the South, but also in the Northeast, Midwest, and West, projects were officially and publicly designated either for whites or for blacks. Some projects were "integrated," with separate buildings designated for whites or for blacks. Later, as white families left the projects for the suburbs, public housing became overwhelmingly black and in most cities was placed only in black neighborhoods, explicitly so. This policy continued one originating in the New Deal, when Harold Ickes, President Franklin Roosevelt's first public housing director, established the "neighborhood composition rule" that public housing should not disturb the preexisting racial composition of neighborhoods where it was placed.

Once the housing shortage eased and material was freed for post–World War II civilian purposes, the federal government subsidized relocation of whites to suburbs and prohibited similar relocation of blacks. Again, this was not implicit, not mere "disparate impact," but racially explicit policy. The Federal Housing Administration and the Veterans Administration recruited a nationwide cadre of mass-production builders who constructed developments that included, on the East Coast, the Levittowns in Long Island, Pennsylvania, New Jersey, and Delaware; on the West Coast, Lakeview and Panorama City in the Los Angeles area, Westlake (Daly City) in the San Francisco Bay Area, and several Seattle suburbs developed by William and Bertha Boeing; and similar developments in numerous other metropolises in between. These builders received federal loan guarantees on explicit condition that no sales be made to blacks and that each individual deed include a prohibition on resales to blacks.

The federal interstate highway system was constructed through urban areas with the explicit purpose of razing and then relocating black neighborhoods to be far from white neighborhoods, or of creating barriers between white and black neighborhoods.

Public police and prosecutorial power was used nationwide to enforce racial boundaries. Illustrations are legion. In the Chicago area, police forcibly evicted blacks who moved into an apartment in a white neighborhood; in Louisville, the locus of *Parents Involved*, the state prosecuted and jailed a white seller for sedition after he sold his home in his white neighborhood to a black family. Everywhere, North, South, East, and West, police stood by while thousands (not an exaggeration) of mobs set fire to and stoned homes purchased by blacks in white neighborhoods, and prosecutors almost never (if ever) charged well-known and easily identifiable mob leaders.

Other forms abound of racially explicit state action to segregate the urban landscape, in violation of the Fifth, Thirteenth, and Fourteenth Amendments. Yet the term "de facto segregation," describing a never-existent reality, persists among otherwise well-informed advocates and scholars. The term, and its implied theory of private causation, hobbles our motivation to address de jure segregation as explicitly as Jim Crow was addressed in the South or apartheid was addressed in South Africa.

Many state policies to enforce residential segregation ended a half-century or more ago. Can we still consider racially separate neighborhoods de jure? I think yes. Equally explicit racial labor market policies ensured that in the mid-twentieth century, when the white working and middle class grew in wealth and income, similarly situated African Americans were denied those opportunities. Government certification for exclusive collective bargaining of unions that openly excluded black workers is one example. Denial for explicitly racial reasons of minimum wage coverage to occupations in which black workers predominated is another. In consequence, most black families, who in the mid-twentieth century could have joined their white peers in the suburbs, can no longer afford to do so. Highways that were once constructed to separate white from black neighborhoods remain in place. A history of state-sponsored violence to keep African Americans in their ghettos cannot help but influence the present-day reluctance of many black families to integrate.

Today, when facially race-neutral housing or redevelopment policies have a disparate impact on African Americans, that impact is inextricably intertwined with the state-sponsored system of residential segregation that we established.

Avoidance of our racial history is pervasive. We ensure the persistence of that avoidance for subsequent generations. In more than 1,200 pages of McDougal Littell's widely used high school textbook *The Americans*, a single paragraph is devoted to twentieth-century "Discrimination in the North." It devotes one passive-voice sentence to residential segregation, stating that "African Americans found themselves forced into segregated neighborhoods," with no further explanation of how public policy was responsible.[14] Another widely used textbook, Prentice Hall's *United States History*, also attributes segregation to mysterious forces: "In the North, too, African Americans faced segregation and discrimination. Even where there were no explicit laws, de facto segregation, or segregation by unwritten custom or tradition, was a fact of life. African Americans in the North were denied housing in many neighborhoods."[15] *History Alive!*, a popular textbook published by the Teachers Curriculum Institute, teaches that segregation was only a Southern problem: "Even New Deal agencies practiced racial segregation, especially in the South," failing to make any reference to what Ira Katznelson, in his 2013 *Fear Itself*, describes as FDR's embrace of residential segregation in return for Southern support of his economic policies.[16]

Socioeconomic integration should certainly be part of a broader assault against economic polarization. But even if this assault made modest progress, geographically separate black communities could be left behind. We are more likely to diminish racial segregation if we reacquaint ourselves with a history that imposes a constitutional obligation to dismantle this de jure legacy.

Talking About Diversity

by James Ryan

I admire Charles Clotfelter's piece about economic and racial segregation, just as I admire his scholarship generally. I also agree with his points about the different normative salience of economic as opposed to racial segregation, the importance of policy with respect to economic (and racial) segregation, and the growth generally (though variably) of both kinds of segregation.

In this brief essay, I want to focus on how we tend to talk about racial and economic segregation at the K–12 level and how this differs markedly from how we talk about the same thing at the university and college level. At the K–12 level, most of the academic—and public—conversation about segregation speaks in terms of costs. The costs are almost always costs borne by poor students or racial minorities. A good example is in Clotfelter's essay, where he writes that "economic segregation almost inevitably means unequal access to the best teachers and other resources." There are two points in this statement: economic segregation has costs, and those costs are borne by the poorer students. The latter point is implicit but perfectly clear, as no one would doubt that it is the poorer kids who lack access to the best teachers and other resources.

And so goes the conversation generally. In most social science studies about segregation, whether racial or economic, the focus is usually on the harms of segregation, and the victims of this harm are racial minorities or poor students. There is nothing wrong with this per se, as segregation does lead to inequalities, and those inequalities (in access to good teachers, safe facilities, educational resources, etc.) tend to disadvantage poorer students and racial minorities. But this is not the only way to talk about segregation, and it may not be the most persuasive. To see why, contrast the conversation about K–12 segregation with the conversation about the same topic at universities and colleges. But wait, you might be thinking, we don't really talk about segregation at universities and colleges. We talk about diversity. You are right, of course, and that is precisely my point. Instead of talking about the harms of segregation in higher education, we talk about the benefits of diversity. There are political and, especially, legal reasons to frame the conversation this way, as the Supreme Court has explicitly approved the use of race in admissions to further campus diversity.

Regardless of the reason for the different focus, notice the effect when the conversation shifts from the harms of segregation to the benefits of integration or diversity. Importantly, the stakes for the audience—what's in it for them—change. When we talk only about harms to poor students, and redressing those harms, middle-income families might naturally wonder: What's in this for my children and me? What might we have to sacrifice in order to help others? One need not be a thoroughgoing cynic to think a conversation focused on addressing the harms to poor children may not galvanize the steadfast support of most middle-income and affluent families.

Suppose, instead, the conversation were about the benefits to every student of attending a racially and economically diverse school. That is, imagine if the conversation were not simply about the costs of racial or economic segregation (costs borne by just one segment of the student body) but about the benefits to all students of attending a racially and economically diverse school. It's not as if we lack research on this topic.[17] It exists, but it does not get as much attention as it should, and there can and should be more of it.

Put plainly, if we want research to influence public policy, my belief is that it will do so when it identifies what economists would call Pareto-optimal policies rather than policies that seem zero-sum. In plainer language, if research can show that all students can benefit from attending diverse schools, I believe that research would be far more influential on public policy than suggesting that a redistribution of resources to poor kids would help poor kids. Don't get me wrong: I believe in educational equity, just as I believe in justice, and I have been writing about these topics my entire career. I just think we should not shy away from opportunities to talk about policies that can actually benefit everyone.

Clotfelter ends his contribution with a call for more research about economic segregation in schools. I completely endorse that call. I would just hope that the focus of that research is on how all students can benefit from attending a diverse school and, just as importantly, on how schools can create and maintain academically successful, socially vibrant, and stable diverse schools. I am not saying, as the song goes, that we should eliminate the negative, but it would help a lot to accentuate the positive.

Notes

1. Otis Dudley Duncan and Beverly Duncan, "A Methodological Analysis of Segregation Indexes," *American Sociological Review* 20, no. 2 (1955): 210–217; David R. James and Karl E. Taeuber, "Measures of Segregation," *Sociological Methodology* 15 (1985): 1–32.
2. Charles Clotfelter, Helen Ladd, and Jacob Vigdor, "Racial and Economic Diversity in North Carolina's Schools: An Update," Sanford School of Public Policy Working Paper, January 16, 2013. www.school-diversity.org/pdf/NC_school_diversity_executive_summary .pdf.
3. Gary Orfield, John Kucsera, and Genevieve Siegel-Hawley, "E Pluribus . . . Separation: Deepening Double Segregation for More Students," Civil Rights Project, September 2012.
4. Of course, there are powerful reasons to want to integrate schools by race having nothing to do with test scores. In a pluralistic democracy, it is important to promote tolerance and reduce racial bias and to prepare students to thrive in a multiracial workforce.
5. Halley Potter, "Updated Inventory of Socioeconomic Integration Policies: Fall 2016," Century Foundation, October 14, 2016, https://tcf.org/content/commentary/updated -inventory-socioeconomic-integration-policies-fall-2016/.
6. "National Education Longitudinal Study of 1988," accessed June 29, 2017, https://nces .ed.gov/surveys/nels88/; National Center for Education Statistics, *Parent and Family Involvement in Education, 2006–07 School Year*, August 2008, Table 3.
7. Douglas N. Harris, *Ending the Blame Game on Educational Inequity: A Study of "High Flying" Schools and NCLB* (Tempe, Ariz.: Education Policy Research Unit, Arizona State University, March 2006), 5.
8. Richard D. Kahlenberg and Halley Potter, "Can Racial and Socioeconomic Integration Promote Better Outcomes for Students?" The Century Foundation and Poverty and Race Research Action Council, May 2012, Figure 2, https://tcf.org/assets/downloads /Diverse_Charter_Schools.pdf.
9. Heather Schwartz, *Housing Policy Is School Policy: Economically Integrative Housing Promotes Academic Success in Montgomery County, Maryland* (New York: The Century Foundation, 2010), Figure 6.
10. National Coalition on School Diversity, Research Briefs, http://school-diversity.org /research-briefs/.

11. Paul Jargowsky, "Concentration of Poverty in the New Millennium," Century Foundation, December 18, 2013, https://tcf.org/content/report/concentration-of-poverty-in-the-new-millennium/.
12. Patrick Sharkey, *Stuck in Place: Urban Neighborhoods and the End of Progress Toward Racial Equality* (Chicago: University of Chicago Press, 2013).
13. Milliken v. Bradley, U.S. Supreme Court 418 U.S. 717, 757 (1974), MR. JUSTICE STEWART, concurring, [418 U.S. 717, 757], Footnote 2.
14. Littell McDougal, *The Americans: Student Edition 2007* (Boston: Houghton Mifflin Harcourt, 2006).
15. Emma J. Lapansky-Werner et al., *Prentice Hall United States History—Modern America*, California Edition (Upper Saddle River, NJ: Pearson Prentice Hall, 2007).
16. Diane Hart, *History Alive! The United States Through Industrialism*, Student Edition (Palo Alto, CA: Teachers Curriculum Institute, 2005); Ira Katznelson, *Fear Itself: The New Deal and the Origins of Our Time* (New York: Liveright, 2013).
17. Genevieve Siegel-Hawley, "How Non-Minority Students Also Benefit from Racially Diverse Schools," Research Brief No. 8, National Coalition on School Diversity, October 2012, http://school-diversity.org/pdf/DiversityResearchBriefNo8.pdf.

PART II

CAUSES OF CONTEMPORARY RACIAL SEGREGATION

Introduction

The three discussions that follow debate the causes of contemporary racial segregation. As both Jackelyn Hwang and Margery Turner note in their essays, there are many reasons to think that segregation should have declined dramatically over the past few decades. First, studies of housing market discrimination show a reduction in the prevalence of explicit forms of discrimination. Second, the income (though not wealth) gaps across racial groups have moderated, even as overall income inequality has widened. Third, surveys consistently suggest increasingly tolerant racial attitudes. Finally, federal housing policy has placed an increasing emphasis on economic integration and the deconcentration of poverty. Yet racial segregation levels, especially black-white segregation, remain high in many U.S. cities. The authors in this section debate the key reasons why segregation has persisted.

Traditionally, arguments about segregation have centered on whether segregation is caused by discrimination, on the one hand, or income differences among and diverging preferences of housing seekers, on the other. The view seemed to be that if segregation is driven by discrimination, it is troubling, but if it is driven by differences in income across racial groups or by the neighborhood preferences of home seekers, then it is largely benign, with housing markets simply operating as markets do, sorting people according to their preferences and ability to pay. But the authors of the essays that follow challenge this simple dichotomy, arguing that the racial preferences of home seekers are not so benign. They offer nuanced takes on the traditional arguments, emphasizing that contemporary segregation is sustained through a collection of factors, including persistent, if more permeable, barriers to mobility, and complex neighborhood preferences rooted in assumptions about largely minority neighborhoods.

Housing Market Discrimination

As noted, one potential explanation for segregation is housing market discrimination, or the differential treatment of minority home seekers by landlords, realtors, home sellers, and lenders. There is ample evidence that such discrimination was pervasive before the passage of the Fair Housing Act and continued after it, and was a central driver of segregation.[1] Margery Turner explains in her essay that national audit studies of housing discrimination show a significant reduction in the prevalence of explicit denials of access to housing on the basis of race, but also indicate that discrimination persists in more subtle forms (see discussion 6). Such discrimination is deeply troubling, and policy makers and advocates should continue to work to root it out at all levels. However, scholars agree that this more subtle form of ongoing discrimination in the marketplace cannot on its own explain the high levels of segregation that we continue to observe in most U.S. metropolitan areas.

Racial Differences in Economic Resources

Another potential driver of segregation, as Solomon Greene suggests, is average differences in economic resources across racial groups. Many black and Latino home seekers may simply not be able to afford to buy or rent in the same neighborhoods as whites and Asians. Even though racial gaps in income have decreased, they remain substantial: in 2015, the median incomes of Asian and non-Hispanic white households in the United States were $77,166 and $62,950, respectively, while the median incomes of Hispanic and black households were $45,148 and $36,898, respectively.[2]

These income differences play some role in sustaining segregation, but again, they cannot explain the full extent of segregation. Considerable research suggests that income differences between blacks and whites account for only a small share of black-white segregation.[3] Sociodemographic variables, taken together, including income, but also education, occupation, household composition, language, and immigration status, likely play a more significant role in shaping segregation levels, perhaps especially for immigrant households. But one study found that even this broad collection of sociodemographic factors could only explain 30 percent of black-white segregation levels in the Bay Area.[4]

That said, researchers have yet to thoroughly investigate the role of racial gaps in wealth (as compared to income), which are vast and have widened since the great recession.[5] The 2016 Survey of Consumer Finances reported a white household median net worth of $171,000, compared to just $20,700 for Latino households and $17,600 for black households.[6] Such enormous disparities in wealth mean that the average white household can afford to buy a significantly more expensive home.

Preferences

What about the role of preferences? For minority-group members, an affirmative desire to live among those who share one's history and culture, and in some cases language, may contribute to segregation. Yet survey evidence provides little support for this ethnic-clustering hypothesis. As Camille Charles notes in her essay, while "they do not want to be 'the only' or one of a very few," most minorities state a preference for racially and ethnically mixed neighborhoods. Ethnic clustering may play a somewhat greater role in the segregation of Asians and Hispanics than that of whites and African Americans, because a larger share of the former are first- or second-generation immigrants who may find that close connections to others who share their language and customs help ease their transition to a new country. In 2012, close to two-thirds of the Asian population and more than one-third of the Hispanic population in the United States were foreign-born.[7] With time in this country, however, preferences for clustering appear to dissipate, as native-born Asian and Hispanic households are less segregated than their foreign-born counterparts.[8] Further, as Turner points out, it is difficult, if not impossible, to distinguish between an affirmative desire to live among coethnics and a fear of the hostility one might encounter when entering predominantly white neighborhoods.

The contributors to the discussions in this section focus most of their attention on the critical role that the residential choices of white households play in perpetuating segregation. But there is considerable disagreement among these contributors, and in the literature more generally, about the specific nature of those preferences. One key disagreement is whether whites avoid living near minorities because of racial animus or because of their perceptions about the neighborhoods lived in by minorities. Some researchers have emphasized the importance of race-based neighborhood stereotypes, suggesting that whites continue to associate the presence of minority neighbors, and in particular black neighbors, with declining property values, disinvestment, and crime.[9] In her essay, Micere Keels pinpoints racialized fears about school quality:

"Not even the most postracial White Americans will reside in mostly minority neighborhoods if it means sending their children to higher-poverty schools." Other researchers have argued that whites have "racial blind spots" that keep them from even knowing much about largely minority areas.[10]

Another key disagreement is whether racial preferences are explicit or implicit. That is, scholars disagree about the degree to which white households are aware of their racial biases and assumptions about minority neighborhoods. For example, while Camille Charles and Richard Ford focus on the explicit views that white households hold about black behavior, culture, and/or neighborhoods, Jerry Kang and Cheryl Staats both emphasize the role of implicit or unconscious bias. As Kang writes, "the segregation of the past can endure into the future simply by the actions of 'rational' individuals pursuing their self-interest with slightly biased perceptions driven by implicit associations we aren't even aware of."

Another important tension is the degree to which racial preferences are malleable and shaped by context. Richard Sander, for example, argues that white preferences differ depending on the demographic history of their metropolitan areas. Whites have historically been more willing to stay in integrated neighborhoods in metropolitan areas in the western United States that have smaller black populations and lack the history of neighborhood racial change found in the rest of the country.[11]

Public Policy

What about public policy in shaping segregation? Public policies, such as the enforcement of restrictive covenants, the disproportionate siting of public housing in predominantly minority areas, and the underwriting requirements for Federal Housing Administration secured loans, have historically played a central role in creating and perpetuating residential segregation in U.S. cities.[12] Most of these practices have since been prohibited, but the residential patterns they created, or facilitated, are sticky and stubborn.

While history is clearly important, current policies, especially at the municipal level, also play a role in perpetuating both racial and economic segregation. Scholars debate which policies are most important. Many, like Solomon Greene and Jon Vogel, emphasize that residents sometimes use the tools of local government, and in particular land-use regulations, to exclude unwanted neighbors. There is broad agreement that such restrictive land-use regulations are becoming more prevalent.[13] Some studies also suggest that these land-use restrictions help to sustain segregation.[14] Residents may not have explicitly racial motivations in supporting restrictions on increased density or multifamily housing; they may be genuinely worried about fiscal burdens or crowded schools. But these restrictions disproportionately exclude minority residents, given their lower average incomes.

$* * *$

The discussions that follow debate these various causes. The differences in these authors' assessments are nuanced, but they matter because they suggest different policy responses. All seem to agree that segregation will not end on its own. Yet there is a sliver of optimism. As Greene and Hwang point out, millennials appear to be more open to living in integrated urban neighborhoods. Gentrification, at least in the short-term, appears to be bringing some integration in its wake, even as it increases housing costs and makes it more difficult for many lower-income households of color to remain in the communities they have long called home. Time will tell whether these millennials will maintain these more liberal attitudes as they age and whether the neighborhoods that are integrating through gentrification will remain stably integrated over time.

The Discussions in Part II

Ending Segregation: Our Progress Today

The first discussion in this section explores why we have not made more progress in reducing segregation. Margery Turner begins the discussion with an overview of the causes of persistent segregation, highlighting the important role that the race-based neighborhood stereotypes held by whites play in perpetuating segregation. The three responders largely agree, though they stress different aspects of those white residential decisions. Camille Charles argues that the nation's troubling history of racial inequality continues to shape white attitudes about black households. Micere Keels emphasizes white households' anxieties about what integration would mean for the schools their children attend. Finally, Jon Vogel echoes Keels's argument, pointing to land-use regulations as a critical tool used by white and affluent households to protect their schools and neighborhoods from perceived threats.

The Stubborn Persistence of Racial Segregation

The second discussion offers four additional, nuanced perspectives on the root causes of segregation within American cities. Jackelyn Hwang starts by highlighting some hopeful trends and progress made in reducing segregation, but, like Turner, she ends by emphasizing how the residential decisions of white households perpetuate segregation patterns. Solomon Greene takes issue with the focus on mobility and choice, arguing that the more important issue may be the white households who stay in place and support exclusionary policies to protect those neighborhoods. Richard Sander reminds us that history and context are critical in driving segregation patterns, and argues that to understand the roots of segregation in different areas, we need to consider the interaction between neighborhood choices and larger demographic forces operating at a metropolitan scale. Jorge Soto emphasizes the role of barriers to the mobility of minority households, and he points to the role of ongoing discrimination by landlords, especially their refusal to house people with criminal records or those using housing choice vouchers, both of which have a disparate impact on the basis of race.

Implicit Bias and Segregation

The third discussion in this section explores the role of implicit bias in perpetuating residential segregation. Jerry Kang starts by arguing that even without explicit racism, the biased perceptions that white households hold about minority households and their communities can sustain segregation. But Richard Ford and Robert Smith challenge Kang's notion that if we could simply make white households aware of their implicit biases, it would inspire a greater moral urgency to address segregation. Ford and Smith contend that white households do not (or would not) feel shame about their biases about minority neighborhoods; indeed, many already acknowledge their views about racial dynamics in neighborhoods and feel justified in their decisions to avoid integrated neighborhoods. Cheryl Staats generally agrees with Kang and stresses the difficulty of breaking down implicit biases.

Notes

1. Douglas S. Massey and Nancy A. Denton, *American Apartheid: Segregation and the Making of the Underclass* (Cambridge, MA: Harvard University Press, 1993); Richard Rothstein, *The Color of Law: A Forgotten History of How Our Government Segregated America* (New York: Liveright, 2017).
2. Bernadette D. Proctor, Jessica L. Semega, and Melissa A. Kollar, "Income and Poverty in the United States: 2015," United States Census Bureau, September 2016, https://www.census.gov/content/dam/Census/library/publications/2016/demo/p60-256.pdf.
3. Reynolds Farley and William H. Frey, "Changes in the Segregation of Whites from Blacks During the 1980s: Small Steps Toward a More Integrated Society," *American Sociological Review* 59, no. 1 (February 1994): 23–45; John Kain, "The Influence of Race and Income on Racial Segregation and Housing Policy," in *Housing Desegregation and Federal Policy* (Chapel Hill: University of North Carolina Press, 1986), 99–118; Stuart

Gabriel and Stuart Rosenthal, "Household Location and Race: Estimates of Multinomial Logit Model," *Review of Economics and Statistics* 71, no. 2 (1989): 240–249; Keith Ihlanfeldt and Benjamin Scafidi, "Black Self-Segregation as a Cause of Housing Segregation: Evidence from the Multi-City Study of Urban Inequality," *Journal of Urban Economics* 51, no. 2 (2002): 366–390; Barrett A. Lee et al., "A Comparison of Traditional and Discrete-Choice Approaches to the Analysis of Residential Mobility and Locational Attainment," *Annals of the American Academy of Political and Social Science* 660, no. 1 (July 2015): 240–260, https://doi.org/10.1177/0002716215577770.

4. Patrick Bayer, Robert McMillan, and Kim Rueben, "What Drives Racial Segregation? New Evidence Using Census Microdata," Yale School of Management Working Paper, July 28, 2004, http://econpapers.repec.org/paper/ysmsomwrk/ysm409.htm.

5. Rakesh Kochhar and Richard Fry, "Wealth Inequality Has Widened Along Racial, Ethnic Lines Since End of Great Recession," *Pew Research Center* (blog), December 12, 2014, http://www.pewresearch.org/fact-tank/2014/12/12/racial-wealth-gaps-great-recession/.

6. Lisa J. Dettling, Joanne W. Hsu, Lindsay Jacobs, Kevin B. Moore, and Jeffrey P. Thompson, "Recent Trends in Wealth-Holding by Race and Ethnicity: Evidence from the Survey of Consumer Finances," FEDS Notes. (Washington, D.C.: Board of Governors of the Federal Reserve System, September 27, 2017), https://doi.org/10.17016/2380-7172.2083.

7. Gustavo López and Jynnah Radford, "Facts on U.S. Immigrants, 2015," *Pew Research Center's Hispanic Trends Project* (blog), 2014, http://www.pewhispanic.org/2017/05/03/facts-on-u-s-immigrants/.

8. John Iceland and Melissa Scopilliti, "Immigrant Residential Segregation in U.S. Metropolitan Areas, 1990–2000," *Demography* 45, no. 1 (February 2008): 79–94.

9. Ingrid Gould Ellen, *Sharing America's Neighborhoods: The Prospects for Stable Racial Integration* (Cambridge, MA: Harvard University Press, 2001).

10. Maria Krysan and Michael D. M. Bader, "Racial Blind Spots: Black-White-Latino Differences in Community Knowledge," *Social Problems* 56, no. 4 (November 2009): 677–701, https://doi.org/10.1525/sp.2009.56.4.677.

11. Farley and Frey, "Changes in the Segregation of Whites from Blacks."

12. Rothstein, *The Color of Law.*

13. Daniel Shoag and Peter Ganong, "Why Has Regional Income Convergence Declined?," Hutchins Center Working Papers, August 4, 2016, https://www.brookings.edu/research/why-has-regional-income-convergence-declined/; Joseph Gyourko and Raven Molloy, "Regulation and Housing Supply," National Bureau of Economic Research Working Paper No. 20536, October 2014, http://www.nber.org/papers/w20536.

14. Rolf Pendall, "Local Land Use Regulation and the Chain of Exclusion," *Journal of the American Planning Association* 66, no. 2 (June 2000): 125–142, https://doi.org/10.1080/01944360008976094; Matthew Resseger, "The Impact of Land Use Regulation on Racial Segregation: Evidence from Massachusetts Zoning Borders," Harvard University, November 26, 2013, https://scholar.harvard.edu/files/resseger/files/resseger_jmp_11_25.pdf; Jonathan Rothwell and Douglas S. Massey, "The Effect of Density Zoning on Racial Segregation in U.S. Urban Areas," *Urban Affairs Review* 44, no. 6 (July 2009): 779–806, https://doi.org/10.1177/1078087409334163.

DISCUSSION 6

ENDING SEGREGATION: OUR PROGRESS TODAY

Why Haven't We Made More Progress in Reducing Segregation?

by Margery Austin Turner

Recent surveys strongly suggest that Americans would prefer to live in more racially and ethnically diverse neighborhoods than they do. So why does residential segregation remain so stubbornly high?

The historical record clearly demonstrates that our nation's stark patterns of racial segregation were established through public policy, including the enforcement of restrictive covenants, local land-use regulations, underwriting requirements for federally insured mortgage loans, and siting and occupancy regulations for public housing. But the dynamics that sustain segregation today are far more complex and subtle. Here's my take on the tangle of factors that perpetuate segregation and undermine the stability of mixed neighborhoods.[1]

First, discrimination constrains minorities' housing search. The most recent national paired-testing study of housing market discrimination finds that minority home seekers (blacks, Latinos, and Asians) are still told about and shown fewer homes and apartments than equally qualified whites. These subtle forms of discrimination limit minorities' information about available housing options and raise their costs of search. But discrimination today rarely takes the form of outright denial of access to housing in predominantly white neighborhoods. So, although discrimination remains a serious problem, it cannot account for the high levels of segregation in most metropolitan housing markets.

Advertising and information sources may also limit housing choices. A small number of studies (all conducted more than a decade ago) suggest that homes in majority-black neighborhoods are advertised quite differently than similarly priced homes in predominantly white neighborhoods and that blacks and whites rely on different sources of information and employ different search strategies.[2] But all these studies were completed before the widespread use of the internet in real estate marketing and information gathering. So we don't know whether disparities in information sources and search strategies between minorities and whites play any significant role in the perpetuation of segregation today. This is an area where we need to learn more.

Affordability barriers contribute to racial and ethnic segregation. Whites on average have higher incomes and wealth (due in part to past patterns of discrimination and segregation) and can therefore afford to live in neighborhoods that are out of reach for many minorities. But these economic differences can only account for a modest share of the segregation that remains today, particularly between blacks and whites. If households were distributed across neighborhoods entirely on the basis of income (regardless of race or ethnicity), levels of black-white segregation would be dramatically lower. So affordability plays a role, but it's definitely not the whole story.

Most minority home seekers prefer mixed neighborhoods. Some people argue that neighborhood segregation today is largely a matter of choice—that minorities prefer to live in neighborhoods where their own race or ethnicity predominates and choose not to move to white neighborhoods. Indeed, the evidence confirms that the average black person's ideal neighborhood has more blacks living in it than the average white person's ideal neighborhood, that few blacks want to be the first to move into a white neighborhood, and that most blacks prefer neighborhoods where their own race accounts for about half the population. But few blacks actually express a preference for living in predominantly black neighborhoods, and it's difficult to disentangle a positive preference for living among other black families from fear of hostility from white neighbors. Surveys suggest that many blacks are hesitant to move to predominantly white neighborhoods primarily because of concerns about hostility—concerns that were painfully reinforced by the shooting of Trayvon Martin.

Many whites avoid neighborhoods with large or growing minority populations. Considerable evidence suggests that the choices of white people play a major role in perpetuating neighborhood segregation. First, very few whites express any interest in moving into neighborhoods that are predominantly minority, probably in large part because predominantly minority neighborhoods have been deprived of the public and private investments that comparable white neighborhoods enjoy. In other words, the legacy of past discrimination and disinvestment puts most minority neighborhoods at a significant disadvantage from the perspective of white home seekers for whom alternative choices abound.

But many whites are also unwilling to move to (or remain in) neighborhoods with smaller, but significant or rising, minority shares. To some extent, this reflects old-fashioned prejudice—an aversion to minority neighbors. And for some whites, living in an area with neighbors of color may be seen as an indicator of lower social status. But survey evidence suggests that these attitudes have declined over recent decades, and today very few neighborhoods (at least in metro areas) remain exclusively white, suggesting that most white households have accepted having at least some minority neighbors.

Nonetheless, many white people fear that a substantial minority presence will inevitably lead to the neighborhood's becoming predominantly minority, with a subsequent downward spiral of declining property values, disinvestment, and crime. These fears cause them to avoid moving into mixed neighborhoods and, in some cases, to flee as minorities move into neighborhoods where they live. This avoidance by whites of neighborhoods that probably look especially welcoming to minority home seekers leads to resegregation and reinforces everybody's expectations about racial tipping.

Given the complexity—and subtlety—of the processes sustaining residential segregation in urban America today, how should public policy respond? In my view, there can be no question that public intervention is essential. But the solutions have to be both nuanced and multifaceted, addressing the interacting barriers of discrimination, information gaps, affordability constraints, prejudice, and fear.

How Do We Reconcile Americans' Increasing Interest in Residential Diversity with Persistent Racial Segregation?

by Camille Zubrinsky Charles

There is mounting evidence that where we live is critically important for our overall life chances—the education of our children, our access to employment, our exposure to crime and environmental toxins, and our physical and mental health. Thus, racial residential segregation has been referred to as "the structural linchpin" in persistent racial inequality in the United States. It is worthy of our continued attention precisely because of its implications for overall well-being and upward socioeconomic mobility. Given our sordid racial history, it comes as no surprise that, on average, blacks in the United States continue to reside in racially isolated neighborhoods over the course of their lives, irrespective of their individual socioeconomic characteristics. Thus, while it is true that racially segregated neighborhoods were, as Turner notes, "established through public policy, including the enforcement of restrictive covenants, local land-use regulations, underwriting requirements for federally insured mortgage loans, and siting and occupancy regulations for public housing," we should not ignore the critical role of earlier and even more dehumanizing racial policies in our history that are key to understanding how we got here and why the path to change has been so slow. To the extent that households' preferences for particular neighborhoods play an important role in perpetuating racial residential segregation, those preferences are not benign. Present-day neighborhood racial composition preferences are infected by the history of racial oppression in the United States.

Blacks in the United States are the only group to have been legally codified as less than full human beings. Later, despite being granted legal recognition as fully human, blacks continued to occupy second-class citizenship status through a series of legally sanctioned policies best known as Jim Crow. Indeed, in terms of our understandings of full citizenship in the United States, blacks only obtained the full rights and protections afforded to U.S. citizens in 1964, 1965, and 1968, with the passage of civil rights legislation. These victories were not won easily, nor did they immediately change what was in "the hearts and minds" of white Americans. Similarly, having finally achieved rights that whites had taken for granted for centuries, blacks were not immediately confident that our nation had solved "the problem of the century" and that they were suddenly free to move about the proverbial cabin.

Trends in racial attitudes confirm decreasing white expressions of racist attitudes but also stubbornly persistent discriminatory attitudes and resistance to antidiscrimination laws. Since the early 1950s, whites' racial attitudes show clear and steady movement away from support for segregationist or Jim Crow principles in the areas of schools, housing, and racial intermarriage. For example, by 1972, fewer than 15 percent of white respondents in the General Social Survey believed that black and white children should attend separate schools, and that fell below 10 percent by the early 1980s.[3] Similar trends are evident with respect to support for laws against intermarriage and the belief that whites have a right to keep blacks out of their neighborhoods; in both cases, support declined from roughly 40 percent in 1972 to about 15 percent in the mid-1990s. Despite these improvements, however, as recently as 2008 nearly one-third of whites opposed laws prohibiting individual homeowners from racial discrimination in the selling of their homes. While this is a significant decline from the two-thirds of whites who held this belief in 1973, it is still a significant minority of whites nationwide. And, before we point to education as the panacea, it should be noted that among highly educated, Northern whites, one in four held this position in 2008.

Whites have largely abandoned beliefs that blacks are biologically inferior to whites; however, they have replaced antiblack stereotypes based on biology with antiblack stereotypes steeped in culture. Thus, the tendency is for whites to believe that blacks are lazy and/or unintelligent not because they are biologically inferior, but because they simply don't value hard work or education. Thus, whites also tend to believe that blacks have only themselves to blame for persistent racial inequality. While it is true that persistent racial residential segregation is the result of a "tangle of factors," we cannot forget that the housing market discrimination that constrains minorities' housing searches, the affordability barriers that contribute to racial/ethnic segregation, and the neighborhood racial composition preferences of all groups are all inextricably linked to racial ideology and racial attitudes.

I point to all of this simply as a reminder of the long-term consequences of racial ideology and racial oppression. A significant minority of whites still adheres to negative racial stereotypes: slightly more than 40 percent of whites believe that blacks tend to be lazy compared to whites, and about one-quarter of whites believe that blacks are "less intelligent" than whites are. Astonishingly, nearly 40 percent of whites believe that individual whites should be able to discriminate against blacks (and likely anyone else) when selling their homes. Most minorities prefer mixed neighborhoods; however, they do not want to be "the only" or one of a very few. Similarly, minority (particularly black) preferences for white neighbors decline to the extent that they perceive whites as "tending to discriminate."[4] These attitudes are the sources of neighborhood racial composition preferences. These attitudes have their roots in a history that still haunts us.

Recent research in political science offers compelling support for a link between present-day racial attitudes and the number of slaves held in Southern counties in the pre-Emancipation South: the larger the slave population, the more negative current residents' attitudes toward blacks.[5] A recent analysis of black-white gaps in earnings and wealth suggests that the "initial conditions at Emancipation and nearly 100 years of segregated schools," along with public policy interventions tied to human capital accumulation and school expenditures, are critical to understanding the persistence of an enormous racial wealth gap.[6] And economists have recently found evidence that, among Africans, "individuals whose ancestors were heavily raided during the slave trade today exhibit less trust in neighbors, relatives, and their local government."[7]

This seemingly unrelated research helps us to understand the endurance of negative racial attitudes and continued opposition to public policies that are viewed as racially redistributive. Moreover, as Mary Pattillo has aptly stated in this book, it underscores the necessity of understanding racial integration as a societal benefit for all Americans, rather than something that only benefits blacks and other disadvantaged groups but is of little or no value for whites. Understanding the lasting impact of slavery and its aftermath on all Americans helps us make sense of emerging research in the area of implicit or unconscious bias, which suggests that individuals can hold (and be sincere in their expression of) egalitarian racial attitudes, while simultaneously exhibiting unconscious racial bias that shapes behaviors in predictable ways.

These realities complicate efforts at reducing racial residential segregation and creating and maintaining stably integrated neighborhoods. Ignoring them all but guarantees more of the same.

Economic Segregation of Schools Is Key to Discouraging Integration

by Micere Keels

My comments focus on economic integration because I believe that desegregation efforts will be stymied for generations to come because of the ways in which race and ethnicity are linked to income and wealth. Not even the most postracial White Americans will reside in mostly minority neighborhoods if it means sending their children to higher-poverty schools.

I teach an undergraduate course that links urban racial and economic segregation to the problems of high-poverty schools. I am at one of the most expensive universities in the United States, a place where students from well-off families come to get the credentials that will secure their place at the top of the economic ladder. However, it is also a place filled with students eager to look beyond themselves and change the status quo. These are the students who take my class. Students vigorously discuss the problems with economic segregation, talk about their volunteer efforts in poor communities, and pledge to not return to the disconnected suburbs in which they grew up. They inevitably become indignant that previous generations have allowed racial and economic segregation to stand.

At this point in the course, I try to get them to viscerally understand why despite their good intentions they, and I, are part of the problem. I ask them to think about their future child and whether, when the time comes, they won't do all that is in their power to give their child every educational resource they can. First the class gets quiet, then they stop making eye contact with me, then they start to squirm and shuffle, and then I let them know that they don't need to answer they just need to remember this moment.

We recently examined whether gentrification benefits the local neighborhood public school, and found that socioeconomic integration of formerly poor neighborhoods did not lead to socioeconomic integration of neighborhood schools.[8] Neighborhood schools were largely untouched by the children of gentrifiers. Furthermore, despite the good, or at least benign, intentions of gentrifiers, neighborhood schools sometimes evidenced marginal harm as they became depopulated and received a smaller share of per-pupil funding.

This is because we are increasingly living in the era of school choice, a well-intentioned idea. However, using school choice to incentivize higher-income families with children to stay in large urban centers means that higher- and lower-income families can live in the same neighborhood without living in the same community. Community means more than geographic proximity. Sharing a school makes parents a community and makes their children school-mates. Sharing a school makes parents shared stakeholders in the quality of that school, and shared stakeholders in each other's children. When I chaperone a field trip, I don't just ensure that my son comes back safely; I help to ensure that all the children come back safely.

I remember taking a policy course from Fay Lomax Cook while in graduate school at Northwestern, and the lecture that I will never forget was the one on how much better systems function when everyone in society understands their stake in the effectiveness of that system. The segregation of schools by income allows those with resources to erroneously believe that their children's fortunes are separate from the fortunes of children attending high-poverty schools.

In part, this is because many mistakenly believe that hoarding resources gives one's children and the children of similar "hardworking" parents the competitive advantage. This may work for one's children in the short run, but in the long run this hoarding of educational resources among a few results in lower overall economic growth.

When I talk with those who grumble about paying to educate "other people's" children, or worry about nonresident children taking advantage of their educational resources, I try to remind them about the interconnectedness of our lives: that when they get old, they will be grateful that their high-school-educated home health worker can read and interpret their doctor's instructions; that they need their garbage man much more than their financial analyst; that their neighborhoods are safer when those at the bottom of society feel they have a stake in it, rather than being crushed by it.

White students are the most segregated group, attending schools where, on average, more than 75 percent of the students are White. Because this has the immediate effect of consolidating economic resources, segregation does not harm White children's test scores, but there is more to schooling than academics. As we come closer to becoming a majority-minority population, the ability to collaborate across racial and ethnic boundaries will be invaluable. This is best accomplished when children grow up in diverse neighborhoods and schools where they learn to appreciate cultural differences, rather than learning to be tolerant of cultural differences as adults.

Exclusionary Zoning and Fear: A Developer's Perspective

by Jon Vogel

In Margery Turner's piece "Why Haven't We Made More Progress in Reducing Segregation?," she identifies numerous factors that have served as challenges to creating the desired outcome of more integrated neighborhoods and schools. As a developer of rental housing in both urban and suburban markets, I have seen firsthand how and why some of these obstacles are put in place, and how they can be overcome.

It is clear that many towns in the Northeast region use their power to control zoning in ways that serve to limit housing opportunity. The reasons for this approach range from perceived fiscal prudence to xenophobia. Whether nefarious motives are at play is really not all that important. It's the disparate impact on minority populations that matters, and potentially appropriate rationales for zoning decisions often fall short of the necessary legal standard, resulting in appropriate oversight by the courts. The bottom line is that municipalities that use exclusionary zoning need to lose their right to control their own destiny. This is how it works in New Jersey under the *Mt. Laurel* jurisprudence. In the *Southern Burlington County N.A.A.C.P. v. Mount Laurel Township*, the New Jersey Supreme Court noted that a municipality's ability to enact zoning regulations is granted by the state to promote the welfare, not of the enacting municipality only, but of all of the state's citizens. Accordingly, every municipality in New Jersey must enable the creation of "an appropriate variety and choice of housing," including options for low and moderate income households, to the extent of the municipality's fair share, and the state must review municipal housing plans to determine whether they meet their obligation to provide that fair share of the state's affordable housing needs.[9] Of course, advocates of inclusion and opportunity need to support more integrative affordable housing policies at the federal level and in state legislatures. However, the courts have done a fine job of serving minorities and the unhoused poor in New Jersey over the past thirty years, and this litigation-based model also needs to be supported and expanded to other states, particularly if real change is to happen anytime soon.

Again, not all towns with exclusionary housing policies are acting with bad intent. Rather, many are facing real or perceived economic challenges, particularly with respect to their school systems. One of the biggest concerns housing developers hear is that new housing will result in financial burdens for existing homeowners, particularly in the Northeast with our already high single-family property tax burdens. We hear questions like "How many school children are expected to live in the new development?" and "Are the projected tax revenues

sufficient to cover the increased costs?" Tax concerns become more complicated when affordable housing is at stake. Race is unquestionably a catalyst in
what is perceived by some to be a zero-sum game. I wish I had never heard the
question, but it bears repeating: "Why do I have to pay to educate their kids?"
Towns that voluntarily embrace inclusion should be rewarded with school
funding and other state funding that eases any burden that growth may cause.
Massachusetts already has a program for this known as 40S, and it is a step in
the right direction.

More importantly, we also must be mindful that the perceived school burdens generally far exceed the reality. This "education issue" requires its own
education of zoning decision makers as to the real impacts, so that fear does not
control the debate. The data show that new market-rate rental housing, particularly in downtown transit-oriented locations, generates relatively few school-
age children, and the few who do move in can often be easily accommodated
within the existing school infrastructure. The use of "average cost per child"
measures to quantify the economic burden of educating one more student is
flawed because marginal costs are much lower. Fixed costs that will not increase
as a result of increased enrollment include senior administrative staff (e.g.,
there will only be one superintendent of the school district) and most facilities
and physical plant costs. Thus, together with some public financial support,
education of decision makers can help bridge the gap between what should be
done to accommodate diversity and integration, and what will be done.

Finally, we need to celebrate success. There are a handful of towns in the
region, including South Orange/Maplewood and Montclair in New Jersey, that
have shown that diversity of housing, income, and race are all worth celebrating. These suburban towns have embraced multifamily housing, and they have
schools that have achieved academic and artistic excellence in a multicultural
setting. The experience of students in these schools is further enhanced by all
that a diverse student body can offer. Meanwhile, rents for luxury apartments in
these towns are among the highest of any location in New Jersey. Having direct
access to the Manhattan employment market via New Jersey Transit helps. But
it is worth noting that embracing diversity does not seem to hurt economic viability; rather, it may actually stimulate demand within the marketplace.

Notes

1. It's important to note that most of the available evidence focuses on black-white segre-
    gation, despite our nation's growing ethnic diversity and significant challenges facing
    Latinos, Asians, and Native Americans.
2. Maria Krysan and Reynolds Farley, "The Residential Preferences of Blacks: Do They
    Explain Persistent Segregation?," *Social Forces* 80, no. 3 (2002): 937–980; Maria Kry-
    san, "Whites Who Say They'd Flee: Who Are They, and Why Would They Leave?,"

Demography 39, no. 4 (2002): 675–696; Maria Krysan, "Community Undesirability in Black and White: Examining Racial Residential Preferences Through Community Perceptions," *Social Problems* 49, no. 4 (2002): 521–543.

3. Lawrence D. Bobo, Camille Z. Charles, Maria Krysan, and Alicia D. Simmons, "The *Real* Record on Racial Attitudes," in *Social Trends in American Life: Findings from the General Social Survey Since 1972*, ed. Peter V. Marsden (Princeton, NJ: Princeton University Press, 2012), 38–83.

4. Bobo et al., "The *Real* Record."

5. Avidit Acharya, Matthew Blackwell, and Maya Sen, "The Political Legacy of American Slavery," *Journal of Politics* 78, no. 3 (July 2016): 621–641, https://doi.org/10.1086/686631.

6. T. Kirk White, "Initial Conditions at Emancipation: The Long-Run Effect on Black-White Wealth and Earnings Inequality," *Journal of Economic Dynamics and Control* 31, no. 10 (October 2007): 3370–3395.

7. Nathan Nunn and Leonard Wantchekon, "The Slave Trade and the Origins of Mistrust in Africa," National Bureau of Economic Research Working Paper No. 14783, March 2009, http://www.nber.org/papers/w14783.

8. Micere Keels, Julia Burdick-Will, and Sara Keene, "The Effects of Gentrification on Neighborhood Public Schools," *City & Community* 12, no. 3 (September 2013): 238–259, https://doi.org/10.1111/cico.12027.

9. Southern Burlington County N.A.A.C.P. v. Mount Laurel Township, 67 N.J. 151 (1975).

THE STUBBORN PERSISTENCE OF RACIAL SEGREGATION

Residential Mobility by Whites Maintains Segregation Despite Recent Changes

by Jackelyn Hwang

A lot has changed in the United States since landmark federal legislation was passed fifty years ago prohibiting discrimination by race in housing and lending. First, since the 1970s, the Black-White high school completion and poverty gaps have declined and the Black middle class has grown substantially.[1] Second, there has been a major shift in housing policy toward poverty deconcentration, characterized by the demolition of high-rise public housing projects, the transformation of public housing into mixed-income developments, and the increase in housing choice vouchers.[2] Third, surveys suggest that negative attitudes toward Blacks have declined and that Whites are more willing to live with minorities compared to the 1970s.[3] Indeed, the prevalence of neighborhoods that are primarily White has been on the decline.[4]

Related to these changes in preferences and policies, as well as large declines in crime and increases in high-skilled jobs across cities, is the increasing prevalence of gentrification—the influx of middle- and upper-class residents moving into low-income neighborhoods—across neighborhoods and across cities in the United States.[5] Stylized images of gentrification often portray it as a process of racial change, where primarily White residents of higher socioeconomic status move into poor, minority neighborhoods. Though not without its fair share of critics, gentrification seems to be racially integrating neighborhoods, at least temporarily.

These significant societal changes should have dramatically reduced the segregation of Blacks and Whites. As debated in the prior discussion, explanations of the persistence of residential segregation in the post–civil rights era generally fall into three categories: socioeconomic differences, housing market discrimination, and residential preferences.

Societal changes suggest that these factors have weakened. Blacks, however, largely continue to live in different neighborhoods than Whites.

So, why are segregation levels still high despite the recent changes?

Although Blacks have made socioeconomic advancements on average since the 1970s, the Black-White gaps in income and wealth remain persistently high.[6] These gaps worsened following the Great Recession,[7] and the share of Blacks in the middle class in the United States has stagnated since 2000.[8] Even these significant socioeconomic differences, however, cannot explain Black-White differences in residential outcomes.[9]

Housing policy shifts that were expected to support greater residential integration have had only weak effects in reducing segregation. A high proportion of Black residents with housing choice vouchers continue to face disadvantages in the housing market, both from a lack of resources and from discriminatory landlord practices. As a result, voucher holders continue to end up in poor and segregated neighborhoods.[10] Moreover, mixed-income developments have had varying success in reducing racial segregation;[11] even as the segregation of poor residents declined somewhat with the deconcentration of subsidized housing, affluent residents became more segregated.[12]

Finally, the growing populations of Asians and Latinos across cities and neighborhoods can explain much of the decline in the prevalence of all-White neighborhoods.[13] White entry into Black neighborhoods is still relatively rare.[14] Recent evidence on gentrification gives reason to question whether gentrification by White movers is making a dent in most minority neighborhoods. National-level studies show that gentrification in predominantly minority neighborhoods is still a rare occurrence;[15] the primary trajectory of low-income, minority neighborhoods is stability.[16] Neighborhoods with greater shares of minorities that do gentrify or that are adjacent to gentrifying neighborhoods are slower to change than neighborhoods with fewer minorities,[17] and the gentrifiers in these neighborhoods tend to be middle-class minorities.[18]

These findings point to how the persistent residential mobility patterns of Whites to avoid minority neighborhoods perpetuate segregation. Fifteen percent of households move each year in the United States; therefore, decisions about which neighborhoods to enter and which ones to exit play an important role in maintaining residential segregation. Despite changing attitudes toward Blacks, Whites still exhibit residential mobility patterns that maintain racially

segregated neighborhoods. Recent studies show that when choosing the neighborhoods in which they would consider living, Whites avoid predominantly
minority neighborhoods.[19] This pattern appears to hold true even in the context
of gentrification. Decisions by developers and policy makers have some role in
shaping where Whites are attracted. Nonetheless, Whites tend to continue to
associate the presence of Black neighbors with poor-quality neighborhoods,
crime, and declining home values,[20] and Whites continue to exit neighborhoods with increasing shares of minorities.[21]

Overall, important changes that, at first glance, should have brought about a
major reduction in residential segregation in the post–civil rights era have had
limited effects. The primary reason for this is the persistent pattern of residential mobility by Whites. Avoiding entry into minority neighborhoods and exit-
ing neighborhoods that begin to diversify reproduces and reifies segregation.
Changes in the socioeconomic status of Blacks, housing policy transformations,
and changing stated preferences have limited effects in producing substantial
shifts in aggregate patterns of segregation as long as Whites continue to exhibit
these patterns of mobility.

We know that segregation comes with a host of negative consequences, particularly for the life chances of minorities living in low-income neighborhoods
and intergroup relations, so how can we promote racial, ethnic, and socioeconomic diversity across all neighborhoods? Policies targeted to people instead
of places, such as housing vouchers, have the potential to move some individuals into neighborhoods with compositions that are different from their
own if implemented effectively, but we cannot rely solely on these types of
policies. After all, White in-movers are unlikely to replace Black voucher holders moving out of low-income, minority neighborhoods. Such neighborhoods
also need substantial place-based investment that can attract residents with
higher socioeconomic status while ensuring that the right policy interventions
are implemented to keep people in place, connect them to the resources and
opportunities that come with reinvestment, and ensure that the development
process is inclusive.

Sticky Preferences: Racial Exclusion's Staying Power

by Solomon J. Greene

In the late 1960s, the economist Thomas Schelling created an early agent-based
computer model to explain the persistence of residential segregation based on
racial preferences.[22] The model was simple but elegant. The inhabitants of a
virtual checkerboard world would be content if their "neighborhood" of nearby
squares had their preferred racial mixture, defined by a "happiness rule" that

could be adjusted from strong to weak preferences for segregation. If inhabitants were unhappy with the racial composition of their neighborhood, they tried to move to a location that matched their desired mix. After simulating a series of moves, Schelling revealed what was at the time a very surprising result: even relatively weak preferences for segregation (such as wanting 30 percent of your neighbors to be of your same race) eventually resulted in complete segregation.

In the decades since, Schelling's model has spawned new thinking and empirical research on why residential segregation persists even after many formal barriers to integration have been lifted and preferences for segregation have weakened across all racial and ethnic groups.[23] Today, you can even play out Schelling's model in an interactive online game call the "Parable of the Polygons," which explains Schelling's theory with colorful anthropomorphic rectangles and triangles. Perhaps more adept at design than suspense, the game developers reveal the lesson of the parable at the outset, proclaiming: "This is a story of how harmless choices can make a harmful world."

Jackelyn Hwang's lead essay in this discussion offers a lower-tech but more nuanced variation on Schelling's parable. According to Hwang, the primary reason that racial segregation persists despite important changes in the post–civil rights era is "the persistent pattern of residential mobility by Whites." Like Schelling's agents (and those portable polygons), Hwang suggests that segregation can be explained by the segregationist preferences of White movers. Hwang's version is more nuanced than Schelling's: her movers may state preferences for integration that aren't borne out by their locational decisions, and she recognizes that developers and policy makers play a role in shaping how attractive neighborhoods are to White movers. But in the end, Hwang insists that today's persistent patterns of segregation are driven by White households' "decisions about which neighborhoods to enter and which to exit."

But what about the White households that *stay*, preferring not to enter or exit because their "happiness rule" is satisfied remaining in neighborhoods rich in amenities but lacking in socioeconomic or racial diversity? And what about the preferences of Blacks and Latinos in the United States, who overwhelmingly prefer to live in integrated environments? Why do they remain unable to access even middle-income neighborhoods with quality schools, low crime, and affordable transportation options and increasingly find themselves "stuck" in neighborhoods of concentrated poverty?

By focusing on the preferences of White movers, Hwang overlooks two crucial drivers of segregation today: the power of White incumbents to exclude low-income people of color from high-opportunity neighborhoods, and the enduring effects of segregation on wealth and prospects for mobility among residents of areas of racially concentrated poverty. Contrary to the premise shared by Schelling and Hwang, these drivers are less about who moves than about who stays.

Let's start with exclusion. Restrictive land-use policies—from density restrictions to local approval requirements—prevent the construction of affordable housing in wealthier, whiter suburban communities in the United States. Although not explicitly race-based, these policies were adopted in the wake of civil rights laws that prohibited overt racial discrimination. They were designed to keep out racial minorities and poor people, and they have proven remarkably successful in doing so. There is an ample body of empirical research demonstrating how land-use controls that limit housing density or prohibit multifamily construction contribute to racial segregation within metropolitan areas in the United States.[24] Even as norms have shifted toward (limited) racial integration, these policies have endured, and they continue to be vigorously defended. We have seen this time and again, from Westchester County, New York to Boulder, Colorado. One need look no further than the backlash to HUD's recent rule interpreting the "affirmatively further fair housing" requirement of the Fair Housing Act of 1968 (which conservative blogs promptly branded the "War on Suburban America") to understand the challenges facing advocates for unwinding exclusionary zoning.[25]

Other forms of exclusion also persist, as documented in earlier contributions to this series. As Margery Turner notes in the preceding discussion, discrimination continues to constrain minorities' housing search, as does limited access to information about housing opportunities in White neighborhoods. Stephen Norman suggests, later in this volume, that discrimination is even more pronounced (and legally tolerated) against housing voucher holders, who are disproportionately people of color. And Jacob Faber draws attention to how exclusion and predation in mortgage markets exacerbate racial segregation, and vice versa.

As Hwang points out, these practices aren't foolproof. The prevalence of neighborhoods that are exclusively White has been on the steady decline.[26] And indeed, some Blacks and other minority groups have gained access to historically White neighborhoods. But they haven't done so in numbers proportionate to their incomes or purchasing power. The average Black family earning more than $100,000 annually still lives in a neighborhood comparable to that of a White family earning less than $30,000.[27]

This brings us to the flipside of the exclusion story: why has poverty become more concentrated along racial lines? As Paul Jargowsky recently found, more than one in four of the Black poor and nearly one in six of the Latino poor live in a neighborhood of extreme poverty, compared to one in thirteen of the White poor—a disparity that has only increased in the wake of the Great Recession.[28]

Hwang implicitly recognizes these differences in neighborhood quality. She points out that White in-movers are unlikely to replace Black voucher holders moving out of low-income, minority neighborhoods. But this may be less about the segregationist preferences of White movers than the devastating conditions under which residents "left behind" in disinvested neighborhoods must endure, absent intervention. The quality of services in these neighborhoods may be so poor that White movers with relatively more wealth and fewer constraints can avoid predominantly minority neighborhoods. But for very low-income Black and Latino families who live in areas of concentrated poverty, "exit" simply may not be an option.[29]

To explain stubborn patterns of racial segregation and concentrated poverty today, we cannot assume that all players are able to exert their preferences equally by making moves across a frictionless checkerboard world. The effects of early forms of discrimination have proven to be more enduring than formal legal changes would suggest. As Daria Roithmayr has demonstrated, "self-reinforcing" differences in wealth and social capital give White families structural advantages over non-White families that determine locational choices for each group. Without intervention, Roithmayr argues, these disparities can "lock in" segregation, even if the constraints of formal discrimination or preferences for segregation are lifted.[30]

But can these patterns become unstuck?

There is some cause for optimism. Both people of color (of all ages) and millennials (of all races) express preferences for integrated neighborhoods, and they are growing into the new American majority.[31] And as Hwang points out, high rates of residential mobility combined with shifting demand for integrated environments should weaken segregation's stronghold.

However, it would be a mistake to assume that evolving preferences and frequency of moves alone will suffice to overcome entrenched patterns of racial segregation in the United States. Intentional strategies must be designed and implemented to facilitate integrationist moves, maintain and support diverse neighborhoods, and affirmatively break down barriers that wall off opportunity and lock too many families of color into areas of distress and disadvantage.

Start with the Micro, Move to the Macro

by Richard Sander

Jackelyn Hwang ably summarizes a large literature on the important and complex question of why levels of housing segregation remain so high. It is very striking, though, how little of the literature she cites offers any detailed, testable answer to this question—a serious failure for a field that has generated a large volume of work. I am hopeful, though, that we are close to some important breakthroughs.

The great mistake of segregation research, I believe, has been its general neglect of locational context. The explanatory phenomena Hwang mentions—socioeconomic differences, discrimination, preferences of groups for integration, and gentrification—are typically measured at the metropolitan level and discussed in national terms. Neighborhoods are, of course, the subject of much excellent ethnographic work, and census tracts usually constitute the unit of analysis in segregation research. But there is a strong tendency not to analyze how what might be called the "supply and demand for integration" plays out at the neighborhood and metropolitan level, how neighborhoods within metropolitan areas vary in terms of their ability to sustain integration, and how these neighborhood effects then aggregate back up to the metropolitan scale. Understanding these "microdynamics" of integration is, I think, the key to building robust, testable hypotheses about the evolution of segregation.

For example, in the 1970s black-white segregation levels dropped sharply in more than half-a-dozen large metropolitan areas.[32] Why did this happen then, and in those particular areas? The timing is clearly connected to the arrival of fair housing laws; there is a wide range of evidence suggesting both that discrimination rates fell sharply in the 1970s and that African Americans moved into white neighborhoods in unprecedented numbers.[33] Desegregation happened, quite simply, when these moves led to stable integration at the neighborhood level rather than rapid, block-by-block racial transition from white to black. So, what were the conditions of stable integration? The crucial variable was the degree to which black moves were dispersed within a metropolitan area, rather than concentrated in just a handful of neighborhoods near existing black districts.

New research that Yana Kucheva (CCNY) and I have conducted shows that urban African Americans migrating from one metropolitan area to another played a crucial role in this process.[34] Compared to blacks moving within a metro area, these "intermetropolitan" migrants were much more likely to move into white neighborhoods some distance away from black enclaves. Plausibly, this was because when intermetropolitan movers arrived at their destination city, they had fewer existing ties to specific neighborhoods or social networks. This tendency—already apparent by the late 1950s—was greatly accentuated by the greater freedom of movement the 1970s brought. In metro areas like San Diego, intermetropolitan black movers accounted for more than a third of all black residents by 1980. Their relatively dispersed movements into white areas appear to have encouraged incumbent blacks to follow, with the result that by 1980 some two-thirds of San Diego blacks lived in neighborhoods that were less than 35 percent black—and virtually all of these neighborhoods remain highly integrated today.

The volume of intermetropolitan black in-migration in the late 1960s and 1970s—which varied largely with the economic growth rate of the receiving metro area, and generally tilted West and South—was important, but so was the relative number of black migrants compared to black incumbents. Substantial in-migration paired with a small incumbent black population meant that a very high proportion of all black moves went to white neighborhoods that were not vulnerable to resegregation. Consequently, metro areas with comparatively small black populations experienced more desegregation than areas with large black populations. Importantly, however, desegregation did not occur only when there was a particular "critical mass" of the right demographic inputs; instead, metro areas desegregated some if they had some favorable demographics, and a lot if they had very favorable demographics. These patterns continued strongly into the 1980s.

There is more to this story than intermetropolitan migration, of course; but space here is constrained, and interested readers can find a detailed discussion in our paper and book.[35] For present purposes, the point is that thinking about how integration happens in local contexts, and in particular the interaction between neighborhood and metropolitan demographic patterns, can produce conceptually rich and testable models, and we now know that these models can account with great precision for actual patterns of desegregation. As we get better at predicting where and how integration happens, we can design a new generation of proactive policies that can catalyze it, and we can even compare the cost-effectiveness of alternative integration strategies. Hwang is absolutely right that housing segregation lies at the core of a host of social ills. Modeling it accurately and designing much better pro-integration strategies are projects that should be at the very center of urban policy making and research.

Persistent Acts of Housing Discrimination Perpetuate Segregation

by Jorge Andres Soto

In her article, Jackelyn Hwang points to research on housing markets and white mobility, but she downplays the historical and contemporary discrimination that restricts the mobility of people of color. For instance, Hwang cites research showing that white people tend to associate the presence of African American neighbors with poor-quality neighborhoods, crime, and declining home values. It would follow, then, that those same perceptions would encourage individual violations of the Fair Housing Act by housing providers and local decision makers.

When housing providers make decisions about prospective applicants based on these prejudices, they illegally lock out people of color and block the opportunity for integration. Paired-audit testing shows that African Americans and Latinos at all income levels continue to encounter housing discrimination.[36] Although enforcement challenges these practices, the overwhelming majority of acts of housing discrimination go unreported because it is difficult to identify discriminatory behavior without paired testing to confirm a difference in treatment.[37]

Housing discrimination has also taken on new forms since the passage of the Fair Housing Act ("the Act") in 1968, as housing providers have used less explicit actions to discriminate, including using proxy criteria for race and ethnicity. For example, housing providers frequently impose blanket bans on renting to individuals with criminal records or screen applicants with criminal records differently, which disproportionately denies housing to people of color, who make up the majority of those involved in the criminal justice system in the United States. Further, discrimination against people who use housing choice vouchers can be a proxy for discrimination based on race and ethnicity. Individuals facing such discriminatory barriers must engage in a prolonged housing search and often end up relying on substandard housing, which tends to be located in chronically poor communities and communities of color.

Any analysis of the persistence of residential segregation is also incomplete without taking into account the weak implementation of the enforcement mechanisms available under the Act to challenge market practices that perpetuate and sustain entrenched patterns of segregation. As Nikole Hannah-Jones notes in her groundbreaking investigative journalism, the Act's promise to eradicate segregation has been largely betrayed since its inception. For the majority of the Act's existence, the responsibility for addressing housing discrimination has fallen primarily on those discriminated against, who had to bring litigation to vindicate their own rights and challenge discriminatory practices more broadly.[38]

Since the Act was passed in 1968, HUD has accepted discrimination complaints through its administrative complaint process, but for twenty years it could only offer conciliation, and, if a respondent refused, HUD had no authority to conduct an investigation. HUD could also refer complaints to state and local government agencies that enforce substantively similar fair housing laws. It was only after the passage of the 1988 amendments to the Act that HUD gained the authority to take actual enforcement actions in administrative complaints. Thus, for a large portion of the Act's existence, fair housing enforcement by the federal government has had virtually no teeth (except in large-scale pattern and practice suits brought by the Department of Justice).[39] The Reagan administration and Congress came to recognize that effective abatement of discrimination could not rely solely upon the willingness of victims of discrimination or local, state, and federal government agencies to enforce the law. President Reagan signed into law the Housing and Community Development Act of 1987, which established the Fair Housing Initiatives Program (FHIP). FHIP supports a network of private, nonprofit fair housing enforcement agencies to advance compliance with the Fair Housing Act, filling the gap in fair housing enforcement not met by government agencies.

Institutional challenges continue to render HUD enforcement largely ineffective. In 2008, national civil rights organizations convened a bipartisan Commission on Fair Housing to analyze the strengths and weaknesses of the Fair Housing Act on its fortieth birthday. The commission—cochaired by former HUD Secretaries Jack Kemp and Henry Cisneros—heard testimony from fair housing practitioners, academics, attorneys, and community groups in five cities to gather information about fair housing enforcement and the persistence of residential segregation.

Perhaps the most sweeping recommendation of the commission's report was to make HUD's Office of Fair Housing and Equal Opportunity (FHEO) an independent agency responsible for enforcement and implementation of the Act.[40] As currently structured, the primary enforcer of the Fair Housing Act, HUD, is also expected to police its own fair housing compliance. An inherent conflict of interest arises when FHEO must police its program office counterparts within HUD, whose responsibility it is to deliver grants to local and state governments and public housing authorities, leaving effective enforcement and compliance at the mercy of competing interests within the agency. Perhaps not surprisingly, HUD's own programs have been criticized for perpetuating racially concentrated poverty.[41]

Amending the Fair Housing Act to protect people with criminal records and those who use housing choice vouchers would restrict some of the proxy discrimination that occurs in the marketplace, but the larger institutional challenges of fair housing enforcement—most fundamentally, the placement of enforcement authority at HUD—continue to fuel the flames of residential segregation.

Notes

1. Pew Research Center, "King's Dream Remains an Elusive Goal; Many Americans See Racial Disparities," Pew Research Center: Social & Demographic Trends, August 22, 2013, http://www.pewsocialtrends.org/2013/08/22/kings-dream-remains-an-elusive-goal -many-americans-see-racial-disparities/; Pew Research Center: Social & Demographic Trends, "The American Middle Class Is Losing Ground," December 9, 2015, http:// www.pewsocialtrends.org/2015/12/09/the-american-middle-class-is-losing-ground/.
2. Susan J. Popkin et al., "A Decade of HOPE VI," Urban Institute, May 18, 2004, http:// www.urban.org/research/publication/decade-hope-vi.
3. Camille Z. Charles, "The Dynamics of Racial Residential Segregation," *Annual Review of Sociology* 29 (2003): 167–207.
4. John R. Logan and Charles Zhang, "Global Neighborhoods: New Pathways to Diversity and Separation," *American Journal of Sociology* 115, no. 4 (January 2010): 1069–1109, https://doi.org/10.1086/649498.
5. Jackelyn Hwang and Jeffrey Lin, "What Have We Learned About the Causes of Recent Gentrification?," SSRN Scholarly Paper (Rochester, NY: Social Science Research Network, July 1, 2016), https://papers.ssrn.com/abstract=2812045.

6. Pew Research Center, "King's Dream Remains an Elusive Goal."

7. Rakesh Kochhar, Richard Fry, and Paul Taylor, "Wealth Gaps Rise to Record Highs Between Whites, Blacks, Hispanics," Pew Research Center: Social & Demographic Trends, July 26, 2011, http://www.pewsocialtrends.org/2011/07/26/wealth-gaps-rise-to-record-highs-between-whites-blacks-hispanics/.

8. Bart Landry and Kris Marsh, "The Evolution of the New Black Middle Class," *Annual Review of Sociology* 37, no. 1 (2011): 373–394, https://doi.org/10.1146/annurev-soc-081309-150047.

9. Charles, "The Dynamics of Racial Residential Segregation."

10. Stefanie DeLuca, Phillip M. E. Garboden, and Peter Rosenblatt, "Segregating Shelter: How Housing Policies Shape the Residential Locations of Low-Income Minority Families," *Annals of the American Academy of Political and Social Science* 647, no. 1 (2013): 268–299.

11. Popkin et al., "A Decade of HOPE VI."

12. Ann Owens, "Housing Policy and Urban Inequality: Did the Transformation of Assisted Housing Reduce Poverty Concentration?," *Social Forces* 94, no. 1 (2015): 325–348.

13. Logan and Zhang, "Global Neighborhoods."

14. Lance Freeman and Tiancheng Cai, "White Entry Into Black Neighborhoods: Advent of a New Era?," *Annals of the American Academy of Political and Social Science* 660, no. 1 (July 2015): 302–318, https://doi.org/10.1177/0002716215578425.

15. Ann Owens, "Neighborhoods on the Rise: A Typology of Neighborhoods Experiencing Socioeconomic Ascent," *City & Community* 11, no. 4 (December 2012): 345–369, https://doi.org/10.1111/j.1540-6040.2012.01412.x.

16. Robert J. Sampson, *Great American City: Chicago and the Enduring Neighborhood Effect* (Chicago: University of Chicago Press, 2012).

17. Jackelyn Hwang and Robert J. Sampson, "Divergent Pathways of Gentrification: Racial Inequality and the Social Order of Renewal in Chicago Neighborhoods," *American Sociological Review* 79, no. 4 (August 2014): 726–751, https://doi.org/10.1177/0003122414535774.

18. Jeffrey M. Timberlake and Elaina Johns-Wolfe, "Neighborhood Ethnoracial Composition and Gentrification in Chicago and New York, 1980 to 2010," *Urban Affairs Review* 53, no. 2 (March 2017): 236–272, https://doi.org/10.1177/1078087416636483.

19. Michael D. M. Bader and Marisa Krysan, "Community Attraction and Avoidance in Chicago: What's Race Got to Do with It?," *Annals of the American Academy of Political and Social Science* 660, no. 1 (July 2015): 261–281, https://doi.org/10.1177/0002716215577615.

20. Ingrid Gould Ellen, *Sharing America's Neighborhoods: The Prospects for Stable Racial Integration* (Cambridge, MA: Harvard University Press, 2001).

21. Logan and Zhang, "Global Neighborhoods."

22. Thomas C. Schelling, "Dynamic Models of Segregation," *Journal of Mathematical Sociology* 1, no. 2 (July 1971): 143–186, at 143, 145.

23. William Easterly, "Empirics of Strategic Interdependence: The Case of the Racial Tipping Point," National Bureau of Economic Research Working Paper No. 15069, June 2009, http://www.nber.org/papers/w15069; David Card, Alexandre Mas, and Jesse Rothstein, "Tipping and the Dynamics of Segregation," *Quarterly Journal of Economics* 123, no. 1 (February 2008): 177–218, https://doi.org/10.1162/qjec.2008.123.1.177.

24. See, for example, Matthew Resseger, "The Impact of Land Use Regulation on Racial Segregation: Evidence from Massachusetts Zoning Borders," unpublished paper, Harvard University, November 26, 2013; Jonathan Rothwell and Douglas S. Massey, "The Effect of Density Zoning on Racial Segregation in U.S. Urban Areas," *Urban Affairs*

Review 44, no. 6 (July 2009): 779–806; Rolf Pendall, "Local Land Use Regulation and the Chain of Exclusion," *Journal of the American Planning Association* 66, no. 2 (June 2000): 125–142.

25. Michael Barone, "HUD's 'Disparate Impact' War on Suburban America," *Townhall*, July 21, 2015, https://townhall.com/columnists/michaelbarone/2015/07/21/huds-disparate-impact -war-on-suburban-america-n2027961.

26. Logan and Zhang, "Global Neighborhoods."

27. Patrick Sharkey, "Spatial Segmentation and the Black Middle Class" 119, no. 4 (January 2014); Sean F. Reardon, Lindsay Fox, and Joseph Townsend, "Neighborhood Income Composition by Household Race and Income, 1990–2009," *Annals of the American Academy of Political and Social Science* 660, no. 1 (July 2015): 78–97, https://doi.org /10.1177/0002716215576104.

28. Paul Jargowsky, "Architecture of Segregation: Civil Unrest, the Concentration of Poverty, and Public Policy," Century Foundation, August 7, 2015, https://tcf.org/content /report/architecture-of-segregation/?session=1.

29. Patrick Sharkey, *Stuck in Place: Urban Neighborhoods and the End of Progress Toward Racial Equality* (Chicago: University of Chicago Press, 2013); Joel Wichtman, "The Failures of Integration: How Race and Class Are Undermining the American Dream, by Sheryll Cashin," *Journal of Catholic Education* 10, no. 4 (June 2007).

30. Daria Roithmayr, "Locked in Segregation," SSRN Scholarly Paper (Rochester, NY: Social Science Research Network, December 2, 2004), https://papers.ssrn.com/abstract =627724.

31. Esther Havekes, Michael Bader, and Maria Krysan, "Realizing Racial and Ethnic Neighborhood Preferences? Exploring the Mismatches Between What People Want, Where They Search, and Where They Live," *Population Research and Policy Review* 35, no. 1 (February 2016): 101–126; Jennifer L. Hochschild, Vesla M. Weaver, and Traci R. Burch, *Creating a New Racial Order: How Immigration, Multiracialism, Genomics, and the Young Can Remake Race in America* (Princeton, NJ: Princeton University Press, 2012).

32. Using the black/white dissimilarity indices published in Douglas S. Massey and Nancy A. Denton, "Trends in Residential Segregation of Blacks, Hispanics, and Asians: 1970– 1980," *American Sociological Review* 52, no. 6 (December 1987): 802–825, the following large metropolitan areas all experienced index declines of 19 or more points: Anaheim /Santa Ana, Denver, Oklahoma City, Phoenix, Riverside/San Bernardino, Salt Lake City, San Antonio, San Diego, and Tucson. Of these, Anaheim/Santa Ana and Riverside /San Bernardino were arguably more "suburban ring areas" than true metropolitan communities.

33. See, for example, Jonathan Zasloff, "Between Resistance and Embrace: American Realtors, the Justice Department, and the Uncertain Triumph of the Fair Housing Act, 1968–1978," *Howard Law Journal* 61, no. 1 (Fall 2017): 69–112. This topic is also explored in depth in Richard Sander, Jonathan Zasloff, and Yana Kucheva, *Urban Pioneers and the Dream of an Integrated Society* (forthcoming).

34. Yana Kucheva and Richard H. Sander, "Black Pioneers, Intermetropolitan Movers, and Housing Desegregation," SSRN Scholarly Paper (Rochester, NY: Social Science Research Network, March 1, 2016), https://papers.ssrn.com/abstract=2757766.

35. Kucheva and Sander, "Black Pioneers, Intermetropolitan Movers, and Housing Desegregation."

36. Margery Austin Turner et al., *Housing Discrimination Against Racial and Ethnic Minorities 2012* (Washington, DC: U.S. Department of Housing and Urban Development, June 2013), https://www.huduser.gov/portal/Publications/pdf/HUD-514_HDS2012.pdf.

37. National Fair Housing Alliance, "Where You Live Matters: 2015 Fair Housing Trends Report," 2015, http://nationalfairhousing.org/wp-content/uploads/2017/04/2015-04-30 -NFHA-Trends-Report-2015.pdf.
38. Nikole Hannah-Jones, "Living Apart: How the Government Betrayed a Landmark Civil Rights Law," ProPublica, June 25, 2015, https://www.propublica.org/article/living -apart-how-the-government-betrayed-a-landmark-civil-rights-law.
39. Jorge Andres Soto and Deirdre Swesnik, "The Promise of the Fair Housing Act and the Role of Fair Housing Organizations," American Constitution Society Issue Brief, January 2012, https://www.acslaw.org/publications/issue-briefs/the-promise-of-the-fair -housing-act-and-the-role-of-fair-housing.
40. National Commission on Fair Housing and Equal Opportunity, "The Future of Fair Housing: Findings," 2008, http://nationalfairhousing.org/wp-content/uploads/2017/04 /Future_of_Fair_Housing.pdf.
41. Stacy E. Seicshnaydre, "How Government Housing Perpetuates Racial Segregation: Lessons from Post-Katrina New Orleans," Catholic University Law Review 60, no. 3 (Spring 2011): 661–718.

DISCUSSION 8

IMPLICIT BIAS AND SEGREGATION

Implicit Bias and Segregation: Facing the Enemy

by Jerry Kang

Social psychologists classify thoughts about social groups into attitudes and stereotypes. An attitude is an evaluative association between a group, such as Whites, and an overall valence that is positive or negative. By contrast, stereotypes are descriptive traits that we probabilistically ascribe to groups. For example, we might think that Asians (social category) are likely to be foreign-born (trait).

When I ask myself about my own attitude and stereotypes toward a particular social group, I assume that I can give myself a complete answer. But decades of scientific research have revealed that we get only part of the story. In particular, we have attitudes and stereotypes that are implicit, in the sense that we have no direct introspective access to them. In other words, in addition to explicit attitudes and stereotypes, we also carry implicit mental associations that cannot be accessed simply by closing our eyes and asking ourselves for an honest accounting. Worse, these implicit social cognitions (ISCs) seem to reflect prejudices and generalizations found in our background culture, even if we expressly reject them as inappropriate or inaccurate.

Experimental social psychologists have accumulated substantial evidence that these implicit biases exist, are measurable, pervasive, and large in magnitude (as compared to explicit biases), and have real-world consequences—at least on the margins.[1] For example, data from millions of participants at Project Implicit, which uses the Implicit Association Test, or IAT (the most commonly used reaction-time measure for implicit biases)[2] reveal that 68 percent of people have an implicit attitude that favors Whites over Blacks, and 72 percent of people have an implicit stereotype that associates weapons more strongly with Blacks than with Whites.[3] Moreover, various studies have revealed that these implicit biases can predict, at least to a small degree, real-world behavior, such as how we evaluate people as job candidates, respond to them through our body language, assess them in terms of threat, mete out penalties, and even treat them as patients.[4]

These findings have myriad implications for the analysis of residential segregation.[5] In this essay, I want to explore in particular how they might change our sense of moral urgency. My intuition is that the intensity of moral urgency felt about residential segregation depends on the degree to which segregation is seen as caused by current racial discrimination. Here, I am using "race discrimination" extremely narrowly—what lawyers call disparate treatment and not merely disparate impact caused collaterally by decisions based on other grounds, such as class.[6] Also, I focus on discrimination taking place today, not the material legacies of discriminatory decisions made decades ago. The reason for this narrow focus is not because I believe that disparate impact or the past are morally or legally irrelevant. Rather, it is because the strongest and broadest public consensus lies against racial discrimination in the form of disparate treatment taking place right now—for example, treating a White family better than an identically situated and qualified Black family in selling a house, renting an apartment, or financing a mortgage.

My sense is that many Americans believe that segregation isn't really caused by racial discrimination taking place today. According to this "common sense," racial discrimination was common in the past (driven by very explicit biases), but today segregation is driven more by simple economics: the rational pursuit of self-interest for oneself and one's family. Most people simply want a safe and clean neighborhood, with good amenities, good schools, and good houses that will keep their property values. People with resources, of whatever race, will select and move into such neighborhoods and away from spaces with crime, blight, disorder, and poverty. According to this commonsense story, racial segregation is just a collateral consequence of the banal fact that well-resourced people (who happen to be disproportionately White) get to exercise their economic choice to move to "good" neighborhoods (again, which happen to be disproportionately White).

This "commonsense" account saps the moral urgency to address racial segregation. First, people have hit civil rights fatigue and stop listening to arguments based on racial discrimination that occurred in the distant past. That was then; this is now. Second, disparate racial impact caused by economically "rational" behavior is viewed as regrettable but understandable, not deplorable. At worst, it's really just the sin of being selfish, and when people are accused of being selfish about their families' welfare, they often respond "Guilty as charged!"

What would generate greater moral urgency? First, evidence that racial discrimination isn't something that happened only in the distant past. This is why audit studies continue to be so important, to demonstrate the ugly fact that players in the housing market, trained to be identical except for race, are often treated differently as renters, home buyers, and borrowers even today.[7]

Second, when average folks like us—not just the large banks or institutional landlords or professional real estate agents—are making housing decisions, we're not actually pursuing rational self-interest based on clinically measured benefits and costs tabulated in a color-blind spreadsheet. To the contrary, our very perceptions of "nice" neighborhoods and "nice" neighbors are infected by implicit bias.

Put it this way: If 68 percent of us associate White people faster with good words than Black people with good words on the IAT, should it be that surprising that we tend to see White neighborhoods as nicer than Black neighborhoods even if they have objectively the same qualities? Robert Sampson and Stephen Raudenbusch carefully documented the social construction of disorder. They meticulously observed the amount of physical and social disorder within neighborhoods (by using official police statistics and video collected from a roaming SUV that systematically recorded street footage). Even controlling for this objective baseline of real disorder, people's perceptions of disorder (both within these neighborhoods and from without) were still influenced by the proportion of racial minorities living in the neighborhood.[8] Conceptually similar findings come from Lincoln Quillian and Devah Pager, who found a correlation between the amount of crime perceived and the percentage of young Black males living in a neighborhood, regardless of the actual crime rates.[9] In sum, people see more disorder and danger where Black and Brown bodies reside—even controlling for actual, objectively measured differences.

Although these studies did not directly measure implicit bias, there are plenty of studies that suggest that implicit attitudes and stereotypes about racial minorities exacerbate these sorts of judgments. For example, a negative implicit attitude makes it harder for us to recognize African Americans as smiling.[10] We also have an implicit stereotype associating Blacks with weapons, which has been correlated with our inclination to shoot Black characters faster in a simulated shooting game.[11] Philip Goff and colleagues have demonstrated the existence of an implicit stereotype linking African Americans with apes. This implicit stereotype has been found to correlate with the degree to which police officers overestimate the age of Black children and also deploy force on Black youth.[12]

These biased perceptions of racial minorities and the spaces they inhabit fuel a predictable self-fulfilling prophecy. On the margins, biased perceptions of fear and dread drive those who have resources to flee, and the disinvestment associated with that flight exacerbates the material conditions that lead people to have greater fear and greater dread.

What might popularization of the implicit bias story do to the national conversation about residential segregation? It shows that family A and family B are being treated differently on the margins today—not in the distant past, not by some faceless bank or housing complex or closed-minded bigot, but by us—even if the two families have identical relevant attributes. We do the same with neighborhood A and neighborhood B, again on the margins, because of how these neighborhoods have been racialized. These "race-space associations," as clearly laid out by Michelle Wilde Anderson and Victoria Plaut, help explain how neighborhoods are stigmatized, with predictable impact on their desirability and their value.[13]

Explicit, stone-cold racists remain a serious problem in residential segregation. But many people think that such racists constitute an endangered species. Adding implicit bias to the story explains why, even without such explicit racism, the segregation of the past can endure into the future simply by the actions of "rational" individuals pursuing their self-interest with slightly biased perceptions driven by implicit associations we aren't even aware of.

We've met the enemy, and it is us.

Focus on Explicit Disparities Instead of Implicit Biases

by Richard Ford

The theory of implicit bias will not help us understand or reverse patterns of segregation. It will only mire us in all-too-familiar, intractable controversies over mental state. Rather than trying to sell a skeptical public on a novel theory of prejudice, we should focus on the institutionalized conditions that produce and sustain inequality and segregation.

Jerry Kang argues that the concept of implicit bias can reveal ongoing discrimination of which most Americans are unaware and this revelation will inspire a sense of moral urgency to address the problem of segregation. But this assumes that most of the bias responsible for segregation is unconscious and unwitting, as opposed to deliberate but concealed. Suppose that although most Americans abhor the type of discrimination they associate with unrepentant bigots, many believe that they are justified in considering lamentable but undeniable racial dynamics. A classic example of such a soft form of discrimination is Reverend Jesse Jackson's notorious admission that even he worries when approached by a group of young black men on a deserted street at night. Many people who would not consider themselves bigots and would not discriminate in other areas of their lives probably have similar reactions. A showing of implicit association can't distinguish unconscious bias from this kind of concealed bias. In fact, the implicit-association research began as a way of smoking out such concealed bias: the original concern that inspired implicit association research was that as prejudice became unacceptable, test subjects would try to conceal their biases from researchers. We won't be able to stir up moral urgency about racial generalizations that many people are aware of and believe are justified.

Consider one of Kang's examples in this light: studies show that many people perceive minority neighborhoods to be more dangerous and disorderly than objectively similar white neighborhoods. Is the problem here that people are unaware that they are making race-dependent evaluations, or is it that they are unwilling to admit that they are making race-dependent evaluations? The idea of a poor, high-crime, minority neighborhoods is so pervasive in our society that I suspect many people consciously believe that it's reasonable to presume that a minority neighborhood is more likely to be dangerous and disorderly than a predominantly white one. When forced to make a high-stakes decision (like purchasing a home—the largest investment most people will ever make) under conditions of uncertainty, most people will consider any available information, even if they know the information is imperfect. Race is a highly imperfect proxy for crime or disorder, but sadly there is some correlation. A rational person could believe that considering race is justified—although, given antidiscrimination laws and social mores, she may be unwilling to admit it.

Even people who do not credit such racial generalizations may well think it prudent to take account of the likelihood that other people will act on them, driving down real estate values and making investments in minority neighborhoods less reliable. It's easy to imagine the vicious cycle that will result: unstable property values make the neighborhood a bad risk, causing banks to withhold prime mortgages; property owners faced with unattractive loan terms are more likely to default; higher foreclosure rates lead to higher numbers of abandoned properties, which are easy marks for vandals, squatters, and illegal enterprises; and, of course, these activities make the neighborhood more dangerous and disorderly than it would otherwise have been, vindicating those who associate minority neighborhoods with crime and disorder. This kind of downward spiral can get going with only a relatively small number of people directly acting on racial stereotypes, supplemented by a larger number of people responding to the risk that other people will act on racial stereotypes or acting on the objective differences created by a downward spiral once it gets going.

In the case of individual buyers, this type of bias is not actionable, and even in the cases of real estate agents, landlords, and lenders subject to antidiscrimination laws, it is very hard to prove. Moreover, bias is far from the only cause of discriminatory practices: nonbiased people contribute to the problem when they react to racially unequal market dynamics such as unstable property values in minority neighborhoods. Focusing on implicit bias will only reinforce the widespread and misguided idea that inequality demands redress only if it is caused by a specific prejudiced mental state, conscious or unconscious.

Eliminating racial injustice will require us to attack the institutional practices and structural incentives that now make racial discrimination rational. Instead of focusing on a subjective and ultimately unknowable mental state, we should focus on objective inequalities and the objective circumstances surrounding contested decisions. We don't need an account of the cognitive mechanism that produced a race- or sex-dependent decision; it is sufficient to demonstrate objectively that the decision is in fact race or sex dependent. Here the social science developments that are most promising are not in psychology, but in econometrics and empirical analysis, which can offer increasingly refined techniques to isolate race, sex, and other variables and determine which decisions depend on them. An objective approach to questions of inequality would blur, if not eliminate, the distinction between disparate treatment and disparate impact, and look for unexplained and unjustified disparities in workforces, renter populations, mortgagees, and other groups covered by antidiscrimination laws. Most important, a focus on objective unjustified inequality would lead us to look beyond individual cases to broad, institutional solutions that would improve the fairness of housing, financial, and labor markets generally. These solutions will not involve convincing individuals that they are unwittingly prejudiced—instead they will involve institutional changes and incentives for socially constructive behavior.

What Do We See When We Look in the Mirror?

by Robert Smith

Jerry Kang tells us that when it comes to housing segregation, we all are the enemy. He argues that this is the case because we have implicit biases that operate without our conscious awareness to negatively impact people of color in all sorts of housing decisions. Awareness of these biases, he argues, would serve as an important step in addressing housing inequities. What if every American understood the role that implicit bias plays in shaping our housing decisions? Would it bolster a moral urgency to eradicate residential segregation? Kang seems to think so. I wish I shared his optimism.

Kang is hands down the most successful translator of implicit social cognition research into the legal literature. So, it comes as no surprise that I agree with much of what he writes. Civil rights fatigue is real and widespread; therefore, arguments about historic injustice tend not to resonate as well as arguments about discrimination in the here and now. Likewise, while old-fashioned blatant racism still exists, discrimination today tends to come from a more nuanced and less explicit place. I also agree that implicit bias provides a partial explanation for the continued existence of residential segregation. It is an effective narrative because it explains discrimination in a world where most of us cannot imagine our families or friends using skin color to make a decision about whether to rent a condo or move into a new neighborhood. The problem, though, is that the causes and harms of housing segregation are simultaneously too complicated and too amorphous to spark a groundswell of moral urgency.

Let's start with the causes of residential segregation. Implicit bias probably influences housing outcomes ranging from individual rental or loan applications to local zoning decisions. But how much responsibility can we assign to it for continued segregation relative to our long and sordid history first of formal discrimination and then of widespread informal, though explicit, racism? Probably not very much. The choice of where to live is a sticky one in two senses that are important here. First, where we live has a strong relationship to our access to basic services like education, transportation, and medical care. It shapes our job options and dictates how frequently and in what capacity we come into contact with law enforcement. Our legacy of overt discrimination dictated where black Americans could live (and continue to live), and we cannot pretend that the dissolution of formal inequality or the decades-long decreases in explicit racism will translate into rapid residential mobility.

Yet even if we assumed that every American family had an equal ability to move to a less segregated neighborhood, the decision of where to reside is still sticky in the sense that our friends, families, and most cherished memories often are strongly tied to the place where we live. These tend to be positive considerations; but in the context of residential mobility, they nonetheless act as constraining forces. We might choose to stay in a racially homogenous neighborhood even though we might not have chosen to live there in the first place had another option been open to us. In sum, then, the legacy of formal discrimination and the stickiness of residential decisions are likely much bigger drivers of modern segregation than is implicit racial bias. Kang acknowledges that implicit racial bias is only part of the segregation puzzle, but my point is a slightly different one: implicit bias is a small enough factor in residential segregation that if people acknowledged the full force of its impact—and then responded in proportion to its harm—we still would have unacceptable levels of residential segregation.

Even the narrow slice of residential segregation that can be attributed to contemporary bias in housing choices probably is not significantly attributable to implicit bias in the strictest sense. Much of the persuasive force of implicit-bias research derives from the fact that most people would not embrace the negative associations that are sparked automatically if we were consciously aware of them and could explicitly weigh their value. In the context of housing choices, do we have reason to believe that Americans would reject the negative mental associations that help to drive the kind of bias that contributes to housing segregation? I doubt it. Indeed, it would not shock me if many white Americans continue to believe, for example, that when a black family (or families) moves into their neighborhood, the price of their own house could fall. I'm not saying that most Americans embrace that the price should drop as a neighborhood becomes more integrated. Nor am I arguing that this perceived "fact" of a future price drop is justifiable. The point is that even if our implicit associations were made explicit, many Americans would not look in the mirror, denounce themselves for making such an association, and act in a consciously race-neutral manner. Thus, while increasing the salience of the implicit-bias narrative could help Americans to understand that automatic associations influence our thoughts and actions without our conscious awareness, it would not do much to reduce residential segregation if the same people would act similarly on the basis of the same associations even if they were made explicit.

This discussion of causation and responsibility misses a larger problem with the idea that increased salience of the implicit-bias narrative would heighten our collective moral urgency. Specifically, I doubt that most Americans fully understand the harm of de facto racial segregation. We have a lot of problems that should spark a sense of moral urgency: teenagers are dying violent deaths in horrifying numbers in the streets of our major cities; veterans are receiving horrendous care from some of our nation's veterans' hospitals. And those are just two ripped-from-the-headlines stories this week. Why should housing segregation deserve a chunk of our finite capacity for moral urgency?

The more serious harm is connected with, but not wholly subsumed by, racial considerations. It goes back to the reality that different neighborhoods receive sharply different public services, enjoy more or less access to jobs and entertainment, and suffer more or less crime and other forms of victimization. It is this broader issue of unequal access to opportunity and security that deserves our sense of moral urgency. While implicit racial bias is a helpful tool for understanding some part of why some families are plugged into the opportunity grid and others are not, the value of an implicit-racial-bias lens diminishes significantly when it comes to evaluating mechanisms for meaningful reform. Implicit bias is a helpful tool in explaining some portion of contemporary discrimination, and awareness of its operation will have some positive effect; if awareness of implicit bias helped change the outcome in 0.5 percent of locational decisions nationally that otherwise would have furthered segregation, that would have a significant impact. Nevertheless, focusing on implicit bias almost certainly is not the shortest path to increasing our collective sense of moral urgency—or, more important, to eradicating the harms that are closely connected with residential segregation.

This last point is an important one for discussions about remedying both segregation specifically and unequal access to opportunity more broadly. Implicit racial bias is compelling and sexy as an academic idea, and its operation has pernicious real-world consequences. There is no doubt that widespread awareness of implicit racial bias would further the goal of equality across a broad range of social contexts, including and perhaps especially in the context of residential segregation. Nonetheless, we need to be very careful that its shimmer does not distract us from harm-specific substantive reforms that ultimately are more likely to bear fruit in terms of alleviating the worst of the ills associated with residential segregation.

Implicit Bias, Intergroup Contact, and Debiasing: Considering Neighborhood Dynamics

by Cheryl Staats

Jerry Kang provides a thoughtful discussion of how the social psychological science of implicit bias can affect how we understand the causes of racial segregation in neighborhoods. Kang explores how the subtle, unconscious nature of implicit bias contributes to the misperception that segregation is not caused by ongoing, current discrimination and thus may diminish any sense of moral urgency in response to the continuing racial division in many communities.

As Kang points out, implicit bias can contribute simultaneously to perpetuating segregation and hiding the present-day discrimination that facilitates that segregation. It is also true that neighborhood dynamics can affect individuals' mental associations and implicit biases. Specifically, diverse neighborhoods can play an important role in reducing bias by facilitating intergroup contact among residents.

With scholarship related to debiasing perceived by some as the "holy grail of implicit race bias research," researchers have studied various interventions designed to change the mental associations that undergird implicit bias.[14] While implicit biases are deeply entrenched, research suggests that implicit associations are malleable and may be changed through conscious efforts that involve intention, attention, and time.[15] One known debiasing strategy is intergroup contact. Stemming from psychologist Gordon Allport's seminal work on intergroup contact theory in the mid-1950s, current research consistently suggests that intergroup contact yields more positive feelings about outgroups and reduces intergroup prejudice.[16]

While other settings, such as schools or workplaces, may yield greater inter-group contact opportunities, neighborhoods may still have a debiasing effect, as they can provide an environment that encourages prolonged interpersonal contact. Research by Nilanjana Dasgupta shows that "being embedded in nat-urally existing local environments that facilitate positive contact with mem-bers of stereotyped groups create and reinforce positive implicit associations, thereby counteracting implicit bias."[17]

Therein lies an unfortunate irony. Implicit biases not only play a role in pro-ducing segregated neighborhoods, but ironically these implicit biases can also contribute to their own perpetuation by limiting the debiasing opportunities that intergroup contact in neighborhoods would create. Instead of turning to their neighborhood context for this debiasing opportunity, individuals living in segregated neighborhoods (particularly those who are cognizant of rela-tionship between biases and one's environment) instead may intentionally seek out other venues for intergroup contact, such as diverse organizations, places of worship, or other "third places" where people congregate outside of home or work, such as barber shops or coffee shops.[18] Furthermore, even for those who live in diverse neighborhoods, it is important to recognize that debiasing effects are elastic and diminish over time if not reinforced.[19] Debiasing requires consistent effort to modify existing mental associations, and intergroup contact such as that facilitated by diverse neighborhoods is just one of many possible debiasing interventions.

Notes

1. Kristin A. Lane, Jerry Kang, and Mahzarin R. Banaji, "Implicit Social Cognition and Law," *Annual Review of Law and Social Science* 3, no. 1 (2007): 427–451, https://doi.org /10.1146/annurev.lawsocsci.3.081806.112748.
2. A. G. Greenwald, D. E. McGhee, and J. L. Schwartz, "Measuring Individual Differences in Implicit Cognition: The Implicit Association Test," *Journal of Personality and Social Psychology* 74, no. 6 (June 1998): 1464–1480.
3. Brian A. Nosek et al., "Pervasiveness and Correlates of Implicit Attitudes and Stereo-types," *European Review of Social Psychology* 18 (2007): 36–88, https://dash.harvard .edu/handle/1/2958438.
4. Anthony G. Greenwald et al., "Understanding and Using the Implicit Association Test: III. Meta-Analysis of Predictive Validity," *Journal of Personality and Social Psychology* 97, no. 1 (July 2009): 17–41, https://doi.org/10.1037/a0015575; John T. Jost et al., "The Existence of Implicit Bias Is beyond Reasonable Doubt: A Refutation of Ideological and Methodological Objections and Executive Summary of Ten Studies That No Man-ager Should Ignore," *Research in Organizational Behavior* 29 (2009): 39–69, https://doi .org/10.1016/j.riob.2009.10.001.

5. Michelle Wilde Anderson and Victoria Plaut, "Property Law: Implicit Bias and the Resilience of Spatial Colorlines," SSRN Scholarly Paper (Rochester, NY: Social Science Research Network, August 16, 2012), https://papers.ssrn.com/abstract=1919766.

6. Whether disparate impacts are legally actionable under Section 804(a) of the Fair Housing Act, 42 U.S.C. § 3604(a), was the subject of the recent Mt. Holly litigation, which settled before the Supreme Court could decide the case. Mt. Holly Gardens Citizens in Action, Incorporated Versus Twp. of Mount Holly, 658 F.3d 375 (3d Cir. 2011) (cert. granted but then dismissed).

7. Margery Austin Turner, Todd Richardson, and Stephen Ross, "Housing Discrimination in Metropolitan America: Unequal Treatment of African Americans, Hispanics, Asians, and Native Americans," in *Fragile Rights Within Cities: Government, Housing, and Fairness*, ed. John Goering (Lanham, MD: Rowman & Littlefield, 2007), 39–60.

8. Robert J. Sampson and Stephen W. Raudenbush, "Seeing Disorder: Neighborhood Stigma and the Social Construction of 'Broken Windows,'" *Social Psychology Quarterly* 67, no. 4 (December 2004): 319–342, https://doi.org/10.1177/019027250406700401.

9. Lincoln Quillian and Devah Pager, "Black Neighbors, Higher Crime? The Role of Racial Stereotypes in Evaluations of Neighborhood Crime," *American Journal of Sociology* 107, no. 3 (November 2001): 717–767, https://doi.org/10.1086/338938.

10. Kurt Hugenberg and Galen V. Bodenhausen, "Facing Prejudice: Implicit Prejudice and the Perception of Facial Threat," *Psychological Science* 14, no. 6 (November 2003): 640–643, https://doi.org/10.1046/j.0956-7976.2003.psci_1478.x.

11. Joshua Correll et al., "The Police Officer's Dilemma: Using Ethnicity to Disambiguate Potentially Threatening Individuals," *Journal of Personality and Social Psychology* 83, no. 6 (December 2002): 1314–1329; Anthony G. Greenwald, Mark A. Oakes, and Hunter G. Hoffman, "Targets of Discrimination," *Journal of Experimental Social Psychology* 39, no. 4 (July 2003): 399–405, https://doi.org/10.1016/S0022-1031(03)00020-9; Jack Glaser and Eric D. Knowles, "Implicit Motivation to Control Prejudice," *Journal of Experimental Social Psychology* 44 (2008): 164–172.

12. Phillip Atiba Goff et al., "The Essence of Innocence: Consequences of Dehumanizing Black Children," *Journal of Personality and Social Psychology* 106, no. 4 (April 2014): 526–545, https://doi.org/10.1037/a0035663.

13. Anderson and Plaut, "Property Law."

14. David Amodio and Saaid A. Mendoza, "Implicit Intergroup Bias: Cognitive, Affective, and Motivational Underpinnings," in *Handbook of Implicit Social Cognition: Measurement, Theory, and Applications*, ed. Bertram Gawronski and B. Keith Payne (New York: Guilford Press, 2010), 353–374.

15. Irene V. Blair, "The Malleability of Automatic Stereotypes and Prejudice," *Personality and Social Psychology Review* 6, no. 3 (August 2002): 242–261; Nilanjana Dasgupta and Anthony G. Greenwald, "On the Malleability of Automatic Attitudes: Combating Automatic Prejudice with Images of Admired and Disliked Individuals," *Journal of Personality and Social Psychology* 81, no. 5 (November 2001): 800–814; Patricia G. Devine, "Stereotypes and Prejudice: Their Automatic and Controlled Components," *Journal of Personality and Social Psychology* 56, no. 1 (1989): 5–18.

16. Gordon W. Allport, *The Nature of Prejudice* (Boston: Addison-Wesley, 1954); Thomas F. Pettigrew, "Generalized Intergroup Contact Effects on Prejudice," *Personality and Social Psychology Bulletin* 23, no. 2 (February 1997): 173–185; Thomas F. Pettigrew and Linda R. Tropp, "A Meta-Analytic Test of Intergroup Contact Theory," *Journal of Personality and Social Psychology* 90, no. 5 (May 2006): 751–783.

17. Nilanjana Dasgupta, "Implicit Attitudes and Beliefs Adapt to Situations: A Decade of Research on the Malleability of Implicit Prejudice, Stereotypes, and the Self-Concept," in *Advances in Experimental Social Psychology*, vol. 47, ed. Patricia Devine and Ashby Plant (Burlington: Academic Press, 2013), 233–279, https://www.researchgate.net/publication /285905888_Implicit_Attitudes_and_Beliefs_Adapt_to_Situations_A_Decade_of _Research_on_the_Malleability_of_Implicit_Prejudice_Stereotypes_and_the_Self -Concept.

18. Chrisopher Peterson, "Happy Places: Third Places," *Psychology Today*, December 1, 2009, accessed July 26, 2017, http://www.psychologytoday.com/blog/the-good-life/200912 /happy-places-third-places.

19. Mahzarin R. Banaji and Anthony G. Greenwald, *Blindspot: Hidden Biases of Good People* (New York: Bantam, 2016).

PART III

CONSEQUENCES OF SEGREGATION

Introduction

A wide variety of important individual outcomes, from life expectancy to life-time earnings, continue to vary by race and by class in the United States. For instance, life expectancy for the white population in 2014 was 3.4 years longer than for the black population, and the difference in life expectancy between the highest- and lowest-earning 1 percent of the population was 14.6 and 10.1 years for men and women, respectively.[1] Among those in the labor force (not adjusted for education), median earnings in 2010 were 32 percent lower for black men and 42 percent lower for Latino men than for white men, and 10 percent lower for black women and 32 percent lower for Latina women than for white women.[2] Why do these basic outcomes differ so significantly by race and class?

One factor that might contribute to these differences is residential segregation. Yet while correlations between residential segregation and individual outcomes in a variety of domains are well established, significant debate remains about the nature of the relationship. The most fundamental question is the degree to which segregation widens disparities, rather than just reflecting them. And even those who have identified evidence that segregation does widen disparities continue to debate the precise mechanisms through which segregation affects individual outcomes.

Residential segregation might widen disparities in outcomes because, at least in the United States, segregation is associated with substantial inequalities in neighborhood amenities, such as the public or private institutions to which one has easy access. Differential access to public investments or services, such as teacher salaries or hospitals, may directly affect the quality of our education or medical care. Further, residential segregation generates associational inequality across groups—in other words, differences in the characteristics of one's neighbors and friends.[3] Segregation may matter for individual outcomes, therefore, because geographic proximity is one of the ways in which our social networks are formed, and those networks shape our education and our employment by determining the information we can access and the referrals that are made on our behalf. It is also possible that segregation matters because it creates particular place-based patterns of social interactions in which our individual decisions may be shaped by our peers and their norms.[4]

This section of the book explores how racial and economic segregation may be connected to concrete consequences across multiple aspects of contemporary life, from health to home finance, and from policing to politics. Three key questions run through these discussions. First, several of the authors consider whether the relationship between segregated metropolitan areas and wider disparities by race and class is causal. Second, if the relationship is a causal one, multiple authors reflect on mechanisms that may connect segregation to inequalities in outcomes. Third, contributors ask what the fragmentation of residential life into different neighborhoods and municipalities by race and class may mean for society as a whole, especially national political life.

Several discussions highlight the association between residential segregation and unequal outcomes in a range of domains and then debate whether segregation itself causes wider disparities, or if segregation and disparities in outcomes by race and class are both driven by a third factor, such as historic inequalities of wealth. Mariana Arcaya and Alina Schnake-Mahl, for example, assert that residential segregation by race and class generates disparities in health outcomes, while Robert Kaestner questions the link between segregation and health disparities, arguing that the evidence for a causal relationship, and potentially any clear relationship at all, is lacking. Arcaya and Schnake-Mahl also raise the possibility that causation may run in the opposite direction: poor health may lead to residence in more economically deprived and racially isolated neighborhoods. In terms of policing, Jeffrey Fagan notes that aggressive policing practices are spatially concentrated and points out that the rate of police stops and the number of misdemeanor arrests of black and Latino individuals are higher than local crime rates would predict; he suggests that segregation facilitates disparities in policing. Monica Bell, meanwhile, suggests that causation at times runs in the other direction: differences in police treatment by race and place contribute to creating segregated residential patterns by steering black and Latino households away from otherwise desirable municipalities where police have a reputation for harsh or discriminatory treatment. In the context of financial services, Jacob Faber argues that residential segregation by race contributed to widespread racial disparities in the rates that banks charged borrowers for mortgage loans leading up to the financial crisis. Stephen Ross questions whether racial disparities in lending were a product of neighborhood-based racial targeting by lenders, suggesting instead that disparities may be produced by wholly different lenders providing different products in different places. In short, across multiple domains, segregation is at least associated with differences in the quality of services or differences in individual outcomes. Contributors, however, debate whether this relationship is a causal one.

The second set of shared questions asks what mechanisms may connect segregation to inequalities in outcomes. John Mollenkopf and Todd Swanstrom focus on how economic segregation (more than racial segregation) has led to the fiscal distress that in turn motivates aggressive ticketing and fines. Similarly, segregation matters for Jeff Smith because it is layered onto a fragmented system of local governments, leading to disparities in the fiscal capacity of governments that directly affect individuals' access to opportunity. Christopher Tinson, however, argues that both segregation and the accompanying disparities are driven by antiblack policy making. In health, Jose Figueroa suggests that one mechanism that may connect segregation to health outcomes is that the quality of health-care services delivered in predominantly black and Latino neighborhoods is consistently lower on objective measures of clinical process compared to the care delivered in predominantly white neighborhoods. Sherry Glied notes that given the variety of ways that segregation could widen health disparities, from differences in mean neighborhood incomes to differences in neighborhood environmental quality, what is actually striking is that disparities by race are not larger than they are given current levels of segregation. Attention to mechanisms, she suggests, must include attention to larger municipal or state-level policy factors that may mediate or mitigate segregation's effects.

Other discussions ask what the fragmentation of residential life in the United States not only into different neighborhoods, but also often into different municipalities, means for society as a whole; some focus particularly on the role that segregation has played in polarizing political life and the need for multiracial political movements in response. For instance, Patrick Bayer and Christina Greer emphasize that the intersection of residential segregation and historic economic inequality makes the mechanisms driving contemporary disparities hard to perceive, and then easy to exploit to undermine support for public goods and institutions. Jennifer Hochschild argues that addressing this "toxic mix of race, place, and poverty" requires moving beyond "old tropes of white racism and black powerlessness" to create multiracial poor and working-class coalitions. J. Phillip Thompson similarly notes the ways in which the spatial distance of residential segregation easily transfers into the social distance of divisive politics and the need for morally rooted, multiracial, class-based organizing in response. Lawrence Bobo expresses alarm at the ways in which empathy appears to be diminishing as economic inequality rises and he highlights the dangers that this decline in empathy poses for democratic politics in a segregated nation.

The Discussions in Part III

Explaining Ferguson Through Place and Race

The first discussion in this series explores in detail the consequences of metropolitan area segregation by race and income in the fragmented St. Louis region,
including the effects of segregation on local government finances, schools, and
policing. The authors suggest that this combination of municipal fragmentation, segregation by race, and concentrated poverty contributed to creating
the context in which an unarmed black teenager, Michael Brown, was shot and
killed by a white police officer, and the context for nationwide protests emphasizing the value of black lives. John Mollenkopf and Todd Swanstrom launch
the discussion arguing that black political participation and enforcement of
civil rights laws alone will not deliver racial or economic equality. The central
battle, they argue, is dismantling the place-based structural policies that create
separate and fiscally unequal communities, such as local government laws facilitating local government secession, land-use laws enabling economic exclusion,
and transportation subsidies for highways encouraging middle-class flight.
They argue that the creation of these fragmented metropolitan structures drives
inequality by both race and class. Agreeing with this emphasis on the intersection of race, place, and poverty, Jennifer Hochschild notes how the growth of
the black middle and upper-middle class may cause unjustified complacency
about inequality in a nation where the poor and the affluent increasingly live in
different worlds. Jeff Smith, a former Missouri state senator, decries the extreme
level of municipal fragmentation in the region and the consequences of thereby
creating weak, inefficient local governments in competition with each other. He
argues that real alliances could be formed, costs saved, and services improved
through municipal and regional consolidation, with a focus on strengthening
government capacity, improving public education, improving law enforcement,
and connecting young people to jobs. Christopher Tinson completes the discussion arguing that race is the central factor in the structural inequality that
Mollenkopf and Swanstrom highlight. In his view, these inequalities within
metropolitan regions must be understood as products of antiblack policy making; the solution lies in advancing the unfinished civil rights agenda.

Segregation and Law Enforcement

Jeffrey Fagan suggests that segregation can facilitate different policing practices.
He argues that policing practices characterized by high rates of pedestrian stops
and arrests for minor criminal misdemeanors are overwhelmingly deployed

in African American or Latino neighborhoods, and that these disparities in police practices can help to reinforce social and spatial boundaries. Further, he argues, it creates a racially unequal criminal-justice tax on everyday activities by people of color in neighborhoods that are predominantly nonwhite. Monica Bell adds that another consequence of racially segregated metropolitan areas is that people of color may then become targets for police profiling in predominantly white areas. Drawing on qualitative research on policing, she describes how higher-income African American and Latino households sometimes report avoiding living in otherwise attractive neighborhoods where police have a reputation for bias or overzealousness. Given the spatial concentration of and disproportionate African American and Latino exposure to violence, Philip Cook notes the trade-off between harsh policing policies that he argues may actually make black and Latino residents overall safer but that also expose black and Latino young men in particular to frequent stops, leading to feelings of abuse and distrust. Anthony Braga turns the spatial concentration of crime into a potential opportunity for more nuanced preventive strategies that can engage neighborhood residents in identifying creative strategies, such as improvements to the physical environment, that can prevent crime and reduce arrests. From this perspective, police strategies focusing on high-risk people or places could be not a form of profiling but a generator of productive community engagement in crime prevention.

Segregation and Health

Robust scholarly debate continues on the relationship between segregation and health. Mariana Arcaya and Alina Schnake-Mahl begin by noting that residents of poor, predominantly minority neighborhoods experience high mortality rates and worse outcomes on numerous measures of health. They point out that one mechanism that could connect residential segregation to disparities in health outcomes is that neighborhood-based health-care systems in segregated areas serve different populations by race, and that those who live in racially isolated neighborhoods have less access to medical care and receive lower-quality care. They also note that poor health itself may make it harder for families to leave disadvantaged neighborhoods. Thus, more equitable access to affordable health care could help not only to address the consequences of segregation but also to encourage greater mobility and integration. Robert Kaestner, however, questions whether segregation is in fact related to disparities in either access to health care or health outcomes. Jose Figueroa focuses on racial disparities in the quality of care, which are well established and could relate to segregation. Consider that just 5 percent of hospitals nationwide care for more than half of all elderly Latino patients and 10 percent of hospitals care for nearly half of elderly African American patients. Sherry Glied asks why, given the multiple mechanisms likely to connect residential segregation and health outcomes, segregation does not have an even larger effect on outcomes. She suggests that some policies that affect health outcomes, such as environmental laws and health insurance policies, operate at the metropolitan or state level, reducing potential neighborhood differences. Additionally, there is the possibility that community cohesion and social supports in more socially homogenous neighborhoods may counter any negative effects of segregation.

Segregation and the Financial Crisis

Jacob Faber starts this discussion with an essay highlighting the stark racial dimensions of the recent housing crisis. He argues that racial segregation played a central role in creating racial disparities by delivering "easily identifiable" markets for subprime mortgage lenders. He goes further to claim that segregation led to a greater overall volume of subprime lending and thus helped to trigger the Great Recession. He suggests that greater economic and racial integration would do more to stop predatory lending than financial education. Ngina Chiteji largely endorses Faber's diagnosis, but she challenges his policy prescription, advocating for more robust financial education as a key tool to combat predatory lending and boost minority wealth. Patrice Ficklin also focuses on policy, emphasizing the role that federal policy and the recently established Consumer Financial Protection Bureau play in fighting redlining and reverse redlining and more generally in enforcing fair lending laws. Stephen Ross challenges Faber's fundamental diagnosis. He agrees that residents of poor, minority neighborhoods disproportionately received subprime loans and disproportionately suffered from the foreclosure crisis, but he questions the link between segregation and the crisis. First, he argues that the number of minority borrowers in disadvantaged neighborhoods was simply too small to have had such a significant effect on the financial system. He also questions Faber's targeting claim, citing research showing that racial disparities are largely explained by standard risk factors and that minority borrowers are generally served by a completely different set of lenders than white borrowers (not by the same lenders offering riskier products in largely minority areas).

Segregation and Politics

Where the first discussion in this section looked at the significance of segregation for politics and policing at the local level in the context of Ferguson, the final discussion examines the relationship between segregation and politics at the national level. J. Phillip Thompson starts by referencing the arguments made by the NAACP lawyers in *Brown v Board of Education* (1954) that segregation "chilled the development in the South of opinion conducive to the acceptance of Negroes on the basis of equality." So too today, Thompson argues, segregation by race and income limits opportunities for cross-class, cross-race interactions that are central to the critical democratic experience of engaging with and learning from those who may be seen as different. Indeed, Thompson suggests that contemporary residential segregation contributes to social distance between groups and scapegoating that distract from a focus on the structural issues that contribute to inequality. He identifies promise in movements that conduct morally based organizing, building common ground across class and race. Patrick Bayer describes how segregation may make politically popular policies focused on choice problematic in that policies that provide greater housing or school choice are likely to yield larger benefits to those who are already advantaged enough to avail themselves of those choices while disadvantaging those whose options are already limited by the geographic sorting by race and income. Residential segregation in the United States allows for individuals to see the fortunes of white communities and communities of color as delinked, and is particularly problematic, Lawrence Bobo writes, at a time when a sense of shrinking opportunity and socioeconomic mobility has appeared to make empathy harder to muster. Bobo argues that addressing segregation is particularly important to enable individual engagement in collaborative multiracial efforts that can assure that working- and middle-class whites see their fates as strengthened, not diminished, by the full inclusion of the growing African American, Latino, and Asian population into society. Christina Greer concludes the discussion by emphasizing how racial and economic segregation contributes to the solidification of political polarization, and that combatting physical segregation and ideological segregation go hand in hand.

Notes

1. Kenneth D. Kochanek et al., "Deaths: Final Data for 2014," *National Vital Statistics Reports* 65, no. 4 (June 2016): 1–122; Raj Chetty et al., "The Association Between Income and Life Expectancy in the United States, 2001–2014," *JAMA* 315, no. 16 (April 2016): 1750–1766, https://doi.org/10.1001/jama.2016.4226.

2. Colin Peterson, Matthew Snipp, and Sin Yi Cheung, "Earnings," *Pathways*, Special Issue 2017, 32–35, https://inequality.stanford.edu/sites/default/files/Pathways_SOTU_2017 _earnings.pdf.

3. Steven N. Durlauf, "Associational Redistribution: A Defense," *Politics & Society* 24, no. 4 (December 1996): 391–410, https://doi.org/10.1177/0032329296024004008.

4. Bryan S. Graham, "Identifying and Estimating Neighborhood Effects," National Bureau of Economic Research Working Paper No. 22575, August 2016, http://www.nber.org /papers/w22575.

EXPLAINING FERGUSON THROUGH PLACE AND RACE

The Ferguson Moment: Race and Place

by John Mollenkopf and Todd Swanstrom

The shooting of Michael Brown, an unarmed black teenager, by a white police officer in Ferguson, Missouri, set off a series of peaceful protests and violent riots that reverberated across the nation—and even the world. The media have largely viewed the turmoil in Ferguson through a racial lens. A half-century after the legislative triumphs of the civil rights movement, it seems as if race relations are as bad as ever. And if old-fashioned racism drives the injustices in Ferguson, then the solutions are clear: enforce civil rights laws, register black voters, take power away from entrenched white political elites, and administer the law fairly.

These steps are necessary, of course, but they are not sufficient for addressing the racial injustices that were exposed by the turmoil in Ferguson. What if blacks have the right to sit anywhere they want on the bus, but no bus runs past their home? What if African Americans have the right to live anywhere they want regardless of skin color, but they can only afford places that suffer from high crime, underperforming schools, and shabby public spaces? What if minorities have the right to vote, but their local government is a "hollow prize": small, fiscally stressed, and lacking in professionalism?

What upholds racial inequality now is not so much person-to-person discrimination but the tangled web of race and class embedded in metropolitan development patterns. In *Place Matters: Metopolitics for the Twenty-First Century*, we, along with coauthor Peter Dreier, document the rise of concentrated poverty and metropolitan inequality.[1] At the same time that black-white segregation has slowly declined,[2] economic segregation has risen.[3] The growth of concentrated poverty is especially striking in the suburbs.[4]

Ferguson has a poverty rate of about 22 percent; on the eastern edge of the town, where the protests took place, the rate exceeds 33 percent.[5] (Ferguson is hardly the poorest municipality in St. Louis County; in fact, seventeen other municipalities have higher poverty rates.) With per capita assessed valuation at only about one-third of the county average, Ferguson is locked in a fiscal cage: if it increases tax rates (to raise revenues to meet needs), it will drive home values down further; but if it does not increase tax rates, it will slowly starve municipal services and the schools.

Fiscally stressed suburbs in St. Louis have tried to finesse this dilemma by turning to alternative sources of revenue. Amazingly, more than one-quarter of Ferguson's budget comes from traffic fines and court fees. Systematic police and judicial practices in poor St. Louis suburbs are balancing their city budgets on the backs of their most vulnerable citizens.[6] Police issue tickets for everything from illegal turns, to driving without insurance, to loud music and "saggy pants." When citizens fail to appear in court because they don't have the cash to pay the fines, a warrant is issued for their arrest. In 2013, the Ferguson municipal court—serving a city of 21,135 people—issued 32,975 arrest warrants for nonviolent offenses. Trapped in an oppressive legal system without a lawyer, people often end up losing their right to drive, their jobs, and their freedom. With good reason, critics have compared it to debtors' prison.

Race adds to the toxic mix. Police systematically target those who look poor, often black people, because they know they are more likely to have an outstanding warrant—and arrest provides additional opportunities to pile on more court fees and fines. Add the fact that fifty out of fifty-three police officers in Ferguson were white (in a city that is two-thirds black), and you have an explosive situation that goes a long way toward explaining the anger that erupted in the protests and riots. Relatively poorly paid and poorly trained white police, who usually do not live in the community, treat peaceful citizens in a remarkably disrespectful—and sometimes, as in the case of Michael Brown, a remarkably brutal—manner.

Race is not the main driver of these oppressive practices. With an all-black city council, black mayor, and majority black police force, the nearby city of Berkeley engages in the same practices as Ferguson, last year generating $111 in traffic fines and court fees per resident and issuing 5,504 arrest warrants.[7]

Whites are also harassed by distressed suburban municipalities. Since one of us (Todd) moved to St. Louis thirteen years ago, he has received a number of minor traffic violations with excessive fines from small municipalities. Todd's solution is simple: He hires a lawyer; the lawyer plea-bargains the ticket down to a nonmoving violation so there are no points against his driver's license; he pays the lawyer about $120 and an inflated fine, say $150, and goes on with his life. It is expensive but low stress. If you are poor and cannot afford a lawyer, however, you can be pulled down into a vortex of fines, arrest warrants, and even imprisonment.

To suggest, as the media and many activists do, that Ferguson's turmoil is rooted in old-fashioned racism misses important points. Electing blacks to Ferguson's city council and hiring more black police officers will help, but it will not address the underlying cause: the growth of concentrated poverty in the suburbs. Not only are the suburban poor, like the central-city poor, isolated from opportunity, but they also face weak governmental and civic institutions that deepen their disadvantage.[8]

Addressing the underlying causes of the unrest in Ferguson will require changing the regional patterns of inequality. As we argue in *Place Matters*, the metropolitan playing field is tilted toward suburban sprawl and urban and inner suburban decline. Governments in the St. Louis region subsidize the flight of middle-class, largely white, families out of the older parts of the region by building highways rather than public transit and giving tax breaks for jobs to decentralize. Exclusionary zoning regulations that outlaw apartments or require large lots for single-family homes prevent poor families from following jobs to opportunity-rich suburbs. These laws need not mention race in order to promote racially disparate outcomes. Because of long-standing, state-sanctioned discrimination against them in job markets and education, African Americans tend to be poorer, and therefore economic discrimination by exclusionary zoning effectively becomes racial discrimination.

Generals are notorious for "fighting the last war." Our concern is that we will make the same mistake in responding to events in Ferguson. In fact, the passage of civil rights laws ended the last war; we won the battle against state-sanctioned racial discrimination. Listening to the coverage of events in Ferguson would make you believe that the civil rights movement failed—that people are as racist as ever. No doubt subtle and subconscious racism still exists. But the underpinnings of racial injustices today are metropolitan development patterns rooted in a tangled complex of private practices and public policies. We need new strategies and tactics for a new war.

What Does Obama's Election Tell Us About "The Ferguson Moment"?

by Jennifer Hochschild

I completely agree with Todd Swanstrom and John Mollenkopf, in both their general claim and their discussion of particulars. The current American racial morass is not the same as the racial divide that persisted for a century after slavery was abolished: civil rights and social welfare laws and their implementation, increasing intraracial economic inequality, demographic transformation, and even changes in whites' racial attitudes have reinvented the old problem of racial inequality and injustice. Our current morass results mainly from the toxic mix of race, place, and poverty, and solutions to it must move beyond old tropes of white racism and black powerlessness. So my comments here will mainly amplify the argument of "The Ferguson Moment."

Electing a black president, twice, did not of course signal that the United States is postracial, whatever that means; countless scholarly writings show that race persists as a causal factor in almost everything that matters. But electing a black president twice does signal some sort of crucial change—the question is what the signal means. I see four meanings relevant to this discussion.

First, enough whites are now sufficiently nonracist that they gave Obama more votes in 2008 than almost any Democratic presidential candidate has received since LBJ's landslide in 1964. Whites' attitudes and, more significantly, behaviors have changed. Second, Obama's victory in both elections depended importantly on votes of nonwhites. That there are now enough nonwhite voters to affect the outcome of a presidential election is evidence of profound changes in law and demography. Third, Obama both instantiates and has had an impact on the growth of a powerful, affluent, self-confident black middle and upper-middle class. African Americans are by no means uniformly poor and struggling; in fact, the Gini index of income inequality is greater within the black population than within any other American racial or ethnic group. Wealth disparities across races remain huge and consequential even among those with high incomes, but it is impossible to ignore the number and impact of people of color in genuinely important public offices.

Fourth, none of these changes has produced much benefit for places like Ferguson or Berkeley, Missouri. Some argue that such changes have actually made things worse for poor blacks in poor communities, since advances for the black middle and upper-middle class and improvement in visible aspects of racial inequality, such as increasing college attendance and declining residential segregation in many areas, might induce unjustified complacency. For example, a Gallup Poll series of questions about whether "race relations will always be a problem for the United States or . . . a solution will eventually be worked out" finds unprecedentedly high optimism among American whites since 2008. Blacks' optimism spiked in 2008, but declined almost to previous levels by 2012.

Even if the improving situation of affluent blacks has not harmed the position of poor blacks, it has complicated intragroup dynamics. A 2007 Pew Research Center survey found about a third of African Americans agreeing that middle-class and poor blacks have "only a little" or "almost nothing" in common; only 22 percent of lower-class blacks saw "a lot" in common. Perhaps this finding hints at growing class conflict among blacks; a year later, an ABC News poll found that upper-income blacks identified more with their race than their class while lower-income blacks identified by class more than by race.[9]

Perhaps these views should not surprise us; as "The Ferguson Moment" implies, the poor really do live in a different world from the affluent. Yet the protests in Ferguson, New York, and elsewhere have evinced a great deal of racial solidarity and not much evidence of a multiracial poor and working-class coalition. Whether such a coalition emerges after the protests die down, or whether the United States continues to follow its well-worn track of race-based antagonisms, remains unclear.

What is to be done? The first thing is to resist the temptation to claim that nothing has changed, that the problem is white racism and black powerlessness, that black communities are only overpoliced and not underpoliced. The second thing is to look much more closely at the question of whether class politics can intersect productively with racial politics, so that poor white (and Latino) suburbs can unite with poor black suburbs in new metropolitan-area configurations. Third, as that possibility suggests, progressives might fruitfully look to states and metropolitan areas more than the federal government for solutions to "The Ferguson Problem." Bruce Katz and Jennifer Bradley argue that "cities and metros are fixing our broken politics and fragile economy. . . . Networks of metropolitan leaders . . . are doing the hard work to grow more jobs and make their communities more prosperous, and they're investing in infrastructure, making manufacturing a priority, and equipping workers with the skills they need."[10] Even if some of this claim is intended more to sell books than to describe reality, there may be crucial seeds of innovation coming from relatively robust cities interacting with depressed suburbs. Growing such seeds is the next civil rights project.

Five Concrete Steps Toward a St. Louis Comeback

by Jeff Smith

In greater St. Louis, decisions of the past created the conditions of the present, which have imbued so many residents with a nihilism about the future. It is a nihilism—a sense that no matter what they do, unseen structural forces will stifle positive change; an exhaustion arising from decades spent as powerless bystanders to policy adoption and implementation affecting their communities; a hopelessness underlined by the horrific image of a teenager mowed down as he raised his hands in surrender—that we must grasp in order to understand what's happening in St. Louis right now.

Todd Swanstrom and John Mollenkopf's diagnosis of this despair's underlying causes largely comports with my assessment a week after Michael Brown's death. They agree that the financial stressors on a hopelessly fractured and increasingly impoverished region have combined with persistent racial inequities in the power structure to create economic, educational, transportation, and criminal justice systems that trap many African Americans in a vicious downward spiral. I outline some of the history underlying these systems in a recent e-book.[11] But since we seem to agree about the root causes, it seems more fruitful here to focus on potential solutions. In pressing President Obama after the 2008 financial collapse, Rahm Emanuel counseled the president, "Never let a serious crisis go to waste." In that vein, it may be the right moment to broach solutions to many of the problems that have long plagued the region.

The first and most obvious policy solution is municipal and regional consolidation. There are currently ninety municipalities in the region, but ten would be more appropriate, along with a larger St. Louis City. Consolidation with other St. Louis County municipalities could help cities like Ferguson reinvest in themselves. Through consolidation, strapped communities could avoid using such a high percentage of their resources for expensive public-safety overhead and obtain more favorable borrowing rates, as a larger size and tax base could reassure potential lenders. Consolidation could also help African Americans compete for a bigger share of the municipal pie and incrementally gain power as larger municipalities increase the importance of broad coalitions and alliances. Finally, consolidation could increase the political talent pool.

In shrinking cities, politics is often a nasty, zero-sum game. But consolidation could create economies of scale, increase borrowing capacity to expand economic opportunity, reduce economic pressures that inflame racial tension, and smash up the old boys' network that has long ruled much of North County. Although consolidation, especially any combination with the City of St. Louis, may be a tough sell to voters in an extremely parochial region, a recent series of reports highlighting the inefficiencies of municipal fragmentation, along with a steady stream of news about Ferguson's incompetence, has shined a light on the impracticality of having fifty-nine police departments in a single county. Now may be the best opportunity in decades to make meaningful progress on merging municipal services and, eventually, entire towns. Reformers must ensure that residents concerned about losing proximity to service providers connect their towns' financial stress to massive service duplication, and that residents grasp the potential to end the hyperpolicing that has caused the frustration (and incarceration) of so many citizens.

A second set of solutions involves law enforcement. The region must overhaul a municipal police and court system that preys on the poor. While the ninety municipalities in St. Louis County make up 11 percent of the state's population, the courts in those municipalities bring in a whopping 34 percent of all municipal court revenue statewide. Twenty of the twenty-one cities in the county that derive at least 20 percent of their revenue from courts are in areas that are predominantly African American. It was difficult enough for black St. Louisans to accumulate intergenerational wealth for the past two centuries because of slavery, Jim Crow, forced residential segregation and disinvestment, price gouging, and restricted employment opportunities. To continue systematically extracting scarce wealth from struggling black citizens, largely to preserve salaried public-sector jobs for predominantly white employees, is unconscionable, and it must change. Recent state legislation reduced the maximum percentage of overall municipal revenue derived from courts to 30 percent from 35 percent; that number should be further reduced to 10 percent, per legislation prefiled by Missouri State Senator Eric Schmitt. This should substantially reduce the pressure on police to cite struggling residents for petty offenses. Also, forgiveness should be offered those who have outstanding warrants for petty offenses; St. Louis City has already taken the lead by forgiving more than 220,000 warrants, and hopefully municipalities throughout North County will follow their example.[12]

Moreover, a police force that looks like the community it serves will be much better able to reestablish trust with residents and implement any policy changes. The fact that public-sector workers aren't required to live within town limits significantly worsens the problem and fuels community resentment; residents see police, prosecutors, and judges as mercenaries brought in to harass them. Adding insult to injury, all of these law enforcement officials—as well as the town clerks and assessors that literally take their money after a court judgment—are paid with the fruits of that harassment. When a Ferguson policeman was caught on tape during one of the protest's first nights referring to the protesters as "fucking animals," it exemplified the fact that many white North County police live far away from the jurisdictions they patrol and see themselves as having little in common with residents of the communities they are supposed to protect. Blacks in North County, while not as poor, on balance, as blacks in North City, almost completely lack political autonomy within many jurisdictions despite compromising majorities of the population. There are preliminary efforts afoot—by both policy makers and philanthropists—to ensure a broader pool of minority applicants for St. Louis County municipal police forces. If these efforts are to have the desired effect, they must create sustainable pipelines through which young black citizens can become police officers—as well as prosecutors and judges. Only then will law enforcement treat subjects as they would their own neighbors, and only then will the system be broadly seen as legitimate by those ensnared in it.

A third key component of any long-term solution to the problems plaguing North St. Louis County is simple: jobs. Estimates of unemployment among young area males vary, but some are as high as 50 percent. As long as most

North County youth graduate from subpar high schools—or, all too often, fail to graduate—they will lack desirable job skills and the social networks that lead to employment.

To help address this, every major St. Louis company—but especially those based in and around Ferguson, including global multinationals such as Boeing, Express Scripts, and Emerson Electric, with market capitalizations ranging from $50 to $100 billion—should immediately hire at least a hundred young people from North County in entry- or midlevel positions and work to create broader employment pipelines for local youth. Several area companies have more than 100,000 employees worldwide; they can easily find room for another one hundred who live within walking distance of their world headquarters.

Emerson Electric has provided a model for local firms by creating a multimillion-dollar program called Ferguson Forward, a wide-ranging education and employment program to support the community with four focus areas: early childhood education, youth jobs, scholarships for college as well as for technical and trade careers, and business-development training. Emerson is partnering with local institutions to develop an early childhood learning resource center to support area preschool programs; supply one hundred jobs for area youth; fund scholarship opportunities for training in business, in science, technology, engineering, and math (STEM) disciplines, and in technical and trade jobs; provide peer mentors and tutors for students; endow scholarships to prestigious Cardinal Ritter Academy, a highly regarded all-black private high school with a nearly 100 percent college-attendance rate; and provide assistance to local small businesses in accounting, finance, legal, logistics, IT, HR, and marketing. These areas are critical to achieving long-term economic inclusion for black St. Louisans, and politicians should shame other local firms into following Emerson's lead.

A fourth solution involves public education. The St. Louis region has some of the finest public schools in the state and some of the worst, and the former must do more to help the latter. The ongoing tragedy of the transfer crisis in the unaccredited Normandy and Riverview Gardens districts—in which suburban superintendents have sought to avoid accepting transfer students from the struggling districts—makes that abundantly clear. There are examples of excellence and dramatic academic improvement among some of the region's poorest students, such as at Cardinal Ritter Preparatory Academy, the KIPP charter schools, and some schools in the Jennings district, which a small minority of Ferguson children attend.[13] We must find the resources and talent to replicate these successes, not just in Ferguson-Florissant but in the Normandy, Riverview Gardens, and St. Louis public schools as well. Until we do, students in unaccredited districts must have the option to matriculate in the school district of their choice, over the vehement objection of many county parents, school boards, and superintendents. Just fifteen years ago, the St. Louis region had the nation's largest voluntary interdistrict school busing program, and there is no reason why the region cannot resurrect a similar transfer program, given the original program's success in increasing the percentage of black students to attend college. If everything else suggested here is accomplished but the education of the region's black youth does not improve, any broader progress will be ephemeral.

Last but not least comes politics. One obvious way for North County black residents to wield more influence over the policy decisions that structure their lives is, of course, to vote. As long as whites continue voting at much higher rates in municipal elections—nearly four times the rate of blacks in Ferguson— disparities will continue. That means a concerted effort to register young voters, since the overwhelming majority of eighteen- to twenty-nine-year-olds in Ferguson are black, is a critical first step, which must go hand in hand with civic education efforts to demonstrate the importance of engagement.

Activists should also seek to change electoral rules. First, they should seek to move municipal elections to the November general election day, instead of the current system of separate municipal elections in the spring, when poorer citizens are less likely to vote. Second, they should work to reform state laws prohibiting recent ex-offenders from voting, which disproportionately affect North County blacks, and to eliminate other obstacles ex-offenders face in voting, such as local registrars' power to require documentation from parole officers before reinstating ex-offenders. Finally, they should work to pass statewide same-day voter registration, which has been linked with higher turnout, especially among younger voters.

None of these proposed solutions is a panacea. But taken together, they have a real chance to begin to heal a region whose wounds have been centuries in the making.

Race, Justice, and the Matters of Black Lives

by Christopher M. Tinson

The ongoing protests in Ferguson, Missouri, in the wake of Michael Brown's killing and the grand jury decision not to indict white police officer Darren Wilson, have shone much needed light on the patterns of U.S.-based racial antagonism. Antagonism best describes the deep-seated and frequently violent tensions concerning race and justice in America.[14] This case and the resistance it inspired have occurred within the long shadow of racial hostility and indifference, defining features of African American experience.

John Mollenkopf and Todd Swanstrom have written a thought-provoking commentary that suggests we give patterns of metropolitan development within cities greater attention in unpacking the significance of what they call "The Ferguson Moment." In other words, place and space matter as much as if not more than race in understanding these events. I would offer a few points that intersect with Mollenkopf and Swanstrom's insights and others that present a different reading of the circumstances of Black life. Where they err is in their discounting of race as a continuing central factor in the processes of structural suppression they highlight. I argue that anti-Black policy making has been the rule in American society, not an accidental or "old-fashioned" feature, but one that is continually reshaped and that guarantees certain material outcomes from a devaluation of difference.

Civil society—lawmakers and ostensibly law-abiding citizens—has historically upheld a logic that linked Blackness with poverty, ghettos, inadequate housing, and poor education. That these have become synonymous with Black life in the United States has established a baseline expectation of Black social deficiency, thus making a notion of Black "success" exceptional. Even when African Americans effectively engage in the electoral process, a right that many fought and died to achieve, it appears new forms of disenfranchisement have emerged in the Supreme Court's gutting of provisions of the Voting Rights Act and active efforts of voter suppression.[15] Not only have Black people been forced to live on the negative side of most social indicators of well-being, America has shown its ability to expand, grow, and develop with said inequity in tow.

As the authors point out, the city of Ferguson has tried to make up for revenue shortfalls through fines and fees generated by writing tickets for a variety of civil violations. The targeting of Black residents for these violations entangles them in whole spiral of further collateral consequences: a simple traffic stop can lead to losing a license, to losing a job or worse, and to further marginalizing Black residents from civic and political participation. However, Michael Brown was not approached and killed over traffic violations, or for allegedly robbing a nearby store. He was killed because he was Black and "threatening" to a white police officer wielding the power of a lethal weapon and badge of legal authority.

In analyzing the racial and class dynamics governing Ferguson, the authors write: "Race adds to the toxic mix. Police systematically target those who look poor, often black people, because they know they are more likely to have an outstanding warrant—and arrest provides additional opportunities to pile on more court fees and fines." The authors position race as an add-on, not as the salient feature that the police observe. "Poor" describes an economic standing, but does not always translate visually. Poor people can present themselves in a variety of forms. By contrast, Blackness is a highly visible marker, and as a result African Americans suffer the brunt of any profiling, regardless of their actual economic position. Although poverty is often used in economic terms, it can describe political circumstances as well. Middle- and working-class Black people across the country also experience political impoverishment in that their rights are often suspended instead of protected.

In this context, race need not be made secondary in order to observe the structural and often deadly dimensions of inequity. Race is central to the structure of contemporary U.S. society. This current movement for justice is rooted in a long history of racial oppression. New forms of anti-Black structural arrangements deprioritize Black people's demands for social advancement. Government policies have supported segregation in housing and education, two essential platforms for advancement. Rewarding residential segregation through "white flight" and restrictive covenants, white backlash against calls for racial redress, and the consolidation of white civic identity and political power under President Reagan all help explain how indifference to long-standing Black suffering and limited aspirational achievement was institutionalized. Unfortunately, this has not only persisted but hardened in the decades since the passage of historic civil rights and voting rights legislation, which was necessary but did not go far enough.[16]

Rather than end with a view of the current energy emerging from Ferguson and other epicenters as "fighting the last war," we can gain more traction by considering current struggles as part of the unfinished agenda of civil rights. One of the unintended consequences of civil rights advancement was that by outlawing segregation it signaled that those institutions and individuals that sought to uphold such practices would have to do so with greater discretion. Ferguson draws attention to some of the localized practices of suppression that have gone unaccounted for or been easily forgotten. The lessons of race and racism are still being learned sixty years after *Brown*, and fifty years after Selma. This paradox—how a society advances on some fronts while actively resisting fundamental changes on others—is one that too few Americans are willing to admit, much less engage.

The Black youth-led, transgenerational, multihued activism in Ferguson, New York, Oakland, and elsewhere under the banner "Black Lives Matter" is not misguided, myopic, or lacking in awareness of the historical roots, government policies, and persistent patterns of inequity and injustice. Enveloped in the vocalized and bodily dissent of this movement one finds deep historical memory, keen insight into gendered forms of anti-Black violence, and firm resolve to challenge the injustices of the status quo in hopes of a liberated future.

Notes

1. Peter Dreier, John Mollenkopf, and Todd Swanstrom, *Place Matters: Metropolitics for the 21st Century*, 2nd ed. revised (Lawrence, KS: University Press of Kansas, 2004).
2. John R. Logan and Brian J. Stults, "The Persistence of Segregation in the Metropolis: New Findings from the 2010 Census," Project US2010 Report, March 24, 2011, http://www.s4.brown.edu/us2010/Data/Report/report2.pdf; Jacob L. Vigdor and Edward L.

Glaesar, "The End of the Segregated Century: Racial Separation in America's Neigh-borhoods, 1890–2010," MI Report, January 2, 2012, http://www.manhattan-institute.org/html/cr_66.htm.

3. Sean F. Reardon and Kendra Bischoff, "Growth in the Residential Segregation of Families by Income, 1970–2009," Project US2010 Report, November 2011, http://www.s4.brown.edu/us2010/Data/Report/report111111.pdf; Rolf Pendall et al., "A Lost Decade: Neighborhood Poverty and the Urban Crisis of the 2000s," Joint Center for Political and Economic Studies, September 2011, http://jointcenter.org/sites/default/files/Lost%20Decade-web.pdf.

4. Elizabeth Kneebone and Alan Berube, *Confronting Suburban Poverty in America* (Washington, DC: Brookings Institution Press, 2013).

5. U.S. Census Bureau, 2008–2012 American Community Survey, https://www.census.gov/data/developers/updates/acs-5-yr-summary-available-2008-2012.html.

6. Radley Balko, "How Municipalities in St. Louis County, Mo., Profit from Poverty," *Washington Post*, September 3, 2014, http://www.washingtonpost.com/news/the-watch/wp/2014/09/03/how-st-louis-county-missouri-profits-from-poverty/; ArchCity Defenders, "Municipal Courts White Paper," November 23, 2014, http://www.archcitydefenders.org/wp-content/uploads/2014/11/ArchCity-Defenders-Municipal-Courts-Whitepaper.pdf.

7. Balko, "How Municipalities in St. Louis County, Mo., Profit from Poverty."

8. Margaret Weir, "Creating Justice for the Poor in the New Metropolis," UCI School of Social Sciences, May 12, 2011, http://www.socsci.uci.edu/newsevents/events/2011/2011-05-12-creating-justice-for-the-poor-in-the-new-metr.php.

9. Pew Research Center, "Blacks See Growing Values Gap Between Poor and Middle Class," November 13, 2007, http://www.pewsocialtrends.org/2007/11/13/blacks-see-growing-values-gap-between-poor-and-middle-class/.

10. Bruce Katz and Jennifer Bradley, *The Metropolitan Revolution: How Cities and Metros Are Fixing Our Broken Politics and Fragile Economy* (Washington, DC: Brookings Institution, 2013).

11. Jeff Smith, *Ferguson in Black and White* (Amazon Digital Services).

12. Nicholas J. C. Pistor, "St. Louis to Forgive About 220,000 Warrants for Nonviolent Municipal Offenses," *St. Louis Post-Dispatch*, October 1, 2014.

13. Elisa Crouch, "Jennings Schools Show Improvement Even as Neighboring Districts Struggle," *St. Louis Post-Dispatch*, September 22, 2013.

14. Frank Wilderson, *Red, White and Black: Cinema and the Structure of U.S. Antagonisms* (Durham, NC: Duke University Press, 2010).

15. Jason Zengerle, "The New Racism: This Is How the Civil Rights Movement Ends," *New Republic*, August 10, 2014.

16. Gary Orfield and Erica Frankenberg, "Brown at 60: Great Progress, a Long Retreat and an Uncertain Future," Civil Rights Project, May 15, 2014, https://www.civilrightsproject.ucla.edu/research/k-12-education/integration-and-diversity/brown-at-60-great-progress-a-long-retreat-and-an-uncertain-future/Brown-at-60-051814.pdf.

SEGREGATION AND LAW ENFORCEMENT

Policing and Segregation

by Jeffrey A. Fagan

The "new policing" has been widely adopted both in the United States and internationally for more than two decades, following a pattern common to the diffusion of innovation.[1] The regime combines advanced analytics to pinpoint allocations of officers, new forms of strict management accountability, and aggressive tactical enforcement of public-order crimes or violations. This third prong, the policing "model," varies from place to place, but generally includes high rates of investigative stops of both pedestrians and vehicles, arrests for minor misdemeanors, and summons for violations of civil ordinances such as open containers of alcohol or tall weeds. Most stops result in no action: no one is arrested or issued a summons, and rarely do the police find weapons or other contraband.[2] The interactions can be noxious if not violent, and the petty and not-so-petty indignities and perceived injustices of these stops can produce a strong sense of legal cynicism and, in turn, withdrawal from cooperation with police.[3]

If arrested, some face a night in jail awaiting a court appearance; others spend longer times in jail if they cannot make bail. Others face repeated court dates to resolve their cases, costing them lost days of work. Once in court, the menu of fines and fees ranges from detention fees to filing fees to drug-testing fees to electronic-monitoring fees, challenging their ability to pay.[4] Many plead guilty simply to escape those intrusions and obligations. Arrest warrants are issued to those who fail to appear for court dates or who are unable to pay fines, transforming what might have been a noncriminal violation into a criminal matter.[5] The stigma costs of a misdemeanor conviction can lead to problems with housing, jury service, employment, and schooling. On top of these burdens, research on the "new policing" leaves some doubt as to its contributions to public safety and urban life.[6]

Also, the effects of the new policing are highly racialized: relative to crime rates, the rate of stops of Black and Latino people is higher than local crime or social conditions would predict in neighborhoods with larger minority population shares.[7] The same is true for misdemeanor arrests.[8] So, when court cases result in monetary fines or fees, the burden falls disproportionately on non-Whites.[9] These fees amount to a racial tax that reaches into the pockets of mostly poor and predominantly minority citizens, deepening any preexisting impoverishment[10] while aggravating racial disparities in criminal justice.[11]

The combination of criminal sanctions and mounting fees tends to reinforce both social and spatial boundaries and, in turn, to deepen racial and economic concentrations in "poverty traps."[12] In effect, the new policing reinforces segregation by imposing a criminal-justice tax on everyday movements and activities. In places as disparate as Ferguson and the South Bronx, the threat of police contacts or criminal sanctions, with both monetary costs and the threat of jailing, raises the transaction costs for Black and Latino residents to move freely within their neighborhoods and as well as when they cross racial boundaries. Because police deployments and actions are racialized and focused in poor and segregated places, police reproduce inequality, racial stratification, and segregation through criminal legal enforcement actions that constrain mobility.[13] In other words, when police routinely intervene in the everyday lives of citizens, they impose interaction costs that deter residents from moving freely.

When police actions produce legal and economic consequences for those already in disadvantaged social positions, those consequences effectively lock them into those positions.[14] Stops and arrests create the risk of heightened police surveillance and harsher treatment in court for any subsequent appearance,[15] and also spill over to bias in the form of exclusion from serving on juries[16] or from college enrollment, attendance, and achievement.[17] Neighborhoods stigmatized by crime and arrests are unattractive for investment, so that economic segregation coincides with residential segregation.[18] Limited access to capital further attenuates the ability of minority business borrowers to invest and multiply their capital, cutting off opportunities for local economic development to the point where the lack of opportunity becomes endemic to the neighborhood.[19] Both the stigma and monetary costs of legal interventions and the dignity costs of police intrusions help to enforce racial boundaries. In other words, stops and arrests beget stops and arrests and "spillover discrimination," simply by stigmatizing a neighborhood as a "high-crime area."[20]

The conflation of racial segregation and economic mobility means that, typically, a Black adolescent or young adult male in a U.S. city lives in very different economic and social circumstances than his White counterpart: different types of schools, different social networks, different levels of access to social capital, leading to crime, different exposure to the police, and a "high risk of physical injury, violent death, and criminal victimization."[21] People in places with high levels of racial fragmentation and income inequality have less access to public goods and lower levels of civic engagement that might alleviate those conditions.[22] Residents of predominantly minority and low-income neighborhoods have limited access to the types of everyday material services (such as libraries, supermarkets, parks, and cultural institutions) that characterize economically better-off places.[23] Several studies report that racial segregation exacerbates the prevalence and severity of health disparities[24] and is a fundamental cause of racial disparities in health.[25] Although research on stressors has not looked (yet) at police treatment, some studies have shown the psychological impact on mental health of harsh interactions with police in the context of new policing.[26]

Research to make these connections is still new, but both theory and data are available to test and elaborate these dynamics. In addition to these indicia of disadvantage, new studies are underway to examine whether policing influences rates of bankruptcy, foreclosure, inequality, and downward mobility. The good news here is that in many places, crime rates remain relatively low compared to earlier decades. The bad news, then, is that policing has become further disconnected from crime, or from judging guilt and innocence, and more closely tied to the racial composition and economic position of neighborhoods. That is indeed bad news.

The Dynamics of Policing and Segregation by Race and Class

by Monica Bell

Across the country, in courts and legislatures and in academia, the geographic concentration of harsh policing and "stop-and-frisk" techniques has recently gained attention. Heavy and sometimes harsh policing is inextricably woven into the experience of daily life in a poor, predominantly black or Latino urban neighborhood. In this way, policing creates dynamics that can lock people into poor, predominantly African American or Latino neighborhoods, as Jeffrey Fagan discusses in his essay. But it also creates dynamics that push others out of whiter and wealthier neighborhoods.

Policing is not necessarily fairer or more effective in whiter or wealthier neighborhoods, at least if you're black, Latino, or poor. Indeed, the high visibility of minorities, especially young black and Latino men and women, can intensify surveillance for people of color who dare venture beyond ethnic enclaves. Sometimes, when minorities are perceived to be out of place in predominantly white neighborhoods, police can be especially harsh, sometimes even using the threat of arrest to expel black and brown people from predominantly white areas.[27] The combination of race and class marginality (thought to be identifiable in clothing, hairstyle, cadence, posture, or even the look in a person's eye) puts particular black and brown people under a special form of threat in a range of middle-class neighborhoods, even in predominantly minority middle-class neighborhoods.[28]

Higher-income African Americans and Latinos might avoid living in otherwise "good" neighborhoods where police have a reputation for harshness or bias. While policing does not singlehandedly cause segregation, the presence and reputation of police in certain neighborhoods sends a message to would-be residents who have choices: Stay away.

In June 2014, before the death of Eric Garner and well before the Black Lives Matter movement reached its zenith, I interviewed Jennifer, a twenty-four-year-old middle-income Latina living outside Dallas, Texas, to ask her about her recent decision to move to a different city nearby.[29] When I'd spoken to Jennifer a year earlier, she had hoped to leave her apartment in part because she felt the neighborhood was too racially homogenous; she desired a more diverse neighborhood. But when Jennifer and her husband actually searched neighborhoods for a home, they tempered their desire for a diverse and low-crime neighborhood with the necessity of avoiding racial profiling from the police. When their realtor showed them a lovely home in a predominantly white suburb of Fort Worth, Jennifer and her husband talked to some friends and family and ultimately concluded that they could not move there. "We liked the neighborhood," Jennifer explained, "It's just like—they kind of told us that the police over there were like, pretty hard." Clarifying what she meant by "hard," Jennifer continued, "Police were like, pretty tough. And when I mean 'tough,' I mean kind of, like, racist." After I asked her to clarify what she meant by "racist," Jennifer continued, "Where they're always pulling over Hispanics and blacks, you know? So we didn't want it."

Jennifer is only one example, but the study produced several stories of black and Latino families who factor the possibility of facing police bias and violence into their assessments of neighborhood livability. When higher-income black and Latino families have to include police bias or harshness as a factor in their decision-making process, their residential options are constrained by race. When lower-income black and Latino families avoid even passing through wealthier and whiter neighborhoods for fear of police profiling—let alone seeking to move to such a neighborhood by, for example, using a housing voucher—their residential options are constrained by race and class.

Understanding this *combination* of policing dynamics—locking certain people into predominantly black or Latino neighborhoods, as Fagan describes, and
pushing them away from more affluent and whiter neighborhoods—is critical
for fully conceptualizing the link between policing and persistent segregation.

The New Policing, Crime Control, and Harm Reduction

by Anthony A. Braga

The "new policing," as described by Jeffrey Fagan, captures a concerning element of the slow drift of the police profession away from community problem-
solving models of policing popularized during the 1980s and 1990s toward
more aggressive enforcement strategies over the past two decades. It is important to note here that the so-called new policing also has desirable elements that
better position police departments to enhance public safety and security. The
police should embrace an analytical approach to understanding crime patterns
and trends. Crime is highly concentrated in small high-risk places, and committed by and against a small number of people who are at high risk of being
the victim of a crime or a party to it.[30] Police managers should also be held
accountable for their performance in detecting and addressing these identifiable risks.

The new policing model unfortunately emphasizes increased law enforcement action over more nuanced prevention strategies that engage the
community. One-dimensional and overly broad police surveillance and
enforcement strategies do little to change the underlying dynamics that drive
serious urban violence and have generally not been found to be effective
in controlling crime.[31] Indiscriminate police enforcement actions also contribute to mass incarceration problems that harm disadvantaged neighborhoods.[32] This is particularly true when such an approach is coupled with a
"crime numbers game" managerial mind-set that promotes yearly increases
in arrest, summons, and investigatory stop actions as key performance measures.[33] Indeed, Fagan makes a strong case that aggressive enforcement strategies in the new policing may heighten racial and economic disparities and
possibly reinforce segregation.

Fagan's essay, however, does not focus on the kinds of crime-control strategies that police executives could pursue in the new policing model that would
help reduce harmful consequences for poor and disadvantaged neighborhoods.
As suggested by former President Obama's Task Force on Twenty-First Century Policing,[34] police strategies that unintentionally violate civil rights, compromise police legitimacy, or undermine trust are counterproductive. This
is precisely why they recommended that law enforcement agencies develop

and adopt policies and strategies that reinforce the importance of community engagement in managing public safety. While community policing programs have not been found to be effective in reducing crime, they have been found to generate positive effects for citizen satisfaction, perceptions of disorder, and police legitimacy.[35] Moreover, community engagement strategies implemented as part of community policing programs can provide important input to help focus problem-oriented policing, hot-spots policing, and focused deterrence approaches, which do seem to reduce crime.[36]

Developing close relationships with community members helps the police gather information about crime and disorder problems, understand the nature of these problems, and solve specific crimes. Community members can also help police prevent crime by contributing to improvements to the physical environment and through informal social control of high-risk people. In this way, police strategies focusing on high-risk people and high-risk places would cease to be a form of profiling and become a generator of community engagement projects.[37] Indeed, a central idea in community policing is to engage residents so they can exert more control over dynamics that contribute to their own potential for victimization and, by doing so, influence neighborhood levels of crime.[38] Preventing crime by addressing underlying crime-producing situations reduces harm to potential victims as well as harm to would-be offenders by not relying solely on arrest and prosecution actions.

Community engagement in developing appropriately focused strategies would help to safeguard against indiscriminate and overly aggressive enforcement tactics and other inappropriate policing activities, which in turn erode the community's trust and confidence in the police and inhibit cooperation. Collaborative partnerships between police and community members improve the transparency of law enforcement actions and provide residents with a much -needed voice in crime prevention work. Ongoing conversations with the community can ensure that day-to-day police-citizen interactions are conducted in a procedurally just manner that enhances community trust and compliance with the law.[39]

Community problem-solving strategies, rather than aggressive enforcement, should be the last prong of the new policing model. In the context of racial and economic segregation, the positive impact of such a policy change could be profound. Reduced mobility driven by fears of undue police attention, financial burdens imposed by fines and other criminal justice system costs, employment and education limitations associated with criminal records, and other negative externalities experienced by residents of disadvantaged neighborhoods would diminish. Effective police-community partnerships could improve the connection of local residents with a range of government and nonprofit resources that promote public safety by improving neighborhood conditions. Safer neighborhoods are more attractive to private businesses that can provide jobs and much-needed goods and services to local residents. In this way, police departments could be key initiators of longer-lasting social and economic changes that undo the harms associated with racial and economic segregation.

The ideals of community policing have been around for a long time. Unfortunately, many police departments do not seem to be embracing these approaches with fidelity to the original principles.[40] It is perhaps not surprising that even though community policing has been widely adopted, at least in principle, substantial conflict between police and the communities they serve continues to occur. It is high time that police departments reinvest in implementing community policing with a much more meaningful commitment to problem-solving and prevention-oriented approaches that emphasize the role of the public in helping set police priorities. By doing so, "new policing" strategies can be oriented toward reducing harm while controlling crime.

High-Volume Stops and Violence Prevention

by Philip J. Cook

Jeffrey Fagan's essay denounces the "new policing" and in particular high-volume "Terry" stops of pedestrians known as "stop, question, and frisk" (SQF). Of course the "new policing" is not that new, and some SQF programs in particular have been discontinued or are under attack. Recent legal challenges in Baltimore, Chicago, New York, and other large cities have now limited its use. In the most prominent example, the federal district court ruled against the programmatic use of SQF by the New York Police Department (NYPD) in the *Floyd* case (2013), in part based on Fagan's finding of frequent violations of the Fourth Amendment's requirement of "reasonable suspicion."[41] In *Floyd* and other legal actions, the legal challenge has also been mounted on the grounds that race was playing an illegitimate role in the police selection of "suspects," in violation of the Equal Protection Clause. SQF suspects are typically youthful minority males, a pattern sometimes justified by the fact that this group is also greatly overrepresented as victims and perpetrators of gun violence in these cities. But it was relatively rare in practice for these stops to find any weapon or other contraband, suggesting ironically that the police were not being selective enough.

The NYPD reported 686,000 SQFs in 2011, but under legal and public pressure, the NYPD has ended high-volume SQF in favor of carefully targeted stops: by 2015, the SQF count had dropped to just 23,000, 3 percent of its peak level. (There was also a drop in misdemeanor arrests during that period, though less dramatic.) More recently, Chicago has experienced a sharp drop in SQFs, apparently as a result of an agreement with the American Civil Liberties Union (ACLU) initiated on January 1, 2016 that, among other things, imposed a greater paperwork burden on officers.

While campaigning for president, Donald Trump touted SQF as an effective crime-control tactic, citing the extraordinary crime drop in New York City under Mayor Giuliani (1994–2001). But in fact there is no obvious correlation between the ramp-up of SQF and the drop in murder and other violence in New York. That decline in violence began before the SQF program and continued after it ended. Chicago experienced a sharp rise in gun homicide rates that coincided with the implementation of the ACLU agreement in January 2016, but that could be just coincidence, since other factors were by no means held constant in this "experiment." For example, the video recording of a Chicago Police Department officer firing sixteen shots at Laquan McDonald was released in late November 2015, and the public outcry may have triggered a defensive reaction by the Chicago police.

To determine whether high-volume SQF "works" to deter gun violence requires better evidence that can isolate the causal effect. In fact, such evidence exists. For example, experimental manipulations of SQF stops in Philadelphia and St. Louis have been analyzed by criminologists, who found substantial reductions in crime in the experimental neighborhood in comparison with control neighborhoods. In high-crime areas, this research shows that aggressive policing improves public safety, at least in the short run.[42]

Thus cities may face a trade-off in the use of SQF. If high-volume stops can make a high-crime neighborhood safer, as appears to be the case, then that benefits the residents both by making them safer and quite possibly by making the neighborhood more attractive for employers and other investors. Given the extent of racial and class segregation in our cities, and the association of demographic factors with criminal violence, the beneficiaries are typically going to be Black or Hispanic.[43] But to the extent that young minority men in that neighborhood are subjected to frequent police stops even if not carrying a weapon, there is every reason for them to feel abused. The costs and benefits fall on somewhat different groups within the same community.

In any event, some courts have been skeptical of this approach, and in some jurisdictions high-volume SQF is no longer viewed as an option. Whether there are other, less noxious approaches to keeping illegal guns off the street remains to be seen. Fagan himself has argued, based on some evidence, that limited police stops based on probable cause (rather than the *Terry* standard of "reasonable suspicion") may accomplish the crime-control effect with a much lower imposition on the residents.[44] Unfortunately, the question of "what works" in violence prevention is going to heat up in many cities if the recent surge of gun violence continues.[45]

Notes

1. Philip B. Heymann, "The New Policing," *Fordham Urban Law Journal* 28, no. 2 (2000): 407–456.

2. Sharad Goel, Justin Rao, and Ravi Shroff, "Precinct or Prejudice? Understanding Racial Disparities in New York City's Stop-and-Frisk Policy," *Annals of Applied Statistics* 10, no. 1 (2016): 365–394, https://papers.ssrn.com/abstract=2572718; Tracey Meares, "Programming Errors: Understanding the Constitutionality of Stop-and-Frisk as a Program, Not an Incident," *University of Chicago Law Review* 82, no. 1 (January 2015), http://chicagounbound.uchicago.edu/uclrev/vol82/iss1/7; Jeffrey Fagan, Greg Conyers, and Ian Ayres, "No Runs, Few Hits, and Many Errors: Street Stops and Racial Bias in Proactive Policing," Paper presented at the Seventh Conference on Empirical Legal Studies, University of California at Berkeley, November 2014.

3. Monica C. Bell, "Police Reform and the Dismantling of Legal Estrangement," *Yale Law Journal* 126 (2017): 2054–2150, https://www.yalelawjournal.org/essay/police-reform-and-the-dismantling-of-legal-estrangement; Robert Sampson and Dawn Jeglum Bartusch, "Legal Cynicism and (Subcultural?) Tolerance of Deviance: The Neighborhood Context of Racial Differences," *Law and Society Review* 32 (1998): 777–804; Matthew Desmond, Andrew V. Papachristos, and David S. Kirk, "Police Violence and Citizen Crime Reporting in the Black Community," *American Sociological Review* 81, no. 5 (October 2016): 857–876, https://doi.org/10.1177/0003122416663494; David S. Kirk and Mauri Matsuda, "Legal Cynicism, Collective Efficacy, and the Ecology of Arrest," *Criminology* 49, no. 2 (May 2011): 443–472, https://doi.org/10.1111/j.1745-9125.2011.00226.x.

4. Alexes Harris, *A Pound of Flesh: Monetary Sanctions as Punishment for the Poor* (New York: Russell Sage Foundation, 2016); Wayne A. Logan and Ronald F. Wright, "Mercenary Criminal Justice," *University of Illinois Law Review* 2014, no. 4: 1175–1226; Katherine Beckett and Alexes Harris, "On Cash and Conviction," *Criminology & Public Policy* 10, no. 3 (August 2011): 509–537, https://doi.org/10.1111/j.1745-9133.2011.00726.x; Katherine Baicker and Mireille Jacobson, "Finders Keepers: Forfeiture Laws, Policing Incentives, and Local Budgets," *Journal of Public Economics* 91, no. 11 (December 2007): 2113–2136, https://doi.org/10.1016/j.jpubeco.2007.03.009.

5. Jeffrey Fagan and Elliott Ash, "New Policing, New Segregation," *Georgetown Law Journal Online* 106 (2017).

6. John MacDonald, Jeffrey Fagan, and Amanda Geller, "The Effects of Local Police Surges on Crime and Arrests in New York City," *PLOS ONE* 11, no. 6 (June 2016): e0157223, https://doi.org/10.1371/journal.pone.0157223; Jeffrey Fagan, "Terry's Original Sin," *University of Chicago Legal Forum* 2016, no. 1: 43–97, http://chicagounbound.uchicago.edu/uclf/vol2016/iss1/3; David Weisburd et al., "Do Stop, Question, and Frisk Practices Deter Crime?," *Criminology & Public Policy* 15, no. 1 (February 2016): 31–56, https://doi.org/10.1111/1745-9133.12172; Richard Rosenfeld and Robert Fornango, "The Impact of Police Stops on Precinct Robbery and Burglary Rates in New York City, 2003–2010," *Justice Quarterly* 31, no. 1 (January 2014): 96–122, https://doi.org/10.1080/07418825.2012.712152; Hope Corman and Naci Mocan, "Carrots, Sticks, and Broken Windows," *Journal of Law and Economics* 48, no. 1 (April 2005): 235–266, https://doi.org/10.1086/425594; Charis E. Kubrin et al., "Proactive Policing and Robbery Rates Across U.S. Cities," *Criminology* 48, no. 1 (February 2010): 57–97, https://doi.org/10.1111/j.1745-9125.2010.00180.x.

7. Jeffrey Fagan and Garth Davies, "Street Stops and Broken Windows: Terry, Race, and Disorder in New York City," *Fordham Urban Law Journal* 28, no. 2 (February 2000):

457–505; Andrew Gelman, Jeffrey Fagan, and Alex Kiss, "An Analysis of the New York City Police Department's 'Stop-and-Frisk' Policy in the Context of Claims of Racial Bias," *Journal of the American Statistical Association* 102, no. 479 (September 2007): 813–823, https://doi.org/10.1198/016214506000001040; Fagan, Conyers, and Ayres, "No Runs, Few Hits, and Many Errors"; Jeffrey Fagan et al., "Stops and Stares: Street Stops, Surveillance, and Race in the New Policing," *Fordham Urban Law Journal* 43 (2016): 539–614.

8. Tammy Rinehart Kochel, David B. Wilson, and Stephen D. Mastrofski, "Effect of Suspect Race on Officers' Arrest Decisions," *Criminology* 49, no. 2 (May 2011): 473–512, http://onlinelibrary.wiley.com/doi/10.1111/j.1745-9125.2011.00230.x/full.

9. Harris, *A Pound of Flesh*; Logan and Wright, "Mercenary Criminal Justice"; Beckett and Harris, "On Cash and Conviction"; Baicker and Jacobson, "Finders Keepers."

10. American Civil Liberties Union, "In for a Penny: The Rise of America's New Debtors' Prisons," October 2010, https://www.aclu.org/report/penny-rise-americas-new-debtors-prisons.

11. Amy E. Lerman and Vesla M. Weaver, *Arresting Citizenship: The Democratic Consequences of American Crime Control* (Chicago: University of Chicago Press, 2014).

12. Robert Sampson and Jeffrey Morenoff, "Durable Inequality: Spatial Dynamics, Social Processes, and the Persistence of Poverty in Chicago Neighborhoods," in *Poverty Traps*, ed. Samuel Bowles, Steven N. Durlauf, & Karla Hoff (Princeton, NJ: Princeton University Press, 2006), 176–203.

13. Aziz Huq, "The Consequences of Disparate Policing: Evaluating Stop and Frisk as a Modality of Urban Policing," *Minnesota Law Review* 101 (2017): 2397–2480.

14. Robert Sampson and Patrick Sharkey, "Neighborhood Selection and the Social Reproduction of Concentrated Racial Inequality," *Demography* 45, no. 1 (February 2008): 1–29.

15. Julia Angwin, Jeff Larson, Surya Mattu and Lauren Kirchner, "Machine Bias," ProPublica, May 23, 2016, https://www.propublica.org/article/machine-bias-risk-assessments-in-criminal-sentencing.

16. Vida B. Johnson, "Arresting *Batson*: How Striking Jurors Based on Arrest Records Violates *Batson*," *Yale Law & Policy Review* 34, no. 2 (2016): 387–424.

17. Alex O. Widdowson, Sonja E. Siennick, and Carter Hay, "The Implications of Arrest for College Enrollment: An Analysis of Long-Term Effects and Mediating Mechanisms," *Criminology* 54, no. 4 (November 2016): 621–652, https://doi.org/10.1111/1745-9125.12114.

18. Paul A. Jargowsky, "Take the Money and Run: Economic Segregation in U.S. Metropolitan Areas," *American Sociological Review* 61, no. 6 (December 1996): 984–998; Jerome L. Kaufman, "Chicago: Segregation and the New Urban Poverty," in *Urban Segregation and the Welfare State: Inequality and Exclusion in Western Cities*, ed. Sako Musterd and Wim Ostendorf (New York: Routledge, 2000), 45–63; Chad R. Farrell, "Bifurcation, Fragmentation or Integration? The Racial and Geographical Structure of US Metropolitan Segregation, 1990–2000," *Urban Studies* 45, no. 3 (March 2008): 467–499, https://doi.org/10.1177/0042098007087332.

19. Darius Palia, "Differential Access to Capital from Financial Institutions by Minority Entrepreneurs," *Journal of Empirical Legal Studies* 13, no. 4 (December 2016): 756–785, https://doi.org/10.1111/jels.12132.

20. Andrew Guthrie Ferguson and Damien Bernache, "The High-Crime Area Question: Requiring Verifiable and Quantifiable Evidence for Fourth Amendment Reasonable Suspicion Analysis," *American University Law Review* 57, no. 6 (2008): 1587–1644.

21. Douglas S. Massey, "Getting Away with Murder: Segregation and Violent Crime in Urban America," *University of Pennsylvania Law Review* 143 (1995): 1203–1232.

22. Alberto Alesina, Reza Baqir, and William Easterly, "Public Goods and Ethnic Divisions," *Quarterly Journal of Economics* 114, no. 4 (November 1999), 1243–1284.

23. John R. Logan, "Separate and Unequal: The Neighborhood Gap for Blacks, Hispanics and Asians in Metropolitan America," *Project US2010 Report*, 2011, 1–22.

24. Tse-Chuan Yang, Yunhan Zhao, and Qian Song, "Residential Segregation and Racial Disparities in Self-Rated Health: How Do Dimensions of Residential Segregation Matter?," *Social Science Research* 61 (January 2017): 29–42, https://doi.org/10.1016/j.ssresearch.2016.06.011.

25. David R. Williams and Chiquita Collins, "Racial Residential Segregation: A Fundamental Cause of Racial Disparities in Health," *Public Health Reports* 116, no. 5 (2001): 404–416.

26. Abigail A. Sewell, Kevin A. Jefferson, and Hedwig Lee, "Living Under Surveillance: Gender, Psychological Distress, and Stop-Question-and-Frisk Policing in New York City," *Social Science & Medicine* 159 (June 2016): 1–13, https://doi.org/10.1016/j.socscimed.2016.04.024; Abigail A. Sewell and Kevin A. Jefferson, "Collateral Damage: The Health Effects of Invasive Police Encounters in New York City," *Journal of Urban Health* 93, Suppl. 1 (April 2016): 42–67, https://doi.org/10.1007/s11524-015-0016-7.

27. Joe Soss and Vesla Weaver, "Police Are Our Government: Politics, Political Science, and the Policing of Race–Class Subjugated Communities," *Annual Review of Political Science*, 2017, http://www.annualreviews.org/doi/abs/10.1146/annurev-polisci-060415-093825.

28. Susan Clampet-Lundquist et al., "Moving Teenagers Out of High-Risk Neighborhoods: How Girls Fare Better than Boys," *American Journal of Sociology* 116, no. 4 (January 2011): 1154–1189, https://doi.org/10.1086/657352.

29. Stefanie DeLuca and Kathryn Edin, "How Parents House Kids," MacArthur Foundation and the Annie E. Casey Foundation, n.d.

30. Anthony A. Braga, "High Crime Places, Times, and Offenders," in *The Oxford Handbook of Crime Prevention*, ed. Brandon C. Welsh and David P. Farrington (Oxford: Oxford University Press, 2012).

31. Anthony A. Braga, Brandon C. Welsh, and Cory Schnell, "Can Policing Disorder Reduce Crime? A Systematic Review and Meta-Analysis," *Journal of Research in Crime and Delinquency* 52, no. 4 (July 2015): 567–588, https://doi.org/10.1177/0022427815576576.

32. Kathryne M. Young and Joan Petersilia, "Keeping Track: Surveillance, Control, and the Expansion of the Carceral State," *Harvard Law Review* 129 (2016): 1318–1360.

33. John A. Eterno and Eli B. Silverman, *The Crime Numbers Game: Management by Manipulation* (Boca Raton, FL: CRC Press, 2012).

34. "The President's Task Force on Twenty-First Century Policing" (Washington, DC: Office of Community Oriented Policing Services, 2015).

35. Charlotte Gill et al., "Community-Oriented Policing to Reduce Crime, Disorder and Fear and Increase Satisfaction and Legitimacy Among Citizens: A Systematic Review," *Journal of Experimental Criminology* 10, no. 4 (December 2014): 399–428.

36. David Weisburd et al., " Is Problem-Oriented Policing Effective in Reducing Crime and Disorder?," *Criminology & Public Policy* 9, no. 1 (February 2010): 139–172, https://doi.org/10.1111/j.1745-9133.2010.00617.x; Anthony A. Braga, Andrew V. Papachristos, and David M. Hureau, "The Effects of Hot Spots Policing on Crime: An Updated Systematic Review and Meta-Analysis," *Justice Quarterly* 31, no. 4 (July 2014): 633–663, https://doi.org/10.1080/07418825.2012.673632; Anthony A. Braga and David L. Weisburd, "The Effects of Focused Deterrence Strategies on Crime: A Systematic Review

and Meta-Analysis of the Empirical Evidence," *Journal of Research in Crime and Delinquency* 49, no. 3 (August 2012): 323–358, https://doi.org/10.1177/0022427811419368.

37. Fagan et al., "Stops and Stares."
38. Wesley G. Skogan and Susan M. Hartnett, *Community Policing, Chicago Style* (Oxford: Oxford University Press, 1997).
39. Tom R. Tyler, *Why People Obey the Law* (Princeton, NJ: Princeton University Press, 2006).
40. National Research Council, *Fairness and Effectiveness in Policing: The Evidence* (Washington, DC: National Academies Press, 2004).
41. Jeffrey Fagan, "*Floyd vs. City of New York*, Expert Report," 2010.
42. Richard Rosenfeld, Michael J. Deckard, and Emily Blackburn, "The Effects of Directed Patrol and Self-Initiated Enforcement on Firearm Violence: A Randomized Controlled Study of Hot Spot Policing," *Criminology* 52, no. 3 (August 2014): 428–449, https://doi.org/10.1111/1745-9125.12043.
43. Songman Kang, "Inequality and Crime Revisited: Effects of Local Inequality and Economic Segregation on Crime," *Journal of Population Economics* 29, no. 2 (April 2016): 593–626, https://doi.org/10.1007/s00148-015-0579-3.
44. Fagan, "Terry's Original Sin."
45. John Donohue, "Comey, Trump, and the Puzzling Pattern of Crime in 2015 and Beyond," *Columbia Law Review* 117, no. 5 (2017): 1297–1354.

SEGREGATION AND HEALTH

Health in the Segregated City

by Mariana C. Arcaya and Alina Schnake-Mahl

Segregation has become an important health risk factor within the field of social epidemiology,[1] and practitioners should consider the complex relationships among health, health care, and segregation. We highlight three salient facets of these relationships: (1) poor, predominantly minority neighborhoods experience disproportionately high mortality rates, as well as worse outcomes on a range of health measures; (2) residential segregation helps give rise to a segregated health-care system, which is associated with worse access to medical care and lower-quality care for those who live in racially isolated neighborhoods; and (3) poor health itself may make it harder for families to leave disadvantaged neighborhoods.

Segregation and Neighborhood Health Disparities

Researchers have found racial isolation to be associated with a host of health risks for black residents, including higher levels of overall mortality, premature mortality, and infant mortality, along with a range of other poor health outcomes such as preterm birth, and low birth weight.[2] In combination with other risks, segregation contributes to striking health disparities over even extremely short distances. In Chicago, a few stops on the L can mean up to a sixteen-year gap in life expectancy, while just six subway stops separate neighborhoods with a ten-year difference in life expectancy in New York City.[3] To be sure, it is difficult to prove that segregation causes poor health. Because neighborhood contexts are (1) transmitted intergenerationally and over the life course and (2) shape crucial individual-level health risk factors, such as socioeconomic position, attempts to isolate the "independent effect" of segregation on health—above and beyond individual factors that are themselves potential products and drivers of segregation—can yield biased results[4] and conceptual confusion.[5] Methodological limitations and some mixed findings aside, many social epidemiologists view residential segregation by race and class as a "fundamental cause"[6] of health disparities because it shapes exposures to critically important health risks and protective factors.[7] On average, disproportionally minority and low-income neighborhoods provide lower-quality educational and employment opportunities, expose residents to a disproportionate burden of unhealthy environmental risks, and may discourage healthy behaviors by forcing residents to navigate degraded built environments and targeted advertising campaigns that encourage consumption of health-damaging foods, alcohol, and other products.[8] To be sure, it is difficult to prove that segregation causes poor health, and much of the existing research only shows an association, but some studies provide evidence of a causal relationship.[9]

Access to Quality Health Care in the Segregated City

While health care would ideally mitigate the health disparities caused by the inequitable patterning of upstream health risks across segregated metropolitan areas, the health-care system itself is often subject to the same inequitable patterning associated with residential segregation. Further, patient-level discrimination compounds disparities in health care between white and black patients. Both segregation and individual factors help explain why racial/ethnic minorities are more likely to experience difficulty accessing care[10] and to receive lower-quality care when they do use the health-care system, even after accounting for access-related factors including insurance status and income.[11]

Predominantly black neighborhoods are more likely to be primary-care shortage areas;[12] they also offer fewer ambulatory facilities, more limited access to physicians, and a lower supply of surgeons.[13] Safety-net hospitals and clinics—health-care institutions that provide a substantial portion of their care to Medicaid or uninsured patients—are more likely to serve predominantly black and high-poverty neighborhoods, and, on average, they exhibit higher rates of adverse patient-safety events than non-safety-net providers.[14] How much of the disparity in outcomes experienced by black versus white patients can be directly attributed to residential segregation? Residential segregation accounts for roughly half the reason that blacks and whites are admitted to different hospitals, while individual characteristics, such as insurance status, account for the other half of our hospital segregation problem.[15] In terms of care quality, about half the variance in at least one key measure of effective care—in this study, eye exams for patients with diabetes—has been attributed to the fact that blacks and whites live in different hospital markets, while 44 percent of the observed disparity stemmed from disparate treatment of blacks and whites within these markets.[16]

Within-geography differences in how black versus white patients experience care, although not attributable to segregation, compound health disparities generated by residential segregation. For example, when blacks and whites present with similar symptoms at cardiac-care centers, blacks receive cardiac catheterizations, bypass surgery, coronary angioplasty, and other lifesaving cardiac interventions at lower rates.[17] Compared to white patients reporting moderate or high levels of pain, black patients reporting equally high pain levels are less likely to receive opioids,[18] and we see racial and ethnic disparities in medical expenditures, which can serve as a proxy for overall intensity of care,[19] after controlling for other demographic, health-status, and socioeconomic characteristics.[20]

Most research on the associations between community racial/ethnic characteristics and health-care outcomes has focused on black isolation.[21] Limited work has found the share of Latinos in a neighborhood to be an inconsistent predictor of health-care outcomes.[22] The consequences of Asian isolation for health care is poorly understood, but the few relevant studies have found a mix of null and positive associations between area-level proportion of Asians and ability to access health care.[23]

Health and Residential Mobility

While it is well recognized that living in high-poverty, predominantly minority neighborhoods likely undermines health, the potential for poor health to reproduce segregation through feedback mechanisms that keep sick residents stuck in poor, racially isolated places, is poorly understood. Managing illness could impede movement out of high-poverty, segregated neighborhoods by reducing capacity to find better-paying work or to explore unfamiliar neighborhoods; lowering risk tolerance for taking on higher fixed monthly costs; depleting financial resources; and increasing dependence on neighborhood-based services and social ties[24]. Evidence that sicker people have a harder time improving their neighborhood environment is limited, but such patterns occurred following Hurricane Katrina, where poor health prior to the storm predicted residence in a higher-poverty neighborhood years later.[25] Data from the Moving to Opportunity experiment offered a chance to examine whether differences in health influenced the likelihood that families that were offered a chance to move from high- to low-poverty neighborhoods with a housing voucher actually did so.[26] Caring for a child with health challenges lowered the odds of moving with a voucher, and those who did use their low-poverty vouchers moved to less affluent areas, on average, than families not reporting that a child in the home had a health challenge.[27]

Conclusions

Research shows that segregation may cause, and is potentially reproduced by, poor health. In response, health care can and should serve as a crucial intervention to weaken the links between segregation and disease. However, evidence shows that the scourge of segregation affects the U.S. health-care system itself. A segregated health-care system combines with medical discrimination and racialized socioeconomic disadvantage to create dramatically unequal experiences in care for black and white patients. Social epidemiologists like to say that "housing policy is health policy," but to the extent that health helps sort families into neighborhoods, health-care policy may also be housing policy. Mitigating the effects of segregation and working toward greater neighborhood integration should include efforts to provide equal-quality, affordable health care across racial/ethnic groups and neighborhoods.

Segregated Health Systems

by Jose F. Figueroa

Mariana Arcaya and Alina Schnake-Mahl highlight important concerns around segregation and its contribution to poor health among minority communities. One issue to focus on further is the average quality of health-care providers serving minority communities and how that may be affecting health outcomes of minority populations.

As the authors point out, an abundance of evidence shows that blacks and Hispanics are much less likely to receive evidence-based care. Underuse of effective care has often been attributed to lack of access to health care,[28] and therefore much of the focus has been on improving access for minority patients—for example, through insurance expansion under the Affordable Care Act.

However, one recent study highlights the complex relationship between minority status and the U.S. health-care system. William Schpero and colleagues found that blacks and Hispanics are actually more likely than whites to receive low-value services[29]—tests and treatments that are considered unnecessary, economically inefficient, and in some cases, outright harmful.[30] Therefore, optimism around reducing disparities in minority communities through increased access alone should be tempered. Further work is needed to determine exactly why minorities are consistently less likely to get things they really need and more likely to get things they may not, even after accounting for differences in insurance and income.

One potential explanation is that providers, including doctors and hospitals, that disproportionately care for minority populations may generally not be as good as others. Care for minority patients tends to be highly concentrated. For example, about 10 percent of U.S. hospitals care for nearly half of all black elderly patients,[31] while just 5 percent of hospitals care for more than half of elderly Hispanics.[32] These minority-serving hospitals tend to provide worse quality of care,[33] with higher rates of hospital readmissions[34] and lower patient-experience scores.[35]

Many are quick to point out, and rightly so, that health-care providers that serve a high proportion of minority patients are dealing with more complex populations with a higher burden of socioeconomic issues. Therefore, it should not be surprising that they perform worse, especially given the lack of risk-adjustment methods that adequately account for social and medical complexity when evaluating quality.

However, minority-serving providers have also consistently underperformed on numerous evidence-based clinical-process measures and are less likely to engage in strategic efforts to improve care for their patient populations. Providers have more control over meeting process measures than over clinical outcomes, so they should arguably be held more accountable for underperformance in these measures. For example, minority-serving hospitals are less likely to adhere to evidence-based clinical processes for common medical conditions like heart failure and pneumonia.[36] They are also generally less likely to invest in health IT systems, hire dedicated care-coordination staff, or engage in postdischarge programs, and they have lower nurse-staffing ratios.[37] Similarly, minority-serving accountable care organizations (ACOs)—groups of doctors, hospitals, and other providers that come together to voluntarily be responsible for the care of a group of patients—also lag in quality performance, including on measures of preventive health and chronic-disease management.[38]

There are exceptions, of course. In some cases, highly ranked academic medical centers in urban areas serve poor and minority neighborhoods. However, this is not often the case for many minority communities across the United States.

What complicates matters more is that payment for health services in the United States is increasingly tied to health-care performance—for example, through alternative payment models like ACOs and hospital pay-for-perfor-mance programs.[39] Institutions that care for minority patients are already more likely to have limited financial resources at baseline, and early evidence sug-gests that minority-serving hospitals and ACOs are much less likely to receive financial rewards under these new programs.[40]

As we consider how to improve the health of minority communities, it is there-fore essential that we take a closer look at the quality of the providers that care for them. Improving access to health care alone is insufficient. Targeted efforts and quality-improvement interventions aimed at minority-serving providers offer one promising approach to improve the health of minority populations.

Why Aren't Segregation's Effects on Health Larger?

by Sherry Glied

Mariana Arcaya and Alina Schnake-Mahl emphasize the importance of racial segregation as a driver of poor health outcomes. Racial disparities in health in the United States are large, pervasive, and persistent. Residential segregation— especially if driven by current or past policy or by the prejudices of advan-taged groups—is clearly terrible for the well-being of disadvantaged groups. It reduces income, education, and access to jobs. It is associated with higher levels of environmental pollution and worse access to healthy foods and exercise facilities. Each of these correlates of segregation has well-understood effects on health, so segregation itself should likewise influence health. Surprisingly, however, research on the association between residential segregation and racial disparities in health outcomes is, as Arcaya and Schnake-Mahl note, methodo-logically limited and somewhat mixed.

The various mechanisms for a robust link between residential segregation and health outcomes are well established, as the authors point out. Health out-comes at the population level are strongly affected by underlying population characteristics, particularly education and income. They are also closely linked to the local environment, particularly levels of air pollution and other toxins. Finally, both hospitals and physicians that serve predominantly minority pop-ulations score worse on measures of provider quality than do those serving primarily white populations.

Paradoxically, however, although one study finds evidence of a causal rela-tionship between segregation and racial disparities in birth outcomes,[41] many analyses of data on health outcomes do not consistently find correspondingly strong links between residential segregation and outcomes. Raj Chetty and his colleagues examine the link between local-area residential segregation (by income) and income disparities in life expectancy.[42] They conclude, "In areas where rich and poor individuals are more residentially segregated, differences in life expectancy between individuals in the top and bottom income quartile were *smaller*" (emphasis added). Chetty and his colleagues focus on income disparities and segregation; no comparable analysis has been conducted focusing on racial segregation. To get a crude sense of how big these relationships might be, I plotted black/white infant mortality disparities at the state level[43] against a measure of state-level black residential segregation.[44] Once again, there was no evident association.

Perhaps a better question, then, is why residential segregation doesn't have much larger overall effects on health outcomes. I can think of a few possible reasons. One is that, as Chetty and his colleagues conjecture, many of the policies and programs that affect health outcomes, such as tobacco taxation, air and water quality, and health insurance laws, operate at larger levels of geographic aggregation than the neighborhood. Even extremely segregated neighborhoods may have good public health infrastructure if they are located in well-functioning, prosperous cities.[45] A second possibility is that social supports and community cohesion operate differently with respect to health in more homogenous neighborhoods.[46] This is particularly plausible in cases where people have the resources and opportunity to move to more diverse neighborhoods but choose not to do so. Third, while measures of technical performance are lower among health-care providers in segregated neighborhoods, there may be offsetting benefits with respect to cultural competence. For example, hospitals serving large Hispanic patient populations will be more likely to have adequate translation services and bilingual providers than will hospitals with few such patients.[47] The long and cruel history of discriminatory and unethical treatment of minority patients by white health-care providers has contributed to a strong level of medical mistrust among black patients, contributing to lower use of preventive and early-stage treatment. Several studies suggest that the availability of minority providers in more segregated areas offsets this mistrust.[48] In sum, the mechanisms Arcaya and Schnake-Mahl highlight are on point, but the connection between the effects of these particular segregation-associated factors and the overall impact of segregation on health requires further study.

Residential Segregation and Health: A Hypothesis Still in Search of Convincing Evidence

by Robert Kaestner

As Mariana Arcaya and Alina Schnake-Mahl note in their essay "Health in the Segregated City," race or ethnicity and poverty are strongly associated

Table 11.1 Proportion of respondents reporting being in fair or poor health versus excellent health

Race/Ethnicity	Fair or poor health		Excellent health	
	Below poverty	Above poverty	Below poverty	Above poverty
Non-Hispanic White	0.28	0.10	0.18	0.30
Non-Hispanic Black	0.31	0.15	0.20	0.25
Hispanic	0.20	0.09	0.23	0.32
Non-Hispanic other	0.22	0.12	0.22	0.29

with health. Table 11.1 demonstrates this well-known fact with data drawn from the 2010 to 2016 National Health Interview Surveys (NHIS).

The figures in Table 11.1 are unsurprising. Being poor is strongly associated with worse self-reported health, and this is true for all racial or ethnic groups. The race/ethnicity-specific differences in health between poor and nonpoor are largest for White persons. Race/ethnicity is also associated with self-reported health (within poverty group). Notably, within each poverty group, differences between White and Black persons are small compared to differences between poverty groups within race. It is also evident that Hispanic persons and those labeled as Other (race) have the best health among the four racial/ ethnic groups.

Similar conclusions apply to two different measures of (poor) health: whether a person has been hospitalized in the past year, and whether the person has had ten or more health-care visits (Table 11.2). Poor persons are much more likely to be hospitalized and to have ten or more visits than nonpoor persons. Here too, within an income group, White and Black persons have similar health, and Hispanic persons and persons of other races (Other) have better health than White or Black persons.

A central thesis of Arcaya and Schnake-Mahl is that residential segregation, independent of race and/or income, worsens health, such as those outcomes shown in Tables 11.1 and 11.2. "Methodological limitations and some mixed

Table 11.2 Proportion of respondents who reported being hospitalized or having ten or more health-care visits

Race/Ethnicity	Hospitalized		Ten or more visits	
	Below poverty	Above poverty	Below poverty	Above poverty
Non-Hispanic White	0.13	0.09	0.19	0.12
Non-Hispanic Black	0.14	0.09	0.16	0.10
Hispanic	0.09	0.05	0.12	0.07
Non-Hispanic Other	0.09	0.06	0.10	0.07

findings aside, many social epidemiologists see residential segregation by race and class as a 'fundamental cause' of health disparities because it shapes exposures to critically important health risks and protective factors."

However, if residential segregation is an independent cause of poor health, as suggested by Arcaya and Schnake-Mahl, then we would expect groups that have the highest rates of segregation to be in the worst health. According to a U.S. Census report, Black persons live in the most segregated (and racially isolated) neighborhoods. Hispanic persons are the group with the next highest rate of residential segregation. Despite these high rates of residential segregation for Black and Hispanic persons, their health is either not very different from, or better than, that of White persons.[49]

Overall, the evidence in Tables 11.1 and 11.2 puts the burden on researchers such as Arcaya and Schnake-Mahl to provide more substantial evidence that residential segregation is a significant cause of health disparities beyond individual-level factors, such as race and income.

It is also worthwhile to highlight a key phrase in the previous quote from Arcaya and Schnake-Mahl: "Methodological limitations and some mixed findings aside. . . ." Social scientists cannot put aside these fundamental issues related to causality to reach conclusions. Credible empirical analyses and a consistent set of findings are required before a conclusion such as "segregation by race and class as a 'fundamental cause' of health disparities" can be drawn.

The sparseness of credible and consistent evidence linking residential segregation to health is illustrated by several quotes from recent studies:

"The health effects of segregation are relatively consistent, but complex. Isolation segregation is associated with poor pregnancy outcomes and increased mortality for Blacks, but several studies report health-protective effects of living in clustered Black neighborhoods net of social and economic isolation. The majority of reviewed studies are cross-sectional and use coarse measures of segregation."[50]

"Socioeconomic status explains much of the association between neighborhood racial segregation and health outcomes."[51]

"In the fully adjusted model . . . higher Hispanic . . . but not Black . . . segregation was associated with higher cause-specific mortality."[52]

Of course, there are some articles that report evidence supportive of the hypothesis that residential segregation is harmful to health,[53] but the bottom line is that the causal link between residential segregation and health is decidedly uncertain.

One argument put forth by Arcaya and Schnake-Mahl is that residential segregation is a cause of inadequate access to health care and of poor-quality health care. The evidence to substantiate this claim is tenuous and based on cross-sectional analyses that have well-known limitations.[54] I am unaware of any study that has linked changes in residential segregation to changes in access/quality of health care for a given person—for example, remaining residents of a transitioning neighborhood. In addition, the link between access (e.g., insurance) and use of care and health remains sparse. For example, results from the Oregon Medicaid Experiment[55] and the more dated RAND Health Insurance Experiment indicate that despite significant increase in the use of health-care services associated with having health insurance (or more generous insurance coverage), there was little differences in health between those with and without insurance (or with less generous insurance).[56]

A second argument of Arcaya and Schnake-Mahl is that residential segregation gives rise to a segregated health care system with low-quality providers serving residents in segregated neighborhoods. However, as shown by researchers from Dartmouth Atlas of Healthcare,[57] the association between the quality of care (provided to Medicare patients) and racial disparities is not strong. "Furthermore, there is no consistent pattern of disparities: some areas may have a wide disparity in one treatment but no disparity in another. The problem of differences in quality of care across regions, as opposed to racial disparities in care, should remain the target of policy makers, as reducing quality disparities would play a major role in improving the health care received by all Americans and by minority Americans in particular."[58]

In sum, the claim that residential segregation (isolation) is an important cause of health disparities net of individual-level factors, such as race and income, is not strong. That does not mean it is not true. There are plausible mechanisms linking residential segregation to health that support the scientific plausibility of the argument.[59] And it is possible (likely) that residential segregation causes poverty and other outcomes that may affect health. Theory and suggestive and inconsistent empirical evidence are reasons to do more research, but they are not sufficient to make causal claims.

Notes

1. Lisa F. Berkman, Ichiro Kawachi, and Maria Glymour, eds., *Social Epidemiology*, 2nd ed. (Oxford: Oxford University Press, 2014); Dolores Acevedo-Garcia and Kimberly A. Lochner, "Residential Segregation and Health," in *Neighborhoods and Health*, ed. Ichiro Kawachi and Lisa B. Berkman (Oxford: Oxford University Press, 2003), 265–287.
2. Michael R. Kramer and Carol R. Hogue, "Is Segregation Bad for Your Health?," *Epidemiologic Reviews* 31 (2009): 178–194, https://doi.org/10.1093/epirev/mxp001.
3. VCU Center on Society and Health, "Mapping Life Expectancy," September 26, 2016, http://www.rwjf.org/en/library/infographics/life-expectancy-maps.html.
4. Thomas A. Glass and Usama Bilal, "Are Neighborhoods Causal? Complications Arising from the 'Stickiness' of ZNA," *Social Science & Medicine* 166 (2016): 244–253.
5. Steven Cummins, Sarah Curtis, Ana V. Diez-Roux, and Sally Macintyre, "Understanding and Representing 'Place' in Health Research: A Relational Approach," *Social Science*

& *Medicine* 65, no. 9 (November 2007): 1825–1838; Richard Mitchell, "How Much Does Place Matter?," *Environment and Planning A* 33, no. 8 (2001): 1357–1361.

6. As described by Link and Phelan, "the essential feature of fundamental social causes, is that they involve access to resources that can be used to avoid risks or to minimize the consequences of disease once it occurs. We define resources broadly to include money, knowledge, power, prestige, and the kinds of interpersonal resources embodied in the concepts of social support and social network." Bruce G. Link and Jo Phelan, "Social Conditions as Fundamental Causes of Disease," *Journal of Health and Social Behavior*, 1995, 80–94, at 87.

7. David R. Williams and Chiquita Collins, "Racial Residential Segregation: A Fundamental Cause of Racial Disparities in Health," *Public Health Reports* 116, no. 5 (2001): 404–416.

8. Williams and Collins, "Racial Residential Segregation."

9. Ingrid Gould Ellen, David M. Cutler, and William Dickens, "Is Segregation Bad for Your Health? The Case of Low Birth Weight [with Comments]," *Brookings Wharton Papers on Urban Affairs*, 2000, 203–238.

10. Robin M. Weinick, Samuel H. Zuvekas, and Joel W. Cohen, "Racial and Ethnic Differences in Access to and Use of Health Care Services, 1977 to 1996," *Medical Care Research and Review* 57, no. 1_suppl (November 2000): 36–54, https://doi.org/10.1177/1077558700 057001S03.

11. Brian D. Smedley, Adrienne Y. Stith, and Alan R. Nelson, eds., *Unequal Treatment: Confronting Racial and Ethnic Disparities in Health Care* (Washington, DC: National Academies Press, 2003).

12. Darrell J. Gaskin et al., "Residential Segregation and the Availability of Primary Care Physicians," *Health Services Research* 47, no. 6 (December 2012): 2353–2376, https://doi .org/10.1111/j.1475-6773.2012.01417.x.

13. Darrell J. Gaskin et al., "Residential Segregation and Disparities in Health Care Services Utilization," *Medical Care Research and Review* 69, no. 2 (April 2012): 158–175, https:// doi.org/10.1177/1077558711420263.

14. Kellee White, Jennifer S. Haas, and David R. Williams, "Elucidating the Role of Place in Health Care Disparities: The Example of Racial/Ethnic Residential Segregation," *Health Services Research* 47, no. 3, pt. 2 (June 2012): 1278–1299, https://doi.org/10.1111 /j.1475-6773.2012.01410.x.

15. Mary S. Vaughan Sarrazin et al., "Racial Segregation and Disparities in Health Care Delivery: Conceptual Model and Empirical Assessment," *Health Services Research* 44, no. 4 (August 2009): 1424–1444, https://doi.org/10.1111/j.1475-6773.2009.00977.x.

16. Katherine Baicker, Amitabh Chandra, and Jonathan S. Skinner, "Geographic Variation in Health Care and the Problem of Measuring Racial Disparities," *Perspectives in Biology and Medicine* 48, no. 1 Suppl. (2005): S42–53.

17. Smedley, Stith, and Nelson, *Unequal Treatment.*

18. Diana J. Burgess et al., "Racial Differences in Prescription of Opioid Analgesics for Chronic Noncancer Pain in a National Sample of Veterans," *Journal of Pain* 15, no. 4 (April 2014): 447–455, https://doi.org/10.1016/j.jpain.2013.12.010.

19. Benjamin Lê Cook, Thomas G. McGuire, and Samuel H. Zuvekas, "Measuring Trends in Racial/ Ethnic Health Care Disparities," *Medical Care Research and Review* 66, no. 1 (February 2009): 23–48, https://doi.org/10.1177/1077558708323607.

20. Benjamin Lê Cook and Willard G. Manning, "Measuring Racial/Ethnic Disparities Across the Distribution of Health Care Expenditures," *Health Services Research* 44, no. 5, pt. 1 (October 2009): 1603–1621, https://doi.org/10.1111/j.1475-6773.2009.01004.x.

21. White, Haas, and Williams, "Elucidating the Role of Place in Health Care Disparities."
22. Carole Roan Gresenz, Jeannette Rogowski, and José J. Escarce, "Community Demographics and Access to Health Care Among U.S. Hispanics," *Health Services Research* 44, no. 5, pt. 1 (October 2009): 1542–1562, https://doi.org/10.1111/j.1475-6773.2009.00997.x; Jennifer S. Haas et al., "Racial Segregation and Disparities in Breast Cancer Care and Mortality," *Cancer* 113, no. 8 (October 2008): 2166–2172, https://doi.org/10.1002/cncr.23828; Jennifer S. Haas et al., "Lower Use of Hospice by Cancer Patients Who Live in Minority Versus White Areas," *Journal of General Internal Medicine* 22, no. 3 (March 2007): 396–399, https://doi.org/10.1007/s11606-006-0034-y.
23. Awori Jeremiah Hayanga et al., "Residential Segregation and Access to Surgical Care by Minority Populations in US Counties," *Journal of the American College of Surgeons* 208, no. 6 (June 2009): 1017–1022, https://doi.org/10.1016/j.jamcollsurg.2009.01.047; Awori J. Hayanga et al., "Racial Clustering and Access to Colorectal Surgeons, Gastroenterologists, and Radiation Oncologists by African Americans and Asian Americans in the United States: A County-Level Data Analysis," *Archives of Surgery* 144, no. 6 (June 2009): 532–535, https://doi.org/10.1001/archsurg.2009.68.
24. Mariana C. Arcaya et al., "Role of Health in Predicting Moves to Poor Neighborhoods Among Hurricane Katrina Survivors," *Proceedings of the National Academy of Sciences of the United States of America* 111, no. 46 (November 2014): 16246–16253, https://doi.org/10.1073/pnas.1416950111.
25. Arcaya et al., "Role of Health in Predicting Moves to Poor Neighborhoods."
26. Jens Ludwig et al., "Neighborhoods, Obesity, and Diabetes—A Randomized Social Experiment," *New England Journal of Medicine* 365, no. 16 (October 2011): 1509–1519, https://doi.org/10.1056/NEJMsa1103216.
27. Mariana C. Arcaya et al., "Health Selection Into Neighborhoods Among Families in the Moving to Opportunity Program," *American Journal of Epidemiology* 183, no. 2 (January 15, 2016): 130–137, https://doi.org/10.1093/aje/kwv189.
28. Smedley, Stith, and Nelson, *Unequal Treatment*.
29. William L. Schpero et al., "For Selected Services, Blacks and Hispanics More Likely to Receive Low-Value Care Than Whites," *Health Affairs* 36, no. 6 (June 2017): 1065–1069, https://doi.org/10.1377/hlthaff.2016.1416.
30. Aaron L. Schwartz et al., "Measuring Low-Value Care in Medicare," *JAMA Internal Medicine* 174, no. 7 (July 2014): 1067–1076, https://doi.org/10.1001/jamainternmed.2014.1541.
31. Ashish K. Jha et al., "Concentration and Quality of Hospitals That Care for Elderly Black Patients," *Archives of Internal Medicine* 167, no. 11 (June 2007): 1177–1182, https://doi.org/10.1001/archinte.167.11.1177.
32. Ashish K. Jha et al., "The Characteristics and Performance of Hospitals That Care for Elderly Hispanic Americans," *Health Affairs (Project Hope)* 27, no. 2 (April 2008): 528–537, https://doi.org/10.1377/hlthaff.27.2.528.
33. Ashish K. Jha, E. John Orav, and Arnold M. Epstein, "Low-Quality, High-Cost Hospitals, Mainly in South, Care for Sharply Higher Shares of Elderly Black, Hispanic, and Medicaid Patients," *Health Affairs* 30, no. 10 (October 2011): 1904–1911, https://doi.org/10.1377/hlthaff.2011.0027.
34. Fátima Rodriguez et al., "Readmission Rates for Hispanic Medicare Beneficiaries with Heart Failure and Acute Myocardial Infarction," *American Heart Journal* 162, no. 2 (August 2011): 254–261.e3, https://doi.org/10.1016/j.ahj.2011.05.009; Karen E. Joynt, E. John Orav, and Ashish K. Jha, "Thirty-Day Readmission Rates for Medicare Beneficiaries by Race and Site of Care," *JAMA* 305, no. 7 (February 2011): 675–681, https://doi.org/10.1001/jama.2011.123; Thomas C. Tsai, E. John Orav, and Karen E. Joynt,

"Disparities in Surgical 30-Day Readmission Rates for Medicare Beneficiaries by Race and Site of Care," *Annals of Surgery* 259, no. 6 (June 2014): 1086–1090, https://doi.org/10.1097/SLA.0000000000000326.

35. Paula Chatterjee et al., "Patient Experience in Safety-Net Hospitals: Implications for Improving Care and Value-Based Purchasing," *Archives of Internal Medicine* 172, no. 16 (September 2012): 1204–1210, https://doi.org/10.1001/archinternmed.2012.3158.

36. Jha, Orav, and Epstein, "Low-Quality, High-Cost Hospitals."

37. Jose F. Figueroa et al., "Safety-Net Hospitals Face More Barriers Yet Use Fewer Strategies to Reduce Readmissions," *Medical Care* 55, no. 3 (March 2017): 229–235, https://doi.org/10.1097/MLR.0000000000000687; Lenny López and Ashish K. Jha, "Outcomes for Whites and Blacks at Hospitals That Disproportionately Care for Black Medicare Beneficiaries," *Health Services Research* 48, no. 1 (February 2013): 114–128, https://doi.org/10.1111/j.1475-6773.2012.01445.x.

38. Valerie A. Lewis et al., "ACOs Serving High Proportions of Racial and Ethnic Minorities Lag in Quality Performance," *Health Affairs* 36, no. 1 (January 2017): 57–66, https://doi.org/10.1377/hlthaff.2016.0626.

39. Sylvia M. Burwell, "Setting Value-Based Payment Goals—HHS Efforts to Improve U.S. Health Care," *New England Journal of Medicine* 372, no. 10 (March 2015): 897–899, https://doi.org/10.1056/NEJMp1500445.

40. Lewis et al., "ACOs Serving High Proportions of Racial and Ethnic Minorities"; Jha et al., "The Characteristics and Performance of Hospitals That Care for Elderly Hispanic Americans"; Matlin Gilman et al., "Safety-Net Hospitals More Likely Than Other Hospitals to Fare Poorly Under Medicare's Value-Based Purchasing," *Health Affairs* 34, no. 3 (March 2015): 398–405, https://doi.org/10.1377/hlthaff.2014.1059.

41. Ellen, "Is Segregation Bad for Your Health?"

42. Raj Chetty, Nathaniel Hendren, and Lawrence Katz, "The Effects of Exposure to Better Neighborhoods on Children: New Evidence from the Moving to Opportunity Project," *American Economic Review* 106, no. 4 (2016): 855–902.

43. T. J. Matthews, Marian F. MacDorman, and Marie E. Thoma, "Infant Mortality Statistics from the 2013 Period Linked Birth/Infant Death Data Set," *National Vital Statistics Reports* 64, no. 9 (August 2015): 1–30.

44. Daniel T. Lichter, Domenico Parisi, and Helga De Valk, "Residential Segregation," in *State of the Union 2016*, ed. David B. Grusky, Marybeth Mattingly, and Charles E. Varner (Stanford Center on Poverty and Inequality, 2016).

45. Chetty, Hendren, and Katz, "The Effects of Exposure to Better Neighborhoods."

46. Christopher R. Browning and Kathleen A. Cagney, "Neighborhood Structural Disadvantage, Collective Efficacy, and Self-Rated Physical Health in an Urban Setting," *Journal of Health and Social Behavior* 43, no. 4 (2002): 383–399.

47. Kellee White, Jennifer S. Haas, and David R. Williams, "Elucidating the Role of Place in Health Care Disparities: The Example of Racial/Ethnic Residential Segregation," *Health Services Research* 47, no. 3, pt. 2 (June 2012): 1278–1299.

48. White, Haas, and Williams, "Elucidating the Role of Place in Health Care Disparities."

49. John Iceland, Daniel Weinberg, and Erika Steinmetz, "Racial and Ethnic Residential Segregation in the United States: 1980–2000," *Census 2000 Special Reports*, August 2002.

50. Kramer and Hogue, "Is Segregation Bad for Your Health?"

51. Joseph J. Sudano et al., "Neighborhood Racial Residential Segregation and Changes in Health or Death Among Older Adults," *Health & Place* 19 (January 2013): 80–88, https://doi.org/10.1016/j.healthplace.2012.09.015.

52. Sandi L. Pruitt et al., "Residential Racial Segregation and Mortality Among Black, White, and Hispanic Urban Breast Cancer Patients in Texas, 1995–2009," *Cancer* 121, no. 11 (June 2015): 1845–1855, https://doi.org/10.1002/cncr.29282.

53. Awori J. Hayanga, Steve B. Zeliadt, and Leah M. Backhus, "Residential Segregation and Lung Cancer Mortality in the United States," *JAMA Surgery* 148, no. 1 (January 2013): 37–42, https://doi.org/10.1001/jamasurgery.2013.408; Asal M. Johnson et al., "The Effects of Residential Segregation and Neighborhood Characteristics on Surgery and Survival in Patients with Early-Stage Non–Small Cell Lung Cancer," *Cancer Epidemiology, Biomarkers & Prevention* 25, no. 5 (2016): 750–758, https://doi.org/10.1158/1055-9965 .EPI-15-1126.

54. Weinick, Zuvekas, and Cohen, "Racial and Ethnic Differences in Access to and Use of Health Care Services."

55. Katherine Baicker et al., "The Oregon Experiment—Effects of Medicaid on Clinical Outcomes," *New England Journal of Medicine* 368, no. 18 (May 2013): 1713–1722, https:// doi.org/10.1056/NEJMsa1212321.

56. Joseph P. Newhouse, *Free for All? Lessons from the RAND Health Insurance Experiment* (Cambridge, MA: Harvard University Press, 1996).

57. Katherine Baicker et al., "Who You Are and Where You Live: How Race and Geography Affect the Treatment of Medicare Beneficiaries," *Health Affairs* Suppl. Variation (2004): VAR33–44, https://doi.org/10.1377/hlthaff.var.33; Baicker, Chandra, and Skinner, "Geographic Variation in Health Care and the Problem of Measuring Racial Disparities"; David C. Goodman et al., "Regional and Racial Variation in Primary Care and the Quality of Care Among Medicare Beneficiaries," September 9, 2010, accessed November 14, 2017, https://www.issuelab.org/resource/regional-and-racial-variation-in-primary-care -and-the-quality-of-care-among-medicare-beneficiaries.html.

58. Baicker, Chandra, and Skinner, "Geographic Variation in Health Care and the Problem of Measuring Racial Disparities."

59. Williams and Collins, "Racial Residential Segregation."

SEGREGATION AND
THE FINANCIAL CRISIS

Segregation Exacerbated the Great Recession and Hindered Our Policy Response

by Jacob Faber

Although the impact of America's Great Recession was widespread, the collapse of the housing market and the subsequent rise in unemployment were highly structured by race. Job loss landed disproportionately on blacks and Latinos; even five years into the recovery, the black unemployment rate was more than twice the white rate and higher than the national rate at the peak of the recession.[1] The distressingly large racial wealth gap also widened during this time, as did disparities in homeownership.[2] The idea that racial and ethnic minorities (and blacks and Latinos, in particular) are more vulnerable during recessions than white Americans is not new. For decades, scholars have pointed to the numerous ways in which racial disparities in education and employment, exposure to crime, and other drivers of opportunity position people of color poorly to withstand economic shocks.

In addition to this "traditional" disparities story, the Great Recession's origin in the mortgage market brought increased attention to the role that financial services play in shaping inequality. Subprime lending expanded rapidly in the late 1990s and early 2000s, making up almost a quarter of all loan originations at its 2006 peak. Racial differences in subprime lending were dramatic. In 2006, black and Latino homebuyers with incomes above $230,000 were more likely to receive subprime loans than white borrowers with incomes around $30,000.[3]

Racial segregation, still a defining aspect of American life a half-century after the adoption of federal fair housing legislation, played a central role in this story.[4] Both subprime lending and subsequent foreclosures were more common in neighborhoods with higher proportions of black and Latino residents.[5] Through both the physical, geographic demarcation of disadvantage and limitations on economic opportunity, segregation created easily identifiable local markets for subprime mortgage lenders (as well as other "fringe" financial services, such as check-cashing outlets) and facilitated the racialized predation and differential treatment admitted by whistleblowers formerly employed within lending companies and evidenced by academic study after academic study.[6]

The geography of subprime lending has an obvious connection to the historic, government-supported, and racist practice of redlining, which funneled affordable mortgages (and massive amounts of wealth) into white suburbs and helped trap poor people of color in ghettos for generations.[7]

Segregation was implicated not only in the causes of the Great Recession, but also in the anemic federal policy response. During the Great Depression—the last time there was a comparable housing market crisis—the federal government dramatically altered the practice of mortgage lending. The response to the contemporary foreclosure crisis has been "too little, too late, and too timid."[8] Recent research by Isaac William Martin and Christopher Niedt shows that despite the scale and scope of the Great Recession, the segregation of neighborhoods and social networks and the concentration of foreclosures in largely minority areas has meant that exposure to the experience of foreclosure is extremely isolated in much of the country.[9] Our likelihood of knowing someone directly affected by the crisis and any resulting interest in enacting policy to alleviate its consequences are shaped by persistent residential segregation. The lack of minority representation among federal policy makers also reflects our segregated society and diminishes the import of minority concerns—such as the foreclosure crisis— within national policy debates. As a result, the political class was able to feel insulated from the greatest housing crisis in a century, and there was (and continues to be) very little political will to effectively address foreclosures.

Much of the retrospective focus has suggested that more financial education would have prevented the subprime boom and subsequent housing market collapse and argues that prospectively it can be a tool to prevent future crises in the mortgage market. While more information is always welcome in a marketplace, the emphasis on education suffers from several important flaws.

First, the extent to which disparities in knowledge about financial products were responsible for subprime lending is unclear. As mentioned previously, high-income blacks and Latinos were more likely to receive subprime loans than even poor whites. The idea that the average African American borrower making a quarter of a million dollars a year was less educated than the average white borrower making a tenth of that is hard to believe. Complementary research found that more than half of subprime borrowers could have qualified for prime loans.[10] These findings strongly suggest that predation and abuse by lenders were at least as significant as borrowers' supposed ignorance. At the very least, this research supports calls for greater transparency regarding lending practices—the expansion of HMDA data collection is a good start.

Second, a focus on the individual borrower ignores the ways in which structural factors, such as segregation and inequality, concentrate economic vulnerability and exacerbate times of crisis. Third, and most important, acceptance of financial education as the primary solution to economic disparities also represents acceptance of a system that permits the exploitation of individuals who lack knowledge or information. "Caveat emptor" regimes have been tried and have failed. In today's complex world, people are presented with too many choices and cannot become experts in every area they need to make choices in. In addition, people—even educated people—are systematically "irrational" when making many important choices. There is just no reason to allow dangerous products on the market and to let individuals sort them out for themselves. Instead, we should work to create more inclusive economic and social systems that foster opportunity and prevent predatory corporate practices.

Deconcentrating poverty and reducing racial isolation have been shown, time and again, to pay enormous dividends for the poor, without consequence for the nonpoor.[11] We've known for more than a century that segregation concentrates vulnerability in communities of color.[12] It connects multiple systems of disadvantage that structure the lived experience and shape lives.[13] The segmented mortgage market, which was fostered by segregation and led to the Great Recession, provided a tragic example of this dynamic. Racial equality in any arena is impossible without a serious effort to desegregate neighborhoods, cities, and regions. Again, although increasing the amount of information available to consumers (and researchers) could create a fairer marketplace, financial education on its own is likely insufficient to prevent economic crises and the inequality-widening effects those crises have. Fostering integrated communities will do far more to create economic opportunity and preempt financial predation.

The Connection Between Segregation, Predatory Lending, and Black Wealth

by Ngina Chiteji

The effects of segregation are more ubiquitous than we realize, reaching into a number of different domains. Researchers have long known that it affects schooling opportunities, access to neighborhood amenities, and even access to jobs in some cases. Jacob Faber's article reminds us that it also has important implications for wealth accumulation.

Faber points out that the racial wealth gap widened after the 2007 recession. The median White family now possesses about thirteen times the wealth of the median non-White family, according to an analysis of Federal Reserve data by the Pew Research Center. At the start of the recession, the ratio was ten. The median White family has ten times the wealth of the median Latino family. The gap was eight prior to the Great Recession. Because wealth is the most comprehensive measure of the resources that a family has available to it, among the "other" drivers of opportunity that Faber's article refers to, wealth is probably the most important device that families can use to shape opportunities for their offspring and to weather shocks.

Because the average American family holds the bulk of its wealth in the form of housing, trends in foreclosures such as those mentioned in Faber's article can be particularly harmful to families. Data from the National Asset Scorecard for Communities of Color Project directed by William Darity and Darrick Hamilton show just how much race structured the likelihood of experiencing the pain of the housing market collapse: they found that Black homeowners were 80 percent more likely to find themselves underwater than White homeowners, and that African American homeowners experienced a 45 percent decline in their wealth, while White homeowners' wealth declined by only 21 percent following the 2007 recession. These data elucidate Faber's claim that segregation meant that minorities were disproportionately harmed by the foreclosure crisis.

That segregation can affect a family's prospects for wealth accumulation is also underscored by research showing that, even in nonrecessionary times, homes in predominately White neighborhoods appreciate much more rapidly than those in predominately Black areas. For example, a recent article by Sandra Newman and Scott Holupka found that home buyers who were African American did not see the types of gains in terms of price appreciation that White home buyers did during the boom years preceding the Great Recession, and their analysis suggests that this outcome can be attributed partly to differences in the rate at which home values rose across neighborhoods.

So what is a society to do? As a researcher interested in helping families build wealth, I would caution Faber not to be too dismissive of financial education efforts. Financial literacy levels are low throughout the United States, and this has implications for much more than mortgages. For example, it also influences people's ability to save adequately for retirement. While researchers and practitioners in the field caution that financial literacy and financial education are complex terms and that measuring literacy levels is not always easy, there does appear to be a consensus in the literature that a sizable fraction of Americans struggle with concepts as basic as interest compounding. If we want widespread homeownership in the United States, it seems important to help ensure that all citizens have the basic skills to determine the true cost of home loans, understand the way their payments will be structured, and identify the degree to which the interest rate that they are offered varies from the prevailing rates. Existing programs to address financial literacy vary. Some take the form of financial counseling programs specifically tied to the home-buying stage (such as the Indiana Neighborhood Housing Partnership's program); others focus on imparting a broader set of financial skills and reasoning abilities at the high school stage, which is important for young people about to enter credit markets for the first time (to buy their first car or to get a college loan, for example). All effective programs should be funded and expanded, given the high rates of financial illiteracy in the United States.

Financial education programs can also work as a supplement to direct market regulation. While it is true that there is no good reason to allow dangerous products to come to market, sometimes it is hard to predict, ex ante, what will be dangerous. If the history of banking has shown us anything, it's that the financial sector innovates at a rapid pace. While one definitely wants regulators who are trying to stay on top of the new products coming to market, it is unrealistic to think that regulatory authorities will be able to anticipate all the problems that could emerge with any given innovation. It will always be important for consumers to be as knowledgeable as possible.

Proposing to expand HMDA data collection is laudable. A more aggressive policy intervention would be to call for principal reduction efforts for homeowners in the communities that were targeted by subprime lenders. While there are potential moral hazard problems to be considered, helping families would arguably be worth the trade-off. After all, moral hazard concerns were waived at times during the financial crisis in order to provide liquidity to several financial institutions.

Faber argues that the financial crisis may have been exacerbated by the segregated nature of U.S. metropolitan areas. Importantly, he also connects the racial differences in housing market outcomes that families experienced during the recent recession to the racial wealth gap. The challenge we face now is how to move forward—both to dismantle segregation and to mitigate its damaging effects on wealth accumulation.

The Contemporary Relevance of Decades-Old Fair Lending Laws

by Patrice Ficklin

In the recent financial crisis, millions lost their jobs; millions lost their homes; and many lost a considerable portion of their household wealth. As so often seems to be the case, communities of color were hit the hardest, with their net worth being approximately cut in half.[14] One of the results of the financial crisis was the creation of the Consumer Financial Protection Bureau (CFPB), through the 2010 Dodd-Frank Wall Street Reform and Consumer Protection Act (Dodd-Frank Act). We at the CFPB have several powerful tools to combat discrimination, including supervisory, enforcement, and regulatory authority over two important fair lending laws: the Equal Credit Opportunity Act (ECOA) and the Home Mortgage Disclosure Act (HMDA).

The Equal Credit Opportunity Act, implemented through Regulation B, prohibits lenders from discriminating on a prohibited basis in any aspect of credit transactions. While the CFPB's efforts to enforce this broad mandate include focusing on a variety of areas, we have consistently prioritized mortgage lending. Homeownership plays a critical role in building wealth for consumers, particularly for communities of color, where the greatest source of wealth is the home.

The Home Mortgage Disclosure Act, implemented through Regulation C, requires certain mortgage lenders to collect and report accurate data about, among other things, the race, ethnicity, and sex of home-mortgage loan applicants and borrowers. The CFPB, other federal regulators, community organizations, state and local agencies, and other entities rely on HMDA data to identify possible discriminatory lending patterns and monitor lenders' compliance with fair lending laws, including the ECOA.

As delinquencies, foreclosures, and other harmful effects of subprime lending unfolded following the financial crisis, it became apparent that communities throughout the nation lacked sufficient information to understand the magnitude of the risk to which they were exposed. Community groups and local, state, and federal officials relied on HMDA data to identify at-risk neighborhoods and develop foreclosure relief and homeownership stabilization programs. However, the limited HMDA data presented challenges for those who attempted to create effective and responsive relief programs.

Accordingly, in response to the mortgage crisis, the Dodd-Frank Act directed the CFPB to expand the HMDA data set to include additional information about applications and loans that would be helpful to better understand the mortgage market. The CFPB recently completed extensive work on changes to Regulation C, expanding the data fields that certain mortgage lenders must collect and report. The new HMDA data fields, which include specific information about borrower credit characteristics, loan terms, and the property securing loans, are designed to serve the purposes of HMDA and to address the informational shortcomings exposed by the financial crisis. The final rule also imposes a new requirement that certain large-volume mortgage lenders report their data to the appropriate federal agency on a quarterly basis, which will enable more timely identification of trends and risks and allow for more effective interventions or other actions.

HMDA disclosures can help the CFPB identify potential discriminatory lending patterns, including redlining. Mortgage redlining is a form of illegal discrimination in which financial institutions provide unequal access to credit, or unequal terms of credit, to applicants or prospective applicants based on the race, color, national origin, or other prohibited characteristics of the people in the prospective borrower's neighborhood. HMDA data help us to identify lenders that appear to deviate significantly from their peers in the extent to which they provide access to credit in communities of color, among other things. In cases where the CFPB observes significant shortfalls in lending to minority communities relative to an institution's peers, we may take action, which may include scheduling an examination or initiating an investigation to further evaluate this redlining risk. We may also take action in cases where data reflect "reverse redlining," or targeting of minority consumers in a geographic area for the provision of credit based on less favorable terms compared to credit provided to nonminorities.

Such fair lending enforcement is not just theoretical. The CFPB, together with the Justice Department, recently resolved claims against Hudson City Savings Bank for engaging in unlawful redlining. This settlement represents the largest redlining settlement in history, as measured by direct subsidies provided to affected communities.

Hudson City's HMDA data provided key information about the bank's lending practices. In addition, the complaint alleged that Hudson City placed its branches and loan officers principally outside of majority Black and Hispanic neighborhoods. Hudson City also focused its limited marketing on neighborhoods with relatively few Black and Hispanic residents and selected mortgage brokers that were mostly located outside of, and did not effectively serve, majority Black and Hispanic neighborhoods.

Pursuant to the settlement, Hudson City will (1) pay $25 million to subsidize mortgage loans made in the majority Black and Hispanic neighborhoods that were redlined, (2) expand the community it serves under the Community Reinvestment Act to include previously excluded majority Black and Hispanic neighborhoods, (3) create two new branches to serve majority Black and Hispanic neighborhoods, (4) spend $750,000 partnering with community-based organizations that provide assistance in majority Black and Hispanic neighborhoods, (5) spend $1 million on increased advertising and outreach in majority Black and Hispanic neighborhoods, and (6) spend $500,000 on providing financial education to residents of majority Black and Hispanic neighborhoods.

Jacob Faber raises the essential point that racial inequality in lending markets remains a challenge, even in the contemporary United States. While decades old, HMDA and ECOA are vital tools for fair lending efforts. We at the CFPB have been working hard to ensure that HMDA and ECOA live up to their potential in facilitating the policing of lending markets and ensuring fair access to credit.

Segregation May Hurt Minorities, but Its Role in the Foreclosure Crisis Is Far Less Clear

by Stephen L. Ross

In his essay, Jacob Faber argues that racial segregation exacerbated the Great Recession. He bases this view on two major premises: (1) that residential segregation is a long-standing feature of U.S. cities that has had significant negative effects on African Americans and (2) that poor African American neighborhoods were disproportionately affected by the subprime lending boom and the foreclosure crisis that followed. Both of Faber's premises are correct, but his conclusion does not follow inevitably, and the evidence indicates that it is overstated.

A long literature, spanning many decades, has documented both the persistence of racial segregation and the negative effects of segregation on African Americans. Meanwhile, mounting evidence demonstrates that African American borrowers were more likely to take out subprime loans and experienced substantially greater increases in foreclosure rates during the crisis. In my work with Patrick Bayer and Fernando Ferreira,[15] we document that most of the racial and ethnic differences in the incidence of high-cost lending are associated with across-lender differences, rather than within lender, even though across-lender differences were relatively unimportant in explaining racial differences in foreclosure. In new analyses for that paper, we show that the vast majority of the across-lender differences in price were attributable to lenders that had very high ex-post foreclosure rates, and that those high-foreclosure-risk lenders served a disproportionate share of minority and subprime-credit-score borrowers and issued a disproportionate share of high loan-to-value ratio loans.

In other work, I have further shown that a low-cost loan originated in a neighborhood and year when many high-cost loans were being originated was substantially more likely to enter foreclosure during the crisis than other low-cost loans in the same location, and this potential spillover of high-cost lending appears to be driven by the market concentration of high-cost lenders in the neighborhood.[16] In addition, I know from firsthand experience reviewing loan documents that loans made to minority borrowers in low-income neighborhoods during the crisis often had severely predatory attributes.

While these patterns are disturbing and should be monitored, the concentrated effects of subprime lending and the foreclosure crisis among minorities and low-income, often segregated, neighborhoods does not imply that the concentration of subprime lending in minority neighborhoods is either the major driver of minority foreclosures or a critical exacerbating factor in the overall foreclosure crisis. The problem with this logic is a classic fallacy of composition.

Most of the observed racial differences in foreclosure are driven by traditional risk factors that are relatively unrelated to the concentration of high-cost lending and foreclosures in largely minority neighborhoods. In other work with Bayer and Ferreira, we find that most of the racial and ethnic differences are concentrated among borrowers who bought their house near the peak of the market (even after controlling for current levels of negative equity).[17] Standard risk factors, such as credit score, loan terms, and metropolitan-wide housing price and employment shocks, explain 80 percent of the racial differences in foreclosure among recent home buyers. Further, the racial differences that remain are primarily concentrated among borrowers who either faced larger employment shocks or were less able to manage an income shock (high expense ratios or low credit scores).

Similarly, even though minority borrowers and disadvantaged neighborhoods were disproportionately affected by the foreclosure crisis, it seems unlikely that those loans were especially important drivers of the overall crisis. The majority of homeowners in this country are white. The majority of minority homeowners are middle- to upper-income minorities living in middle-income, suburban communities. Further, when we consider capitalization, rather than the number of loans, a huge fraction of the market capitalization of the mortgage market is outside of the types of neighborhoods that I have seen most victimized by predatory lending, neighborhoods where housing prices tend to be low. Recent work by Manuel Adelino, Antoinette Schoar, and Felipe Severino is especially informative on this point.[18] They document that the expansion of mortgage credit during the crisis was spread evenly over the entire income distribution and that the share of mortgage dollars in delinquency attributable to low-income groups actually fell during the crisis. Therefore, it is my view that the vulnerable populations of minority and low-income borrowers that were clearly disproportionately and unfairly affected by subprime lending activities were simply too small to be a major driver of the macroeconomic crisis.

Notes

1. Valerie Wilson, "Projected Decline in Unemployment in 2015 Won't Lift Blacks Out of the Recession-Carved Crater," Economic Policy Institute Briefing Paper #393, March 26, 2015, http://www.epi.org/files/pdf/81754.pdf.
2. Rakesh Kochhar and Richard Fry, "Wealth Inequality Has Widened Along Racial, Ethnic Lines Since End of Great Recession," Pew Research Center, December 12, 2014, http://www.pewresearch.org/fact-tank/2014/12/12/racial-wealth-gaps-great-recession/; Skylar Olsen, "A Black & White Story, Unchanged for 115 Years," Zillow Research, 2015, https://www.zillow.com/research/homeownership-by-race-8851/.
3. Emily Badger, "The Dramatic Racial Bias of Subprime Lending During the Housing Boom," CityLab, August 16, 2013, http://www.theatlanticcities.com/housing/2013/08/blacks-really-were-targeted-bogus-loans-during-housing-boom/6559/.

4. John R. Logan and Brian Stults, "The Persistence of Segregation in the Metropolis: Findings from the 2010 Census," Project US2010 Report, March 24, 2011, http://www .s4.brown.edu/us2010/Data/Report/report2.pdf.

5. Vicki Been, Ingrid Ellen, and Josiah Madar, "The High Cost of Segregation: Exploring Racial Disparities in High-Cost Lending," *Fordham Urban Law Journal* 36, no. 3 (January 2009): 361.

6. Stanford Center on Poverty and Inequality, Income Segregation Maps, accessed August 8, 2017, http://inequality.stanford.edu/income-segregation-maps; Raj Chetty et al., "Where Is the Land of Opportunity? The Geography of Intergenerational Mobility in the United States," National Bureau of Economic Research Working Paper No. 19843, January 2014, http://www.nber.org/papers/w19843; Jacob William Faber, "Banking on Distress: The Expansion of Predatory Financial Institutions During the Great Recession," Association for Public Policy Analysis & Management, November 6, 2014, https://appam.confex.com/appam/2014/webprogram/Paper10835.html#; Michael Powell, "Bank Accused of Pushing Mortgage Deals on Blacks," *New York Times,* June 6, 2009, http://www.nytimes.com/2009/06/07/us/07baltimore.html?pagewanted=all; Jacob W. Faber, "Racial Dynamics of Subprime Mortgage Lending at the Peak," *Housing Policy Debate* 23, no. 2 (2013): 328–349, http://www.tandfonline.com/doi/abs/10.1080/105 11482.2013.771788; Sewin Chan et al., "The Role of Neighborhood Characteristics in Mortgage Default Risk: Evidence from New York City," *Journal of Housing Economics* 22, no. 2 (June 2013): 100–118, https://doi.org/10.1016/j.jhe.2013.03.003; Jacob S. Rugh, "Double Jeopardy: Why Latinos Were Hit Hardest by the US Foreclosure Crisis," *Social Forces* 93, no. 3 (March 2015): 1139–1184, https://academic.oup.com/sf/article -abstract/93/3/1139/2332222/Double-Jeopardy-Why-Latinos-Were-Hit-Hardest-by; Matthew Hall, Kyle Crowder, and Amy Spring, "Variations in Housing Foreclosures by Race and Place, 2005–2012," *Annals of the American Academy of Political and Social Science* 660, no. 1 (2015): 217–237.

7. Ta-Nehisi Coates, "The Case for Reparations," *Atlantic,* June 2014, https://www.theatlantic .com/magazine/archive/2014/06/the-case-for-reparations/361631/.

8. Dan Immergluck, "Too Little, Too Late, and Too Timid: The Federal Response to the Foreclosure Crisis at the Five-Year Mark," *Housing Policy Debate* 23, no. 1 (2013): 199–232.

9. Isaac William Martin and Christopher Niedt, *Foreclosed America* (Stanford, CA: Stanford University Press, 2015).

10. Rick Brooks and Ruth Simon, "Subprime Debacle Traps Even Very Credit-Worthy," *Wall Street Journal,* December 4, 2007, http://www.wsj.com/articles/SB119662974358911035.

11. Raj Chetty, Nathaniel Hendren, and Lawrence F. Katz, "The Effects of Exposure to Better Neighborhoods on Children: New Evidence from the Moving to Opportunity Experiment," *American Economic Review* 106, no. 4 (April 2016): 855–902; Len Albright, Elizabeth S. Derickson, and Douglas S. Massey, "Do Affordable Housing Projects Harm Suburban Communities? Crime, Property Values, and Taxes in Mount Laurel, NJ," *City & Community* 12, no. 2 (June 2013): 89–112; Rucker C. Johnson, "Long-Run Impacts of School Desegregation & School Quality on Adult Attainments," National Bureau of Economic Research Working Paper No. 16664, January 2011, http://www.nber.org /papers/w1666; Heather Schwartz, "Housing Policy Is School Policy: Economically Integrative Housing Promotes Academic Success in Montgomery County, Maryland," in *The Future of School Integration: Socioeconomic Diversity as an Education Reform Strategy,* ed. Richard Kahlenberg (New York: Century Foundation Press, 2012).

12. William Edward Burghardt Du Bois and Isabel Eaton, *The Philadelphia Negro: A Social Study* (Philadelphia: University of Pennsylvania Press, 1899).

13. Patrick Sharkey and Jacob W. Faber, "Where, When, Why, and for Whom Do Residential Contexts Matter? Moving Away from the Dichotomous Understanding of Neighborhood Effects," *Annual Review of Sociology* 40, no. 1 (July 2014): 559–579, https://doi .org/10.1146/annurev-soc-071913-043350.

14. Rebecca Tippett et al., "Beyond Broke: Why Closing the Racial Wealth Gap Is a Priority for National Economic Security," Center for Global Policy Solutions, 2014, https:// globalpolicysolutions.org/wp-content/uploads/2014/04/BeyondBroke_Exec_Summary .pdf.

15. Patrick Bayer, Fernando Ferreira, and Stephen L. Ross, "What Drives Racial and Ethnic Differences in High Cost Mortgages? The Role of High Risk Lenders," Review of Financial Studies 31, no. 1 (January 2018): 175–205.

16. Stephen L. Ross, "Minority Borrowers, Subprime Lending and Foreclosures During the Financial Crisis," 2015, https://www.dallasfed.org/~/media/documents/cd/events /2015/15intentross.pdf.

17. Patrick Bayer, Fernando Ferreira, and Stephen L. Ross, "The Vulnerability of Minority Homeowners in the Housing Boom and Bust," American Economic Journal: Economic Policy 8, no. 1 (February 2016): 1–27.

18. Manuel Adelino, Antoinette Schoar, and Felipe Severino, "Loan Originations and Defaults in the Mortgage Crisis: The Role of the Middle Class," Review of Financial Studies 29, no. 7 (July 2016): 1635–1670.

SEGREGATION AND POLITICS

Politics in a Racially Segregated Nation

by J. Phillip Thompson

The white working class spoke up on November 8, 2016, to say that they'd lost confidence in the leadership of both political parties. Their opinion did not hinge on Hillary Clinton's or Donald Trump's policies; Trump did not even articulate discernible policies. The white working class voted on the declining quality of their lives and resentment from a history of failed promises. Trump promised to blow up Washington, and most white voters supported him in doing so. White working-class activism could someday open up political space for beneficial forward-looking change; but it will be disastrous if neofascism instead fills the void. Some people believe that the word "neofascism" cannot be applied to the United States, given the vaunted strength of liberal democracy. I am among those who think that legalized racial segregation *was* a form of neofascism, so a renewal of neofascist policies is quite thinkable. Trump's flirta-tion with the far right is, by my lights, a grave concern.

What happens next largely depends on the orientation of the white working class toward blacks, Latinos, and other nonwhite, and non-Christian, work-ers. What is their current orientation? In spite of the many questionable opin-ion polls that have prompted naïve proclamations of white racism's demise, I tend toward a long historical view. I agree with W. E. B. Du Bois that capi-talism created not one, but two, proletariats: one of color, and the other white.

The white proletariat was accorded the privilege of not being enslaved, the duty to police nonwhites via regular (police, military) and irregular (Klan, militia) means, and the honor of rubbing elbows with wealthy whites in restaurants or in the 'White Only' sections of trains. This type of racial repression was constitutive of capitalism, of American democratic institutions, and also of citizen identities. Repression fosters in human beings a lack of empathy for those whom you repress—hence protest slogans like "Black Lives Matter" and "Ain't I a Woman" and "I Am a Man." Absence of empathy for nonwhites is the living white supremacist legacy. For many whites, such as those who found it impossible to accept Barack Obama as their president, whiteness goes to the heart of what it means to be an American. This is not only true of the right. The U.S. labor movement, for example, has never embraced the U.S. antebellum antislavery movement as a *labor* movement (as if slavery were not about labor). Doing so would mean that abolitionism and the Civil War were milestones in *their* history, that Harriett Tubman and Sojourner Truth were *their labor* leaders. It would force them to face up to the white male domination of labor's identity. Few labor unions have engaged these issues, which helps explain the contemporary orientation of white workers. White workers may have moved past Jim Crow expressions of racism, but a majority display little regard for the lives of blacks, Latinos, Muslims—those, who along with others, are most directly threatened by Trump's election.

Racial segregation perpetuates white supremacist identity and blocks unity among working people. NAACP lawyers argued in *Brown v. Board of Education* (1954) that segregation "chilled the development in the South of opinion conducive to the acceptance of Negroes on the basis of equality."[1] There is little reason to doubt that they were right. De facto segregation of public schools continues to thrust aside the critical democratic experience of learning and conversing with racial Others during the formative years of human and citizen development. Racial segregation in housing provides little opportunity for whites and blacks, Latinos, Muslims, and others to know each other. In the absence of personal familiarity with the Other, stereotypes often take hold. Workers are less likely to recognize commonalities in their values—concern for family, respect for hard work, willingness to help others—with those of other racial groups and religions. This social distance is easily transferred into scapegoating and divisive politics.

White workers are unhappy on three points: capitalism led by Wall Street has failed them; politicians of neither party represent ordinary working people; and for some, blacks, Latinos, and Muslims (maybe Jews too) are threatening to whites and must be controlled.

During the election, Trump gave voice to all three complaints. Clinton could not credibly remake herself as a champion of ordinary working people. Nor did her campaign seize on Trump's racism to mount strong field operations in black communities. This left many black activists with the strong impression that Clinton took black voters for granted while chasing white workers moving to the right—a long-standing complaint that began with Bill Clinton. Hillary Clinton came to symbolize the fact that economic hurt in America stems from a *structural* problem—a "pay-to-play" politics that endangers democracy. While Wall Street ideally rewards promising entrepreneurs and efficiently run businesses and is supposed to spread risk across sectors and geography, its focus is on making short-term profits for investors (and themselves). Workers no longer trust Wall Street to self-regulate or to ensure economic prosperity for the majority. Workers aren't wrong: the not-so-surprising result of financial deregulation and the loosening of campaign finance regulation has been a spectacular leap in the wealth and political importance of the financial sector, while income has declined for workers and investment in education, workforce training, infrastructure—things that don't generate quick payoffs but really could make America great—has languished. At the same time, widening segregation by income has meant that economic and political elites are less and less likely to share their neighborhoods and their neighborhood schools or infrastructure with working-class or middle-class households.

What Is Needed to Advance Democracy?

Remarkably, some of the most hopeful notes concerning American democracy have been sounded by black leaders, from King to Obama, arguing that the arc of history bends toward justice. Their confidence in ultimate justice is not based on historical precedent—neither they nor we have experienced a nation or world full of social justice—but they have Dewey-like faith that whites, blacks, and others will recognize their common humanity via personal engagement in working together. Along this line, there are several promising movements across the country embracing what I call "morally based organizing." The Service Employees International Union (SEIU), for example, began a racial-justice engagement program among its members two years ago, in which workers in interracial gatherings described the problems they saw, invited speakers, read materials, and held focused small-group conversations about how to make change. There have been many positive results: SEIU's mostly white correction officers in Michigan supported (mostly black) prison inmate protests earlier this year; 80 percent of SEIU members voted for Clinton, whereas almost half of AFL-CIO members voted for Trump.

With white-supremacist nationalism on the rise, it is critical right now to engage working people across race in morally based organizing, with deliberations (schools of practical democracy) about questions that go to the contested fundamental underpinnings of politics: "Who should be allowed to live in this country?" "Do we want to live together, or racially segregated?" "What kind of economic opportunity must we create for working people?" "How can we make sure government represents the people?" How to convene the public when the majority (including a majority of blacks and Latinos) is dispersed in segregated suburbs is a pressing practical issue. What is clear is that out of these deliberations must come immediate actions to save and change democracy.

The Enduring Legacy of Our Separate and Unequal Geography

by Patrick Bayer

Our connections to the world and each other have a profound influence on our perceptions, attitudes, and beliefs. It's simple, really—we are hardwired to care about the people with whom we share regular contact. We do this instinctively, with little effort, often without even thinking about it.

But empathy and compassion become so much harder at any sort of distance, even for those with the best of intentions. It is hard to walk a mile in someone's shoes when we scarcely know the path they must travel.

One of the most painful illustrations of the power of human connectivity is our centuries-long struggle with racism in America. Racism is a disease that both creates and feeds on separation—fueling the lack of connection that in turn perpetuates it.

That racism creates separation is obvious from even the most cursory glance at American neighborhoods and schools. Black and white families that are identical in every other way routinely inhabit completely different spaces within our cities and society. And it is exactly this separation that allows racism to persist over generations. When we are disconnected, it takes intentional effort to see each other as individuals, and it becomes all too easy to see those of another race as fundamentally different, other, inferior.

Segregation based on race would be distressing enough on its own, but when combined with our vastly unequal history, it has especially dire consequences. The separation that racism creates works to preserve the inequities experienced by each generation, passing them to the next in a way that is far too little diminished.

The following fact from John Logan about the geography of race and poverty in the United States makes this point in a direct and striking way: The average black family with an income *above* $75,000 lives in a neighborhood with a higher poverty rate than the average white family with income *below* $40,000.[2] Sean Reardon, Lindsay Fox, and Joseph Townsend illustrate this point in even richer detail. They show that while median neighborhood income increases with household income for each race and ethnicity, the line for black households lies far below that of whites, implying that black households (at every income level) live in much lower income neighborhoods—with the accompanying lower-quality schools, higher crime rates, and worse access to jobs—than comparable white households.[3]

This separate and unequal geography has profound implications for both current and future generations. It forms the conditions that foster the vastly uneven application of law enforcement and criminal justice, gives rise to systematic differences in the quality of schools that black and white children attend, and geographically correlates race and poverty in a way that is difficult for many observers to tell apart, further driving racial misperceptions and racism itself.

It is precisely this powerful combination of separation and historical inequity that makes the aggregate force of racism so unequal. While any individual might hold racist attitudes or beliefs, the collective impact of these attitudes works to preserve the material advantage of those favored by history—ultimately slowing the speed with which social and economic differences dissipate over generations.

This separate and unequal geography also has profound implications for our national politics, as J. Phillip Thompson develops in detail in his essay. The great distances that divide our country by race and ethnicity—city versus suburbs, rural versus urban—make it easy to exploit white racism to drive down support for a whole range of public goods and institutions. Support for these policies is undermined by presenting them as largely benefiting an undeserving other—an other that distance and ignorance make all too easy to caricature and dehumanize.

The perspective that racism and segregation are really just two sides of the same coin and that their impact is not neutral given historical inequities also has far-reaching implications for policy more generally.

It suggests, for example, that housing and schooling policies that provide "choice" rather than resources naturally yield greater benefit to those who can take full advantage of the increased opportunities than to those whose choices are effectively limited by the collective action of racial sorting.

It also implies that the rush—by politicians and the courts—to declare America a postracial society and dismantle remedies designed to protect the basic rights of African Americans is incredibly premature, whether related to affirmative action, voting rights, criminal justice, or school segregation. The impact of "race-neutral" policies in the presence of ongoing racism and enduring inequality is anything but race-neutral.

And it illuminates one final point—that to continue our progress toward a truly color-blind society, policy must actively and aggressively target racial segregation wherever it appears. For the act of separating itself not only reinforces existing racial inequality but also serves as a clear and disheartening marker of the great force that racism retains in our society.

Linking Multiracial Coalitions and Class-Based Appeals

by Lawrence Bobo

Three aspects of Phil Thompson's essay immediately and strongly resonate for me. First is his clear, and I believe well-founded, apprehension that we stand on the verge of a serious wave of American neofascism. Donald Trump's victory in the recent presidential election ushers into power a dangerous demagogue with no real experience with or commitment to democratic institutions and processes. Instead, he is a man of privilege, entitlement, and a long history of discrimination and exploitative dealings with real working people. The anger and intolerance of many of his most ardent supporters, when joined with Trump's profound disregard for democratic norms and procedures, do not bode well.

Moreover, as long as we still live in a racially segregated nation, the fortunes of black and Latino communities will lack an obvious and tight connection to the fate of white communities. Individuals will thus continue to form their sense of personal and larger political interests in a manner heavily structured around boundaries of race. Race will inevitably remain one of the principal levers of political motivation and action in America.

These two developments would be less worrisome if empathy was in great abundance in the American mass public. But in the context of rapid social change, worsening economic inequality, and a material sense of shrinking opportunity and mobility, empathy—the willingness to put oneself in another person's shoes—has been in short supply. Instead, we inhabit a political climate in which a presidential candidate denounced an entire national-origin group as "rapists," "murderers," and "drug dealers"; in which that same candidate called for building a wall against a long-standing neighbor and ally and elicited deafening howls of support; in which this same candidate raised the possibility of excluding from entry to the country all the members of one of the world's great religious traditions; in which the very same candidate routinely belittled and even bragged of assaulting women; and in which, despite this stunning collection of outrages and more, this candidate rose to be freely elected to the highest office in the land. No, empathy would indeed seem to be in exceedingly short supply.

If I dissent from the analysis Thompson has given us—and it is a rather modest dissent—it concerns his insistence on the central importance of the white working class. This bespeaks a mistaken analysis of what happened in the 2016 election and of what ought now to be the strategy for the years ahead. Hillary Clinton did not lose because the white working class turned on her with special force. I see those defections as at least no more significant than those that occurred in the case of Jimmy Carter in 1980, or Walter

Mondale in 1984, or Michael Dukakis in 1988. The problem, as Thompson put it, is that "Clinton could not credibly remake herself as a champion of ordinary working people."

We should all be acutely mindful that Hillary Clinton won the popular vote by a substantial margin yet made strategic errors that cost her the Electoral College. Indeed, the actual vote margin across the three states of Wisconsin, Michigan, and Pennsylvania was so exceedingly small that it is fully explained by lower African American turnout, and lower support among those who did turn out, in just three cities (relative to Obama's 2012 performance): Milwaukee, Detroit, and Philadelphia. The story of 2016 is not some new rebuke to Democrats or to a progressive coalition coming from the white working class—not at all. It is, in my assessment, the failure of a democratic nominee to effectively claim and excite the full multiracial coalition—black, white, Latino, Asian, and more—that elected Barack Obama in 2008 and comfortably reelected him in 2012. Guarding against a repeat of that failure is what should concern us most— to wit, a candidate with a robust, topline, front-and-center economic message and credible profile as a critic of Wall Street, the big banks, unchecked corporate power, and the top 1 percent is the real remedy.

Yes, there is work to be done to assure that working- and middle-class whites do not see their fates as weakened by a demographically changing population or by better opportunities and fuller inclusion for African Americans, Latinos, and Asians. Neither special coddling of the white working class nor continued marginalization of the legitimate aspirations of minority workers is the answer. It is exactly the sort of personal engagement in multiracial collaborative efforts that Thompson calls for, truly working together for the common good, that is what we most urgently need. Yet the racial segregation that continues to characterize our nation may just get in the way.

A Nation Divided Still: How a Vote for Trump Says More About the Voter Than About the Candidate Himself

by Christina Greer

The impact of the 2016 election will be felt for generations to come. For those who sought to blow up Washington, their motivations for voting for Trump illustrate the cognitive dissonance white voters have when it comes to "government" and the services that government actually provides and has provided them for generations. Lest we forget, "government" encompasses public schools, dutiful police (in their communities), the GI Bill (which likely assisted many of their fathers or themselves), and assistance when needed (public and environmental) when in times of crisis.

Jesse Jackson argued that real economic change and advancement are not possible because poor whites consistently choose their racial status over their economic status.[4] Trump played into the racial hierarchy "advantage" for poor whites. But segregation facilitated their parochialism. Segregation blinds white Americans and prevents them from seeing their fellow Americans as equal or deserving of the same benefits they have enjoyed. Segregation blocks empathy and leads whites to hold Blacks, Latinos, and others accountable for the ills in their communities, rather than seeing the neighborhood disparities as byproducts of historical, systematic, and institutional practices, policies, and laws that created these inequities in the first place.

The Trump strategy, while often framed as initiatives from the far right, extends well beyond the right-wing fringes of the Republican Party. The current retrograde policies of the Trump administration are made possible, and will succeed, because of the silence from the middle of the ideological spectrum, voters and elected officials alike. There is a tendency to focus primarily on white working-class voters when attempting to understand the politics of a racially segregated nation. To focus only on white working-class voters is to lose sight of the role that middle-class and upper-class whites have played and continue to play in the racial agenda of the new Republican Party. Racial and economic segregation continue to permeate almost all levels of the democratic experiment, which continues to calcify the deep polarization in this country.

I agree with Thompson in that whiteness "goes to the heart of what it means to be an American." However, the heart of the American foundation is also based on capitalism, anti-Black racism, white supremacy, patriarchy, and segregation. The neofascist and racist animus that currently divides the country extends beyond the white working class and helps explain why the white middle class (including white middle-class women) voted for Trump.[5]

Even while taking the history of this nation and the current racially polarized political climate into account, there are some promising moments on the horizon. Organizations like Project South and the Black Alliance for Just Immigration (BAJI) are forging multiclass, multistate, and intergenerational movements across the country. They focus primarily on leadership development of all members, connecting communities both locally and globally, building political, economic, and educational power at the grass roots, and providing a space for diverse Black groups to connect and advocate. These organizations and others like them are moving away from the "civil rights model," which has been a historically heteronormative Black male leadership model, one still too often replicated in large Black-led organizations.

America has been and continues to be void of empathy with respect to people of color in this country. One can look to past signs of "No N-ggers. No Jews. No dogs" and the current iterations, signs, and postings by white voters (of all classes), which some dismiss as merely expressions of "economic anxiety."

Immediate actions to save and change democracy are imperative. Structural inequality is now reinforced by a swift-moving far-right agenda that seeks to roll back progressive and inclusive policies, while the systems of the separation of powers and checks and balances are challenged by executive branch bullying. The rules have changed, and therefore, so must our strategies. A winning strategy must encompass both electoral and protest politics. Most fundamentally, we must begin by bringing communities together by combating both the physical and ideological segregation of this nation.

Notes

1. *Brown v. Board of Education of Topeka*, 347 U.S. 483 (1954).
2. John R. Logan, "Separate and Unequal: The Neighborhood Gap for Blacks, Hispanics and Asians in Metropolitan America," *Project US2010 Report*, 2011, 1–22.
3. Sean F. Reardon, Lindsay Fox, and Joseph Townsend, "Neighborhood Income Composition by Household Race and Income, 1990–2009," *The Annals of the American Academy of Political and Social Science*, 660, no. 1: 78–97, https://doi.org/10.1177/0002716215576104.
4. Arthur Kretchmer, "Jesse Jackson: A Candid Conversation with the Civil Rights Leader," *Playboy*, November 1969, reprinted February 24, 2014, accessed November 20, 2017, http://playboysfw.kinja.com/jesse-jackson-a-candid-conversation-with-the-civil-rig -1528367166.
5. Jane Junn astutely explains how these white female voters have been hiding in plain sight and have consistently chosen to vote in line with their elevated racial status over their gender. Jane Junn, "Hiding in Plain Sight: White Women Vote Republican," *Politics of Color*, November 13, 2016, http://politicsofcolor.com/white-women-vote-republican/.

PART IV

POLICY IMPLICATIONS

Introduction

The preceding parts of this book have focused on the causes and consequences of segregation. This section considers what we should do about it. The twelve discussions that follow debate whether and how to reform housing and community-development policies to further integration—or, at a minimum, at least not exacerbate segregation. The discussions cover a lot of ground, but the differences in opinion center on a few fundamental issues.

The first disagreement is about how actively and extensively the government should intervene in the market to foster integration. Should the government develop policies that explicitly aim to encourage integration, or should it simply enforce antidiscrimination laws? And how broadly should we interpret discrimination? Should the government focus on combating only intentional acts of discrimination, or also unintentional policies that have the effect of exacerbating segregation or denying access to housing and neighborhoods on the basis of race? This disagreement clearly pits those with a more libertarian bent against those supporting more interventionist government policies. The essays by Richard Epstein and Edward Glaeser are good examples of arguments for more limited government involvement. At the other extreme, Desmond King's essay is an example of a much more interventionist perspective. To some extent, the disagreement is rooted in different beliefs about the value of economic and racial integration. How much do economic and racial integration benefit society, and how much should we be willing to trade off other priorities to achieve integration?

The second, and related disagreement, centers on scale, or the extent to which the benefits of integration depend on the scale at which integration occurs. Should we be aiming for integration at the level of the building, the neighborhood, or the jurisdiction? For example, Carol Lamberg argues that economic integration is most essential at the jurisdictional level, while Mark Joseph highlights the promise of mixed-income buildings.

A third fundamental dispute that runs through policy debates on segregation is whether neighborhoods with high concentrations of poor residents are inherently unhealthy places to live. Some, like Lawrence Vale and Nick Kelly, posit that all communities have the potential to be thriving, nurturing environments, as long as they receive meaningful investments in infrastructure and services. Others, like john powell, take the view that in our highly unequal society, neighborhoods can only provide meaningful opportunities for advancement if they house higher-income residents who can connect their neighbors to jobs and social networks, provide useful information, and wield the political power necessary to attract both public and private investment.

A fourth and related disagreement is how best to address concentrations of poverty and disadvantage: investing in building opportunities in distressed communities or supporting individual families and helping them move to neighborhoods with more resources. To some extent, this comes back to the previous dispute about whether neighborhoods of concentrated poverty can be enriching places to live. But even those who advocate for the importance of economic and racial integration quarrel over the best means to achieve it. Should we invest in disadvantaged areas to attract higher-income residents and create communities of choice where households of all types will want to live, or should we help low-income families move to higher-income areas, either by building affordable housing in such areas or by providing subsidies to individual families to help them move there? The discussions led by Rob Sampson and by Raphael Bostic and Sheryl Whitney offer insightful new contributions to this long-standing debate.

The final series of disagreements that increasingly pervade policy debates on segregation concern gentrification. Some welcome gentrification as a potential pathway to creating integrated communities. Surely, in the short run, the movement of higher-income households into lower-income urban neighborhoods will foster economic integration. Gentrification can potentially foster racial integration too, as it often involves white households moving into largely minority neighborhoods, at least in the past decade in the United States.[1] But many doubt that gentrification will lead to stable, integrated communities over the longer term, and call for different forms of intervention. Some, like Rachel Godsil, maintain that policies should focus on protecting individual households from displacement, allowing them to stay near their friends, families, and communities. Others, like Lance Freeman, emphasize that gentrification is largely driven by a shift in the composition of who is moving into a neighborhood, and policies should therefore focus on ensuring a diversity of housing types affordable to different income levels. Finally, Rafael Cestero and Errol Louis highlight disagreements about whether neighborhood change is inevitable and about the extent to which governments should prioritize slowing that change and stabilizing communities.

Many of the disagreements that surface in the discussions that follow are expressions of these core issues of contention as applied to particular urban policies. In some cases, authors may be on the same side of these fundamental disputes but disagree about the best way to achieve their shared goals—say, stabilizing neighborhoods facing gentrification pressures, or enriching extremely poor neighborhoods.

It is worth noting that the policy landscape shifted rapidly after the 2016 presidential election, as the Trump administration sought to roll back Obama-era fair housing policies, such as the Small Area Fair Market Rents Rule, the Affirmatively Furthering Fair Housing Rule, and potentially the rule regarding the disparate-effects standard of the Fair Housing Act. Although the thrust of federal policy making has changed, fair housing advocates have challenged attempts to roll back these policies, and cities and states across the country continue to wrestle with the policy issues discussed here as they craft their own strategies to address segregation and disparities in access to opportunity.

The Discussions in Part IV

The Future of the Fair Housing Act

The first two discussions in this section address fair housing law. The first discussion debates the degree to which the Fair Housing Act should apply to policies that have a "disparate impact" (or negative effect) on groups protected by the act, even when there is no explicit intention to discriminate. Shortly after these authors wrote their essays, the Supreme Court, in a five-to-four opinion authored by Justice Kennedy, confirmed, in *Texas Department of Housing and Community Affairs v. The Inclusive Communities Project* (2015), that disparate-impact claims were indeed cognizable under the Fair Housing Act. But the debates about what constitutes a disparate impact, how to prove that a policy causes a disparate impact, and the degree to which courts should second-guess decisions that state and local governments make in their housing programs are hardly settled. Alan Jenkins starts by arguing that to be effective in advancing open and inclusive communities, the Fair Housing Act must prohibit not only intentional acts of discrimination but also policies that have a disparate impact on minority groups, such as exclusionary zoning. Richard Epstein, by contrast, challenges the use of a disparate-impact standard altogether, arguing that it is not the business of the courts or the federal government to second-guess the decisions that state and local governments make in good faith when trying to implement already complicated federal housing programs. Dennis Parker agrees with Jenkins, emphasizing that proving disparate-impact claims is a difficult task, and that the standard represents "a careful, measured way of protecting all Americans from discrimination." Susan Ann Silverstein focuses on the ways in which unintentional discrimination can exclude people with disabilities and argues that the ability to bring disparate-impact claims under the Fair Housing Act is essential to ensure that disabled and older adults are able to make housing choices that afford them the opportunity to live full and independent lives.

The opinions in the *Inclusive Communities* case echo some of the divides expressed in these essays. The Court held that disparate impact claims are consistent with the text and purpose of the Fair Housing Act of providing "a clear national policy against discrimination in housing" (ICP 17) and are important "in moving the Nation toward a more integrated society" (ICP 24). The Court noted that disparate-impact liability "permits plaintiffs to counteract unconscious prejudices and disguised animus that escape easy classification as disparate treatment" (ICP 17), an explicit recognition of the significance of implicit bias. At the same time, Justice Kennedy articulates a need for "safeguards," stating that "[d]isparate-impact liability mandates the 'removal of artificial, arbitrary, and unnecessary barriers,' not the displacement of valid governmental policies" and that the FHA should not be used "to force housing authorities to reorder their priorities" (ICP 18). Despite the Court's repeated affirmation of disparate-impact liability, the insurance and banking industries have consistently challenged the disparate effects rule that HUD issued in 2013, and HUD in 2018 announced that it was seeking public comment on proposed amendments to the rule.[2]

Affirmatively Furthering Fair Housing

The second discussion also relates to fair housing, covering the Final Rule on Affirmatively Furthering Fair Housing (AFFH) that the U.S. Department of Housing and Urban Development (HUD) issued in July 2015 to implement the portion of the Fair Housing Act that requires all federal executive agencies and all recipients of federal housing and urban development funding to take affirmative steps to address segregation and disparities in access to opportunity. The authors all generally welcome the new rule, and the fact that it requires state and local governments to engage with the public in open conversations about segregation and how to dismantle it. But some, like Michael Allen, bemoan the fact that the rule has few teeth to ensure that state and local governments comply. Allen calls on local advocates to mobilize to ensure that local governments are following through on complying with the rule and fulfilling their commitments. Angela Glover Blackwell embraces Allen's call to action but has more faith in the power of the rule, and the discussion and scrutiny of local data it requires, to motivate local leaders to take actions to foster inclusive communities. Michael Bodaken and Ellen Lurie Hoffman warn against abandoning efforts to invest in high-poverty, largely minority communities and highlight the importance and value of preserving existing affordable housing, much of which is located in high-poverty areas. Edward Goetz endorses Allen's call for a ground game, but he also emphasizes the importance of targeting the exclusionary practices of high-income, predominantly white communities rather than challenging efforts to build affordable housing in poor and predominantly minority neighborhoods.

The rule has continued to generate debate. Forty-nine municipalities submitted Assessments of Fair Housing under the new AFFH Rule between August 2015 and January 5, 2018, when HUD suspended implementation of the AFFH Rule until 2020 and then subsequently withdrew indefinitely the tool that municipalities had been required to use to submit their Assessments of Fair Housing. The National Fair Housing Alliance, the Texas Low Income Housing Information Center, and Texas Appleseed sued, alleging that HUD had failed to follow the requirements of the Administrative Procedure Act and was violating the Fair Housing Act. At the time of publication, the case remained pending.

Balancing Investments in People and Place

The next set of discussions focuses on whether federal urban policy should prioritize individual people or places. Raphael Bostic and Sheryll Whitney argue that the crux of the disagreement between the two camps is differing views of the importance of ending racial segregation *per se*. From Bostic and Whitney's perspective, policy makers must support both types of efforts. Nancy Andrews and Dan Rinzler emphasize the need for coordinated, cross-sectoral, and sustained investments in the housing, services, and environments of disadvantaged communities. Erin Boggs, meanwhile, leans toward supporting efforts to open up housing choices in lower-poverty neighborhoods, arguing that the status quo is far from balanced and, at least in Connecticut, offers very few affordable housing options outside of high-poverty and majority-minority communities that have long suffered from disinvestment. Rolf Pendall points out the stark regional differences in growth patterns around the country and calls for policy approaches that are more sensitive to regional context—in particular, empirically grounded assessments of how cities and neighborhoods are likely to grow in the future.

Addressing Neighborhood Disinvestment

The discussion led by Robert Sampson covers similar ground but offers fresh perspectives. Sampson emphasizes the mounting research evidence about the costs of concentrated disadvantage. He calls for balance but offers a new proposal: to give cash assistance to poor households that have lived in high-poverty neighborhoods for an extended period of time, suffering from what he calls compounded disadvantage. All three respondents largely agree with Sampson's endorsement of both people- and place-based approaches, though with different emphases. Richard Florida emphasizes the need for an even more ambitious and broad-based public investment to create stable, decent-paying jobs, affordable housing, and functioning public transit. Rosanne Haggerty calls for improving basic public services and making durable investments in high-poverty neighborhoods, which she argues will ultimately save taxpayer money by reducing the amounts the government would have to spend on health care, child protection, and criminal justice. Michael Stoll also highlights the importance of jobs, but rather than providing direct subsidies to attract businesses, he argues for broad-based investments in early education, school reforms, and criminal-justice reforms, which will disproportionately help residents of poor neighborhoods, reduce the stigma of those areas, and ultimately help to attract employers.

Place-Based Affirmative Action

In this discussion, Sheryll Cashin offers a proposal to target residents of high-poverty neighborhoods for assistance. Specifically, she argues for replacing race-based affirmative action in college admissions with a policy that would give special consideration to students living in high-poverty neighborhoods or attending high-poverty schools. She argues that such a policy would be not only more politically palatable but also more effective in targeting disadvantaged students and redressing the harms of segregation. George Galster is sympathetic to the motivation for Cashin's proposal but predicts that it would ultimately do little to remedy the underlying structural inequality it aims to address and might instead set up for failure students coming from the lowest-performing schools. Rather than "tinkering" with admissions policies, he advocates for efforts to improve the inadequate public schools that most students of color attend. Desmond King also sees the need for a more far-reaching intervention to meaningfully address racial inequalities. In contrast to Cashin's proposal, which is deliberately race-blind, he calls for explicitly race-sensitive measures. Gerald Torres draws on the example of the Texas Ten Percent Plan to endorse Cashin's proposal as a way to create genuine opportunities for children throughout the state.

Selecting Neighborhoods for Low-Income Housing Tax Credit Developments

The next set of discussions concerns place-based subsidized housing—particular housing developments that offer homes at below-market rents to households earning incomes below some threshold. The first discussion centers on what neighborhoods we should target for affordable-housing development through the Low-Income Housing Tax Credit (LIHTC), which has become the largest source of support for affordable housing in the United States. In his lead essay, Adam Gordon argues that states should adjust their allocation criteria to give greater priority to LIHTC projects in neighborhoods with access to good schools, jobs, and transit and to ensure that those developments built in high-poverty areas are part of a comprehensive revitalization effort. Robin Hughes counters that developing in higher-income areas is more expensive and will thus lead to fewer units of affordable housing. Further, she maintains that many low-income neighborhoods, especially those experiencing gentrification pressures, desperately need affordable housing, and fair housing advocates should be careful not to condemn all new affordable housing slated for low-income areas. Kathy O'Regan, who at the time was assistant secretary for policy development and research at HUD, makes an important distinction between rehabilitation and new construction, and argues that states should be more strategic in their use of LIHTC dollars in high-poverty areas, focusing on preserving existing affordable housing and adopting concrete guidelines for the kind of "concerted community revitalization" that should accompany such investments. Denise Scott, like Hughes, cautions against cutting off credits to high-poverty areas, arguing that tax credits go further there and that LIHTC developments in themselves trigger revitalization in distressed areas.

Public Housing and Deconcentrating Poverty

This discussion examines what we should do about the poor physical conditions and the concentration of poor residents found in traditional public housing developments. In their lead essay, Lawrence Vale and Nick Kelly argue that we should not rush into replacing all public housing with vouchers or mixed-income housing, but instead invest in improving the physical conditions and management of developments to make them "truly decent places to live." Robert Chaskin largely agrees with their argument and holds out hope that investments in public housing, coupled with educational support and job training, could significantly improve environments. That said, he also points to a need for policies that explicitly target the structural factors that perpetuate racial segregation and lead black and Latino public housing residents to be far more likely to live in high-poverty communities. Drawing on his influential research on the Moving to Opportunity Program, Nathaniel Hendren also emphasizes the costs of living in high-poverty areas and the benefits of moving to lower-poverty areas. While he agrees with Vale and Kelly that we should not abandon all efforts to improve distressed neighborhoods, he argues we need more research to identify the most effective ways to do so. Finally, John Powell counters that physical revitalization will do little to address the economic and social deprivation found in many public housing developments. He argues that to improve the life chances of poor families, we should invest instead in mobility programs that help poor families reach communities that offer a different set of opportunities and social networks.

Creating Mixed-Income Housing Through Inclusionary Zoning

This debate focuses on mixed-income housing, inspired by the controversy in New York around "poor doors," or separate entrances for the residents of the affordable apartments that developers receiving zoning bonuses or tax incentives are required to include in their otherwise market-rate buildings in affluent Manhattan neighborhoods. Edward Glaeser calls such separate entrances "inherently jarring," but he poses a more fundamental challenge to such inclusionary housing strategies, questioning whether the benefits delivered by mixed-income housing are large enough to outweigh the very high costs of housing a few low-income households in such expensive buildings. Ben Beach defends inclusionary housing (though not poor doors), not so much because it delivers mixed-income buildings, but because he views it as a critical tool to create affordable housing choices in affluent neighborhoods. Similarly, Mark Joseph highlights the many barriers—above and beyond cost—that prevent low-income households from reaching high-opportunity neighborhoods. He holds out hope for mixed-income housing—with shared entrances, amenities, and governance—as a strategy not only to create more equitable access to neighborhoods, but also to build truly integrated and diverse communities. While Carol Lamberg appreciates the goal of building communities, she maintains that the far more important goal is to build as many decent, safe and affordable homes as possible given the tremendous need. In her mind, the challenge is not the diversity of individual entrances, buildings, or even neighborhoods, but the diversity of New York City as a whole, which is gravely threatened by the high cost of housing.

Neighborhoods, Opportunities, and the Housing Choice Voucher Program

The next two discussions center on the housing choice voucher program, which provides subsidies to eligible low-income households who rent homes on the private market. In theory, housing choice vouchers promote choice by allowing households to use their rent subsidies in any unit available through the private market that meets HUD's housing quality standards. In practice, however, voucher holders disproportionately live in high-poverty neighborhoods. The authors here consider different tactics to enable more voucher holders to reach low-poverty areas. Barbara Sard and Phillip Tegeler argue strongly for the need to encourage such moves and propose a number of strategies, including rewarding housing authorities that place more of their voucher families in low-poverty areas, minimizing barriers for voucher holders to cross jurisdictional lines to access units in higher-opportunity neighborhoods, and supporting supplemental assistance to families trying to make such moves. Stefanie DeLuca endorses the need for such mobility assistance, pointing out that voucher holders face highly constrained searches and, absent assistance, will seek homes in low-income neighborhoods where they are easier to find. The practitioners in this discussion, Sandra Henriquez and Stephen Norman, both endorse the mobility goal but push back on the proposals for reform, arguing that, in the current budget-constrained climate, the resources these proposals would take would actually undermine the more fundamental goal of the voucher program: to provide sound, affordable homes to as many low-income households as possible. They suggest that opening up low-poverty areas will take more than reforming the voucher program and will require addressing broader structural barriers and investing in fixed, subsidized units as well.

Making Vouchers More Mobile

Robert Collinson argues for another specific voucher reform: replacing the current metropolitan-area-wide rent caps with voucher rent limits that are set at the zip-code level, called Small Area Fair Market Rents. He points out that anchoring subsidy levels to rents in a zip code will increase the potential voucher subsidy in low-poverty areas while reducing it in higher-poverty areas, thereby simultaneously encouraging and enabling more households to settle in low-poverty, resource-rich communities. He points to research he conducted with Peter Ganong showing that the adoption of Small Area Fair Market Rents in Dallas led voucher holders to move to significantly safer and lower-poverty neighborhoods at no added cost to the government. Demetria McCain endorses Collinson's call for neighborhood-based rent caps and argues that there is substantial untapped demand among low-income families to move to safer areas with better schools. But she emphasizes that Small Area Fair Market Rents are insufficient; they must be supplemented by counseling to help families move. Rachel Fee and Diane Yentel both agree that Small Area Fair Market Rents are promising but argue for additional support and protections for voucher holders remaining in low-rent areas, as they are likely to see rising rents as their subsidies are reduced. Fee underscores the particular difficulty faced by voucher holders in tight housing markets like New York who, faced with such limited options, are likely to get stuck paying higher rents in the same high-poverty neighborhoods.

In November 2016, shortly after the authors wrote their essays, HUD published a final rule regarding Small Area Fair Market Rents, making their adoption mandatory in twenty-four metropolitan areas and optional everywhere else. The agency then suspended the mandatory implementation of Small Area Fair Market Rents less than one year later under the new administration. Fair housing organizations sued, and the federal district court reinstated the rule, finding that HUD had neither the authority nor compelling reasons to suspend implementation.

Gentrification and the Promise of Integration

The final two discussions consider appropriate responses to gentrification. Rachel Godsil advocates for targeting vouchers to long-term residents in gentrifying neighborhoods to help protect them against rising rents. The three responders appreciate her call for government action, but all three assert that her proposal falls short. Lance Freeman counters that while Godsil's proposal would help allay displacement fears, it would do little to help maintain stable integration in the longer run. Brad Lander goes even further than Freeman, maintaining that a voucher program could ultimately be self-defeating, as subsidies might put upward pressure on rents and further burden those whose incomes are just above the threshold to qualify for assistance. Both Freeman and Lander argue for a broader set of policies, including inclusionary zoning and place-based subsidized housing, to ensure longer-run integration. Olatunde Johnson underscores the difficulty of deciding which neighborhoods and residents would be eligible for vouchers—and when—and argues instead for creating an inclusive process to engage residents in crafting community plans that can foster and sustain economic and racial diversity.

Community Preferences and Fair Housing

The last discussion debates the merits of giving priority to neighborhood residents who apply to live in new subsidized housing units in their community. Rafael Cestero argues that such community preferences are an important tool in fighting displacement and supporting community stability in high-cost cities, as they help to allow residents who wish to remain in their communities to do so. Errol Louis disagrees, contending that preserving the fabric of neighborhoods in highly segregated cities like New York is preserving the fabric of racially homogenous communities—in other words, sustaining segregation. He also views community preferences as inherently unfair, as they exclude low-income families facing displacement who just do not happen to live near any new subsidized housing. Robert Schwemm makes a legal case against community preferences, arguing that they likely violate the Fair Housing Act by imposing a disparate impact on minority groups when less discriminatory options are available to support the same goals. Sam Tepperman-Gelfant acknowledges the fair housing arguments against community preferences but argues that we should think differently about their use in gentrifying areas. He maintains that in low-income areas facing gentrification, community preferences can help to temper displacement and promote stable integration over the longer term.

Notes

1. Ingrid Gould Ellen and Lei Ding, "Advancing Our Understanding of Gentrification," *Cityscape* 18, no. 3 (2016): 3–8, https://www.huduser.gov/portal/periodicals/cityscpe/vol18num3/guest.pdf.
2. U.S. Department of Housing and Urban Development, "Reconsideration of HUD's Implementation of the Fair Housing Act's Disparate Impact Standard," June 20, 2018, https://www.federalregister.gov/documents/2018/06/20/2018-13340/reconsideration-of-huds-implementation-of-the-fair-housing-acts-disparate-impact-standard.

DISCUSSION 14

THE FUTURE OF THE FAIR HOUSING ACT

As We Celebrate Fair Housing Month, the Fair Housing Act Is at Risk

by Alan Jenkins

As we celebrate Fair Housing Month, the Fair Housing Act is at risk.

This is Fair Housing Month, commemorating the bedrock civil rights principle that we all deserve the opportunity to choose a home and neighborhood free from discrimination. April is Fair Housing Month because on April 11, 1968, President Johnson signed the Fair Housing Act of 1968 after months of ideological gridlock. The legislative breakthrough came only when, on April 4th of that year, the Act's champion, Dr. Martin Luther King, Jr., was murdered

Note: As discussed in the introduction to part IV and recognized in discussion 15, on June 25, 2015 (after these contributions were written) the Supreme Court, in an opinion authored by Justice Kennedy, held 5-4 that claims of discrimination based on the disparate impact of a policy on a protected group are cognizable under the Fair Housing Act. The decision, however, also sought to limit the reach of disparate impact claims by reminding litigants of the need to establish a causal connection between a specific policy and the challenged disparity and by reminding courts that remedies should strive to eliminate disparities through race-neutral means. Many of the subsidiary questions raised in this discussion continue to be litigated in lower courts and, at the time of publication, the current administration was seeking to amend the disparate effect rule that HUD had promulgated in 2013, presumably to limit its scope.

in Memphis. In the wake of that tragedy, and growing demands for action, Congress came together to pass the 1968 Act.

Today, almost fifty years later, the Fair Housing Act is again at risk. In a case from Texas pending before the U.S. Supreme Court, the justices may be poised to greatly weaken the Act. An adverse decision would undermine America's progress toward a nation of open and inclusive communities and our national values of equal opportunity for all.

A full and effective Fair Housing Act serves the nation well, prohibiting discrimination based on race, religion, gender, national origin, disability, or family status. It has helped to break up long-standing patterns of segregation and fostered diverse, prosperous communities. It has helped to create and preserve housing that is affordable to working families of all races and backgrounds. It has offered true inclusion to people with disabilities in communities around the country. And it has been one of the few successful tools for holding big banks accountable for the subprime lending abuses that crashed our economy just a few years ago.

This progress should be allowed to continue, and more remains to be done. Antiquated zoning restrictions, for example, still hamper the construction of homes that working people can afford, and disproportionately exclude families of color. Real estate agents and landlords still often make assumptions about people's ability to pay based on stereotypes instead of facts. And we've seen that big banks like Wells Fargo, Bank of America, and PrimeLending have systematically marketed risky subprime mortgages to people of color, including those who can well afford market-rate loans.

Addressing those challenges requires a Fair Housing Act that prohibits both intentional bigotry and unjustified policies that exclude or segregate in practice. For more than four decades, lower courts have agreed that the Act does just that. The U.S. Department of Housing and Urban Development, which is charged with enforcing the Act, has concurred. Despite this consensus, however, the U.S. Supreme Court will decide in the coming weeks whether to require proof of a decision maker's subjective discriminatory intent to prove a violation of the Act.

Requiring proof of intent would badly damage the Act's effectiveness. In the twenty-first century, people rarely announce their intention to discriminate. Moreover, some of the most harmful fair housing violations involve the thoughtless perpetuation of past discrimination. Consider for example, the many municipalities in which minority neighborhoods are geographically isolated from opportunities like quality schools, good jobs, and public transportation. Land-use decisions that deepen those patterns should go forward only if municipalities show that they advance important objectives, and absent less discriminatory alternatives. Requiring proof of active discriminatory animus would remove that scrutiny and allow harmful practices to continue.

Other types of decisions can be equally harmful. In a recent fair housing case from Ohio, for example, a bank denied a pregnant woman a mortgage that she could afford because she planned to take paid maternity leave and would be away from work several weeks. People with disabilities, who often lack a record of continuous employment despite having adequate resources, often face similar obstacles.

In a Louisiana case, a parish approved an ordinance shortly after Hurricane Katrina prohibiting property owners from renting to people who were not family members or related by blood. Since 93 percent of current homeowners were white, the provision would have excluded African Americans seeking to relocate when their homes were damaged by the storm.

A strong and effective Fair Housing Act is needed to ensure that thoughtless and unnecessary barriers like these do not block the path to opportunity. If the Supreme Court fails to recognize that reality, it will fall to Congress and the president to restore the Act to its intended reach.

The Unintended Consequences of Fair Housing Laws

by Richard A. Epstein

Alan Jenkins, the executive director of the Opportunity Agenda, has written an all too one-sided defense of the fair housing laws. His major error is to assume that the goals of the law, however laudable, can be achieved by the coercive means that the government wishes to employ. The legal issue at stake in *Texas Department of Housing and Community Affairs v. The Inclusive Communities Project* is whether it is possible to prove a violation of the Fair Housing Act of 1968 without producing any evidence of an intention on the part of government authorities to engage in acts of discrimination.

I have written at length elsewhere on the technical aspects of this case and the complex statutory framework in which the federal government closely monitored the distribution of federal funds into certain low-income areas. It simply challenges credibility to think that the Texas Department violated the Fair Housing Act because of its good faith effort to comply with the complex dictates of the Low-Income Housing Tax Credit program. Imposing any comprehensive federal judicial oversight on how Texas should run its program would require a huge expenditure of state and national funds that could be spent far better in dealing with the housing needs of the poor. It is simply false to assume that a statement of laudable ends of social and racial integration insulates the means chosen from criticism by those on the other side.

Indeed, in *Inclusive Communities*, the real culprit is the U.S. Department of Housing and Urban Development (HUD), whose key regulations make hash of the much narrower statutory language. Even if Jenkins were correct on the need for a disparate-impact standard, which he is not, it would not be appropriate for HUD to unilaterally change the law. That responsibility lies with Congress. Yet before acting, Congress should ask whether the Fair Housing Act has had the unambiguously favorable consequences that Jenkins attributes to it. On that score, the picture is more complex than his glowing defense of the law suggests.

Here are some of the complications. The first question is whether the Fair Housing Act has in fact been able to do two things: break patterns of segregation and increase the levels of affordable housing for working-class families. It is hard to give a clear verdict on the first of these questions because, wholly apart from the passage of the Fair Housing Act, there have been major changes in social attitudes on a wide range of questions that operate independently of the law. Allocating the influence that each of these sources has on changes in residential patterns is difficult to do. That task becomes especially demanding over time, given that the major gains from enforcement of the Fair Housing Act occurred during the early years after its passage. The questions of de facto segregation, and its causes and effects are much more difficult to disentangle.

Regarding the second goal, there is no reason to think that any affordable-housing program works to achieve its intended goal of expanding housing opportunities for poor and working-class families. These programs are beasts to run because they require extensive and continuous oversight of rental units to see that the right applicants are slotted into the right groups. Indeed, it is uncertain whether the Fair Housing Act has led to any, let alone significant, increases in the level of affordable housing for low-income families. It is hard to believe that these low-income-housing programs will crank out more affordable housing units if they are saddled with an additional layer of rules and regulations.

The situation is only more difficult because a rigorous affordable-housing regime requires that resumes be updated to take into account shifts in income and family status after the individual units are rented. The entire process slows down the renting of new units, and thus the willingness of developers to expand the total supply of housing units. There is no more congested housing market than New York City, where aggressive enforcement of affordable-housing programs tends to drive developers from the residential real estate market into the commercial market, where these restraints are not present.

There is a clear moral from the unhappy experience of skyrocketing rents in New York, which imposes heavy burdens on new arrivals to the city's tight housing market. Yet Jenkins does not have a kind word to say about the ability of markets to expand housing opportunities. In so doing, he ignores the most powerful change agent in society. What is needed is for heavily regulated communities like New York City to cut back on their ornate approval processes so that new housing projects can start with a minimum of time and effort. There are all too many efforts to deride "trickle-down" housing. But that unfortunate epithet should not be allowed to conceal this essential truth. The best and surest way to drive down housing costs is to increase the available supply of housing units, which in a place like New York City means eliminating rent-stabilization programs and slimming down the permitting process. The race-targeted initiatives championed by Jenkins come in a distant second place.

Let's Stick with What Works

by Dennis Parker

Nearly fifty years ago, Congress passed the Fair Housing Act as a way of confronting the problems of residential segregation and conditions of poverty that blocked access to opportunity for communities of color and led to bitterness, frustration, and civil unrest.

From the outset, the bipartisan sponsors and supporters of the Fair Housing Act recognized that, given the pervasiveness and complexity of housing discrimination, it was necessary to prohibit all forms of discrimination, not only those that resulted from discriminatory intent, but also acts neutral on their face that had a discriminatory effect.

The future efficacy of the Fair Housing Act as a tool in fighting the full range of housing-related discrimination is now in question as we await the decision of the United States Supreme Court in *Texas Department of Housing and Community Affairs v. The Inclusive Communities Project*, a case challenging the use of the disparate-impact standard—a standard that focuses on actions that have an unfair impact and lack business necessity, and one that has long been accepted by all of the courts of appeals in the country.

This standard has been a vital tool in combating discrimination. Persistent housing segregation is one clear indication of the need for its continued existence. An adverse ruling in the case also threatens to undermine the Fair Housing Act's effectiveness in fighting more subtle, but still harmful, policies and practices.

One striking example of the continuing need for an effective way of addressing the increasingly subtle ways in which groups protected by the Fair Housing Act are denied equal access to housing can be seen in the wake of the economic crisis of 2008. During the run-up to the crisis, discriminatory lending practices became increasingly prevalent, including providing high-cost subprime loans to members of communities of color who actually qualified for prime loans. In 2005, 55 percent of all subprime borrowers had sufficiently high credit scores to qualify for prime loans, and these borrowers were disproportionately people of color. A joint report from HUD and the Department of the

Treasury found that, as of 2000, "borrowers in black neighborhoods [were] five times as likely to refinance in the subprime market than borrowers in white neighborhoods," even after controlling for income. Even more striking was the finding that "borrowers in upper-income black neighborhoods were twice as likely as homeowners in low-income white neighborhoods to refinance with a subprime loan."[1]

These communities had previously experienced a long history of intentional discrimination in the form of racial steering, redlining, and lack of access to financial institutions offering fair borrowing options. The new practice of extending mortgages on predatory terms added new injury to the old. The combination of the new abusive lending practices and the history of redlining and systematic disinvestment resulted in a foreclosure crisis that had a particularly serious impact on communities of color and reversed many of the economic gains that had been realized by those communities over the past half-century. The only legal redress for the policies that facilitated this discrimination, such as compensating originators more for high-cost loans, is a disparate-impact claim, because no individual would be able to demonstrate the discriminatory consequences of these policies that fueled the subprime bubble without relying on evidence of their collective, broad impact. Cases challenging the lending practices that brought about the economic crisis that threatened the economy as a whole, but had particularly serious consequences on individuals and communities of color, illustrate that the disparate-impact standard is a careful, measured way of protecting all Americans from discrimination. After plaintiffs have shown that a policy or practice has a disproportionate impact on protected classes, defendants have the opportunity to demonstrate that there is a substantial legitimate reason for the practice and policy. Policies only violate the fair housing act if they have no legitimate justification or if there is a less discriminatory way to achieve the same purpose.

By permitting the consideration of impact as well as goals and the means of achieving those goals, the disparate-impact standard permits challenges to barriers that prohibit equal access to fair housing. It is common sense that any policy that unnecessarily excludes people from housing on the basis of their religion, gender, race, ethnicity, family status, disability, or other protected criteria should be set aside in favor of one that serves everyone's needs fairly, effectively, and without discrimination. The disparate-impact standard is a commonsense way of assuring effective and equal fair housing opportunity, and its use should be protected. To do otherwise would undercut decades of progress and betray the efforts of the people nearly half a century ago who sought to assure fairness and equality in housing by passing the Fair Housing Act. Should the Supreme Court take steps that threaten the continuing vitality of this important statue, the president and Congress should take whatever steps are necessary to restore its role as a critical tool for achieving equality and fairness.

An Aging Population Relies on the Fair Housing Act for Independence and Community Living

by Susan Ann Silverstein

The older population is growing at an unprecedented rate. By 2030, one in five Americans will be age sixty-five or over; by 2040, the number of Americans age sixty-five and over will double, from 40 million in 2010 to 81 million. The aging population is also becoming more diverse, driven by both changing demographic trends and increasing immigration. Given current racial disparities in wealth, the higher proportion of minority older households means that there will be more households entering old age with fewer resources and higher mortgage debt, as well as other housing disparities that are often the result of past discrimination. Older African Americans, for instance, are more exposed than other age groups to residential segregation and to neighborhoods with higher levels of poverty and lower levels of amenities important to health, such as access to fresh food, transportation, and open spaces. Even long-term residential care, such as assisted living and nursing homes, remains racially segregated, with African Americans receiving lower levels of care and exhibiting worse health outcomes.

Meanwhile, the prevalence of disability increases with age: more than half of people over sixty-five have a disability. To age with dignity and maintain their quality of life, older adults need housing that is affordable, accessible, and well located. If possible, almost all prefer to age in place in their own homes. If they must relocate for cost savings or accessibility, older adults want to do so on their own timetable, not at the whim of a landlord or on conditions circumscribed by the adverse effects of rules based on outmoded, misguided, or uninformed opinions or decisions of housing providers, politicians, or government officials. Rules that prohibit scooters or companion animals on residential property are relics of a time prior to the movement for civil rights for people with disabilities, as are zoning laws that prevent building ramps or policies that dictate how many people with disabilities can live together.

Building on the civil rights movements for disability rights and racial justice, older people all over the country have relied on the Fair Housing Act to ensure that they have equal access to housing that is affordable, appropriate, and accessible to them as they age and where they can have the services they need provided to them in their communities rather than in an institutional setting. Age is not a protected class under the Fair Housing Act. Nevertheless, older persons, like all Americans, are protected from discrimination based on their race, color, national origin, religion, sex, family status, or disability. Discrimination can sometimes take subtle or hard-to-identify forms, even though the policy that facilitates the discrimination occurs openly and in plain sight, as the following case illustrates.

More than twenty-five years ago, a social worker in a nursing home called my legal-services office about a sixty-four-year-old resident who was desperately trying to get out. There was no longer a medical need for her to be there. Her doctors agreed her care could easily be provided in an apartment in the community. So the worker helped Ms. Cason apply to the local housing authority for an apartment she could afford in a senior high rise. When she called me, the social worker asked what she could do about the rejection Ms. Cason had received, which stated that before Ms. Cason could move in, she had to prove she was "capable of independent living" by living in the community on her own for eighteen months.

What was happening to Ms. Cason was wrong and unfair, but it was not on its face illegal or discriminatory. In fact, it was a neutral, general rule applied to anyone applying to the housing authority's high-rise apartments, usually set aside for those sixty-two and older. Only after other clients were interviewed and admissions data examined did it become clear that the housing authority's policy had the effect of discriminating against people with disabilities. They were the ones applying from rehab centers, from nursing homes, or from living with their families, and thus bearing the burden of the eighteen-month rule. *Cason v. Rochester Housing Authority* became the first disparate-impact case decided under the Fair Housing Amendments Act of 1988 (FHAA).[2] As a result of that case and others like it, many people with disabilities who would have been barred from living in the community were able to move from nursing homes and other institutional settings to apartments and fully partake in community life.

Twenty-five years after the *Cason* decision, the ability of the Fair Housing Act to provide for the full inclusion of people with disabilities in the community is at risk if the Supreme Court rules that it will no longer be possible to challenge rules and policies based only on their discriminatory effect. In passing the FHAA, Congress understood that discrimination against people with disabilities often results from indifference or stereotypes, not explicit discrimination, and that it would be necessary to outlaw actions or policies that had the effect or operated to discriminate. "Independent living" policies similar to those challenged in *Cason* continue to exist in many segments of the senior housing market. As an example, many professionals I know who rely on assistive technology and personal attendants are prohibited by these rules from moving into many retirement communities, despite earnings and backgrounds similar to those of their professional peers. These policies will be difficult to challenge if the Supreme Court eviscerates disparate impact.

Older people are also vulnerable to racial discrimination. This summer, the first residents of the Gardens neighborhood expect to move into their new one-floor, age-friendly, affordable homes in Mt. Holly, New Jersey. These plaintiffs settled their lawsuit against the Township of Mt. Holly shortly before the

Supreme Court was scheduled to hear their case in December 2013. The Gardens in Mount Holly, New Jersey, was a community of mostly minority, lower-income, older homeowners. The Township of Mt. Holly decided that the neighborhood, where a substantial portion of the Township's minority residents lived, was "blighted" and planned to force out all of the residents, demolish the neighborhood, and transfer it to a private developer to build townhomes that most existing residents would be unable to afford. The residents challenged the Township's redevelopment plan because it called for the complete demolition of their homes and dispersal of their community; furthermore, the cash payment they would receive would never allow them to become homeowners again in the current market or to pay for care they might need as they aged.

The Third Circuit Court of Appeals found that the Gardens' residents had sustained their initial burden of showing that the Township's redevelopment plan adversely discriminated against the plaintiffs based on race. After that decision and before the Supreme Court heard the case, the Gardens' residents and the Township came to an agreement on a new redevelopment proposal. As in the original, challenged plan, the new redevelopment plan includes commercial and residential units and creates economic development potential for the Township. In contrast to the original plan, however, it does not displace residents from the community, is cost neutral for residents, and allows all of the Gardens' older residents to age in place. Many of the oldest residents, some who have lived there since the community's founding during World War II, would certainly be looking at scattered nursing homes now had a showing of intent been required to challenge even such an overwhelmingly, wholesale discriminatory plan.

The Fair Housing Act is essential to ensuring that older Americans have the housing they need to live high-quality, independent, financially secure lives. Their continued ability to challenge policies that limit their full inclusion in the community without the necessity of proving intent must not be limited.

Notes

1. U.S. Department of the Treasury and U.S. Department of Housing and Urban Development, "Curbing Predatory Home Mortgage Lending," June 1, 2000, https://www.huduser.gov/portal/publications/hsgfin/curbing.html.
2. Cason v. Rochester Housing Authority 748 F. Supp. 100 (W.D.N.Y. 1990).

DISCUSSION 15

AFFIRMATIVELY FURTHERING FAIR HOUSING

HUD's New AFFH Rule: The Importance of the Ground Game

by Michael Allen

On July 13, 2015, the U.S. Department of Housing and Urban Development (HUD) promulgated a final rule on Affirmatively Furthering Fair Housing. Coming nearly six years after the groundbreaking *Westchester* litigation,[1] which exposed the county's flagrant violations of its civil rights obligations, many advocates expected HUD to adopt a "law enforcement" approach that would require state and local governments and public housing authorities to strictly comply with those obligations, on pain of losing their federal funds (which, in fiscal year 2015, amounted to more than $38 billion).[2]

What HUD produced is a final rule long on "carrots," but painfully short on "sticks." To compound that problem, HUD does not currently have—and is very unlikely to acquire—sufficient resources to police the compliance of 1,200 block-grant recipients and 3,400 public housing agencies. As a consequence, the promise of the Affirmatively Furthering Fair Housing (AFFH) mandate is likely to be realized only in communities where grassroots and legal advocates mobilize and create their own enforcement strategies. The success of the final rule will depend on this grassroots mobilization, on a community-by-community basis, all over the country. This means that advocates, collectively, need to step up to the plate and provide the tools and resources for a sustained "ground game."

When Congress passed the Fair Housing Act of 1968, it gave HUD the power to withhold, condition, or terminate federal funding to recipient state and local governments that engaged in discrimination or failed to "affirmatively further fair housing."[3] In its role as funder and regulator, HUD has what some federal courts have termed "immense leverage" to secure compliance with civil rights objectives.[4] This power is critical, because the Fair Housing Act does not give private litigants a right to enforce this obligation in court. As Judge Stephen Breyer noted nearly thirty years ago, this AFFH mandate "imposes . . . an obligation to do more than simply refrain from discriminating. . . . This broader goal [of truly open housing] . . . reflects the desire to have HUD use its grant programs to assist in ending discrimination and segregation, to the point where the supply of genuinely open housing increases."[5]

In part because HUD was a defendant in a number of AFFH cases early on,[6] and in part because of a general agency queasiness about withholding federal funds from local governments, HUD did not promulgate regulations until 1995.[7] Since then, as an explicit regulatory precondition to their eligibility for federal funds, recipients have been required to certify that they will comply with AFFH and other federal civil right laws.[8] Many have done so without a full understanding of what is required by these certifications, knowing that HUD would not challenge their validity. Many recipients simply ignored their civil rights certifications and continued to receive and spend billions of dollars in federal funds to build affordable housing in disadvantaged neighborhoods, where they faced less resistance and where families were often consigned to another generation of poverty, crime, and failing schools. We have made precious little progress in ending discrimination and segregation over the past five decades, in part because HUD has generally refrained from using its "immense leverage" to secure those objectives.[9]

While HUD's final rule plows some new ground, it does not revolutionize the field. The final rule sharpens a recipient's obligations to identify and overcome segregation-based impediments, but its overall tenor is one of collaboration rather than enforcement. In fact, although the final rule leaves in place HUD's powers to withdraw funding in the face of noncompliance,[10] HUD's media rollout of the final rule repeatedly emphasized that "enforcement is a last resort."[11]

On the positive side, the final rule makes explicit—for the first time—that every state and local government (and every public housing authority) that receives HUD funds must take "meaningful actions, in addition to combating discrimination, that overcome patterns of segregation and foster inclusive communities free from barriers that restrict access to opportunity based on protected characteristics."[12] Those actions must "address significant disparities in housing needs and in access to opportunity, replacing segregated living patterns with truly integrated and balanced living patterns, transforming racially and ethnically concentrated areas of poverty into areas of opportunity, and fostering and maintaining compliance with civil rights and fair housing laws."[13] Now, theoretically at least, every community that receives federal grants for housing and community development will be required to have an honest conversation about segregation and devise a local plan to dismantle it.

The final rule replaces the long-ignored Analysis of Impediments with a new framework—the Assessment of Fair Housing, or AFH—through which recipients must identify, analyze, and overcome barriers to fair housing choice, and ties it to other planning processes through which federal, state, and local resources are allocated. In other words, it creates a fair housing lens for all of a participant's decisions about housing and community development needs. Beginning in April 2016, HUD grant recipients must submit AFHs to HUD, which can reject noncompliant AFHs and impose a range of sanctions for noncompliance, up to and including withholding federal funds. As my firm has found since the *Westchester* decision, the prospect of losing federal funds because of civil rights noncompliance tends to bring recalcitrant recipients to the table, often more effectively than conventional civil rights litigation.[14]

The new framework requires greater reliance on data (which will be supplied by HUD), greater transparency and public participation in the development of the AFH, and greater accountability with respect to expanding housing choice. Most important, it will require recipients to initiate and follow through on jurisdiction-specific community conversations about race, segregation, and access to opportunity areas.

While the final rule is not what many of us had hoped for, it does provide a foundation on which civil rights advocates can build antisegregation campaigns at the local level. Local capacity building will require community education and organizing by fair housing advocacy organizations, financial support from the philanthropic sector, and lawyers prepared to bring enforcement actions.

My firm stands ready to do its part. Anyone else with me?

A Call to Action to Embrace and Enforce the AFFH Rule

by Angela Glover Blackwell

As a Black girl growing up in St. Louis in the 1950s and 1960s, I experienced segregation firsthand. Though segregation controlled where I could live, learn, play, and pray, I was fortunate enough to live in a mixed-income Black neighborhood, with a good school, safe streets, prospering Black-owned businesses, and civic engagement. Many other Black St. Louis residents were not as fortunate. Discrimination forced them into very poor segregated neighborhoods that were cut off from opportunity. My experience illustrates how, even in the face of adversity (in this case, the demoralizing, destructive policy of segregation), all communities have the potential to thrive if they have access to certain basic ingredients for opportunity.

Segregation has long been abandoned as official federal policy, but this has not been enough to create greater opportunity for most communities of color. Instead, the footprint of segregation—and the selective government disinvestment that persisted for decades—are painfully visible today. Most of the economically integrated Black neighborhoods of my childhood have disappeared, becoming areas of concentrated poverty. Today, a child born in primarily Black north St. Louis can expect to die sixteen years earlier than a child born in an affluent, predominantly White suburb just one zip code away. This startling disparity, though not uncommon in many American cities, is a testament to the depth of the problem, and the complexity of the solutions required to address it.

That is why the newly released AFFH rule is so important. It recognizes that successful housing policy cannot exist in a vacuum; it must be part of a larger vision for connecting residents to opportunity.

Overcoming decades of discriminatory policies and practices that created and perpetuated today's racial inequities requires housing policies that do more than seek to prevent ongoing segregation. We must also proactively counteract segregation's legacy by linking struggling communities to the basic resources— quality housing, good schools, healthy environments, living-wage jobs—that any community needs to thrive. The Fair Housing Act (FHA) of 1968 was written with this intention in mind, but has repeatedly fallen short. The arrival of the AFFH rule injects new awareness, tools, and momentum into fair housing policy—and it is crucial that the federal government use its full authority to embrace and enforce the rule.

Michael Allen's main contention is that this rule is "long on 'carrots,' but painfully short on 'sticks,'" necessitating grassroots mobilization on a community-by-community basis to police the rule locally, where HUD will likely lack the resources to do so itself. As a result, the new rule, in Allen's words, leans toward "collaboration rather than enforcement" and "plows new ground . . . but does not revolutionize the field."

While Allen is undoubtedly right that HUD's willingness to enforce this new rule will be crucial to its success, the power of the spirit of collaboration should not be underestimated. The "stick," while necessary, is not sufficient for enacting meaningful change if it is wielded without collaboration with local leaders and communities. Moreover, while the mere existence of the rule may not revolutionize housing practice, the tools it provides to local leaders—the Assessment of Fair Housing and the local, disaggregated data—have immense potential to revolutionize those leaders' ability to push for equity in housing, transportation, education, and other areas of community life. Without HUD as a careful watchdog, the AFFH rule may fail to reform housing practice among reticent grantees (and civil rights litigation will likely play a key role here), but for the rising generation of local leaders who are eager to address inequity in their jurisdictions, this rule can be a game changer.

I have seen firsthand the potential of a collaborative AFFH process play out in rural towns, midsize and large cities, and tribal reservations across the country. In the five years preceding the release of the AFFH rule, my organization worked with HUD and seventy-four regions to test out the assessment and data tools that have now been incorporated into the final rule. As under the current rule, local leaders and advocates were provided with tools to measure which neighborhoods lacked key resources (proximity to transit, good schools, job opportunities, clean air, etc.) and a framework through which these findings could be incorporated into city planning processes. In Seattle, this translated into a new regional food-distribution hub in the Rainier Valley to bring new jobs and healthy-food access to neighborhoods where both were lacking. In New Orleans, the framework resulted in public-transit service hours that would better meet the needs of lower-income shift workers in the health-care and hospitality industries.

In these and other jurisdictions, the AFFH pilot served as the catalyst that spurred the assessments, discussion, and convening of local stakeholders. But the outcomes were only possible because of ongoing collaboration between local government, community leaders, private-sector partners, and intermediaries, such as nonprofits, local universities, and infrastructure agencies. While the AFFH rule requires that grantees take "meaningful actions . . . [to] foster inclusive communities," it will always be these local partners, working in concert with HUD grantees, who help determine the nature of that meaningful action and provide the energy and dedication to put it in place.

Having watched these collaborations play out throughout the country, I am filled with hope that the next fifty years of the Fair Housing Act, fueled by this new rule, will be revolutionary. Allen is not wrong to point out that the United States has made "precious little progress in ending discrimination" since 1968, but the AFFH rule is also being launched at a moment of great demographic, political, and economic change for America. In the 1960s, America was 15 percent people of color. Today it is 37 percent, and a majority of children under five are of color. While the Fair Housing Act was born of a moral obligation to end discrimination, the AFFH rule arrives at a time when the United States can no longer ignore the economic imperative that accompanies the moral one. So long as people of color are a growing share of the workforce and population, America's ability to build towns, cities, and regions where all children can reach their full potential will be a direct determinant of the success and prosperity of the entire nation. The AFFH rule is a crucial lever that advocates, local government, philanthropists, and the private sector can pull to make that vision a reality. That is why my organization's response to Allen's call "Is anyone else with me?" is a resounding, enthusiastic "Yes!"

The Need for a Balanced Approach to Fair Housing

by Michael Bodaken and Ellen Lurie Hoffman

We appreciate Michael Allen's thoughts on the need for local organizing, education, and capacity building to ensure that the U.S. Department of Housing and Urban Development's (HUD) Affirmatively Furthering Fair Housing (AFFH) rule is implemented and enforced appropriately. We agree that local communities should identify barriers to fair housing and devise strategies to ensure that all residents can choose the housing that is best for themselves and their families.

Like Allen, we welcomed the Supreme Court's milestone ruling upholding the use of disparate impact as a legal argument in fair housing cases and HUD's release of the AFFH rule to help communities meet fair housing obligations. The National Housing Trust (NHT) works in partnership with civil rights organizations to support and protect fair housing laws. In the summer of 2015, we joined other advocates in opposing attempts in Congress to block funding necessary to implement the AFFH rule, and we will continue to urge Congress to fully fund its implementation.

As we reflect upon Allen's comments about enforcing the AFFH rule, we urge careful consideration of precisely what we are enforcing. Many fair housing advocates promote mobility policies to help low-income minorities move out of inner cities and resettle in more affluent suburban communities. Mobility strategies are an indispensable tool for providing opportunity, but they are not sufficient to meet the needs of all residents of distressed urban communities. Not all of these families can be relocated to affluent communities, and many would prefer not to leave their neighborhoods. We favor a "mobility plus" strategy, providing residents the choice to move while also working with other residents to transform distressed urban neighborhoods into diverse, high-opportunity communities with access to transit and jobs.

We believe preserving affordable housing is the obvious first step to addressing our nation's affordable rental housing crisis. For every new affordable apartment created, two are lost to deterioration, abandonment, or conversion to more expensive housing. Without preserving existing affordable housing, we fall two steps back for every step we take forward. In distressed neighborhoods, preserving affordable housing can catalyze the revitalization of an entire community. Saving decent, affordable housing means saving a critical community asset. It also signals the reversal of years of neglect and disinvestment and can spark the public-private investment that is essential for community revitalization.

Both the Supreme Court decision and HUD's AFFH rule uphold a "balanced approach" to fair housing, which embraces both mobility strategies and housing preservation and community revitalization. Indeed, HUD's AFFH final rule specifically embraces "a balanced approach to fair housing." The rule highlights the value of preserving affordable housing in "high poverty" neighborhoods: "HUD's rule recognizes the role of place-based strategies, including economic development to improve conditions in high poverty neighborhoods, as well as preservation of the existing affordable housing stock, including HUD-assisted housing, to help respond to the overwhelming need for affordable housing." The rule also provides, "A program participant's strategies and actions . . . may include various activities . . . including . . . targeted investment in neighborhood revitalization or stabilization; preservation or rehabilitation of existing affordable housing; promoting greater housing choice within or outside of areas of concentrated poverty and greater access to areas of high opportunity; and improving community assets such as quality schools, employment, and transportation."

NHT has worked for decades to renovate and preserve existing affordable rental homes so that low-income families can live in integrated neighborhoods with access to opportunities. In wealthier suburbs or high-cost cities, we protect affordable housing that is at risk of losing its affordability because of gentrification. Thus, in Washington, D.C., we worked with low-income tenants in an affluent area to preserve their homes near million-dollar condos.

In other instances, we have engaged with residents, local governments, and community-based organizations to preserve affordable housing and invest in neighborhoods that have experienced disinvestment and neglect. Our investments have helped to maintain long-term affordability for affordable properties, improved the energy efficiency and safety of these buildings, and created a healthier environment for low-income residents. We have developed after-school tutoring programs for resident children, built on-site computer labs to allow parents to improve their technological literacy and pursue education and job training, and planted gardens to allow residents to grow and enjoy healthy food.

Instead of abandoning the communities where low-income families live, we strive to transform them into areas of opportunity. These communities have value, and as fair housing advocates, we cannot simply promote efforts to move people out. Many residents want to remain in their neighborhoods. NHT is dedicated to preserving their affordable homes and thereby helping to improve the communities in which they exist.

We strongly support distributing federal resources in a manner that allows low-income people to make housing choices that are best for themselves and their families, to increase their access to opportunity. Federal, state, and local governments agree with this balanced approach to housing investment.

Let's create effective solutions together.

The Right Target for Fair Housing Advocacy

by Edward Goetz

Michael Allen calls for a sustained "ground game" in which advocates across the country "mobilize and create their own enforcement strategies" to leverage HUD's new rule on Affirmatively Furthering Fair Housing (AFFH). His own actions have led the way in showing what that ground game can look like. Those interested in racial equity in housing owe a debt of gratitude to Allen and his firm for the work they did in producing the *Westchester County* settlement. Jurisdictions that conspire, through a combination of land-use controls and investment decisions, to exclude affordable housing and thereby exclude the populations dependent on that housing should, as Allen argues, find themselves in jeopardy of losing federal funding.

I, too, would like to see the fair housing movement incorporate more grassroots activism. It is important, however, to choose the right targets. Fair housing advocacy is best directed against intransigent communities that continue to exclude affordable housing or people of color, pressing for greater housing opportunities where they do not currently exist.

Fair housing goals are ill served by instead challenging central-city revitalization efforts and community development activities. Some of Allen's own advocacy has made this mistake, including his complaints against the cities of Minneapolis and Saint Paul (see, for example, *Metropolitan Interfaith Coalition on Affordable Housing (MICAH) v. City of Minneapolis*, and *MICAH v. City of St. Paul*). Efforts to reduce the public resources going to poor and predominantly minority neighborhoods are counterproductive. Even if those challenges are successful on their own merits, they do nothing to get housing built in exclusionary communities where it is needed. Denying affordable housing in neighborhoods that are deemed to have "too much" of it already in no way compels exclusionary communities to change their practices. Some may think that they can find support for such an approach in HUD's recent AFFH rule or in the Supreme Court's 2015 decision in *Texas Department of Housing and Community Affairs v. The Inclusive Communities Project, Inc.*, but both of these acknowledge the legitimate place of community development initiatives that direct investment to low-income neighborhoods and to communities of color.

Segregation by income in this country is greatest at the high end of the income distribution, and racial isolation is greatest among whites.

The grassroots activism Allen urges should be the sustained advocacy necessary to create opportunities for affordable housing in high-income, predominantly white, exclusionary communities. Let's hope that is where the movement focuses.

Notes

1. "In the face of the clear legislative purpose of the Fair Housing Act, enacted pursuant to Congress's power under the Thirteenth Amendment as Title VIII of the Civil Rights Act of 1968, to combat racial segregation and discrimination in housing, an interpretation of 'affirmatively further fair housing' that excludes consideration of race would be an absurd result." United States ex rel. Anti-Discrimination Center v. Westchester County, New York, 495 F.Supp.2d 375, 387–88 (S.D.N.Y. 2007). "[T]he central goal of the obligation to AFFH [is] to end housing discrimination and segregation." United States ex rel. Anti-Discrimination Center v. Westchester County, New York, 668 F.Supp.2d 548, 564 (S.D.N.Y. 2009). The author was cocounsel for the plaintiff-relator in the *Westchester* litigation.
2. HUD's final appropriations for FY 2015 provided approximately $4.5 billion in HUD block-grant funding for state and local governments and $33.5 billion in public housing and rental-assistance funding to public housing authorities and similar agencies.
3. See 42 U.S.C. §3608(e)(5). See also 42 U.S.C. §§5304(b)(2), 5306(d)(7)(B)(Housing and Community Development Act of 1974, as amended); 42 U.S.C. §12705(b)(15) (consolidated planning); 42 U.S.C. §1437C-1(d)(16) (public housing). HUD has promulgated regulations implementing the AFFH requirements for entities receiving block-grant and public housing funds. See 24 C.F.R. §§570.602; 91.225, 91.325, 91.425, 903.7(o).
4. NAACP v. Sec'y of Housing and Urban Development, 817 F.2d 149, 156 (1st Cir. 1987).
5. NAACP v. Sec'y of Housing and Urban Development, 817 F.2d 149, 155 (1st Cir. 1987).
6. See, for example, NAACP v. Sec'y of Housing and Urban Development, 817 F.2d 149, 155 (1st Cir. 1987).
7. 60 Fed. Reg. 1896 ff. (January 5, 1995).
8. These include Title VI of the Civil Rights Act of 1964, Section 504 of the Rehabilitation Act of 1973, and Section 109 of the Housing and Community Development Act of 1974.
9. To be fair, whether through the phenomenon of "industry capture" or because of a political reluctance to disrupt funding to state and local governments, most federal agencies have had a poor record of using funding leverage to secure such objectives. See, for example, Eloise Pasachoff, "Agency Enforcement of Spending Clause Statutes: A Defense of the Funding Cut-Off," *Yale Law Journal* 124, no. 2 (November 2014): 248–335; Olatunde C. A. Johnson, "Beyond the Private Attorney General: Equality Directives in American Law," *NYU Law Review* 87, no. 5 (November 2012): 1339–1413. As this article was going to press, the Second Circuit affirmed HUD's authority, pursuant to the "old" AFFH regulations—24 C.F.R. § 91.500(b)—to withhold block-grant funds because Westchester County's AFFH certification was "inaccurate" and without supporting evidence. Cty. of Westchester v. U.S. Dep't of Hous. & Urban Dev., 802 F.3d 413, 435 (2d Cir. 2015).
10. See, for example, 24 C.F.R. §§91.500(b) (HUD approval action); 570.304 (making of grants); 570.485(c) (making of grants); 570.601 and 570.602 (civil rights certification requirements); 570.904 (equal opportunity and fair housing review criteria); 570.910–570.913 (corrective and remedial actions).

11. *PBS NewsHour*, July 9, 2015, accessed August 20, 2015, http://www.pbs.org/newshour/bb/new-rules-require-cities-fight-housing-segregation/.
12. 24 C.F.R. §5.152 (definition of "Affirmatively furthering fair housing").
13. 24 C.F.R. §5.152.
14. See, for example, Conciliation Agreement between Texas Low Income Housing Information Service et al. and the State of Texas, May 25, 2010, http://www.relmanlaw.com/docs/Texas-AFFH-Final-Conciliation-Agreement-signed-by-HUD.pdf (resolution governing $1.7 billion in disaster-relief funding); Conciliation Agreement between Latino Action Network et al. and the State of New Jersey, May 30, 2014, http://www.relmanlaw.com/docs/New-Jersey-Conciliation-Agreement-signed-5-30-2014.pdf.

BALANCING INVESTMENTS IN PEOPLE AND PLACE

Creating Opportunity for Minority and Low-Income Families

by Raphael Bostic and Sheryl Verlaine Whitney

The election of an African American president notwithstanding, American society continues to have significant sensitivities about race and class. The lack of venues to openly, honestly, and safely face and wrestle with these concerns allows them to float under the radar screen. As a consequence, our workplaces and social circles have embedded messages about race and class that can create tension, distrust, and suspicion. These undercurrents make finding effective solutions when problems arise difficult and complex. Mary Pattillo's essay on integration in this volume makes the point clearly. Depending on your vantage point, your perception of race, class, power, and opportunity can differ substantially—meaning that what one person believes is a good action or policy might be viewed as less rosy, or even detrimental, by another person.

It is against this backdrop that we are trying to craft public policies to improve the conditions of poor and minority families and communities. Advocates hold very different perspectives on the best way to achieve the shared goal of increased access to opportunity and a better quality of life. And the debates can get quite fierce. For this reason, the pursuit of equitable community development took more of Raphael's attention than anything else while he was assistant secretary of policy development and research at HUD and remains an issue of deep personal concern and commitment for both of us.

Many of those advocating for increasing access to opportunity can be roughly divided into two groups offering different perspectives. Those who focus on the negative effects of racially concentrated poverty emphasize the need to support housing mobility, making it possible for residents to leave segregated neighborhoods with high concentrations of poverty and move to communities with greater economic and institutional resources. Those who focus on the negative effects of economic isolation emphasize place-based investments that can improve the built environment, social institutions, and the economic growth of urban neighborhoods.

So why is this an argument, when the "obvious" answer is to do both? There are many reasons why this conversation continues. We will touch on a few of the biggest ones. The first is a lack of consensus on what success should look like and what the priority should be. One camp argues that racial segregation is the primary problem and that decreasing segregation should carry the greatest weight in assessing local actions. The other, alternative view holds that improving the conditions in poor, largely minority, isolated neighborhoods is critical—at least as important as the goal of reducing segregation. This view emerges in part from the serious concerns about improving conditions in slums, which has historically been the driver of housing policy in the United States. The ongoing debate is in part a debate about which of these goals should hold more sway.

This lack of a unified definition of success is closely related to a second issue, which is a perception that current federal housing programs give virtually no attention to segregation concerns. Take the low-income housing tax credit program, for example, which is the largest federal affordable housing program. Many low-income housing tax credit (LIHTC) developments are located in poor, isolated, minority neighborhoods, and the program actually gives bonuses for developments located in such areas. There are no comparable bonuses for projects sited in more affluent areas in which few minorities reside. The imbalance—some would call it a bias—is clear. And some argue that this bias is a key reason why meaningful change on the issue of segregation does not occur. The status quo is merely perpetuated. Yet those who support investing in communities rarely face or embrace such arguments. This is a source of additional tension.

These are technical issues involving the nuts and bolts of program design and implementation, but other challenges are also important, perhaps even more important. Primary among these is that these discussions are about more than race and class. Culture is very much present. We are strengthened, nurtured, and comforted within our community context. This is the blessing of multiculturalism, but also its curse. On our good days, we see other traditions as valuable and interesting; on our bad days, they are a source of suspicion and mistrust. We have seen many conversations shut down as people around the table are overcome by visceral reactions to feelings that their culture, experiences, and voice are being disrespected or disregarded.

Language and perception are significant hurdles. Many residents of poor, impoverished neighborhoods hear in the antisegregation emphasis on housing mobility an implied statement that they are the problem and that they and their communities have limited or no value. Having to move involves significant costs for the families that have to make the transition, and many feel that these costs have not been adequately recognized or appreciated. Underlying this is a question: if poor minority families are bearing much, if not most, of the cost, are we not saying that they are the problem? We must confess that we were shocked the first time we heard a fair housing advocate describe a minority neighborhood with concentrated poverty as being "impacted," suggesting implicitly that the presence of poor minority families is a malady to be treated and eliminated. To many, this smacks of blaming the victim, and it heightens tensions.

To be clear, though, this issue is about more than just language. There remain serious questions about whether the proposed policy remedy is the right one. It was striking that many participants in the Moving to Opportunity program did not stay in the "opportunity neighborhoods" to which their vouchers gave them access, but instead ultimately settled in neighborhoods that were physically closer to their existing networks and only slightly better than their old neighborhoods along key dimensions such as poverty rate and school performance. In thinking about mobility programs, perhaps more attention needs to be given to the value of "neighborhood," the social networks and institutions that communities have formed over time, and how this should be incorporated into program design.

A final reason why arguments persist in this area is the feeling that we are living in a zero-sum game. There are not enough resources, so any hint that some might be diverted to another use must be resisted vehemently. Consider again the tax credit program. In California, credits are already heavily oversubscribed under the framework that currently exists. If one were to broaden the scope of eligible projects, a difficult situation would become even more dire. And do we have to mention the community development block-grant program, whose funding has been cut by more than 25 percent in the past three years? Resource availability is a real issue.

All of these legitimate reasons notwithstanding, we can't help but think that there should be a way to reconcile these two different approaches, both of which ultimately share the same goal of furthering opportunities and reducing economic and racial inequality. We are hopeful that HUD's "Affirmatively Further Fair Housing" (AFFH) rule may become a template that helps advance the ball. But practitioners and advocates in the field must get on board. Otherwise, we think the prospects for meaningful collaboration and coordination remain bleak. There have been some very good efforts, but more is needed—much more.

Holistic Place-Based Investments

by Nancy O. Andrews and Dan Rinzler

"A child's course in life should be determined not by the zip code she's born in, but by the strength of her work ethic and the scope of her dreams."

—Barack Obama

When President Obama invoked the ideal of an equal playing field in his remarks on the fiftieth anniversary of the War on Poverty, he also underscored the powerful role that neighborhoods continue to play in brokering Americans' life chances. Even as our everyday existence has become increasingly networked through advances in technology, our home addresses still largely determine our educational opportunities, employment prospects, and chances at good health.

Not all neighborhoods provide the same supports, and place-based resource disparities play a major role in perpetuating inequality in the United States. Plenty of research over the past few decades has detailed the damaging effects of concentrated poverty, as well as the central role of racial discrimination in perpetuating harmful, multigenerational exposure to localized risks such as violence and other sources of stress and trauma. All too often, the people who live in places of concentrated poverty have never had any other real options—they are stuck there, without much choice.[1]

This uneven playing field persists five decades after the passage of the Fair Housing Act. Even as the landscape of opportunity across metropolitan areas is shifting, many pockets of urban concentrated poverty remain, and new ones are developing in suburbs.[2] Nearly half of all African American children live in neighborhoods with poverty rates over 30 percent,[3] and around one-fifth of all Americans live in areas with very limited access to good jobs, quality housing, a clean environment, healthy food, and opportunities for physical activity.[4]

These challenges merit a comprehensive policy response that leverages the power of places in shaping access to opportunity and exposure to risk. Our strategies must also confront the racial history underlying patterns of neighborhood disadvantage, and adapt to the particular needs of vulnerable populations that have experienced long stretches of entrenched poverty.

Place-based investments should continue to be a central component of this policy response. Altering the landscape of where people live is only part of the equation—the other part is changing the landscape itself.

Mobility strategies that expand access to high-opportunity areas for low-income families and racial minorities are important and deserve our support.

But even if efforts to expand low-income people's housing "choice sets" are wildly successful, most people will still remain in relatively poorer areas for the foreseeable future because of both supply- and demand-side barriers, as well as personal preferences. Allowing such deep neighborhood resource disparities to persist is unsustainable, both from a moral standpoint and in light of the social and economic downsides of underinvesting in human and physical capital.

In sum, both approaches are needed in different places and at different times. The community development field will amplify its impact by recognizing the vital role played by mobility strategies and making common cause with human capital programs (long believed to be outside our purview). But it also must continue to identify and invest in the most effective place-based strategies. This is no easy task, but to do less is to shy away from the mission that led us to our practice in the first place. We are morally obligated to face up to the complexity required to truly change lives and futures. Luckily, some themes have emerged that can help us find the way forward.

For example, we have learned that "mono-line" strategies—such as building affordable housing or increasing access to fresh food—are important building blocks, but are not enough to make a significant positive impact in low-income communities if pursued in isolation. This is especially true for the most vulnerable populations that have endured successive generations of neighborhood disadvantage, and who face a range of challenges that extend beyond a single area for potential investment.

Instead, current best practices emphasize comprehensive approaches that combine and coordinate sustained, long-term investments in multiple areas— such as affordable housing, early childhood education, quality schools, access to primary medical care, and a range of social supports—and track progress toward common goals over time, adjusting course when necessary. Organizing efforts that build power and self-direction among residents are also critical during both design and implementation stages.

When capable systems integrators or "quarterbacks" have led these integrated approaches, the results have been impressive. Examples include the East Lake Foundation's transformation of the East Lake neighborhood in Atlanta and Neighborhood Centers, Inc.'s efforts across the Houston metropolitan area. Funders have also begun to adapt to silo-busting efforts on the ground. At the federal level, the Sustainable Communities Program and Promise Zones are two examples of the kind of interdepartmental, cross-sectoral collaboration that is needed from the public sector to support integrated strategies. More of these kinds of funder-level adjustments would be welcome.

We would also argue that the most advanced place-based investments are actually place-conscious, to use a term and framework advanced by Margery Turner and other scholars at the Urban Institute.[5] While focusing investments in a specific location, place-conscious strategies also leverage opportunities and partners outside the physical neighborhood—such as regional economic development strategies, or efforts to expand the geographic range of subsidized housing stock—as well as plan for how the area might evolve over time. Our organization's work around regionally scaled, equitable transit-oriented development is one example of how this framework can be implemented.

In response to Raphael Bostic and Sheryl Whitney's eloquent prompt, it is worth noting here that mobility practitioners focused on expanding housing choices have actually gone through some of the same learning processes as the place-based community developers we have described. For example, they have come to realize the importance of substantial service components—and also that positive impacts on vulnerable people's lives require sustained investment over time, and can take many years to take hold. The same is true of investments in places.

In fact, the higher-performing mobility programs currently in operation are by definition comprehensive and place-conscious. They leverage multiple place-based benefits, such as high-performing schools and safe streets, but also seek to help families align a range of needs across multiple locations and institutions, such as accessing work and child care.

It turns out that people- and place-based strategies aren't so different after all—and that each, at this point, is probably misnamed as such. Going forward, the field should frame them as complementary elements of a broader policy response to combat neighborhood disadvantage. The constrained fiscal and political environment around our work should motivate us to at least entertain the idea of joining forces.

A Case for Choice: Looking at Connecticut

by Erin Boggs

Raphael Bostic and Sheryl Verlaine Whitney provide a broad overview of the challenges facing efforts to improve life chances for low-income and minority populations. Connecticut offers an important real-world example of these challenges.

By a number of different measures, Connecticut is one of the most ethnically, racially, and economically segregated states in the country. Segregation has created neighborhood environments that are starkly different in terms of school quality, public safety, and job access, just to name a few. As assessed by the Kirwan Institute, 81 percent of Blacks and 79 percent of Latinos live in lower-opportunity areas, compared to 25 percent of Whites and 44 percent of Asians.[6]

Affordable subsidized housing, which could potentially provide access to higher-opportunity neighborhoods, is simply not available at sufficient levels

Table 16.1 Connecticut LIHTC by race, poverty, and R/ECAP (By tract)

Demographic served	Total units	Units in dispropor-tionately minority areas	Units in high-poverty areas	Units in R/ECAP
All	20,018	73%	73%	40%
Family	13,560	76%	76%	37%
Elderly	4,740	58%	55%	36%
Supportive	734	96%	96%	63%

in areas where schools are thriving and streets are safe. Only 31 out of Connecticut's 169 towns have at least 10 percent affordable housing as defined by state law.[7] Other factors, such as the incentive structure of the housing choice voucher program, also severely limit housing choice.

The location of units created with the assistance of the low-income housing tax credit (LIHTC; see table 16.1) is typical of patterns in other forms of subsidized housing that we see in Connecticut, where upwards of 70 percent of government housing subsidy program units are located in the 6 percent of the state that is minority-concentrated. Likewise, 40 percent of LIHTC units are in the 1 percent of the state that qualifies as racially/ethnically concentrated areas of poverty (R/ECAPs) as defined by HUD, again similar to patterns in other housing programs.

Many interests, including well-intentioned efforts to revive struggling neighborhoods and blatant efforts to keep low-income people and people of color out of thriving suburban communities, converged to generate development after development in areas of minority and poverty concentration, which in turn deepened minority and poverty concentration. It is striking that in the Hartford region, every single area that was redlined by the government in 1937 is a very low opportunity area today.

We can debate what the proper balance is for high- versus low-opportunity area housing subsidy placement, but clearly we are far from striking that balance now. In crafting a solution, we must work to undo the decades of policies that created deep imbalance in the distribution of opportunity. Fair housing advocates strongly support investment in and improvement of neighborhoods harmed by histories of disinvestment. What we object to is the continuing disproportionate placement of low-income housing units in such neighborhoods, which perpetuates segregation, further concentrates poverty, undermines community reinvestment, and deprives families of the opportunity to choose housing in lower-poverty areas.

Some people have argued that many families might choose to remain in more racially, ethnically, and poverty concentrated areas. I wholeheartedly agree that this should be an option. What is missing, however, is the ability for low-income families of color to have any kind of real choice between staying and moving to a neighborhood that is less concentrated—and many families desperately want to make such moves. In 2012, Stefanie DeLuca of Johns Hopkins and I gathered together housing choice voucher holders in Connecticut to discuss housing choices. Two things were apparent from these discussions: Many people wanted to move but could not. Primary motivating factors for moving were fear for children's health and safety and the desire for a quality education. And there was clear consensus, even among people who did not want to move, that there should, at an absolute minimum, be a choice.

So how do we address these concerns, along with others like preserving hard units of subsidized housing and revitalizing struggling areas?

1. **Understanding Connections:** One initial step is to understand that these goals of revitalizing struggling areas and fostering access to opportunity are connected. Unless we plan, build, and design programs with choice as the centerpiece, we will continue to invest in struggling areas in a manner that, at best, fails to produce serious life improvements or, at worst, displaces people only to reconstitute areas of poverty concentration elsewhere. By setting the stage for voluntary poverty deconcentration, we will allow our revitalization efforts to convert lower-opportunity areas into areas with greater access to resources critical to success in life. In this sense, the solution is not a zero-sum game—it is simply a smart strategy. Consider again the redlining/opportunity map of Hartford. While millions of dollars have been invested in failed efforts to "revitalize" Hartford since 1937, no serious money has been spent to create housing choice. Hartford remains the fourth poorest city in the country. It needs investment and community development that goes beyond subsidized housing.

2. **Let's Get on the Same Page and Advocate Together:** Another crucial point to recognize is that much of the challenge is rooted in an overall lack of affordable housing. Many heroes in the housing movement have dedicated their lives to finding the funding necessary to address this critical need, yet the shortage of affordable housing continues to grow. The more advocates can come to some consensus on the issue of choice, the more we can move on together to push for more housing resources. It is important to also recognize that a portion (although certainly not all) of the need for affordable housing is generated by exclusionary zoning and other restrictive policies that have blocked the creation of affordable housing in higher-opportunity areas.

3. **Learning from Each Other:** My experience as part of a Sustainable Communities Initiative grant in the Hartford region made it clear to me that there is a lot that affordable housing proponents, town and regional planners, developers, and fair housing advocates can learn from each other. Fair housing advocates need to understand the dire housing need, cost considerations,

transportation factors, and political considerations that drive where housing is currently placed in order to either challenge underlying assumptions or craft better solutions that meet both the needs of partners and fair housing policy priorities. For example, here in Connecticut, some of the resistance to higher-opportunity housing was coming from stakeholders who believed there were no employment opportunities in the suburbs. By analyzing data on job trends, fair housing advocates were able to demonstrate that, in many areas, jobs were growing only in higher-opportunity suburbs. Thus, higher-opportunity affordable housing would actually bring low-income families closer to jobs. As another example, conversations with developers revealed how insurmountable zoning barriers are in some towns, prompting exploration of ways to create higher-opportunity affordable housing that can fit even highly restrictive zoning regimes (such as the purchase of scattered site properties).

4.   **It Takes a Movement and Legal Advocacy:** Politics matter. Those of us who care about fair housing and housing choice must continue to improve how we present the data, information, and personal stories so as to help policy makers and the general public understand that housing is not just a roof and four walls but a significant driver of life outcomes, primarily because of its location. Through making these links, we will gain greater support, not just for more affordable housing, but for more equitably located affordable housing. That said, when education and advocacy efforts are insufficient, we must be prepared to bring legal action. In many parts of the country, it is people who are in the minority racially or ethnically who experience the most negative effects of imbalanced housing policy. The fair housing laws that are intended to prevent this de facto violation of civil rights must remain a sharp and ready tool in our toolbox.

Prepare for Divergent Metropolitan Futures

by Rolf Pendall

As Raphael Bostic and Sheryl Verlaine Whitney note, fair housing and community development interests don't always align. It's true in advocacy, in academia, and even within government. After a cogent description of these tensions and a reasonable explanation for why they persist, Bostic and Whitney close with optimism: "There should be a way to reconcile these two different approaches." What might that way be?

In practice, the answer depends on context, as U.S. regions are on divergent trajectories. Across the Great Lakes region, one city after another has lost thousands of people over the past twenty years—especially people in their twenties and thirties, who have moved not just to Great Lakes suburbs but to other parts of the nation as well. On net, many of the region's metropolitan areas have already lost population, and these losses will accelerate as mortality begins to claim large numbers of baby boomers, unless economic rebirth does more than just slow outmigration. The result may already be emerging as a "generational housing bubble," as Dowell Myers and SungHo Ryu have called it.[8] In regions facing this generational reorientation of their housing markets, the main housing problem is not high housing prices—the existing stock costs much less to buy than it does to build—but a housing surplus. Even as housing demand has waned, housing supply has grown. For every household Michigan added between 2000 and 2010, its communities issued more than four residential building permits for new construction.

Efforts to rebuild old neighborhoods are likely to fail for both fair housing and community development if this overbuilding does not stop. To shore up community development efforts, cities will need to demolish abandoned, obsolete, and unwanted housing to balance demand and supply, even if new construction at the fringe is controlled. It would take monumental, regionally coordinated initiatives to balance housing supply and demand to the extent that large numbers of white households would move into predominantly African American neighborhoods. Considering the implausibility of such initiatives, fair housing goals will need to be met through housing measures (e.g., tenant-based assistance) and transportation mechanisms (e.g., affordable and reliable access to automobiles) that will allow low-income African Americans to move to higher-opportunity neighborhoods. Additional efforts also need to build the capacity of the workforce to move into jobs being vacated by retiring baby boomers and to reorient and stabilize regional economic bases.

Other regions, however, are still growing fast; depending on immigration reform and economic recovery, we could grow by another 50 million people by the 2030s even as the boomers pass away. As my colleague Margery Austin Turner and I have written, just fifteen large and diverse regions accounted for three-quarters of the nation's growth in people under twenty years old between 2000 and 2010. This growth is already transforming formerly white/black regions into complex multiracial areas in which cities and suburbs alike are increasingly diverse. Community development in these contexts needs to take a "both-and" approach. The prospect of millions of new residents represents a dramatic opportunity to meet both fair housing and community development goals in fast-growth regions like Houston, Dallas, Atlanta, Charlotte, Raleigh, and Austin. Cities, states, and the federal government can enact policies and make investments to encourage community development that refreshes older, affordable neighborhoods for new generations, taking pains to ensure their continued affordability as their favorable position in sprawling regions makes them more valued locations. They can ensure the construction of new neighborhoods and districts with mixed land uses and housing types, with housing affordability built in from the start. Efforts to ensure affordable and reliable car access can play a critical role in meeting community development and fair housing goals in these regions too.

Regardless of the regional context, our policies for community development and fair housing need to be reoriented so that they anticipate the future. Too often, we make policy through a foggy rearview mirror rather than using data and wisdom to look out the windshield to how our regions, cities, and neighborhoods are likely to change in the coming decades. We can already see the territory we're entering, one in which metropolitan areas are growing more diverse and aging, thanks to projects like PolicyLink's National Equity Atlas, the Brookings Institution's Metropolitan Revolution and Diversity Explosion, and the Urban Institute's Mapping America's Futures. Using such tools, policy makers, researchers, and the public will be able to take that longer-term future view and develop fresh approaches that justify Bostic and Whitney's optimism.

Notes

1. Patrick Sharkey, *Stuck in Place: Urban Neighborhoods and the End of Progress Toward Racial Equality* (Chicago: University of Chicago Press, 2013).
2. Elizabeth Kneebone and Alan Berube, *Confronting Suburban Poverty in America* (Washington, DC: Brookings Institution Press, 2013).
3. Annie E. Casey Foundation, "Data Snapshot on High-Poverty Communities," February 1, 2012, http://www.aecf.org/resources/data-snapshot-on-high-poverty-communities/.
4. Elaine Arkin et al., "Time to Act: Investing in the Health of Our Children and Communities," Robert Wood Johnson Foundation, January 2014, http://community-wealth.org/content/time-act-investing-health-our-children-and-communities.
5. Margery Austin Turner et al., "Tackling Persistent Poverty in Distressed Urban Neighborhoods," Urban Institute, July 11, 2014, https://www.urban.org/research/publication/tackling-persistent-poverty-distressed-urban-neighborhoods.
6. The Kirwan Institute assessed eleven data points to assign each census tract in Connecticut to one of five opportunity levels. These data points reflect neighborhood qualities that lead to success in life and include educational indicators (math and reading scores and educational attainment), economic indicators (unemployment rates, percent of people on public assistance, percentage job increase, mean commute time), and neighborhood/housing quality indicators (neighborhood vacancy rate, crime rate, homeownership rate, poverty rate). Kirwan Institute, "People, Place and Opportunity: Mapping Access to Opportunity in Connecticut," November 2009, http://www.kirwaninstitute.osu.edu/reports/2009/11_2009_CTOppMapping_FullReport.pdf.
7. Connecticut General Statute Section 8-30g, the Affordable Housing Appeals Act, creates a builder's remedy for proposals to build housing with at least 30 percent affordable units that are rejected by towns with less than 10 percent affordable units. Under the Act, housing that is counted toward the 10 percent exemption includes any housing created with government assistance, housing occupied by people qualifying for and using

government housing assistance, housing purchased with the help of a state-financed mortgage, housing that is deed-restricted for people earning 80 percent of median income or less paying 30 percent or less of their income toward rent, and similarly deed-restricted mobile homes and accessory apartments.

8. Dowell Myers and SungHo Ryu, "Aging Baby Boomers and the Generational Housing Bubble: Foresight and Mitigation of an Epic Transition," *Journal of the American Planning Association* 74, no. 1 (January 2008): 17–33, https://doi.org/10.1080/01944360701802006.

DISCUSSION 17

ADDRESSING NEIGHBORHOOD DISINVESTMENT

Move Up or Out? Confronting Compounded Deprivation

by Robert J. Sampson

The sharp neighborhood divide in American society has been under an intense spotlight lately, prominent in stories of the police use of deadly force and high rates of incarceration in black communities, the loss of middle-class neighborhoods while poor and "1-percent" neighborhoods increase, and the fact that upward economic mobility depends in no small part on where one grows up. Many pundits have professed surprise at the magnitude of spatial inequality in our nation's cities.

But we should not be surprised or feign surprise. Spatial inequality has a long history in America, and a rich vein of research foretold the current state of affairs.[1] We know, for example, that poor neighborhoods have long been disproportionately subjected to institutional disinvestment, violence, joblessness, criminal-justice sanctions, poor health, underperforming schools, and other forms of disadvantage—what we have conceptualized as "compounded deprivation."[2] Not only is inequality spatially organized and compounded, but there is mounting evidence that prolonged exposure to concentrated disadvantage undermines early child development, which in turn predicts later critical outcomes like the formation of human capital skills, involvement in crime, and general health and well-being.

Much attention was drawn recently to a major study showing that neighborhoods also serve as an important platform for long-term economic mobility.[3]

It is unnerving—but again should not be surprising—to learn from this evidence that Baltimore, the site of considerable unrest after the death of Freddie Gray, scores at the bottom of all U.S. cities in its rate of upward economic mobility. Concentrated poverty, income segregation, violence, poor schools, and low social capital all appear to play a role in explaining why neighborhoods matter for getting ahead in life.

It follows, then, that just as schools cannot be fairly saddled with the responsibility of solving all family and neighborhood ills, criminal-justice reform alone will not end the problem of compounded deprivation. Even if the prison doors were to swing open tomorrow, the multidimensional and persistent poverty in places like West Baltimore would await those coming home. Meanwhile, the long-term effects of concentrated disadvantage on today's young children have yet to manifest themselves.

What to Do?

The enduring neighborhood effect implies that we need to consider policies that confront the spatial foundations of compounded deprivation. One way to think about potential policy responses is to separate them by units of intervention—individuals or communities. Put in terms commonly used, should ameliorative policies target people or place?

The people-based approach to reducing spatial inequality focuses on individual residential mobility—attempting to move individuals out of poor communities and into middle-class or even rich areas. One strategy is giving housing vouchers to induce residents to move away from areas of concentrated poverty, as occurred in the famous Moving to Opportunity (MTO) experiment.[4] The front-page print headline in the *New York Times* reporting new results on the MTO and another study on moving neighborhoods laid bare the policy takeaway: "Change of Address Offers a Pathway Out of Poverty."[5] A new voucher program in Dallas is even more coercive: "To sharpen the prod, the government has also cut subsidies for those who do not go."[6] Let us call this the "move out" approach.

By contrast, the place-based tactic is to intervene holistically at the scale of poor neighborhoods or communities themselves. Instead of moving poor people from their homes, the goal is to renew the existing but disinvested and often troubled neighborhoods in which they live with an infusion of resources. In theory at least, people can stay in place at the community level but still "move up."

Person-based versus place-based interventions have been the subject of much debate that goes well beyond the scope of this short essay, but a concise summary is that there is no "magic bullet" intervention at either level. Mobility programs like MTO have shown some positive effects, but the evidence is still

uncertain overall; meanwhile, although neighborhood income-mixing has sur-
faced as a favored policy tool and is the subject of growing scholarly discussion,
research is sparse and has produced conflicting results. It is also not clear that
"scaling up" voucher mobility programs to the national level is feasible—can we
afford to move tens of millions of residents? There are also worries that concentrated poverty would simply be shifted to other locations if mobility programs
crossed a threshold of program participation.

And there is a deeper issue that deserves reflection. Taking a cue from Mary
Pattillo's provocative and insightful contribution at the beginning of this volume, I would like to consider the notion that living among the poor is not by
itself the problem. Put another way, are rich neighbors really necessary as role
models? When poor individuals are asked about problems in their communities or why they want to move, the answers turn on issues like violence, drugs,
gangs, and poorly performing schools. This is an important finding, for what it
suggests is that what many poor residents want is not to live near the rich, but
rather to have the community resources of the better-off. This is not surprising, because like many Americans, the poor value the family ties, friendships,
churches, and traditions that are tied to their communities.[7] We can extend this
idea in a thought experiment. Suppose a poor community had safe streets, well-
funded schools, and decent housing. Would we still insist that residents move
out? Would the residents want to move? These questions become more salient
when we consider the literature on the disruption caused by forced residential
mobility and community destruction.

Although community-level or place-based interventions have a mixed
record of success, the data on persistent inequality point to the need for new
thinking on sustained interventions at the neighborhood level. It is surprising how few neighborhood policies take the long view; most interventions
are single-site or time-constrained, with outcomes measured locally and in
the short run. As Patrick Sharkey has argued, we need durable investments in
disadvantaged urban neighborhoods to match the persistent and long-standing
nature of institutional disinvestment that such neighborhoods have endured
over many years.

Several strategies to improve communities are logical candidates for retool-
ing with an emphasis on sustained investment. Candidates include violence
reduction, integrated with community policing and prisoner reentry programs
that foster the legitimacy of criminal-justice institutions; integrated community-based social services that recognize the multidimensional nature of poverty; code enforcement and crackdown on landlord disrepair and illegal eviction
practices; enhanced protections against housing discrimination; and educational
reform and support for healthy child development in high-risk, poor communities. Hybrid interventions that seek to create a more equitable mix of incomes,
such as the HOPE VI mixed-income intervention, also make logical sense.

The accumulated evidence tells us that what is needed are not just local policies targeted at specific communities, but rather a large-scale set of interventions, sustained over time and targeted to many, or ideally all, disadvantaged communities. A long-term focus is also consistent with the emerging body of research, noted previously, that demonstrates the critical importance of early childhood development for later well-being and economic mobility. National interventions by the federal government in many cities, such as Choice Neighborhoods and Promise Neighborhoods, are to date relatively small-scale and unevaluated, but they may prove useful in informing the next generation of place-based interventions.

People and Place

A different policy option is to give cash assistance or reduced tax rates to those in compounded deprivation—that is, poor residents who also live in poor or historically disinvested areas. Cash assistance or tax relief could also be combined with jobs training or public-works job creation. The logic behind this idea is that poor individuals who have lived for an extended period in poor neighborhoods have accumulated a set of disadvantages very different from those of poor individuals who have otherwise been surrounded by the resources of better-off neighborhoods.

Racial inequality cannot be set aside in this discussion. African Americans, more than whites or Latinos, have historically borne the brunt of differential exposure to compounded deprivation, and the data show that this continues to the present day. Our recent longitudinal study in Chicago found that 16 percent of black young adults were living below the poverty line and in a neighborhood with more than 30 percent poverty, compared to virtually no whites and less than 2 percent of Latinos.[8] The prevalence of compounded poverty among blacks is higher than the national average of individual poverty and greater than the prevalence of marriage in our sample. It is not just extreme poverty; blacks are also much less likely to live in mixed-income communities than either whites or Latinos.

These challenges could be addressed, and communities potentially preserved, even with a policy targeted at all qualified persons regardless of race. The ecological impact would disproportionately benefit minorities, and unlike MTO-like voucher programs, such a policy would allow poor residents to remain in place, if desired, while at the same time increasing their available income. Extra income would, in effect, lower the neighborhood poverty rate and, in theory, lead to longer-run social investments in the community among stayers. Length-of-residence requirements could be imposed to counteract attempts to game the system by in-movers, and incentives to move could remain an alternative for residents wishing to leave.[9]

Encouraging trends give hope to the idea that revitalizing disadvantaged communities through place-based interventions and individual tax or job policies is not naïve. For one thing, contrary to stereotypes, disadvantaged communities have latent collective efficacy (e.g., organizational capacities, reservoirs of informal social control) that is otherwise suppressed by the cumulative disadvantages built up after repeated everyday challenges.[10] The further good news is that some of the challenges that have accrued to disadvantaged communities have abated. Violence is down dramatically, people are moving back into cities, racial segregation is down, and immigration is changing the nature of many neighborhoods. Taken together, these facts suggest real prospects for the increased sharing of neighborhoods across race and class boundaries in urban areas that not too long ago were written off or were thought to be "dying." These trends raise the possibility that with sustained policy interventions, the "black-white" gap that has dominated the urban scene for so long may decline.

There is nothing intrinsic about policy that prevents us from intervening at the community level while attending to the realities and dignity of individual choice. Voucher mobility programs are important and should remain, but rather than privileging a potentially coercive "move out" approach, the time has come for sustained policy investments that give poor individuals an equal chance, if desired, to "move up" in place.

We Need a New National Urban Policy

by Richard Florida

It is no surprise that Rob Sampson—one of the finest minds ever to wrestle with the challenges of the city and the role of neighborhoods in structuring our life chances—would stimulate such an important conversation on our urban and national future. Here, he poses what is perhaps the fundamental question urbanists and policy makers must grapple with: Should we favor "people-oriented" policies, as many economists have argued, that move people, particularly young people, out of disadvantaged places and relocate them in neighborhoods with better schools and public services? Or should we focus on "place-oriented" policies that build up disadvantaged neighborhoods and make them better and stronger? This is one of the most vexing issues in urban policy, and it is one that I have personally struggled with. My own view is shaped not just by my own urban scholarship but by my life experience.

Let me explain. I was born in Newark, New Jersey, to working-class parents. My father, a child of the Great Depression and a veteran of World War II, worked in an eyeglasses factory in Newark's Ironbound District, starting at age thirteen. In 1960, when I was a few years old, my parents moved from

Newark to North Arlington, New Jersey, in search of a better environment for my brother and me.

North Arlington was a different world from Newark—its streets were cleaner and safer, its schools were better, and its demography was whiter—but it was still a rough-and-tumble place, one-third Italian American, one-third Irish American, and one-third Polish American. I fought my way through grade school, where I had to hide the fact that I was smart. By high school, my peers were involved in all sorts of things we think of now as urban pathologies—using and dealing drugs, committing petty crimes, and getting girls pregnant.

When I was seventeen, I applied for and received a Garden State scholarship to Rutgers, and it changed my life. I was lifted out of my old tough-guy peer group and transported into an environment where I could learn and thrive. I not only earned my degree, but I found my great passion. While I went on to complete a doctorate and become a professor of urban studies, any number of my old peers went to drug rehab, to prison, or worse. Some overdosed; others were killed. I am sure that if I had I stayed in that environment, some ill event would have come my way too, no matter how hard I tried to avoid it. My own upward mobility was not only a consequence of my parents' incredible commitment, but also of those two moves, especially the second one.

All of this is a long way of saying that I agree with Sampson's conclusion that a two-pronged approach is best. In the short term, it makes sense to both continue and expand existing people-oriented strategies that enable talented kids to get away from the overwhelmingly negative peer and neighborhood effects that they would otherwise be exposed to. But we also need a longer-term strategy that supports much more substantial investments than we are making to improve disadvantaged neighborhoods. The kids I grew up with in North Arlington may have been tough and misdirected, but they had real talent that, unfortunately for them and for society, went untapped. Most of the kids who were left behind in Newark didn't have a chance. Some of my own extended family that remained there dropped out of high school; more than a few are no longer with us.

It's become a commonplace to say that cities in and of themselves are a force for change and that mayors can do it all. But the scale of investment that I am envisioning goes far, far beyond anything that our mayors and cities can do by themselves: To get there, we need a new kind of national urban policy. Our existing policies are holdovers from an older age, when central cities had been devastated by the flight of people and jobs to the suburbs.

With the rise of the postindustrial knowledge economy, the job market has bifurcated into well-paid knowledge work for about a third of the workforce and precarious and contingent low-paid service work for more than half of it. At the same time, the old hole-in-the-donut pattern of hollowed out urban cores surrounded by increasingly well-off suburbs has become a patchwork, with zones of concentrated advantage juxtaposed with zones of concentrated disadvantage across suburbs and cities alike, the geographic manifestation of our deepening economic polarization. The most desirable locations in terms of schools, public services, natural and built amenities, job opportunities, and physical and social mobility are occupied by the already advantaged. The left-over spaces and the peripheries where the less advantaged are forced to live are rife with neighborhood effects that compound their disadvantages.

Beyond the interventions that Sampson describes, we need an urban policy that is attuned to this new reality—and that can help to change it. What we need is a new growth model that is as ambitious and as far-reaching as our post–World War II commitment was to creating a middle class. We need to reknit the safety net and ensure that everyone has access to good, family-supporting jobs that are the equivalents of my father's factory job. That means upgrading the 70 million low-wage service jobs that are concentrated in our cities. It means a renewed commitment not just to building more big buildings, as so many urban economists already advocate, but also to building housing that is afford-able for people who earn significantly less than the median. It means invest-ments in transit to connect our cities to our suburbs and the unemployed and underemployed to better jobs and services, and in high-speed rail to connect less fortunate metros to more thriving ones. It means massive new investments in education. And it means investing in the places left behind, just as Sampson lays it out. All in all, it means a combined approach to both people and places.

Sampson gets it. Now it's time for our nation's policy makers to listen and get it too.

Leave No Neighborhood Behind

by Roseanne Haggerty

People or place? Which is the source of persistent poverty, and therefore where and how do we intervene? Variations on this question have occupied social scientists and policy makers for a long time, with one, then the other viewpoint moving in and out of favor. In his essay, Robert Sampson helps us to move past this circular debate and focus on the complex but liberating truth: it's both.

Few have done more than Sampson to reveal the effects of place and of human agency on the symptoms of persistent poverty in American cities. His monumental study, "Project on Human Development in Chicago Neighbor-hoods," identified "collective efficacy" as the social glue that underlies healthy communities. Collective efficacy is typically explained as social cohesion, or the willingness of residents to act on behalf of their neighborhood. Will neighbors band together to prevent a firehouse from closing? Will adults hold young people to observance of the neighborhood's social norms? Sampson's research documented that neighborhoods with high collective-efficacy scores are likely to protect and support their residents' aspirations, regardless of the neighborhood's relative wealth.

Yet the presence, or absence, of high collective efficacy is typically reflected in the physical environment as well. Is a neighborhood filled with blighted property? Is the local park well maintained? What does the physical evidence say about the quality of public services in a place, particularly if government is a large local property owner?

The interplay between people and the places they live is complicated. The effects of concentrated disadvantage are undeniable. In the two neighborhoods where Community Solutions works—Brownsville in Brooklyn, New York, and Northeast in Hartford, Connecticut—life expectancy lags that of nearby wealthier communities by ten years or more, and young people are far more likely to spend time in jail than in a college classroom. But you don't need to see the statistics to know that residents of these communities have been assigned the failure track. Walk around these places and see vacant and poorly maintained housing, poor-quality markets, overgrown lots, untended parks. Look in vain for a cultural facility in either neighborhood. Take note of the shabby and inaccessible subway station in Brownsville and the absence of any bus shelters in Northeast.

The physical deficits of these places are like marbles thrown in the path of families' aspirations. Since few residents own their homes, or own a car, they are more dependent than residents of wealthy communities on well-functioning public goods and services: vigorous code enforcement to hold landlords accountable for the quality and safety of rental housing; well-functioning public transportation to get to decent food markets and jobs; safe and well-maintained parks for children who don't have their own yards to play in. Yet even to the naked eye, it's clear that the opposite is the case: there is inadequate attention paid to the delivery of basic public services or the maintenance of public goods in these places.

In the midst of the long-standing neglect of these neighborhoods, and all the evidence showing that the sensible thing to do is to move out, fast, I've come to appreciate that there's a lot more at stake: the people part.

In Brownsville, our team, made up principally of longtime residents of Brownsville's (neglected) public housing, ends each team meeting with the cheer "11212!" (our Brownsville zip code). My colleagues remind me regularly that it's possible to want a better life for your children and for your community, and that you shouldn't have to sacrifice one for the other.

Earlier this year, I was meeting with Erin Boggs of the Open Communities Alliance at our office in Northeast. She was sharing her study on housing segregation in Connecticut and the grim findings that, to an extreme degree, persons of color are trapped in the state's lowest-opportunity neighborhoods. Erin had surveyed residents who were desperate to leave these neighborhoods. That is surely true. Yet just earlier that day, my colleague John Thomas, a lifelong resident of the neighborhood, had introduced me to members of the Northeast youth council, which is cleaning up vacant lots and creating a greenbelt of community gardens, as well as working with the Friends of Keney Park, residents who are determined to renew this grand and neglected part of the neighborhood they love.

Erin and I agreed that what is missing are good options.

We should make it easier for families wishing to move to what are now higher-opportunity neighborhoods to do so. And we should make every neighborhood an opportunity neighborhood, to make it possible, as Sampson suggests, to "move up in place."

This is not some vague dream. I grew up in a well-functioning neighborhood where public services worked well, and I live in one now. Most of us do. Delivering effective public services is something that we know how to do in this country. Improving the delivery of basic public services in high-poverty neighborhoods is an obvious place to begin.

"Durable investments," as Patrick Sharkey describes, are also proven tools in the community development toolbox. Why not make major investments in health, library, early childhood, cultural, and sports facilities in these communities? Why not focus education, employment, and housing initiatives in a coordinated way on the places where the gaps are greatest?

The sad truth is that we currently spend a fortune on managing the effects of neglect in these communities. There is good evidence that a comprehensive investment approach is a win-win. Not only would it enable more citizens to contribute to our communities and economy, but it could sharply reduce the amounts now spent on criminal justice, child protection, and health care in these neighborhoods. And these steps to create the conditions that make opportunity an authentic promise would signal hope—a precondition to growing collective efficacy in a community.

Sampson is to be thanked for freeing us from unproductive debate over people or place, and for again pointing the way to a more nuanced and actionable approach to poverty and opportunity.

Jobs: The Missing Piece

by Michael Stoll

I read Robert Sampson's essay with great interest. Sampson's emphasis on the concept of compounded deprivation is important because differentiating poverty experiences—from that which is fleeting and/or occurring in non-poor neighborhoods to that which is deep-seated, possibly multigenerational, and in areas in extreme disadvantage along multiple dimensions—is useful for research and even more important for shaping policy intervention and design.

Sampson argues that poverty through compounded deprivation requires a unique policy response that centers on people- *and* place-based approaches. Although I agree that such a dual focus is sensible, I believe that in addressing compounded deprivation, Sampson somewhat overlooks the need to improve physical and social access to (quality) jobs. Suffice it to state that employment obviously has numerous individual, household, and community economic development benefits, and that lack of employment opportunities has played a devastating role in producing neighborhoods characterized by compounded deprivation. This suggestion complements Sampson's call for people- and place-based strategies that focus on improving prosocial institutions such as schools and reducing social problems such as violence, drugs, and gangs, as well as considering cash assistance or tax relief.

What people- and place-based policies can increase access to employment? Like Sampson, I think people-centered policies that help poor people move to areas of opportunity should be supported but not prioritized. Even though most employment growth takes place in areas distant from the neighborhoods where most poor people live, and distance to jobs does matter in influencing employment, especially for the less skilled,[11] "move out" initiatives such as the Moving to Opportunity demonstration program still may not be the most effective use of resources, particularly given research results pointing to disappointing effects on employment.[12] Further, recent policy changes already make it easier for housing choice voucher recipients to use vouchers in different jurisdictions. Thus, if the program were expanded, many would choose to move to areas of opportunity (especially if coupled with greater incentives for "landlord take-up" in these areas and/or enforcement of laws prohibiting discrimination against voucher holders).

As for place-based approaches, incentive policies that attempt to lure or create private-sector jobs in areas of compounded deprivation are probably a comparatively inefficient approach. Research on enterprise or, more recently, empowerment zones demonstrates that it costs a lot of taxpayer money to bring or to create just one job in a zone; even then, many job gains come from companies migrating from just outside to just inside the zone, so that there is little net increase in employment in a region.[13] A recent example of competition among Western states for Tesla's new car-battery plant that Nevada recently won makes the point on cost and inefficiency. Nevada provided Tesla $1.2 billion in tax incentives over a ten-year period for what amounts to, at worst, 6,500 direct jobs in the Tesla plant or, at best, 22,500 jobs, including the indirect jobs created by the existence of the Tesla plant. A simple back-of-the-envelope calculation indicates that this subsidy amounts to between \$54,000 and \$184,600 per job (without appropriate discounting).[14]

What to do then? Conceptually, there is another people-based policy that can have place-based impacts at the same time—but this one does not require moving people out. This people-based approach focuses on extremely poor people while keeping them in place, and its effectiveness rests on the fact that those in neighborhoods characterized by compounded disadvantage are spatially concentrated. Therefore, targeting the extremely poor would have disproportionate spatial benefits. This strategy is likely to be all the more effective if combined with strategic place-based (more than likely public) investments that are not necessarily direct job-creating efforts but rather investments in social and physical infrastructure that, in turn, incentivize employers to locate to areas they've historically shunned.

What kind of policies could these be? Policies such as high-quality universal preschool will have a disproportionately positive impact on extremely poor neighborhoods where residents face inconsistent and/or low-quality child care. Economic development in these areas could occur not only through the strategic site selections of centers in extremely poor areas, which in turn would create jobs for caregivers, but also by better preparing children for primary schools, thereby making primary school more efficient for harder-to serve-children. Policies that target extremely poor students in primary and secondary schools by providing more money per student (as California recently did for those in high-poverty neighborhoods, because equal educational opportunity requires unequal resources) can have this same impact. Combined with ongoing and other school-based and teacher reforms that aim to increase student achievement and skill sets, these efforts should in the medium to long run improve the skill sets of those in extremely poor areas and increase employer interest.

Ongoing criminal-justice reforms at the state and local levels that "get smarter" on crime—such as changing sentencing and parole practices, abandoning mandatory minimum sentences, and creating incentives to redefine the use of state prison systems—and then using budgetary savings from these efforts to further invest in crime-preventing activities such as diversion programs, community drug courts, or the hiring of more (community) police (as my colleague Steven Raphael and I have advocated) will continue to put downward pressure on already falling crime rates in tough neighborhoods.[15] This combined with an increase in ex-offender rehabilitation and training programs will begin to add employable (mostly) young men to neighborhoods destabilized in the past by draconian incarceration policies.

Finally, these efforts, combined with smart, strategic public investments in extremely poor areas, such as public hospitals, libraries, and light rail routes or other public transit options, to name a few, could begin to add value and attract employer interest, especially in those areas that are proximate to centers of economic and creative activity. Doing so would require electing forward-thinking public officials who see public expenditures as investments.

Combined, these activities could raise the location profile of areas characterized by compounded deprivation and attract businesses. However, low- and mixed-income housing investments must be part of that policy mix to limit harmful impacts of gentrification; doing so would require local government to be smart about incentivizing infill development and relaxing outdated zoning codes that restrict repurposing of existing older commercial structures for residential development.

Notes

1. Barrett A. Lee et al., eds., "Special Issue: Residential Inequality in American Neighborhoods and Communities," *Annals of the American Academy of Political and Social Science* 660 (June 2015), accessed August 8, 2017, https://us.sagepub.com/en-us/nam/the-annals-of-the-american-academy-of-political-and-social-science/book249079.
2. Kristin L. Perkins and Robert J. Sampson, "Compounded Deprivation in the Transition to Adulthood: The Intersection of Racial and Economic Inequality among Chicagoans, 1995–2013," *Russell Sage Foundation Journal of the Social Sciences* 1, no. 1 (2015): 35–54.
3. Raj Chetty and Nathaniel Hendren, "The Effects of Neighborhoods on Intergenerational Mobility: Childhood Exposure Effects and County-Level Estimates," May 2015, https://scholar.harvard.edu/files/hendren/files/nbhds_paper.pdf; Raj Chetty, Nathaniel Hendren, and Lawrence F. Katz, "The Long-Term Effects of Exposure to Better Neighborhoods: New Evidence from the Moving to Opportunity Experiment," May 2015, http://www.nber.org/mtopublic/final/MTO_IRS_2015.pdf.
4. Another variant is to tear down poor communities and disperse residents, as occurred in the Robert Taylor Homes or Cabrini Green projects in Chicago.
5. David Leonhardt, Amanda Cox, and Claire Cain Miller, "Change of Address Offers a Pathway Out of Poverty," *New York Times*, May 4, 2015, A1.
6. Binyamin Appelbaum, "Vouchers Help Families Move Far from Public Housing," *New York Times*, July 7, 2015, https://www.nytimes.com/2015/07/08/business/economy/housing-program-expansion-would-encourage-more-low-income-families-to-move-up.html.
7. See also Bostic and Whitney, earlier in this volume.
8. Perkins and Sampson, "Compounded Deprivation in the Transition to Adulthood."
9. Robert Sampson, "Individual and Community Economic Mobility in the Great Recession Era: The Spatial Foundations of Persistent Inequality," Paper presented at the Federal Reserve Conference on Economic Mobility, Washington, DC, April 2, 2015.
10. Robert J. Sampson, *Great American City: Chicago and the Enduring Neighborhood Effect* (Chicago: University of Chicago Press, 2012).
11. Elizabeth Kneebone and Natalie Holmes, "The Growing Distance Between People and Jobs in Metropolitan America," Brookings, March 24, 2015, https://www.brookings.edu/research/the-growing-distance-between-people-and-jobs-in-metropolitan-america/.
12. One reason for the disappointing employment effects is that many MTO participants moved to areas not very dissimilar from their old neighborhoods. See John Quigley and Steven Raphael, "Neighborhoods, Economic Self-Sufficiency, and the MTO Program"

in *The Brookings-Wharton Papers on Urban Economic Affairs: 2008*, ed. Gary Burtless and Janet Rothenberg Pack (Washington, DC: Brookings Institution Press, 2010).

13. David E. Dowall, "An Evaluation of California's Enterprise Zone Programs," *Economic Development Quarterly* 10, no. 4 (November 1996): 352–368.

14. "Inside Nevada's $1.25 Billion Tesla Tax Deal," *Reno Gazette Journal*, September 16, 2014, http://www.rgj.com/story/news/2014/09/04/nevada-strikes-billion-tax-break-deal -tesla/15096777/.

15. Steven Raphael and Michael A. Stoll, "A New Approach to Reducing Incarceration While Maintaining Low Rates of Crime," Brookings, May 1, 2014, https://www.brookings .edu/research/a-new-approach-to-reducing-incarceration-while-maintaining-low -rates-of-crime/.

DISCUSSION 18

PLACE-BASED AFFIRMATIVE ACTION

Place Not Race: Reforming Affirmative Action to Redress Neighborhood Inequality

by Sheryll Cashin

Race-based affirmative action should be reformed to help those actually disadvantaged by segregation. There are many ironies about affirmative action as it is currently practiced in selective higher education. First, it does nothing to help most black and Latino students, the vast majority of whom will attend nonselective institutions, if they enter higher education at all. Second, it tends to benefit highly advantaged students of color, disproportionately children of immigrants, who tend to live in integrated settings. Those blessed to come of age in poverty-free havens have access to highly selective K–12 education that sets them up well to enter selective higher education. Those who live outside of advantaged neighborhoods and networks—as do most African American and Latino children—must overcome serious structural disadvantages, including underresourced schools with less experienced teachers, fewer high-achieving peers to raise expectations and model the habits of success, and exposure to violence. A third irony is that race-based affirmative action engenders resentment, particularly among whites, that makes it more difficult to garner support for public policies that will redress the structural barriers that most children of color face.

I argue that colleges and universities have an ethical obligation to consider high-achieving students from underresourced places. Currently, only

42 percent of Americans live in a middle-class neighborhood (down from 65 percent in 1970). Only 30 percent of black and Latino families do. For some time, advocates of race-neutral strategies have focused on class or on first-generation college attendance as a means of achieving socioeconomic, if not racial, diversity. However, class-based affirmative action that focuses only on family income does not capture the structural disadvantages that cause opportunity hoarding in American society. Place locks in advantages and disadvantages that are reinforced over time. Geographic separation of the classes puts affluent, higher-opportunity communities in direct competition with lower-opportunity places for finite public and private resources. And affluent jurisdictions are winning.

Increasingly, highly educated families with multiple degrees are also segregating into their own environs, places thick with what I call "college-knowledge." Children, like my own, that grow up surrounded by doctors, lawyers, prize-winning journalists, and World Bank economists rise easily on the benefits of shared networks and practices that lead to success. Economic segregation is rising fastest among blacks and Latinos. Anyone who can afford to buy their way into a high-opportunity neighborhood or school usually does. Only seventeen counties in the United States currently boast a population with more than half college graduates—places that elite college recruiters flock to. The college educated used to be much more evenly dispersed in American society. Yet there are high-achieving students in inner cities, struggling suburbs, and rural hamlets, too. A high-achieving student from a low-opportunity place (e.g., where more than 20 percent of their peers are poor) is deserving of special consideration, regardless of his or her skin color. No one deserves affirmative action simply because he has dark skin or because her parent is an alumnus of her dream school. In addition to helping high-achieving students who are actually disadvantaged, place-based affirmative action has the benefit of encouraging rather than discouraging cross-racial alliances among the majority of Americans who are locked out of resource-rich environments.

In my 2014 book, *Place not Race: A New Vision for Opportunity in America*, I cite the example of the Texas Ten Percent Plan and the coalition of strange bedfellows that supports it.[1] The plan guarantees admission to a public college to graduating seniors in the top 10 percent of every high school in the state. It was enacted by the Texas legislature, after a temporary court ban on race-based affirmative action, with the support of blacks, Latinos, and a lone rural Republican who realized that his constituents were not gaining entrance to the University of Texas. The law ended the dominance of a small number of wealthy high schools in University of Texas admissions, and it changed the college-going behavior of high achievers in remote places that had never bothered to apply to the University of Texas at Austin. Of course, parents in wealthy school attendance zones have repeatedly attacked the plan as unfair, but in the Texas House of Representatives, white Republicans from rural districts, blacks, and Latinos strongly support the plan and have insulated it from repeal. The end result is a successful public policy that enhances opportunity across the state and a more cohesive politics—at least on the issue of access to higher education. Percentage plans are not the only solution, but this illustrates the type of transformative policies and politics that diversity advocates could achieve with fresh thinking.

In addition to giving special consideration to coming from a low-opportunity neighborhood or school, I argue that the entire admissions process should be scrubbed of unfair exclusionary practices that do not promote the university mission. Standardized tests should be optional or not used at all. Instead, admissions offices should focus on cumulative high school GPA and the noncognitive attributes—grit, resilience, scholarly dedication, and a willingness to forgo recreation for academics—that most reliably predict success. Financial aid should be based solely on need, not so-called merit. Legacy preferences should be abolished, as has been done by the University of California and other institutions that no longer consider race in admissions. As I explain throughout my book, systems of opportunity increasingly work only for people who are already advantaged, and colleges and universities have an ethical obligation to mitigate these trends or at least not to reinforce them. Hopefully, we will soon reach a tipping point where colleges and universities and the people who love them throw off the oppressions of rankings and throw a hammer into the whole admissions process and start breaking things—to restore common sense, fairness, and real opportunity to America.

Reforming Affirmative Action at Universities Misses Deeper Problem

by George Galster

Sheryll Cashin has done a magnificent and timely public service by offering a cogent critique of affirmative action as traditionally practiced in U.S. higher education and advancing a clever, provocative alternative that is based not on race but on place characteristics of applicants. I fundamentally agree with the motivation for her critique and the logic of her proposed solution. Unfortunately, I do not believe that her proposal would do much about the fundamental sources of economic inequality across racial lines, which are the inadequacies of the primary and secondary school systems that most Latino and African American students attend.

"Affirmative action," defined as giving positive weight to a student's nonwhite racial status as a consideration for admission to a selective institution of higher education, is, as Cashin notes, a blunt instrument for remedying the ills promulgated by the racist structures of American political economy and the generations of private and public discriminatory acts that reinforced it. Though I decry the spate of recent Supreme Court decisions that further restrict the consideration of race in admissions, I can accept Cashin's assertion that affirmative action has become a "wedge issue" that is being used effectively by conservative forces to frustrate attempts to enact a wider range of redistributive social policies.

I also agree that if selective universities were to substitute for race the attributes of applicants' place (school and/or neighborhood with concentrations of poor households, for example), racial minorities would likely benefit disproportionately. There is a massive and growing body of literature that place-based characteristics (school and public-service quality, institutional infrastructure, environmental quality, exposure to violence, peer and role models) are increasingly shaping the opportunities for our children and youth. Sadly, Latino and African American youngsters are disproportionately exposed to the worst geographic environments in all the aforementioned domains. To acknowledge in the university admissions process the achievements made by students struggling against such constraining places is indeed appropriate and fair.

I could quibble with the likelihood that selective universities will follow Cashin's advice by substituting admission standards based on place and "soft" attributes of applicants for quantifiable measures of student body "quality" (such as standardized test scores) because of the American fetish with measurable rankings. But that would detract from the core of my concern: misdiagnosis. Implicit in Cashin's argument is the notion that the central problem of racial disparity to be overcome is that selective universities are no longer going to offer as many admission slots to Latino and African American applicants if they cannot consider race in the process. This problem is not trivial, but it pales in comparison to one that is much more fundamental: the inability of primary and secondary schools to prepare the majority of Latino and African American students for productive roles in the modern economy and success in postsecondary education. Put differently, the segregated, poverty-concentrated, and typically underresourced public schools that most students of color attend prepare them poorly to attend, thrive in, and graduate from any university, let alone selective ones.

Let me illustrate with the case of my own employer, Wayne State University, located in Detroit. For decades, the only requirement for entrance was a diploma from an accredited Michigan high school. It was essentially an "open university"—nonracial affirmative action on steroids. The result was a tremendously racially diverse undergraduate student body. Unfortunately, it was also a tremendously diverse student body in its ability to do college-level work. Not surprisingly, the failure rate among Latino and African American students was epidemic, and their rate of graduating within five years was scandalously anemic. Admitting marginally qualified applicants may make sense from the perspective of marketing the university as an "opportunity institution," but it does a financial and psychological disservice to those it sets up for failure.

Cashin offers persuasive arguments for maintaining minority students' access to selective universities through their adoption of place-based admission criteria. Unfortunately, the more fundamental shortcomings of the American educational system vis-à-vis the vast bulk of Latino and African American students impinge at the primary and secondary school levels. Tinkering with the bases for affirmative action at selective universities will do nothing to address these basic problems.

Keeping the American Federal State Active: The Imperative of "Race-Sensitive" Policy

by Desmond King

In her passionate dissent in *Schuette v. Coalition to Defend Affirmative Action* (2014), Supreme Court Justice Sonia Sotomayor defended the need for a continuing American federal state role in affirmative action. Justice Sotomayor argued for the continuing need for "race-sensitive" measures, specifically in university admissions, but in principle in other spheres of society too. They are appropriate because of America's history of denying equal political rights to African Americans and other racial minorities, because of the endurance of deep material racial inequalities, and, Justice Sotomayor added, because race matters so much in daily experiences: "race matters to a young man's view of society when he spends his teenage years watching others tense up as he passes, no matter the neighborhood where he grew up."[2]

Race-sensitive measures—often described as "race-conscious" or "race-targeted" policies—are widely unpopular with most white voters but receive support from at least 60–70 percent of African American and Latino voters. Rogers Smith and I argue that two racial policy alliances dominate approaches to addressing enduring material racial inequalities: advocates of so-called color-blind policies and their adversaries, who advance race-conscious measures. These two positions overlap with modern America's historically exceptional partisan polarization: Republicans aligning with color-blind arguments and Democrats with race-conscious positions. This alignment between preferences for policies dealing with racial inequality and partisan polarization is unusual historically (both parties had pro- and anti-civil-rights reformers from the 1880s until the 1980s) and makes the challenge of devising public policy intensely difficult. The majority of justices on the Supreme Court—Republican appointees—have made clear their hostility to affirmative action policies, leaving the minority of justices—Democratic president nominees—constantly embattled when defending measures or policies designed to promote racial equality. Thus, where Sotomayor reinforces the urgency of race-sensitive policies in the federal government's initiatives to try to get on top of enduring material racial inequality, Chief Justice John Roberts reiterates in the same judgment the color-blind stance he first articulated in *Parents Involved in Community Schools v. Seattle School District No. 1* (2007): "the way to stop discrimination on the basis of race is to stop discriminating on the basis of race." The color-blind and race-conscious policy alliances are engaged—to the minimal extent there is engagement—in a dialogue of the deaf.

In this setting, Sheryll Cashin makes a valuable and welcome contribution to the debate on what affirmative action should look like in the current political era. Cashin advances a richly defined basis for modern affirmative action, linking her proposal (that the criteria for such measures as university admissions should be based on residential area) to the sources of enduring racial inequality increasingly recognized by social scientists—in this case, the bundle of restrictive traits labeled as "neighborhood effects" by such scholars as Patrick Sharkey and Robert Sampson and featured in the work of scholars of entrenched residential segregation, such as Camille Charles, and its class consequences, such as Mary Pattillo. Cashin gives the Texas Ten Percent admissions scheme as an example. She argues for a scheme that will focus on low-opportunity neighborhoods (defined as more than 20 percent of residents in poverty), independent of a household's race. Such a scheme might win Court endorsement because the color-blind majority can interpret it as a class- rather than race-based stance.

But such color-blind schemes for affirmative action are in danger of offering too limited an approach to material racial inequality for several reasons. First, they neglect the searing entrenched character of racial segregation in residential and educational patterns in the United States. Nothing short of a national program combining targeted community development high-investment measures combined with a national program of coercive affirmative action quotas will begin to reduce this embedded infrastructure of inequality. The significant desegregation of schools since the late 1960s and decline in hypersegregated residential patterns can't mask the persistence of segregation; for example, those school districts released from court-ordered integration mandates since the 1990s have demonstrated a remarkable tendency to resegregate without provoking any objection from the Supreme Court majority in its consideration of related cases. While the statistics on housing desegregation point to a desegregation trend, we still have a long way to go. Ironically, the University of Texas Ten Percent scheme could only exist because residential and education segregation is so deep.

Second, as Justice Sotomayor's dissent implies, racial discrimination and prejudice—though greatly reduced—remain salient in modern America. This can be measured, for instance, in the revealed preferences of Americans by race or ethnicity about what sort of neighborhoods they wish to live in. Almost all respondents express a preference for living in integrated neighborhoods, but few—especially households with children—actually do so, as Northwestern University sociologist Lincoln Quillian shows in his research. It can also be measured in the role of implicit racial bias and patterns of racially disparate impact, measurement of which is limited by judicial rulings, but which are nonetheless observable in health statistics, in labor-market participation and unemployment levels, and in criminal-justice outcomes. Brown University political scientist Michael Tesler has also shown in recent papers how much attitudes about race continue to influence electoral choices, particularly on such issues as President Obama's health-care reform.

Cashin offers a timely intervention into a critical public-policy challenge: how to devise policies that effectively address enduring material racial inequalities. Her proposal is an imaginative attempt to find a political space between the partisan and policy divisions represented in color-blind and race-conscious frameworks, and this sort of pragmatic engagement is to be welcomed. The issue it leaves us to consider, however, is how to deal with the structural and political forces producing the conditions of segregation that make such middle-way schemes necessary in the first place. Cashin is quite right to formulate a policy proposal requiring intervention by the American federal state (working in liaison with universities), but this intervention will have to be much more far-reaching and race sensitive to materially advance racial equality.

Race and Place

by Gerald Torres

Yi Fu Tuan was a geographer at Minnesota when I taught there in the law school. When thinking about the arguments advanced by Sheryll Cashin, I thought of Yi Fu Tuan's books *Space and Place* and *Landscapes of Fear*.[3] In those books, Tuan discusses the experience of place and the anxieties that places create. He is careful to stress that the nature of a place is derived as much from its meaning as from its brute social or physical characteristics. We know a place in many ways, and often they provide a kind of compass, both real and imagined, that guides us in our further interpretations of the world and conditions our experience of new places.

For example, when I am asked where I am from, I often say "the real California"—not the California of the tourist ad, although that place too, but the California of steel mills, orchards, hard cities, and race riots; of hardworking people and limitless sunshine; of race and class conflict and of loving kindness. But what it meant for me was an orientation toward the future that has colored everything ever since. It was a place where I did not have to wonder about belonging because I was of it. Its richness of experience, its thickness with human relations, matched its biologic fertility, and that fertility was expressed in the diversity of life and of landscape, whether natural or created. The scale of life, and thus the scale of promise, were larger. I can be certain that the California I miss no longer exists, although aspects of it still do.

The spirit of that promise was tapped in the search for alternatives to race-conscious affirmative action after the Hopwood case. My ruminations on Tuan bolstered my impulse to discuss the Texas Ten Percent Plan (TTP); after all, I had a front-row seat in its creation and implementation. The TTP was born in the antagonisms of racial politics in a state that is not only a former slave state and part of the Confederacy, but that was also part of another country and home to native people displaced by one wave of European colonists after another. The complex history of the state has left it with a deep populist bent and a geography that is racially, ethnically, and economically segregated. Its populism led to the adoption of a constitution that committed itself to creating opportunity through education, though it took litigation to make the commitment real.

The TTP is a further expression of that commitment. It measured excellence by assessing whether graduates had done everything asked of them. If they did, then they could go on to the university. One high school might be better than another, but you couldn't blame the students; they had cleared the challenges put in front of them. By making the guarantee universal, the TTP ensured that every part of the state could be represented in the entering class of the flagship university. But it also meant that ultimately those students would transform the university as well as themselves. The university really could become an engine of change in the lives of a vast cross section of Texans, and it would stop serving only a small slice of the population. Those who valued the university would have to reject the idea that it existed to serve only the economic elite of the state. It would have to serve all Texans, and it would have to become a better university to do it. The University of Texas had to make space for kids from the small towns of West Texas or the Rio Grande Valley as well as the big cities like Dallas, Houston, or San Antonio. Excellence does not know those boundaries, just as excellence does not know the boundaries of race, nationality, or class. And this reimagining of opportunity would create a new politics that enabled people to link hands together with those they might never have thought of as having the same interests or sharing the same fate.

So what does this have to do with Cashin's arguments? Only this: she is right. There has to be a new way to approach how our social places are constructed. Where we are from and where we are going are places constructed by law, too. We have to imagine them as sources of change that facilitate the creation of a political space that can be open to the possibility of democratic richness and where the promise of an open future can take root.

Notes

1. Sheryll Cashin, *Place Not Race: A New Vision of Opportunity in America* (Boston: Beacon, 2014).

2. Schuette v. Coal. to Defend Affirmative Action, Integration & Immigrant Rights & Fight for Equal. By Any Means Necessary (BAMN), 134 S. Ct. 1623 (2014).

3. Yi-fu Tuan, *Landscapes of Fear* (New York: Pantheon, 1979); Yi-Fu Tuan, *Space and Place: The Perspective of Experience* (Minneapolis: University of Minnesota Press, 2011).

SELECTING NEIGHBORHOODS FOR LOW-INCOME HOUSING TAX CREDIT DEVELOPMENTS

Tax Credits Can and Should Build Both Homes and Opportunity

by Adam Gordon

The Low-Income Housing Tax Credit (LIHTC) program has built more homes affordable to lower-income renters than any federal program in American history. Yet there has been far less robust discussion and policy innovation around how to best focus this expansive program than one would expect given LIHTC's scale. It is time to better ensure that LIHTC builds not just homes, but also opportunity. A new study by HUD's Office of Policy Development and Research prepared by the Furman Center, along with other recent research and experience, provides an empirical framework for how to use LIHTC to expand opportunity.[1]

Incredibly, in the first twenty years after its creation as an untested idea in the omnibus Tax Reform Act of 1986, LIHTC accounted for one-third of all rental homes built in the United States. More than 2.5 million homes have been created or preserved through the program. It is imperative that any future tax reform keep LIHTC in place as a policy experiment that has worked—much better than most people thought it would at the start.

As a credit against federal taxes, LIHTC is administered by the Department of the Treasury, rather than by the Department of Housing and Urban Development. Treasury has given each state's housing finance agency essentially free rein in where they allocate the credits. Perhaps as a result, the LIHTC program has often been left out of debates about federal housing policy—even though, for creation and preservation of rental homes, it essentially is the federal government's housing policy. The statute establishing the LIHTC program requires each state to produce a Qualified Allocation Plan (QAP) establishing how it will divide up its allocation of funds, and also mentions a number of general allocation criteria. Treasury has never issued regulations that further clarify these criteria, and how they relate to broader federal obligations such as the Fair Housing Act. As a result, each state has been basically on its own to come up with its QAP, with widely varying results.

Given the prominence and success of LIHTC, it is time to ask whether the incentives of the program have been structured correctly to make sure that federal dollars are used most effectively. How does one identify housing that does more than just provide physical shelter? How can we make sure that LIHTC also connects people to opportunity and builds strong, diverse communities?

The NYU Furman Center study empirically demonstrates that these QAPs matter. The study focuses on the relationship between criteria in the QAP and the share of LIHTC funds going to low-poverty, medium-poverty, and high-poverty neighborhoods. Concentrations of poverty, and segregation by race and ethnicity, have generally been linked to lower earnings and fewer educational and economic opportunities. While many people may choose to live in or stay in concentrated-poverty neighborhoods where they have strong roots, others would like to move to seek better schools or safer neighborhoods. The Furman Center study measures the degree to which the LIHTC program provides a range of choices rather than siting LIHTC units only in high-poverty neighborhoods.

According to the study, QAPs matter—a lot. Among the twenty-one states studied, allocations of LIHTC homes to low-poverty (under 10 percent poverty) neighborhoods ranged from an astonishing 0 percent in Mississippi to 47 percent in New Jersey. And states that had shifted their QAP system over the previous decade to place greater emphasis on lower-poverty neighborhoods generally saw significant results.

Most strikingly, New Jersey a decade ago allocated only 12 percent of its tax credits to low-poverty neighborhoods. In 2003, New Jersey changed its QAP to emphasize higher-opportunity neighborhoods as part of the mix and subsequently saw a 34-percentage-point jump in the share of LIHTC units in low-poverty neighborhoods. Other states such as Massachusetts and Texas saw similar, though more modest, results from changes to their QAPs. Meanwhile, states such as Indiana and Maryland that made it harder for proposals that located homes in low-poverty areas to win the competition for tax credits—for instance, Maryland added additional hurdles by requiring local governments to sign off on developments even if they fully complied with local zoning—saw significant decreases in the share of LIHTC units built in low-poverty areas.

How did New Jersey do it? My organization, the Fair Share Housing Center, along with two NAACP branches and the Camden City Taxpayers Association, sued the New Jersey Housing and Mortgage Finance Agency in 2003 over its QAP. We alleged that New Jersey's record of allocating LIHTC homes over the first fifteen years of the program violated state and federal civil rights laws. Notably, 20 percent of tax credit units had been allocated to Camden, one of the poorest cities in the country, even though Camden has less than 1 percent of New Jersey's population. Camden community groups brought the lawsuit because many (though not all) of these homes were built not as a result of community demand, but rather because developers from outside the community saw isolated areas of Camden as profitable places to buy land for very little money and get LIHTC funding. Although the federal LIHTC statute requires states to prioritize urban developments that are part of a comprehensive revitalization plan, that rarely happened.

In response, before the case ever got to argument, the New Jersey Housing and Mortgage Finance Agency (HMFA) changed its QAP. HMFA head Sean Closkey devised a system in which developers whose proposals sited homes in low-poverty, high-opportunity communities would get a significant share of credits—roughly 60 percent. Meanwhile, the remaining credits would be prioritized for urban neighborhoods. The system also placed significant priority on preservation of aging existing affordable housing, with LIHTC providing a capital infusion for renovation and extended affordability, as part of the overall allocation system. This priority ended up involving both neighborhood categories: while older New Jersey subsidized housing was predominantly in poorer neighborhoods, a significant number of suburban and rural developments also needed preservation.

In the view of the NAACP chapters and the Camden City Taxpayers Association that brought the suit, these changes, while making some progress, did not sufficiently prioritize higher-opportunity communities nor truly focus on comprehensive revitalization in urban areas. The court ultimately agreed that the Housing and Mortgage Finance Agency had a duty, in its administration of the QAP, to comply with the federal Fair Housing Act and to affirmatively further fair housing. The court, however, deferred to the agency's changes, finding that they were sufficient to meet that duty.

While the changes from our perspective were not enough, they had a big impact. As the Furman study shows, the allocation of tax credits to lower-poverty neighborhoods jumped from 12 percent to 47 percent of all allocations after the changes were adopted. As a result, more than five thousand households have had an opportunity to live in communities that they would not have otherwise been able to access. A recent book by Doug Massey and several Princeton colleagues, *Climbing Mount Laurel*, suggests that many of those households have had better educational, economic, and mental-health outcomes as a result.[2] And demand has been huge: three- to five-year waiting lists are typical. In the meantime, significant funds have still gone to projects in higher-poverty communities, still in amounts more than their share of the state's overall population, though the differential is not as extreme as it was prior to 2003, when Camden received twenty times as much funding as its share of the population.

After a new head of the New Jersey Housing and Mortgage Finance Agency, Tony Marchetta, was appointed in 2010, he set out to revise the QAP for the first time since the litigation. He aimed to maintain a balance between access to higher-opportunity communities and community revitalization, while doing more to target the most critical projects in both areas. After extensive discussions with nonprofit and for-profit developers, smart-growth organizations, housing authorities, and other stakeholders, the resulting new QAP, adopted in 2013, does much more to target urban areas facing gentrification and to prioritize lower-poverty areas with the best schools, job access, and transit.

Many other states can learn from what we have done in New Jersey. While the solutions to more effective use of LIHTC will not be identical in every state, the results in very different kinds of states in the Furman Center study show that QAPs do matter. Changes to the QAP can encourage more opportunities in lower-poverty neighborhoods throughout the nation that encourage racial and economic integration, while also addressing the threats of gentrification to existing affordability and encouraging comprehensive community revitalization.

The federal government should also do more to encourage more effective use of the single biggest federal housing production program. That does not mean that the federal government should write QAPs; states need to have the flexibility to address their local situations. But the federal government should ensure that every QAP affirmatively furthers fair housing and does not simply reinforce existing concentrations of poverty and racial segregation. And the federal government should set standards so that comprehensive community revitalization means something beyond just a box that developers check. Thirty years into the LIHTC program, it is time to acknowledge the program's vast scope, significance, and successful model for building homes—and make sure that its resources are used effectively.

Yes, and . . . Don't Abandon Poor Residents of Gentrifying Neighborhoods

by Robin Hughes

Yes, federal housing policy, including the Low-Income Housing Tax Credit (LIHTC) program, should encourage the production and preservation of affordable homes in high-income, low-poverty neighborhoods. The LIHTC programs should also encourage the development and preservation of affordable housing in lower-income communities where there is a strong demand for affordable homes and, simultaneously, a deep need for this critical economic stimulus. This is especially true in communities that are experiencing gentrification, where long-term lower-income residents are being displaced just as access to better education and economic opportunities are increasing in their community.

I am concerned when the development of much-needed affordable homes in lower-income neighborhoods is threatened by opponents who argue that affordable housing developments in these communities contribute to the concentration of poverty, thus violating fair housing laws and the civil rights of future residents. My organization recently experienced this very challenge to its Rolland Curtis Gardens residential community in South Los Angeles.

Rolland Curtis was owned by a private owner who allowed the property's affordability covenants to expire with the intent to convert the property to market-rate student housing for the nearby University of Southern California. Moreover, the property sits adjacent to bus and light-rail transit systems and is located next to the largest private employer in the city (USC) and in an emerging commercial and retail development corridor driven by the university. In short, there are few locales that provide greater access to local and regional jobs, as well as economic opportunities.

With the support of our community-based partner and local land trust, Abode Communities gained control of the property. Given the site's tremendous potential, Abode Communities has proposed increasing the density to 140 affordable homes to maximize the number of low-income Angelenos who can take advantage of the potential benefits. We worked closely with the families who currently reside at the property, who engaged in the redevelopment plans and will have the right to return to the newly developed property, which will remain affordable thanks to the subsidies provided by LIHTC and other public financing programs.

While we were in the midst of securing land-use entitlements for Rolland Curtis, a small group of opponents submitted an appeal to the city planning commission. The appeal was supported by a letter from two prominent professors putting forth an argument that siting affordable housing in a high-poverty neighborhood that lacked quality schools and access to employment opportunities "may serve to trap lower-income families in a vicious cycle of poverty and further destabilize poor communities." This was simply the wrong argument for the wrong neighborhood. Our team was able to successfully defeat the appeal with, among other things, strong support from local residents who have witnessed firsthand the displacement of lower-income families as a result of gentrification. But it could have resulted in the loss of needed affordable homes in a neighborhood with increasing opportunities.

That said, in addition to building and preserving housing like Rolland Gardens in gentrifying low-income neighborhoods, I believe we also need to find ways to get more affordable housing built in higher-income, lower-poverty neighborhoods. In Los Angeles, there are significant barriers to creating such housing. First, it can be difficult to find appropriately zoned land. Second, the cost to build in many low-poverty communities is prohibitive. Land costs alone can drive a project's costs to levels where affordable rents are very difficult to achieve. Third, the land-use approval process is often protracted, which is costly, and low-poverty neighborhoods often have well-organized and mobilized groups of NIMBYs that can extend this time considerably, introducing even more costs. Taken together, these factors make producing affordable homes in low-poverty neighborhoods a daunting task.

So how do we make changes to the LIHTC program and QAPs to encourage the production and preservation of affordable housing in lower-poverty areas? Clearly, increasing the competitiveness of these developments for the existing LIHTC program is part of the solution. However, increasing the overall size of the federal tax credit program and linking this increase to incentives that target production and preservation in low-poverty areas is needed. By doing so, state allocating entities would be able to increase the amount of tax credits going into these developments without reducing the level of financial support that is especially needed in lower-income communities.

As Adam Gordon noted, the LIHTC program has been successful accounting for one-third of all rental homes built in the United States since the program's inception. Because it is often not profitable for the market to build housing for low-income residents, one might argue that if not for tax credit programs, most affordable homes would not have been built. I know this might be over simplifying matters, but why not let the LIHTC program be just that—a housing program? The success of the LIHTC program is evident both in the sheer number of homes built over the past thirty years and in the number of high-quality, affordable homes for lower-income renters.

Research Can and Should Play a Role in More Effective Use of LIHTC Resources

by Kathy O'Regan

Adam Gordon's excellent essay ends with a challenge to the federal government to do more "to encourage more effective use of the single biggest federal government housing production program." As a federal official leading HUD's Office of Policy Development and Research (PD&R), I want to start where he ended, with that challenge. PD&R's goal in funding the study he references was essentially that—to examine the effectiveness of using QAPs to achieve one goal of LIHTC: providing affordable housing in areas of greater opportunity. While there has been considerable work simply examining QAPs, and another body of work describing the locations of LIHTC developments, to date there has been very limited work drawing credible connections between the two.

That is the first key contribution of this report: assessing the relationship between location outcomes and specific features of QAPs likely to affect tax credit siting in high- or low-poverty neighborhoods. Using allocation data on competitive ("9 percent") credits for twenty-one states, the authors examined five categories of changes in QAPs between 2002 and 2010: prioritization of opportunity neighborhoods; proximity to amenities; importance of community approval; investing in high-poverty neighborhoods; and avoiding concentration of assisted housing. Changes were scored in terms of whether they would increase or decrease siting in low-poverty areas and on the likely magnitude of those effects.

Statistical models using a composite measure of changes in QAPs found that states that increased priorities for higher-opportunity areas saw significant increases in the share of developments allocated tax credits in low-poverty areas, decreases in the share in high-poverty areas, and decreases in the average neighborhood poverty rates surrounding LIHTC developments. As Gordon says, QAPs matter—and that is very important to know. QAPs are meant to be the mechanism through which states achieve their local priorities for LIHTC, consistent with federal requirements.

Exactly which features of the QAPs are most effective is harder to learn through this purely quantitative assessment across only twenty-one states. When broken out individually, none of the five components of the index meets standard levels of statistical significance, which is not surprising with such a small sample and the inevitable noise in the data. There is, however, suggestive evidence that three components might shape locational patterns—these elements achieved near statistical significance (at the 15 percent level) in three models. Specifically, prioritizing high-opportunity neighborhoods and avoiding concentration of assisted housing each showed signs of mattering for increasing access to low-poverty neighborhoods. Meanwhile, stronger community approval measures, which may act as a local veto on developments, were associated with higher average neighborhood poverty rates for tax credit developments.

These last sets of results are just suggestive at this point, but they lead to the second contribution of this study—as a starting point for further exploration on the specific actions taken by states and their experiences. The report contains descriptions of each of the QAP changes undertaken, providing an inventory for states and interested parties to consider and learn from. To that end, HUD discussed this report directly with many state housing agencies at the

National Council of State Housing Agencies' (NCHSA) most recent gathering in Los Angeles, just one means of getting information into the hands of those who can use it. Supporting and disseminating research on topics core to HUD's mission—including housing programs we don't administer—is PD&R's charge. Indeed, such knowledge creation is a quintessential public-sector role, and in this case I would argue a federal one. That was recognized in the Housing and Economic Recovery Act's requirement that state HFAs submit tenant data annually to HUD. It is a role we should take up more consistently.

Of course, there are limits to this study and what can be learned from it. Let me focus on one feature in particular, which also connects to how we should and should not interpret the results. As noted by the researchers, data limits prohibit distinguishing between new construction and rehabilitation. Rehabilitation is frequently part of preserving affordable housing, itself a key LIHTC goal because of its cost effectiveness and benefits for existing tenants. Such housing, however, is more likely to be in higher-poverty neighborhoods. In this report, prioritizing preservation is scored as lowering access to low-poverty neighborhoods. Does that mean preservation should not be prioritized? No, it does not.

LIHTC is meant to meet many goals. Any individual development may be contributing primarily to only a subset or one of those goals. Simply said, the inclusion of priorities in QAPs to support additional goals, such as preservation of affordable housing and leveraging the tax credit for community revitalization, can be completely consistent with federal priorities.

The study may, however, help us understand trade-offs between goals and help identify ways to minimize them. Not all applications that help meet one goal come at the direct cost of another goal; it may be possible to find projects that meet multiple goals. Gordon's essay notes that while New Jersey's preservation of existing affordable housing predominately occurred in high-poverty neighborhoods, over time it has also encompassed suburban development, in essence lowering the trade-off on two key goals. Exploiting opportunities for meeting multiple goals within one project would stretch limited resources further.

Ensuring that states' criteria for allocating credits more clearly match intended outcomes would also improve targeting. Here I want to focus on the federal requirement to prioritize applications in Qualified Census Tracts (QCTs) with "concerted community revitalization plans." As frequently noted, no federal agency has issued guidance on what constitutes such a plan. That has resulted in many states staying silent and, by default, all applications in QCTs receiving some type of preference, regardless of whether there is evidence of a revitalization plan. That is not the intent of the federal requirement, and this may well increase the prevalence of tax credit developments in high-poverty neighborhoods without the added benefit of contributing to revitalization.

Other states, however, have stepped into that gap and defined concerted community revitalization plans, and those definitions are described in an appendix to the study. While the study does not assess the effects of adding those definitions, adding definitions has the potential for targeting state allocations to those projects in QCTs where the goal of revitalization is more likely achieved. This is more consistent with federal priorities and, I suspect, those of states.

I am sympathetic to the call for more federal action. In the meantime, this federally funded study is meant to arm state HFAs and advocates with some evidence for better accomplishing one key affordable housing goal: improved access to higher-opportunity areas.

Building More Than Housing

by Denise Scott

It's hard to believe a program little known beyond community development circles is now central to the national debate about poverty. And yet, the Low-Income Housing Tax Credit (LIHTC) is increasingly viewed as a tool to promote economic mobility for the poorest Americans.

It is clear why—the housing credit helps finance almost all affordable rental housing in the country. Over the past three decades, it has leveraged more than $100 billion in private capital to build 2.7 million rental apartments in urban, rural, and suburban areas. By almost any measure, it has been a tremendous public policy success.

But because the program primarily directs resources to low-income neighborhoods, some people are asking whether it has also reinforced segregation and concentrations of poverty in certain places.

It's a tough question. It speaks to this country's history of housing discrimination and the legacy of high crime, struggling schools, and poor health it has left us. We know that some children benefit from moving to neighborhoods with less poverty. We also know that some families are deeply rooted in their communities and want to raise the standards of living in the places they call home. State and local housing finance agencies (HFAs) that allocate the housing credit need to balance these two opportunities as they craft their Qualified Allocation Plans to respond to gaps in their local housing landscape.

At the same time, we shouldn't overlook the fact that the housing credit has an antipoverty impact that goes well beyond the number of apartments built. The credit spurs considerable economic development that engages the private market in places long starved for capital. It lays the groundwork for new businesses, health centers, schools, parks, and jobs. Because of this broad reach, a dollar of LIHTC capital typically has a much greater impact in low-income areas than it does in other places. It isn't just residents of these projects that benefit—so, too, do nearby neighbors and business owners in low-income areas.

Harlem might be the best example of how investments using the housing credit—especially those led by neighborhood nonprofits—have spurred new stores and restaurants, improved schools, cleaned-up parks, and expanded access to health care. Indeed, as Harlem has gentrified, the housing credit has helped ensure that low-income people can still afford to live there to enjoy the benefits.

Versions of that experience can be found in communities across the country. In Boston's Roxbury neighborhood, early investments in housing continue to drive steady progress. And in Washington, D.C.'s Brookland neighborhood, LIHTC capital has helped fuel an arts-centered revitalization near the local metro station. It's not that the credit has eradicated poverty—some people still struggle to find good jobs, and crime is still a concern. But incomes are on the rise, and people generally feel safer. These are communities that now offer opportunities to residents.

Congress recognized this kind of added value several years ago with specific policies to boost housing tax credit projects in deeply distressed communities. At the Local Initiatives Support Corporation, we have seen billions of dollars in housing credit investments spur billions more in commercial development and community programs that improve safety and expand economic opportunity. It is as evident in Oakland and Houston as it is in Duluth and Providence.

Nationally, the LIHTC program is responsible for an estimated 96,000 new full-time jobs and $9.1 billion in local income each year. It eliminates blight—the kind that lingers, spreads, and destroys local economies. It helps attract new customers to local businesses and nudges out crime. It improves nearby property values and expands tax receipts to support city services.[3] And it is vital for preserving affordable housing, so that when a neighborhood does start to turn around, longtime residents aren't priced out.

If we push too many credits beyond low-income areas, we lose those wide-ranging benefits. What's more, simply allocating credits to projects in more prosperous areas isn't enough to spur affordable housing development there. Market forces, local zoning ordinances, and intensified local opposition often make these projects more costly to develop and/or significantly lengthen the development timeline. We think LIHTC projects can be one piece of an effort to decentralize poverty. But they aren't quick roads to economic diversity, at least not on their own.

So, let's be thoughtful—and practical—as we debate this issue. What can we do right now to create more options for low-income families, wherever they might live?

Expand the LIHTC program: The Bipartisan Policy Center has recognized the value of the LIHTC investments and recommends a 50 percent increase in credits to help meet existing demand—which, depending on the state, is typically three to four times current tax credit limits. If we want to encourage more affordable housing in higher-income areas, it's critical that we not strangle our ability to revitalize troubled communities in the process. Expanding the overall LIHTC program gives us the chance to accomplish both.

Develop incentives to support mobility: It's unrealistic to expect poor families to just pick up and move to projects in so-called high-opportunity areas—those with better schools and less crime. They don't have the resources to do so. HUD should consider incentives that help projects support mobility, including counseling and help for families to relocate if they so choose. State QAPs could then align with those incentives.

Facilitate voucher portability and enforce "source of income" regulations: The federal housing choice voucher program should give very low income families the chance to move into healthier communities. But voucher holders often face administrative hurdles and widespread discrimination, leaving most with apartments in or near the same areas where they have always lived. Local housing authorities should work together to make sure vouchers are portable. And jurisdictions should consider whether they need new legislation to discourage or prohibit discrimination against voucher holders while educating landlords and enforcing existing antidiscrimination laws and policies.

In a resource-constrained environment, this is a high-stakes debate. Unless we plan to raze troubled neighborhoods or turn them over for total gentrification, we need to deal with the myriad challenges they face. It will take a thriving LIHTC program to tackle deeply entrenched poverty and build the kind of economic stability that reaches beyond any one development effort. We should be advocating for ways to expand the program to reach more people and more places so both have a chance to thrive.

Notes

1. Ingrid G. Ellen, Keren Horn, Yiwen Kuai, Roman Pazuniak, and Michael David Williams, *Effect of QAP Incentives on the Location of LIHTC Properties: Multi-Disciplinary Research Team Report* (Washington, DC: U.S. Department of Housing and Urban Development, 2015).
2. Douglas S. Massey, Len Albright, Rebecca Casciano, Elizabeth Derickson, and David Kinsey, *Climbing Mount Laurel: The Struggle for Affordable Housing and Social Mobility in an American Suburb* (Princeton, NJ: Princeton University Press, 2013).
3. Ingrid Gould Ellen and Ioan Voicu, "Nonprofit Housing and Neighborhood Spillovers," *Journal of Policy Analysis and Management* 25, no. 1 (2006): 31–52.

PUBLIC HOUSING AND DECONCENTRATING POVERTY

From Public Housing to Vouchers: No Easy Pathway Out of Poverty

by Lawrence J. Vale and Nicholas F. Kelly

American public housing for families, launched in an era of "separate but equal," now too often just seems to be equally separated. In many cases, it is racially and economically segregated from more prosperous parts of the city; and in many other cases, when it is well located, it gets prioritized for redevelopment, usually leading to a reduction of low-income units and accelerated gentrification. Meanwhile, low-income households face a double problem in many American urban areas: wages lag behind housing affordability, and the affordable housing supply lags well behind demand. Of those who are income eligible for a deep housing subsidy, only a lucky 23 percent receive one.[1]

Unfortunately, many of those deeply subsidized units are located in areas of high poverty, and contribute to its concentration. Neighborhoods of concentrated poverty, commonly defined as census tracts with poverty levels of 40 percent or higher, are strongly associated with long-lasting negative effects on life chances.[2]

This has launched ongoing debates over the last forty-plus years about whether (or how) to fix "the projects"—and how best to replace them with public-private initiatives centered on new roles for vouchers and private developers.[3] St. Louis officials staked out one extreme in 1972 by launching the iconic implosion of Pruitt-Igoe, but in most places the demise of public housing has proceeded more slowly and stealthily. Neglect, disinvestment, institutional mis-management, vacancy, and attrition have resulted in more gradual implosions, even as some cities, such as New York, have valiantly resisted this trend.

In the 1990s and 2000s, conventional wisdom held that mixed-income communities offered the best alternative solution, yet the centerpiece of this strategy—HUD's HOPE VI program—has received mixed reviews at best. At a time when three-quarters of eligible low-income households receive no housing subsidy, HOPE VI and related demolition efforts have led to the loss of about 20 percent of the nation's conventional public housing stock, which peaked in the early 1990s at 1.4 million units.[4] Proponents of HOPE VI stress the value of neighborhood investment (which has been enhanced by HOPE VI's place-based successor, Choice Neighborhoods).[5] Scholars have found increased resident satisfaction among those who relocated to HOPE VI devel-opments compared to their former public housing developments.[6] However, studies have also repeatedly found a lack of social mixing in these deliberately engineered mixed-income communities,[7] coupled with some evidence that the mixing that does occur has been discriminatory and dysfunctional because of class-linked conflicts and racialized misunderstandings.[8]

Given the troubled history of HOPE VI, it is hardly surprising that policy makers and politicians are eager to find evidence that there might be better alternatives to project-based solutions. This helps explain the widespread atten-tion given to a study published in 2016 by economists Raj Chetty, Nathaniel Hendren, and Lawrence Katz, which extended the analysis of the Moving to Opportunity (MTO) experiment and found later-in-life economic benefits for children who move out of public housing with vouchers before the age of thirteen.[9] This creative and careful analysis represents a major contribution to the study of how neighborhoods affect the life chances of children. However, as important as this study is, it has been taken to mean much more than the authors themselves actually claim. We believe that it is crucial to put the results of MTO in the broader context of poverty in the United States, as well as the actual choices facing policy makers.

First, the results of the study have been interpreted in the press as an important vote of confidence in mobility alternatives to "concentrated pov-erty."[10] But ten years after the MTO experiment began, the average poverty levels of the neighborhoods where the MTO voucher takers eventually moved (28.3 percent for those who had initially moved to "low-poverty" neighbor-hoods, 29.2 percent for those who moved with traditional vouchers) were not much different from the average poverty levels of the neighborhoods where those who had initially stayed on in public housing had ended up (33 percent).[11] The authors do show that children, over the course of their childhoods, were on average exposed to neighborhoods with lower poverty rates than the control group.[12] However, these modest results are hardly a ringing endorsement for making large investments based on the presumed value of dispersal from "concentrated poverty."

Some results that Chetty et al. find to be statistically significant may be less socially significant for low-income residents than they seem—and thus less policy relevant. For instance, the study encouragingly found that those under age thirteen whose families left public housing with vouchers to live in low-poverty neighborhoods were more likely to go to college. This is important—but the statistically significant difference is between 16.5 percent for those who were not offered vouchers and 19 percent for those who used vouchers.[13] Both numbers remain quite low—about one-third of the national average.[14] Perhaps additional investment in pre-college tutoring provided on-site in public housing—as has been done with some success—might be a simpler and more cost-effective way to enhance upward mobility through college than a reliance on vouchers.[15]

Similarly, the Chetty et al. study found that children who moved out of public housing before age thirteen had higher incomes in their twenties than those not offered the vouchers. But the average income they had in their mid-twenties was still about $15,000—instead of $11,000 for those not offered these vouchers to move out of public housing. Again, this statistically significant finding represents a substantial 31 percent increase in wages for low-income families—but it also suggests that these individuals are still deeply impoverished and therefore unlikely to be able to afford a move into any form of market-rate private-sector housing. Is being merely very poor instead of extremely poor enough to call this finding sufficient to influence policy?[16] It's clearly an encouraging trend, but hardly a guarantee that vouchers have launched these young adults on a pathway out of poverty. Again, one may ask whether concerted job-training programs in public housing, targeted to those in their late teens and early twenties, might do at least as much as vouchers to improve income and enhance the capacity of residents to afford to leave public housing.[17]

Most troubling of all, the Chetty et al. study found that older children (those who were between thirteen and eighteen at the time the experiment) were slightly worse off economically if they received vouchers and moved to low-poverty areas than individuals who were not offered such vouchers.

The Chetty et al. study offers support for targeted voucher programs. But as important as the gains in college enrollment and income are for MTO families, the gains are not necessarily significant enough to translate into clear choices for policy makers. Seen most positively, the study implies that future policies should focus on offering vouchers to households with younger children. Moreover, if even a modest reduction in exposure to high-poverty neighborhoods could yield a modest increase in long-term incomes, investment in more extensive and extended supports intended to enable families to remain longer in low-poverty neighborhoods could yield large benefits. Yet both of these policy adjustments risk introducing a new paternalism that presumes voucher recipients will not know how to make their own neighborhood choices.

In the meantime, we do not know how the effects for voucher recipients documented by Chetty et al. compare to the experiences of households that benefit from placed-based investments. Researchers should develop a way to look empirically at the longitudinal outcomes of former public housing residents who move out with vouchers versus those who move into revitalized and well-managed public housing sites. Instead of assuming and furthering the false polarity and trade-off between place-based and mobility-based investments in reducing poverty and segregation, more targeted comparative research is needed to assess the benefits of each approach.[18]

For now, in the absence of stronger evidence that targeted vouchers restricted to low-poverty neighborhoods improve the well-being of families over and above place-based revitalization efforts, policy makers should not give up on public housing. Instead, they should focus on improving the physical conditions and management of public housing developments to make them once again truly decent places to live.

Housing Policy Is a Necessary but Insufficient Response to Concentrated Poverty

by Robert J. Chaskin

Lawrence Vale and Nicholas Kelly sound a useful note of caution regarding the potential for housing vouchers and mobility programs to significantly address the problem of concentrated poverty. The authors suggest that the recent (and much heralded) findings by Raj Chetty, Nathaniel Hendren, and Lawrence Katz regarding the longer-term positive economic effects on adults who moved when they were young children as part of the MTO demonstration program need to be understood in light of the magnitude of these effects. They draw a useful contrast between social and statistical significance. Although incomes may have risen for these young movers as compared to those not offered vouchers, Vale and Kelly point out, these increases fall far short of moving them out of poverty, except in the narrow sense of the Census definition, which at about $12,000 per year for an individual leaves people still quite poor. They may be less poor than they would have been without the voucher, but they are still largely very poor (earning roughly $15,000 annually) and living in largely poor neighborhoods. An excess of enthusiasm for the potential of mobility programs to move people out of poverty, along with the disappointing results emerging from efforts to replace large-scale public housing with mixed-income developments, Vale and Kelly argue, lead to a false dichotomy that pits place-based responses against relocation policies. The relocation narrative undermines support for ongoing investment in public housing that might still provide safe, decent, affordable homes for the poor.

Vale and Kelly's critiques on this front are important. There may well be benefits to promoting housing mobility for the very poor, but embracing housing vouchers too enthusiastically as a preferred solution to concentrated poverty has clear risks. In addition to the limited social benefits of marginally increasing material well-being for the poor, there may well be potential social costs. Beyond the paternalism inherent in mobility programs noted by the authors, relocated public-housing residents may, for example, incur losses associated with disconnection—from social networks, access to social support, and institutional associations.[19]

The problems associated with large-scale public housing and the contribution it has made to increasing concentrated urban poverty in many cities is clear, but I agree with Vale and Kelly that the wholesale abandonment of public housing is not the answer. Certainly the policies they note as having potential on this front—investing in the physical stock and focusing on the effective management of public housing; educational support and job training for public housing residents—are important to support. The Jobs-Plus demonstration project provides one example; it promoted significant earnings increases for public-housing participants relative to the comparison group.[20]

Renewing a commitment to public housing can also provide an important counterbalance to affordable-housing policy characterized by an overreliance on market mechanisms. Whether manifested via vouchers or mixed-income redevelopment, this dependence on the market creates inherent constraints on achieving the social goals of lifting families out of poverty and integrating them into "better," more economically diverse neighborhoods.[21] Housing is a foundational need (even if it is not recognized nationally in the United States as a fundamental right) and is an essential part of the social safety net for the poor, yet affordable housing is vastly undersupplied. More than 50 percent of households with incomes below the poverty line spend more than half of their income on rent, and of those, 67 percent receive no housing subsidy.[22] There is a clear role for public policy to address the need for affordable housing. It must be done, of course, without reproducing—or exacerbating—concentrated poverty and the segregation and isolation of the poor. Some promising strategies on this front include direct provision of public housing—through, for example, new investment in scattered-site public housing—and the strengthening of inclusionary zoning policies to allow for both (a) a higher percentage of affordable-unit setasides and (b) lower AMI definitions of "affordable" in order to provide units for lower-income households.[23]

However important affordable housing is, we also need to examine the fundamental limitations of housing policy as a response to urban poverty.

Researchers and policy makers should recognize the need for broader investment in neighborhoods themselves. Affordable-housing development can be effectively coupled with broader efforts at community development, but even this broadened policy must be coupled with a renewed attack on the structural factors that create and reproduce urban poverty. Inequalities in access to quality education, the absence of living-wage employment for those with limited education and skills, and a range of institutional barriers (from discrimination to incarceration to lack of access to higher education) that face the urban poor—especially poor people of color—all contribute to the persistence of urban poverty and the difficulty of plotting a path toward self-sufficiency and social and economic mobility. Although affordable housing is clearly an important contributor to the well-being of poor families, housing policy cannot, as historian Michael Katz points out, "substitute for policies that tackle poverty head on."[24]

Finally, racial inequality deserves separate attention. Although Vale and Kelly characterize public housing as "racially and economically segregated from more prosperous parts of the city," most of their discussion of policies is silent on race, as are contemporary policy frameworks like HOPE VI and MTO. Race may be implicit, but the principal focus is more centrally placed on poverty deconcentration and economic integration. Although about a third of the public-housing population in the United States is white, the vast majority of public-housing residents living in high-poverty neighborhoods are either black or Hispanic, and these families are three times as likely to live in neighborhoods of 40 percent poverty or greater than their white counterparts.[25] The issue of race and the structural nature of racial disadvantage, too, need to be addressed "head on."

Effects of Moving to Opportunity: Both Statistically and Socially Significant

by Nathaniel Hendren

There are large differences in individuals' economic, health, and educational outcomes across neighborhoods in the United States. In two recent studies, my collaborators and I have shown these differences primarily reflect the impact of childhood exposure to growing up in these areas.

Our first study illustrates how every year a child spends growing up in a better neighborhood improves her outcomes in adulthood. Analyzing the experiences of more than five million families that move across areas while their children are growing up, we show that exposure to better[26] neighborhoods increases earnings in adulthood, increases college attendance, decreases incidence of teenage births, and increases the likelihood of marriage.

This suggests two potential policy directions for increasing childhood exposure to good neighborhoods: (1) improve neighborhoods or (2) help families in bad neighborhoods move to better neighborhoods. In the spirit of (2), our second study examines the Moving to Opportunity (MTO) experiment. This randomized controlled trial conducted by the Department of Housing and Urban Development in the mid-1990s provided vouchers to families living in high-poverty public housing developments to help them move to lower-poverty neighborhoods.

Earlier work studying MTO had not found much economic impact on those who were teenagers and adults at the time of obtaining a voucher. However, if one believes that places matter in proportion to the length of time a child is exposed to a good neighborhood, then the youngest children (who are just now at the age of entering the labor market) should reap the largest gains from moving to a better neighborhood.

In contrast to the portrayal of our results discussed in Vale and Kelly, we believe the impact of giving families a voucher to move to a lower-poverty neighborhood on the adult outcomes of their young children is large—statistically, economically, and socially. Young children whose families were given vouchers to move to lower-poverty neighborhoods saw 31 percent higher earnings, were more likely to attend college, generally attended more selective colleges, and today are on a higher earnings growth trajectory. In their lifetime, we estimate these children will earn $302,000 more relative to young children whose families were not provided such a voucher.

In addition, these children are today living in better neighborhoods, and those who are women are more likely to be married and less likely to have had an out-of-wedlock birth, suggesting the effects may persist into future generations. From a cost/benefit perspective, children are currently paying more than enough back to the government in taxes to cover the cost of providing those vouchers and counseling to their parents to help them move to the new neighborhood. One dollar spent on helping families move to better neighborhoods appears to pay us all back in the future.

In short, we find large effects of giving families with young children vouchers to move to lower-poverty neighborhoods. As noted by Vale and Kelly, some families who initially moved to lower-poverty neighborhoods eventually chose to move back to higher-poverty neighborhoods. This wrinkle makes the magnitudes of MTO on children's adult outcomes all the more impressive, as one would expect even larger impacts of policies that sustained longer exposure to better neighborhoods. It also suggests that future policies might achieve even stronger results if they provide greater support to help families sustain their moves to opportunity. More generally, the results suggest that targeting vouchers to families with young children could be particularly effective at improving upward mobility in the United States.

MTO provides a concrete policy example of how we can improve the adult outcomes of disadvantaged youth by helping them increase their exposure to better neighborhoods while growing up. But Vale and Kelly are correct to point out that this fact does not necessarily mean public policy should abandon the goal of improving neighborhoods, and opt solely for moving families out of the bad neighborhoods.

The trade-off between place-based and people-based policy is of fundamental importance, but unfortunately there is a dearth of empirical research needed to assess this trade-off. For example, our MTO results have not focused on any effects of moving families out of bad neighborhoods on the residents left behind; nor have we studied the effects on the surrounding residents in the destinations to which these families go. This is not because such effects are unimportant, but rather because they are hard to identify empirically given their dispersed nature. Similarly, more work should be done to study the long-run effects of policies aimed at improving public housing and low-income neighborhoods, along the lines suggested by Vale and Kelly.

But one thing is clear: giving families with young children living in poverty the opportunity to move to better neighborhoods can dramatically improve the later-life outcomes of these disadvantaged youth. While future work will hopefully illuminate whether other policies can provide similar or greater benefits, MTO provides a useful benchmark against which alternative policies should be judged.

Moving (Both People and Housing) to Opportunity

by John A. Powell

Housing is the hub of opportunity in America. A home is more than a roof over one's head or a place to live; it is an access point into a school system, a neighborhood, parks and recreational facilities, safe environments, jobs, and grocery stores. Racial and economic segregation pushes too many families off the ladder of upward mobility and extends the distance between the rungs of the ladder for those who can stay on.

Evidence is mounting that economic segregation is on the rise and that any progress we may have made in abating racial segregation is slowing, if not reversing. The average white resident of a metropolitan area resides in a neighborhood that is 75.4 percent white, 7.9 percent Black, 10.5 percent Hispanic, and 5.1 percent Asian; in contrast, a typical African American resident lives in a neighborhood that is 34.8 percent white, 45.2 percent Black, 14.8 percent Hispanic, and 4.3 percent Asian. The "exposure" of the average African American to the majority white population is thus 35, a figure that has not improved since 1950.

The evidence is now greater than ever that mobility strategies are the best way to improve individual and family life chances. Life chances are shaped by many inputs. As a result, many place-based strategies, such as reinvesting in public housing, are insufficient to transform the full range of resource deprivations that accrue in the lowest-opportunity environments. With the exception of renovating or rehabilitating public housing sited in neighborhoods with declining rates of poverty and improving conditions, physical investments simply won't dramatically change individual and family life chances. In contrast, mobility strategies, properly supported, show great promise.

The recent research of Raj Chetty, Nathaniel Hendren, and Lawrence Katz on the Moving to Opportunity demonstration finds profound improvements in lifetime earnings and educational attainment. Lawrence Vale and Nicholas Kelly are right to point out some of the limitations of the MTO experiment, such as the fact that it generally involved only modest reductions in the neighborhood poverty levels to which recipients moved. Indeed, moving to lower-poverty environments may have limited benefits if the move is insufficient to overcome the so-called "spatial mismatch" of jobs and residence faced by far too many low-income adults of color. Many of the relatively short MTO moves were also insufficient to escape the "undertow" of neighborhood relations and extended networks that shape, if not circumscribe, the life chances and outlook of too many high-poverty-neighborhood residents.

Vale and Kelly remind us that for these reasons the initial results for the MTO experiments, in at least some cities, were disappointing along several key dimensions, including safety and mental health. In contrast, the moves following the *Hills v. Gautreaux* litigation were much more dramatic and pulled families out of the networks of their former neighborhoods.[27]

That is why I advocate for an opportunity-based housing approach. An opportunity-based model looks beyond single indicators like poverty and considers the full range of factors that shape life outcomes, including access to transportation, job opportunities, and the safety of the environment. Only by considering a broader range of indicators can we overcome the limitations of the MTO experiment and move toward a more equitable society.

An opportunity-based approach does not always recommend a mobility strategy over a place-based approach, but rather directs attention to communities of opportunity. When public housing rehabilitation occurs in gentrifying neighborhoods with access to public transportation, it can be used to connect residents to opportunity and improve life chances while reducing displacement. When, however, public housing units are situated in high-poverty, low-opportunity environments, reinvestment strategies are unlikely to succeed.

Notes

1. Will Fischer and Barbara Sard, "Chart Book: Federal Housing Spending Is Poorly Matched to Need," Center on Budget and Policy Priorities, 2013, updated March 7, 2017, https://www.cbpp.org/sites/default/files/atoms/files/12-18-13hous.pdf.

2. Elizabeth Kneebone, "The Growth and Spread of Concentrated Poverty, 2000 to 2008–2012," Brookings Institution, July 31, 2014, http://www.brookings.edu/research /interactives/2014/concentrated-poverty; Jeffrey D. Morenoff, Robert J. Sampson, and Stephen W. Raudenbush, "Neighborhood Inequality, Collective Efficacy, and the Spatial Dynamics of Urban Violence," *Criminology* 39 (2001): 517–558.

3. Lawrence J. Vale and Yonah Freemark, "From Public Housing to Public-Private Housing: 75 Years of American Social Experimentation," *Journal of the American Planning Association* 78, no. 4 (September 2012): 379–402, https://doi.org/10.1080/01944363.2012 .737985.

4. Edward G. Goetz, *New Deal Ruins: Race, Economic Justice, and Public Housing Policy* (Ithaca, NY: Cornell University Press, 2013).

5. Henry G. Cisneros and Lora Engdahl, eds., *From Despair to Hope: Hope VI and the New Promise of Public Housing in America's Cities* (Washington, DC: Brookings Institution Press, 2009), http://www.jstor.org/stable/10.7864/j.ctt1280sf.

6. Susan J. Popkin, Diane K. Levy, and Larry Buron, "Has HOPE VI Transformed Residents' Lives? New Evidence from the HOPE VI Panel Study," *Housing Studies* 24, no. 4 (July 2009): 477–502, https://doi.org/10.1080/02673030902938371.

7. R. J. Chaskin and M. L. Joseph, "Building 'Community' in Mixed-Income Developments: Assumptions, Approaches, and Early Experiences," *Urban Affairs Review* 45, no. 3 (January 2010): 299–335, https://doi.org/10.1177/1078087409341544.

8. Lawrence J. Vale, *Purging the Poorest: Public Housing and the Design Politics of Twice-Cleared Communities* (Chicago: University Of Chicago Press, 2013); Erin M. Graves, "The Structuring of Urban Life in a Mixed-Income Housing 'Community,'" *City & Community* 9, no. 1 (March 2010): 109–131, https://doi.org/10.1111/j.1540-6040.2009.01305.x; Naomi McCormick, Mark Joseph, and Robert Chaskin, "The New Stigma of Relocated Public Housing Residents: Challenges to Social Identity in Mixed-Income Developments," *City & Community* 11, no. 3 (September 2012): 285–308 https://doi.org/10.1111 /j.1540-6040.2012.01411.x.

9. Raj Chetty, Nathaniel Hendren, and Lawrence F. Katz, "The Long-Term Effects of Exposure to Better Neighborhoods: New Evidence from the Moving to Opportunity Experiment," *American Economic Review* 106, no. 4 (2016): 855–902.

10. Bob Davis, "Economist Raj Chetty's Proposals on Inequality Draw Interest on Both Sides of the Political Aisle," *Wall Street Journal*, October 21, 2015, http://www.wsj .com/articles/economist-raj-chettys-proposals-on-inequality-draw-interest-on-both -sides-of-the-political-aisle-1445383469.

11. Jens Ludwig et al., "Neighborhoods, Obesity, and Diabetes—A Randomized Social Experiment," *New England Journal of Medicine* 365, no. 16 (October 20, 2011): 1509–1519, https://doi.org/10.1056/NEJMsa1103216.

12. Chetty, Hendren, and Katz, "The Effects of Exposure to Better Neighborhoods."

13. Chetty, Hendren, and Katz, "The Effects of Exposure to Better Neighborhoods."

14. Nationally, 80 percent of high school entrants for the class of 2014 graduated from high school, and about 66 percent of those went on to college in 2014, so we estimate a college attendance rate of just over 50 percent. Lyndsey Layton, "National High School Graduation

Rates at Historic High, but Disparities Still Exist," *Washington Post*, April 28, 2014, https://
www.washingtonpost.com/local/education/high-school-graduation-rates-at-historic
-high/2014/04/28/84eb0122-cee0-11e3-937f-d3026234b51c_story.html; Floyd Norris, "Fewer
U.S. Graduates Opt for College After High School," *New York Times*, April 25, 2014, http://
www.nytimes.com/2014/04/26/business/fewer-us-high-school-graduates-opt-for
-college.html.

15. Lawrence J. Vale, *Reclaiming Public Housing: A Half Century of Struggle in Three Public
    Neighborhoods* (Cambridge, MA: Harvard University Press, 2002).

16. While some scholars have examined this question, it remains understudied. The
    research that explicitly compares voucher holders and residents living in revitalized
    public housing developments suggests that voucher holders are faring comparatively
    poorly. Chetty et al. conduct a cost/benefit analysis to justify the policy, but the amount
    of money saved by the government may not be justified if other policies move people
    out of poverty more effectively.

17. Other place-based initiatives that may help include interventions such as the Promise
    Neighborhoods program and the Choice Neighborhoods program (which succeeded
    and expanded upon HOPE VI), both of which emphasize educational goals.

18. Robert J. Chaskin et al., "Public Housing Transformation and Resident Relocation:
    Comparing Destinations and Household Characteristics in Chicago," *Cityscape* 14, no. 1
    (2012): 183–214; Susan J. Popkin et al., "CHA Residents and the Plan for Transforma-
    tion," Urban Institute Brief #02, January 2013, https://www.urban.org/sites/default/files
    /publication/23376/412761-CHA-Residents-and-the-Plan-for-Transformation.PDF.

19. Xavier de Souza Briggs, "Brown Kids in White Suburbs: Housing Mobility and the
    Many Faces of Social Capital," *Housing Policy Debate* 9, no. 1 (January 1998): 177–221,
    https://doi.org/10.1080/10511482.1998.9521290; Xavier de Souza Briggs; Susan J. Popkin,
    "The HOPE VI Program: What Has Happened to the Residents," in *Where Are Poor
    People to Live?: Transforming Public Housing Communities*, ed. Larry Bennett, Janet L.
    Smith, and Patricia A. Wright (Armonk, NY: M. E. Sharpe, 2006), 68–90; Sudhir Ven-
    katesh, and Isil Celimli, "Tearing Down the Community," Shelterforce, November 2004,
    https://shelterforce.org/2004/11/01/tearing-down-the-community/.

20. Howard Bloom, James A. Riccio, and Nandita Verma, "Promoting Work in Public
    Housing: The Effectiveness of Jobs-Plus," MDRC, March 2005, http://www.mdrc.org
    /publication/promoting-work-public-housing.

21. Robert J. Chaskin and Mark L. Joseph, *Integrating the Inner City: The Promise and Perils
    of Mixed-Income Public Housing Transformation* (Chicago: University of Chicago Press,
    2015).

22. Matthew Desmond, "Unaffordable America: Poverty, Housing, and Eviction," *Fast
    Focus*, no. 22-2015 (March 2015), https://www.irp.wisc.edu/publications/fastfocus/pdfs
    /FF22-2015.pdf.

23. Chaskin, and Joseph, *Integrating the Inner City*.

24. Michael B. Katz, "Narratives of Failure? Historical Interpretations of Federal Urban Pol-
    icy," *City and Community* 9, no. 1 (March 2010): 13–22.

25. National Low Income Housing Coalition, "Who Lives in Federally Assisted Housing?,"
    Housing Spotlight 2, no. 2 (November 2012), http://nlihc.org/article/housing-spotlight
    -volume-2-issue-2.

26. In contrast to many common ways of defining good or bad neighborhoods, our results
    utilize an outcome-based measure of neighborhood quality using prior residents. We
    show that children who move to places where the prior residents do well in terms of
    some characteristic (e.g., earnings in adulthood) are also more likely do well (e.g., have

higher earnings) the earlier they move to that area. In practice, our results suggest five characteristics of places that tend to produce better outcomes for children with low-income family backgrounds: more social capital and civic engagement, stronger family structures as measured by the fraction of two-parent households, less racial and economic segregation, less income inequality, and higher-quality schools.

27. In 1976, the Supreme Court ruled that HUD could be required to create a metropolitan area-wide housing voucher mobility program to remedy its discriminatory conduct in Chicago. Hills v. Gautreaux, 425 U.S. 284 (1976).

DISCUSSION 21

CREATING MIXED-INCOME HOUSING THROUGH INCLUSIONARY ZONING

There Are Worse Things in Housing Policy Than Poor Doors

by Edward Glaeser

Poor doors, which ensure that wealthy residents of buildings don't have to mix with the less prosperous inhabitants of on-site affordable housing, are inherently jarring. Their very existence reminds us of the stark inequality of New York and the world. But poor doors did not create that inequality, and they may even be a reasonable middle ground between complete integration of rich and poor and the economists' standard wish: cash transfers plus free choice.

We can't properly evaluate poor doors because we don't really understand the benefits of integrating at the building—or door—level. Sadly, New York and other cities are making their affordable-housing policy without the knowledge needed to make trade-offs between freedom and desegregation. Even more sadly, this is proceeding without even a firm commitment toward obtaining that knowledge.

To understand the economics of poor doors, it helps to start with Milton Friedman's logic about cash versus in-kind transfers. The Friedman view is that policies aimed at aiding the poor should give them more choices, not less, given a fixed amount of public spending. Economics has, after all, had a bias toward liberty since the eighteenth century.

Allowing welfare recipients to be "free to choose" pushes against housing vouchers, food stamps, and Medicaid, and replaces them all with some sort of cash program, like a negative income tax. In the New York context, Friedman's reasoning suggests that the current requirements of providing on-site affordable housing units should be replaced with a tax on development that should be used to provide cash transfers to the poor. Naturally, Friedman might also wonder (as I do) whether taxing development is sensible in a city where housing supply seems so limited relative to demand.

Paternalistic logic is usually given as the reason for in-kind transfers, but I think that's the worst possible argument for in-kind transfers. Paternalism suggests that the state should correct the bad choices of the poor, but I don't always make such great choices myself, and I'm not at all eager to surrender my liberty. After all, whatever behavioral ticks trouble private decision making will also trouble public decision making. Voters are not known for their hyperrationality. Moreover, as there is no obvious definition of the "right choice," other than the choice that individuals make, paternalism occupies an empirics-free zone, where values rather than data determine the path of policy.

The better argument for in-kind transfers is that they generate spillovers for people other than the aid recipients. Taxpayers seem to prefer it when welfare recipients consume nice healthy stuff, like food and health care, instead of free cash that can be used on all sorts of seedier pleasures. There was outrage when the $2,000 FEMA debit cards provided to the victims of Hurricane Katrina were spent at strip clubs. Housing-linked assistance is one way of ensuring that money gets spent on things that taxpayers value.

If welfare recipients drink their payments, this may lead to more emergency room visits that generates costs that others bear. If they spend more on housing, this may mean that they brighten their children's economic prospects. Raj Chetty's recent Ely lecture documents that the children of the Moving to Opportunity housing-voucher recipients have better adult outcomes, at least if they were sufficiently young when their parents moved to a better neighborhood.[1] These externality effects can be measured, and that measurement can then help us weigh the spillover benefits from nudging toward housing against the losses that come from restricting parents' choice sets by not giving them cash.

Yet even if we buy this argument for housing assistance, that doesn't imply that the public sector should try to control where people use that housing assistance. Accepting the value of in-kind housing aid does not mean that aid recipients need to live in shiny new luxury apartment buildings. The fifty-year-old idea behind vouchers is that housing works best if people can choose their own units.

But the structure of New York's on-site affordable housing requirements essentially means that developers provide affordable units using extremely expensive real estate.

The market value of the unit being provided through the affordable-housing program is likely to be far higher than the cost of providing decent housing somewhere else in the city. Again, the economists' argument is that the aid recipient would surely be better off receiving the cash difference between the rent of the affordable unit in the fancy unit and the market rent that could be charged on that same unit. Yet on-site affordable-housing requirements push for affordable units to be placed in expensive new structures, even if the structure's owners are allowed (sometimes) to create poor doors.

A secondary issue with on-site affordable housing units is that these units will fix their inhabitants in place. The world-class bargain that the inhabitants are receiving will stop them from moving, and if they get rich, then they typically won't be kicked out either. This makes on-site affordable housing a particularly inflexible form of providing aid.

There is one plausible economic argument for on-site affordable-housing requirements, and one more political argument. The economic argument is based on the value of integration. According to this argument, affordable-housing recipients benefit by being close to all that prosperity. Moreover, the prosperous may become better people if they live near a more diverse set of neighbors.

The more political argument is that it is hard to make a case for new housing projects based either on their tax revenues or on the equilibrium argument that more units promote marketwide affordability. Pointing to the affordable units provided in the program provides a more tangible example of how the project is helping at least some poorer people.

I buy the political argument, but since I dislike supporting bad policies because they are good politics, I hope that there is a better case for on-site affordable housing.

The economic argument for integrating at the building level is harder because of an absence of evidence. Certainly, there is abundant evidence on the downsides of citywide segregation, but it is less clear that we need poorer people living in every fancy building in the city. Before expanding a program of on-site affordability, it would make more sense to do a serious evaluation of its benefits. Indeed, the fact that affordable units are so desirable means that they could be provided by lottery, which would be an ideal opportunity for serious analysis. Lotteries would have the added benefit of making the process fairer and less nepotistic.

Poor doors seem to reduce the integration benefits of on-site affordable housing and kill the political benefits of such housing altogether. If the primary reason for building on-site affordable housing is to win the support of naturally NIMBYist neighbors, then poor doors should clearly be banned. If the value of on-site affordable housing is that it brings the benefits of integration, then this also requires evidence. I don't know if any such benefits exist, let alone whether they are eroded by the presence of a poor door.

The economic case for cash transfers is straightforward, but the more restrictive the form of aid, the higher the hurdle should be for providing evidence showing that the benefits exceed the costs. We are coming to a point where we can properly evaluate the spillovers from housing-related aid, especially on children.

Yet affordable housing in high-end buildings may be the ultimate in-kind transfer. I can't think of any other government program that provides as much of a bonus as a cheap apartment at the Mandarin Oriental. Before embracing these programs with even more enthusiasm, we need to be sure that integration at the building level really brings any benefits. Maybe New York would be much better off if developers just paid taxes that were used to fund citywide housing vouchers.

Inclusionary Housing Delivers Diverse Neighborhoods and a Better New York

by Ben Beach

In responding to Edward Glaeser's essay about inclusionary housing, let me start with a point of agreement. For reasons set out below, I think cities should strive for economic and racial diversity across all neighborhoods. Thus I appreciate Glaeser's noting the "abundant evidence on the downsides of citywide segregation." However, in weighing what policy approach best enhances freedom for low-income people, Glaeser fails to account for important benefits of inclusionary housing strategies.

The housing market in some neighborhoods in New York is increasingly out of reach for low- and even moderate-income households, and the new construction taking place in those neighborhoods only brings more unaffordable units. In the Park Slope/Carroll Gardens neighborhood, a Furman Center report indicates the 2012 median rent among recent movers was $2,054, the rent burden among low-income renters was 52.5 percent, and the 2013 median sales price was $691,000.[2]

Under these circumstances, while low-income people may not necessarily want to live in a luxury building, inclusionary housing may be the only way to allow them to stay in or enter such expensive neighborhoods. Inclusionary housing requirements mean developers must set aside as affordable housing a portion of new units that they construct, either in the building or in close proximity. ("Poor doors," which I find morally repugnant in no small part because of their similarities to Jim Crow–era measures, are separate entrances for residents of inclusionary affordable units and thus lie somewhere in between on-site and off-site housing.)

The conclusion that inclusionary programs are effective policy tools for ensuring diversity across neighborhoods finds support in a 2012 RAND study of eleven such programs. That study found that 75 percent of the affordable units created through the programs were located in low-poverty areas, compared to a range of 8 to 34 percent for other types of affordable-housing programs.[3]

Research also shows that inclusionary housing programs, which are currently in place in nearly five hundred cities and counties across the country, create demonstrably positive impacts for low-income families. A 2010 report regarding Montgomery County Maryland's inclusionary housing program (established in 1973) found that the program succeeded in integrating low-income children into low-poverty neighborhoods and schools for sustained periods of time, resulting in improved academic outcomes.[4] Further, a study early on found that the program had substantially promoted racial integration in the county, with people of color occupying significant percentages of the inclusionary units interspersed with market-rate units.[5]

A 2010 review of the literature on inclusionary programs found that low-income residents of mixed-income communities experienced a range of benefits such as more job contacts, more race- and gender-diverse job networks, higher levels of occupational prestige with their housing, reduced stress, greater levels of self-esteem, and improved health and educational outcomes. These benefits did not arrive through social interaction with upper-income neighbors, which occurred infrequently, but because of the environment and amenities (such as low-poverty schools) made available through inclusionary programs.[6]

Of course, the policy details matter. As the Real Affordability for All campaign in New York City has noted, set-aside units need to be affordable to families at all income levels, especially to those whose housing needs are greatest. Similarly, off-site affordable units need to be built just as quickly as market-rate units.

I suspect Glaeser and I also agree that all residents of a city benefit when low- and moderate-income people have more economic freedom to make choices about where they live. When people aren't at risk of displacement because of housing costs, neighborhoods are more stable, businesses are better able to retain employees, and schools have lower turnover rates. When people can afford to live near where they work, they are able to drive less, which reduces traffic and air pollution.

There are many potential routes to providing these choices, including preserving the stock of existing restricted affordable housing and public housing, which is critical. Fees on market-rate development to finance new affordable-housing development offer another valuable tool increasingly in use in cities. But in places where rising rents and luxury development predominate, inclusionary housing strategies may be essential to ensuring that these neighborhoods remain a choice for some low-income households.

Separate but Equal Redux: Resolving and Transcending the Poor-Door Conundrum

by Mark L. Joseph

> *When you suddenly find your tongue twisted and your speech stammering as you seek to explain to your six-year-old daughter why she cannot go to the public amusement park that has just been advertised on television, and see tears welling up in her little eyes when she is told that Funtown is closed to colored children, and see the depressing clouds of inferiority begin to form in her little mental sky . . . then you will understand why we find it difficult to wait.*

—Dr. Martin Luther King, Letter from a Birmingham Jail, 1963

Like so many others, I was shocked and troubled to learn that fifty years after Dr. King wrote of the deep humiliation of segregation, there are policies in place in New York City sanctioning a twenty-first-century version of separate and unequal. I imagined a parent in a "poor-door" building today, trying to explain to a child why they had to use a separate entrance into their building, why they could not use the fitness center, pool, or playroom, or why they could not store their belongings in the storage room used by other building residents. Rather than the emergence of the dream that this book is revisiting, there would be a parent's nightmare of "depressing clouds of inferiority."

This is an especially poignant moment for this particular discussion topic as we commemorate the fiftieth anniversary of the Selma march and President Obama exhorts us to remember the "meaning of America" and "the idea of a just America, a fair America, an inclusive America, a generous America." These lofty principles are at the forefront of Mayor de Blasio's Housing New York plan, for which his cover letter speaks of "knitting communities together" and making New York "a city where everyone rises together . . . where our most vulnerable, our working people, and our middle class can all thrive." [7]

In his essay opening this discussion, Edward Glaeser acknowledges the "jarring" nature of the existence of poor doors and concedes that perhaps they should be banned. But, true to the eminent economist that he is, he steers quickly away from squishy issues of social justice and racial equity and focuses on elucidating why the question of poor doors, and indeed the whole notion of the "in-kind transfer" of affordable housing, is a complex and problematic policy approach. He makes several points with which I agree, but ultimately disregards some fundamental realities that make his predilection for the silver bullet of "cash transfers" ultimately unconvincing.

First the common ground. Glaeser and I agree that "there is abundant evidence on the downsides of citywide segregation." As Patrick Sharkey notes in the opening discussion of this book, "confronting racial segregation should be seen as one way to weaken a core mechanism by which racial inequality is maintained and reproduced in America." Second, we agree that there are compelling economic and political arguments for integration within buildings. There is room to parse these arguments more thoroughly, and my review of the theory and research has found that mixed-income developments hold more promise for improving social order and enhancing the quality of amenities and services than for social capital formation and role modeling.[8] Third, we agree that poor doors would seem to "reduce the economic benefits" and "kill" any political benefits. Finally, I fully agree with Glaeser that "we need to be sure that integration at the building level really brings any benefits," and we currently have far from enough evidence to make a conclusive case for or against poor doors.

So where do our points of view diverge? My first, and most stark, point of contention with Glaeser regards his yearning for a policy that would provide a cash transfer to the poor to facilitate their "freedom" rather than engineering desegregation and inclusion. Give them cash and they'll find the choice that's best for them, or at least give them a voucher and don't constrict their choice to a "shiny new luxury building." He makes, on the face of it, the persuasive argument that the "market value of the unit being provided through the affordable housing program is likely to be far higher than the cost of providing decent housing somewhere else in the city." Here's the problem: as a vast literature on neighborhood effects has made clear, quality of life and access to opportunity come from housing and the neighborhood context and amenities with which it is bundled.

Is Glaeser's cash transfer large enough to pay not only for high-quality New York City housing, but also for quality schooling, neighborhood safety, quality retail services and amenities, and employment opportunities? And how does his cash transfer address housing discrimination, limited information to guide a citywide search, and transaction costs? De Blasio's "Housing New York" plan makes the point clearly: "The inequality and lack of diversity in many neighborhoods means that some families do not have access to the education, jobs, and other opportunities others enjoy. It also means that low income households often are unable to find homes in the neighborhoods in which they would like to live."[9] As Sherrilyn Ifill states in this book's first discussion: "we should also recognize the pragmatic reality that housing integration may be the most foolproof way to ensure the equitable allocation of public services and development dollars for black children and families." In the same discussion, Mary Pattillo goes further, calling for the "real stuff of equality: wages that support a family, and income maintenance in the absence of work; schools that compensate for inequalities in family resources; policing that does not always have its finger on the trigger."

Second, in my view, Glaeser underestimates the potential harm that could be rendered by settling for "partial integration," what he refers to as possibly "reasonable middle ground" between full integration and his preferred cash transfers. While he has a point that poor doors don't create inequality, they certainly exacerbate it, promoting a phenomenon that Robert Chaskin and I call "incorporated exclusion" in our book, *Integrating the Inner City*, on the mixed-income transformation of high-rise public housing in Chicago.[10] Residential integration without "ensuring participation and advancing inclusion," as Olatunde Johnson urges in her contribution to this book's discussion of gentrification, can generate a sense of stigma and marginalization.[11] Glaeser fails to note that the impact of poor doors often extends well beyond assigning separate entrances and lobby areas to exclusion from fitness centers, pools, playrooms, rooftop gardens, and storage areas.

My final point will surely dismay Glaeser and others willing to accept the poor-door compromise. A growing body of research on mixed-income housing suggests that banning poor doors would only be a first level of intervention required to make good on Mayor de Blasio's aim of "knitting communities together." In addition to truly mixed-income buildings, there will need to be proactive property management, inclusive governance and voice for residents, and community building to identify common ground and establish shared norms and expectations for what I call effective neighboring. Why has mixed-income housing yielded disappointing results thus far? In part, in my view, because not enough has been done to "activate the mix" and leverage the economic diversity for the benefit of all residents.

Speaking of common ground, back to two clear implications on which Glaeser and I can agree: there should be immediate efforts, both informal and more rigorous, to build knowledge and evidence about the demographics, well-being, and experiences of residents in poor-door buildings, and there should be a longer-term evaluation leveraging the lottery assignment process for affordable units to test the effects of inclusionary housing on low-income households. In addition, I would urge city administrators to incentivize, support, and press private developers and their property managers to activate the mix through proactive and intentional strategies to avoid exclusion and stigma and promote engagement and opportunity.

In his Selma speech, President Obama declared that "with effort, we can roll back poverty and the roadblocks to opportunity. . . . But we do expect equal opportunity . . . if we really mean it, if we're willing to sacrifice for it."[12] This is a useful framing of the policy challenge ahead. Can private developers be convinced to sacrifice some profits in order to promote inclusion? Will enough higher-income residents be willing to sacrifice exclusivity and the comfort of homogeneity? Will low-income residents be willing to sacrifice the comfort of familiar social surroundings and accept greater scrutiny? And can property managers adapt from the relative simplicity of a homogenous (or segregated) clientele and accept a broader role as community builders? Much stands to be learned as the fifty-year quest for racial and economic integration in America now takes center stage in New York City.

Housing Priorities: Quality Is More Important Than the Number of Entrances

by Carol Lamberg

I disagree with many of the assertions in Edward Glaeser's essay. Let me start with one of the more modest claims he makes—that separate doors for low-income residents are "inherently jarring." I just got back from looking at the door in question. It's a nice door. It even has a steel canopy. It does not look like a service entrance or anything.

The person who thought up the term "poor door" can really turn a phrase. The brouhaha around 40 Riverside Place would not exist if the building had been described simply as a moderate-income building adjacent to a luxury condominium.

Many affordable developments in New York are located next to luxury buildings. Condominiums and rental buildings have separate entrances. Hotels and condos also have separate doors. So what's the big deal?

Settlement Housing Fund, from which I retired last year after thirty years as executive director, created excellent mixed-income developments for families. These buildings provide well-maintained, permanently affordable housing, and the surrounding neighborhoods have improved dramatically. The developments "work" physically, economically, and socially because of sound investments by government and assiduous management and maintenance. One can evaluate success by physical inspection and review of financial statements, including promptness of rent payments. I have seen many other successful mixed-income developments owned by nonprofit and for-profit entities throughout the United States. Although we like the mixed-income model, we would never oppose developments for specific populations, as long as the buildings are secure and well maintained.

In addition to developing and owning buildings, Settlement Housing Fund acts as marketing agent for the low-income portions of "80/20" rental buildings owned by luxury developers who benefit from tax-exempt financing. Some of the recent projects benefited from very low interest rates, especially those with adjustable rates. The 1984 Tax Act requires the lower-income units to be scattered through buildings with this kind of financing. The bottom line is so good that developers line up to obtain the financing for 80/20 buildings—mix or no mix.

In spite of my lifelong belief in mixed-income buildings, I do not think it is a "holy grail" issue. I do not find 100 percent moderate-income buildings objectionable and would not sacrifice any affordable housing just because the entrance is around the corner from the luxury building that provided its financing. The need for affordable housing is too serious to get caught up in relatively unimportant issues. This is especially true when developers can provide more affordable units by creating separate buildings or wings. We spend too much time arguing about how to subsidize housing instead of fighting for the resources needed to allow every American to live in a decent, safe, affordable home.

Glaeser would disagree. In his contribution here and in his book *Triumph of the City*, he prefers to alleviate poverty by giving out cash to low-income individuals, allowing free choice as to how the cash is spent.[13] I agree that a guaranteed minimum income would be great. However, it would not solve the housing crisis in New York City, where only the super-rich can afford market-rate rents.

Glaeser is not a fan of subsidized housing. This puzzles me, because he grew up in New York, where successful subsidized buildings abound. The great Mitchell Lama buildings, the cooperatives sponsored by United Housing Foundation, and buildings renovated or constructed with federal, state, and local funds allow the city to remain diverse. We need many more affordable housing units, with good management and maintenance. Although some subsidized buildings are a mess, almost all the buildings that I have seen are cherished by their residents and their neighbors.

From years of observation, I believe that mixed-income housing and community building can stimulate upward mobility, especially when housing is combined with neighborhood amenities and programs, such as the college counseling program at one of Settlement Housing Fund's buildings. It would be great for someone in academia to examine this theory.

Notes

1. Raj Chetty, "Behavioral Economics and Public Policy: A Pragmatic Perspective," *American Economic Review* 105, no. 5 (May 2015): 1–33, https://doi.org/10.1257/aer.p20151108.
2. Sean Capperis et al., "State of New York City's Housing and Neighborhoods in 2013," NYU Furman Center, 2014.
3. Heather Schwartz, Lisa Ecola, Kristin J. Leuschner, and Aaron Kofner, *Is Inclusionary Zoning Inclusionary? A Guide for Practitioners* (Santa Monica, CA: RAND Corporation, 2012). Unfortunately, other affordable-housing programs tend to create units in high-poverty areas, perhaps especially in high-cost areas. As the Furman Center recently reported, "since 2000, just six percent of new subsidized affordable rental units have been located in Manhattan below 96th Street, compared to 17 percent of subsidized rental units built in the 1970s." Ingrid Gould Ellen and Max Weselcouch, "Housing, Neighborhoods, and Opportunity: The Location of New York City's Subsidized, Affordable Housing," NYU Furman Center, 2015.

4. Heather Schwartz, "Housing Policy Is School Policy: Economically Integrative Housing Promotes Academic Success in Montgomery County, Maryland," in *The Future of School Integration*, ed. Richard D. Kahlenberg (New York: Century Foundation Press, 2012).

5. Florence W. Roisman, "Opening the Suburbs to Racial Integration: Lessons for the 21st Century," 23 *W. New Eng. L. Rev.* 65 (2001). A study of Davis, California's inclusionary program reached a similar conclusion about racial integration (Alexandra Holmquist, "The Effect of Inclusionary Housing on Racial Integration, Economic Integration, and Access to Social Services: A Davis Case Study," University of California Davis, Masters Thesis, 2011.)

6. Innovative Housing Institute. "Inclusionary Housing Survey: Measures of Effectiveness," November 2010, http://inclusionaryhousing.ca/wp-content/uploads/sites/2/2014/10/IHI-InclusionaryHousingSurvey-2010.pdf.

7. City of New York, "Housing New York: A Five-Borough, Ten-Year Plan," 2014, http://www.nyc.gov/html/housing/assets/downloads/pdf/housing_plan.pdf.

8. Mark L. Joseph, Robert J. Chaskin, and Henry S. Webber, "The Theoretical Basis for Addressing Poverty Through Mixed-Income Development," *Urban Affairs Review* 42, no. 3 (January 2007): 369–409, https://doi.org/10.1177/1078087406294043.

9. City of New York, "Housing New York."

10. Robert J. Chaskin and Mark L. Joseph, *Integrating the Inner City: The Promise and Perils of Mixed-Income Public Housing Transformation* (Chicago: University of Chicago Press, 2015).

11. Robert Chaskin, Amy Khare, and Mark Joseph, "Participation and Decision-Making in Mixed-Income Developments: Who Has a Say?," 2012, http://nimc.case.edu/research/scans-and-briefs/participation-and-decision-making-in-mixed-income-developments-who-has-a-say/; Amy T. Khare, Mark L. Joseph, and Robert J. Chaskin, "The Enduring Significance of Race in Mixed-Income Developments," *Urban Affairs Review* 51, no. 4 (July 2015): 474–503; Naomi J. McCormick, Mark L. Joseph, and Robert J. Chaskin, "The New Stigma of Relocated Public Housing Residents: Challenges to Social Identity in Mixed-Income Developments," 2012, https://www.infona.pl/resource/bwmeta1.element.wiley-cico-v-11-i-3-cico1411.

12. Maya Rhodan, "Read the Full Text of Obama's Speech in Selma," *Time*, March 7, 2015, http://time.com/3736357/barack-obama-selma-speech-transcript/.

13. Edward Glaeser, *Triumph of the City: How Our Greatest Invention Makes Us Richer, Smarter, Greener, Healthier, and Happier* (New York: Penguin, 2011).

NEIGHBORHOODS, OPPORTUNITIES, AND THE HOUSING CHOICE VOUCHER PROGRAM

Children and Housing Vouchers

by Barbara Sard and Phillip Tegeler

Ideally, our federal rental housing programs should give low-income children and their families the opportunity to live in safe, healthy neighborhoods with access to high-performing schools. However, our housing programs are not currently well structured to achieve this goal. The unbalanced distribution of subsidized housing for families is partly a historical legacy of segregation, but it also results from ongoing policies and program structures.

Among our federal housing programs, the housing choice voucher program is unique, because the subsidized family is not tethered to a specific location. In theory, voucher families can choose to move to lower-poverty neighborhoods, even crossing municipal and school district lines. As we will describe, the housing choice voucher program has given children better access to quality neighborhoods than HUD "project-based" programs, but it is still falling far short of its potential.

Support for the work described in this contribution has been generously provided by the William T. Grant Foundation, the MacArthur Foundation, the Century Foundation, the Annie E. Casey Foundation and the National Science Foundation.

Why Children Need Safe, Healthy Neighborhoods and Good Schools

Children need housing that is stable, affordable, and free from environmental toxins. But housing location also matters for children's health and development. A growing body of research over the past several decades suggests that stress and exposure to violence in high-poverty neighborhoods can affect children's cognitive development, school performance, mental health, and long-term physical health. These effects occur both directly and indirectly by influencing, for example, the mental health and parenting practices of parents. Children in high-poverty neighborhoods are also more likely to be exposed to health hazards such as lead-based paint, vermin, and pollution and, as a result, are more likely to suffer from asthma and the serious effects of lead poisoning. Conversely, low-poverty neighborhoods tend to be free of these environmental stressors and often have resource-rich, higher-quality schools. Low-income children tend to perform better in schools where many of the students are from higher-income families, teachers are more skilled, staff morale is high, and student turnover is low. Poor children who have the opportunity to live for a long duration in low-poverty neighborhoods with high-quality schools appear to perform significantly better than those who do not.

These conclusions have clear implications for housing policy. For our colleagues in community development, they point to the compelling need to revitalize poor neighborhoods, improve public safety, reduce concentrations of poverty, and improve school performance in high poverty schools. But there is also another important message for housing policy—we should be doing more to help families choose safer, "higher-opportunity" neighborhoods that offer educational and other long-term advantages for children.

In a recent essay in the American Medical Association's *JAMA Pediatrics* journal, Johns Hopkins Professor Craig Pollack and his colleagues summarize the growing evidence on the damage to children's development associated with growing up in extremely poor neighborhoods and ask this same question: why aren't we doing more to help families with young children move to safer environments? They point to the Baltimore Housing Mobility Program as an example—a voluntary program that is now focused on helping very low income families with young children move to low-poverty, nonsegregated areas with high-performing schools.[1]

The Potential Value of the Housing Choice Voucher Program for Young Children

Research by the Center on Budget and Policy Priorities (CBPP) finds that in 2010, only 15 percent of the nearly four million children in families that received rent subsidies through HUD's three major rental assistance programs—the housing choice voucher (HCV) program, public housing, and Section 8 project-based rental assistance—lived in low-poverty neighborhoods, where fewer than 10 percent of the residents have incomes below the poverty line. The typical (or median) family with children that received federal rental assistance lived in a census tract that was 23 percent poor. A greater share of such children (18 percent) lived in extreme-poverty neighborhoods (where at least 40 percent of the residents are poor).[2]

The HCV program has performed better than HUD's project-based rental assistance programs in enabling families with children to live in lower-poverty neighborhoods. One in five families with children participating in the HCV program (20.2 percent) used their vouchers to live in a low-poverty area in 2010. These families were disproportionately white, as a share of the total number of voucher families—but while having a voucher makes little difference in a poor white family's ability to live in a low-poverty neighborhood, it makes a large difference for minority families. More than twice the share of poor black children and close to double the share of poor Hispanic children in families receiving vouchers, lived in neighborhoods with less than 10 percent poverty in 2010, compared with poor black and Hispanic children generally.

HCV families are also much less likely to live in an extreme-poverty neighborhood, where at least 40 percent of the residents are poor. More than a third (35 percent) of family-occupied public housing units and 22 percent of family-occupied privately owned units with project-based assistance are in extreme-poverty neighborhoods. A much smaller share of families that receive rental assistance through the HCV program—10 percent—live in these neighborhoods.

Nevertheless, nearly half of families with children use vouchers in poor neighborhoods that may diminish children's economic prospects and future health, and a quarter of a million children in the HCV program are living in the most troubled neighborhoods, despite the better options that having a voucher should make available to them. Increasing poverty and concentrations of the poor since 2010 likely mean that the current situation is worse than these data indicate. A 2012 PRRAC/Furman Center report found that an alarming 24.9 percent of voucher families with children were living near the lowest-performing elementary schools, and more than 40 percent were living near very high poverty schools (in many metro areas, these rates are much higher).[3]

In spite of these trends, HUD policy makers and local program administrators have the ability to enable a much larger share of families to use vouchers to access high-opportunity neighborhoods, without any need for new federal legislation.

What HUD Needs to Do for Children in the Housing Choice Voucher Program

The mounting evidence on the impact of housing location on low-income families, particularly children, and the performance of federal rental assistance programs on location-related measures lead us to recommend two near-term goals for federal rental assistance policy. In the next several years, all federal rental assistance programs should provide measurably expanded opportunities for families to choose affordable housing outside of high-poverty neighborhoods and measurable progress for families with children of all racial and ethnic groups to move to low-poverty, safe communities with high-performing schools.

Even in the current fiscally constrained environment, we can make substantial progress toward these goals in the next few years, without action by Congress or additional funding. Federal, state, and local agencies can make four sets of interrelated policy changes that will help families in the housing choice voucher program live in better locations.

1. *Create strong incentives for local and state housing agencies to achieve better location outcomes.* Federal policy should provide incentives for agencies to reduce the share of families using vouchers in extreme-poverty areas and increase the share residing in low-poverty, high-opportunity areas. HUD could do this in three ways: by giving added weight to location outcomes in measuring agency performance, reinforcing these changes with a strong fair housing rule—the rule that will revise HUD grantees' planning for how to achieve outcomes that further fair housing goals—and rewarding agencies that help families move to high-opportunity areas by paying these agencies additional administrative fees.

2. *Modify policies that discourage families from living in lower-poverty communities.* Many HCV program policies—at both the federal and local levels—have the effect of encouraging families to use their vouchers in poor and often racially concentrated neighborhoods. HUD should finalize its rule on public housing agencies' obligation to affirmatively further fair housing and revise federal policies (like the metrowide "fair market rent" system) to facilitate families' moving to higher-opportunity areas that aren't racially concentrated. And at least where necessary to help families move from extreme-poverty, highly racially concentrated neighborhoods to higher-opportunity communities with less poverty, HUD should require agencies to identify available units in these lower-poverty communities and extend the search period for families seeking to make such moves.

3. *Minimize jurisdictional barriers to families' ability to choose to live in high-opportunity communities.* HUD should modify the HCV program's

administrative geography to substantially reduce the extent to which the boundaries of housing agencies' service areas impede the program's ability to promote access to higher-opportunity neighborhoods. HUD could substantially lessen these barriers by encouraging agencies in the same metropolitan area to unify their program operations and by simplifying "portability" procedures.

4. *Assist families in using vouchers to live in high-opportunity areas.* To expand housing choices in safe, low-poverty neighborhoods with well-performing schools, state and local governments and housing agencies should adopt policies—such as tax incentives and laws prohibiting discrimination against voucher holders—to expand participation by landlords in these neighborhoods in the HCV program and to encourage interested families to use their vouchers in these areas. Such assistance for families could include financial incentives to offset the additional costs of moving to high-opportunity areas, mobility counseling, and programs to expand access to cars and other transportation to and from these areas.

While HUD works to reform the HCV program (its largest rental assistance program), it has the opportunity to move even more quickly in three smaller programs that rely in large part on vouchers for their success. First, the Moving to Work (MTW) demonstration program gives thirty-nine public housing agencies budgetary flexibility and freedom from many HUD regulatory requirements. MTW has an explicit statutory goal of "increasing housing choices," which has never been defined or implemented by HUD. As HUD is considering extending MTW contracts beyond 2018, it should require better outcomes from participating agencies' HCV programs. Second, the Rental Assistance Demonstration enables public housing agencies to leverage private funding to rehabilitate and preserve their properties and provides residents (for the first time) a choice to move with tenant-based rental assistance. If implemented well and expanded with strong HUD guidance, this program could help many more families live in higher-opportunity neighborhoods. Finally, HUD's Choice Neighborhoods Initiative provides funding to revitalize distressed HUD-funded properties as a means to support the broader goal of improving residents' lives and conditions in the surrounding neighborhoods, with parallel investments in education and safety from partner agencies. Choice Neighborhoods expressly requires participating agencies to offer housing-mobility counseling to the families it serves—yet the evidence of program performance to date has been mixed. CBPP's 2014 report discusses these policy recommendations and their rationale in more detail.

This focus on geographic-mobility goals (or increasing families' ability to remain in affordable housing in neighborhoods that meet these goals) is not intended to imply that policy makers should not pursue broader strategies to increase incomes, enhance safety, and improve educational performance in very poor areas. But the unfortunate reality is that we know relatively little about what types of interventions are effective at transforming extremely poor, disadvantaged neighborhoods. Moreover, broader economic development and revitalization strategies take many years and are likely to be very costly. The bottom line is that we need to rebalance our seriously out-of-balance housing policies and pursue both neighborhood-revitalization and housing-mobility strategies simultaneously. The well-being of literally millions of children depends on it.

Why Don't More Voucher Holders Escape Poor Neighborhoods?

by Stephanie DeLuca

Barbara Sard and Phil Tegeler argue the case for why high-quality neighborhoods and homes are important for child development, and suggest how we should leverage the housing choice voucher (HCV) program to help families reach such communities. In order to implement their strategies and take other innovative directions in housing policy, it is essential to understand what makes it difficult for families to use their vouchers to reach low-poverty communities in the first place. We know that there are important supply-side barriers, such as the relative scarcity of affordable housing in neighborhoods with high socioeconomic opportunity, as well as the higher cost of units in these communities (some exceeding HUD's fair market rent). However, in theory, voucher holders still have available affordable housing options to choose from in many neighborhoods pending landlord approval. Yet research on the residential destinations of voucher holders shows that what happens in practice is different. Why? What does the process of finding and choosing housing look like for voucher holders up close? For more than ten years—alongside my colleagues and students—I have been conducting fieldwork in several cities to answer these questions. In-depth interviews and fieldwork with hundreds of families reveal that the strategies, experiences, and constraints of poor families shape whether and how housing policies can connect families to communities of opportunity. Here are some of the lessons we've learned.

1.   *Poor families rarely choose when to move and where to live.* In recent work, we find that almost 80 percent of recent moves among poor families are sudden and often happen for reasons outside of their control.[4] The most common factors that "push" families to move include problems with landlords and poor housing quality. Sometimes landlords sell buildings out from underneath families with little notice, or a dwelling unit can become uninhabitable after significant flooding, vermin infestation, or fire from electrical problems. These unforeseen events force parents to make quick and desperate decisions about

where to live, to make sure their children don't go homeless. The situation can be complicated even for families with housing vouchers. Failed housing inspections (to meet federal housing quality standards) can also cause families to leave their unit when landlords do not cooperate with needed repairs. Another unpredictable move comes when a family finds out they're finally off the years' long voucher waiting list. This is good news to be sure, but the lottery-like lucky break comes with a hidden stressor—a time limit. Public housing agencies generally give voucher recipients sixty days to find an eligible unit before their voucher expires and is given to the next family in line. While that sounds like a lot of time, our fieldwork suggests that it easily gets eaten up, as families wait days to hear back from landlords about listed units and drive around looking for rental signs. This is even more difficult for employed parents, who have fewer days and hours to devote to the search. The unpredictable nature of residential moves adds to the time crunch to find a place (either to keep children housed or avoid losing the voucher), leading families to take what they can find, quickly. Unsurprisingly, many of these units are in poor and segregated communities similar to those where new voucher holders already live. In other words, instead of leading to gains in neighborhood quality, these reactive moves reproduce geographic inequality.

2. *Time-pressured search processes rely on quick and easy sources of information for sure-bet units.* When families suddenly find themselves with a voucher and limited search time, they rarely gamble on the longer, more difficult process of finding housing in more affluent areas. Why search somewhere uncertain and unknown while the clock is ticking? Instead, they rely on lists provided at the public housing agency and websites like GoSection8.com or on the easy referrals from friends, family, and even former landlords.[5] These resources provide the benefit of a shortcut to available units but can severely narrow search parameters to only those neighborhoods where landlords have advertised their properties as "Section 8 welcome"—often racially segregated, high- or moderate-poverty areas, with lower-quality schools. Families also know that these landlords will not turn them down because of their vouchers, a demoralizing experience for the families we've followed. Since it's legal to refuse to rent to a voucher holder in all but a handful of states and cities, this approach makes good sense. Families are faced with an implicit trade-off: searching in higher-opportunity neighborhoods where they must navigate unfamiliar places with unknown landlords while their time is running out, risking potential homelessness through the loss of their precious subsidy, versus searching in lower-opportunity neighborhoods where they are more likely to find an available unit in time.

3. *When faced with resource constraints, families often make the tough trade-off and sacrifice neighborhood quality for dwelling-unit characteristics.* One of our most striking findings is that poor families make decisions about where to live

based on the unit first, not the neighborhood.[6] For example, Holly Wood finds that when deciding where to live, parents focus first on meeting the basic needs of housing, because aspects of the dwelling unit are crucial for how they think good parents provide for their family. Mothers prioritize renting a single-family home or townhouse, rather than an apartment, because these houses tend to have private entryways (which increase safety), a backyard (which allows safe and enclosed space for children to play), a basement (which gives older adolescents independent space and reduces conflict with younger siblings), and multiple floors (to manage noise and give space for homework and privacy). Of course, these larger houses are much easier to afford in higher-poverty, inner-city areas, where families can get more "bang for the buck." However, this forces the difficult trade-off between unit and neighborhood quality.

This trade-off also extends to school quality. Parents first secure the best housing quality they can afford, within a neighborhood they deem "safe enough," and then they think about where children can go to school.[7] Often families prefer the school nearby, especially if that location makes transportation to work or child care easier to juggle. If they find that a child's school is unsafe, or not meeting educational needs, parents look to the addresses of family members or transfers to exercise school choice. These strategies make sense for getting by in dangerous neighborhoods—making sure the housing unit is adequate for raising children and keeping them indoors can protect against exposure to violence and crime. Thinking about schooling options after making a residential move also makes sense when faced with the immediate need to house your family and the limited search time in which to do so. However, these strategies suggest that housing policies cannot assume families will search the whole menu of metropolitan neighborhoods as possible destinations, or maximize neighborhood and school quality at the expense of housing size or amenities when they are given the chance to move to new communities.

4. *Families need a combination of housing subsidies and sustained housing counseling to learn about the benefits of different kinds of communities, to search for affordable quality housing in these areas, and to remain in these neighborhoods.* We've learned that families that have spent years living in high-poverty communities learn to adapt and survive there in the face of tough trade-offs, often in the absence of housing assistance. However, when given the voucher alongside extensive mobility and housing-search counseling, families will move to neighborhoods of opportunity and many will stay there.[8] Families that have escaped public housing and high-poverty neighborhoods through major mobility programs have expressed profound psychological and emotional relief after moving, and many recognize the benefits of safety and better schools for their children.[9] Recent work on the Baltimore Mobility Program has shown that when provided with a housing voucher, coupled with extensive counseling, search assistance, and security-deposit aid, families will not only relocate to

higher-opportunity neighborhoods, but remain there long after program requirements. Even more striking, perhaps, is that their subsequent moves are focused on ensuring both neighborhood quality and high-performing schools.[10] Living in these opportunity-rich neighborhoods raises expectations for what neighborhoods, homes, and schools can provide and brings new criteria, such as school quality, neighborhood "quiet," and ethnic diversity, into consideration when thinking about where to live, even when facing difficult trade-offs.

Children and Housing Vouchers: A Policy Maker's Perspective

by Sandra B. Henriquez

The housing choice voucher program provides rental assistance that enables low-income households to rent apartments in the private market. Besides making homes affordable in real estate markets throughout the country, the voucher program creates choice, allowing families to decide where they want to live. It is this ability to choose that makes the program attractive. Families receiving a voucher are able to use the same criteria we all do when deciding where to live: quality of the neighborhood, proximity to family and social supports, location of religious and educational institutions, transportation, health care, and crucially, the availability and cost of housing opportunities.

The commentary written by Barbara Sard and Philip Tegeler cites a number of compelling statistics showing that a child's zip code is highly correlated with her future success. Changing a child's zip code just might change a child's future, but we need more research to understand what features of neighborhoods matter most and which interventions provide the most benefit to children's long-term outcomes, such as increased educational opportunities, access to better jobs, reduced involvement with the social-service and criminal-justice systems, improved health, and wealth creation through homeownership and other means.

The authors underscore the potential value of a reformed housing choice voucher program in helping families move to more enriching neighborhoods. When considered together, the evidence suggests that the U.S. Department of Housing and Urban Development (HUD) may be missing a significant opportunity. The proposed reforms have merit, and many could be incorporated into the voucher program. However, advocates have the luxury of not having to balance their reform positions with the realities of the funding, operation, and administration of the voucher program itself.

HUD must balance competing goals with the voucher program. One such goal is a real reduction in homelessness. In addition to funding for special purposes, such as vouchers to reduce chronic and veterans' homelessness, HUD must decide how best to use its limited appropriations to support current program participants and to add new participants who sit on waiting lists for years at high risk of becoming homeless. Tegeler and Sard encourage housing-mobility counseling programs to assist families in moving into higher-opportunity areas. Funding for such counseling comes either from the voucher program or, as the writers suggest, from a city's community-development or HOME block-grant programs, which are already overcommitted. Creating incentives in the program to encourage landlords to lease to voucher holders and to encourage administering agencies to achieve better locational outcomes may also require money, thereby shrinking existing funding.

Should the program (1) house as many families as possible, given the funding, so that they can avoid homelessness or afford the rent; or (2) house a lesser number of families in higher-opportunity but more expensive communities? For example, in one existing voucher program with counseling, the cost of a voucher being used in opportunity communities is twice the national average. The counseling assists families in making informed choices about their potential moves and provides support for them as they venture into less welcoming neighborhoods, but it comes at a steep cost. Use of voucher funding for expenses other than actual rent subsidies means fewer families housed.

A number of other conditions, beyond HUD's control, affect the ability of voucher holders to reside in communities with low poverty concentrations. The supply of rental housing, the availability of transportation, the adherence of municipalities and of landlords to fair housing laws in both spirit and intent, and the attitude of neighbors, for instance, can both affect the ability of voucher holders to find housing in areas with higher opportunity and shape the effects of that move on their family's well-being.

Some models to overcome such barriers exist. One was set in motion when a housing developer wanted to build market-rate homes in a town in the western United States. Crucial municipal legislation required that a portion of units be affordable. Together with a strong nonprofit organization, the partners worked to create a new neighborhood in an idyllic location about fifteen miles outside of a large metropolitan center, with access to public transportation. In this wide-open, green-grass, blue-sky setting, the nonprofit and for-profit homebuilders invested significantly in the local schools. The public schools are among some of the best in the state. Concerned about their property values as voucher-holding families moved in, a few residents moved out in response, but most remained and were joined by other new residents, willing to build a welcoming, inclusive community. When the murkier issues of race and class presented themselves, people who believed in the goal of integrated housing worked to overcome them.

This community was developed with intentionality. Inclusive zoning made the affordable housing possible, and advocates and educators worked to ensure that the entire community shared experiences and felt welcomed. For instance, a sought-after day-care provider operates in the community, drawing parents of modest and not-so-modest means together, participating in the lives of their children. As these children grow up and go to school together, they will benefit from a richer educational environment that can make other opportunities possible.

In short, there are broader structural problems, such as a shortage of affordable rental housing, a lack of accessible public transportation, and continuing resistance to economic and racial integration, that challenge voucher-program outcomes, even with counseling. Working on these structural problems may be more important than adding counseling or other expensive supports to the voucher program, which will inevitably reduce the number of households that can be served. Both fair housing advocates and HUD should be at the forefront of encouraging municipalities to address these obstacles, and both HUD and local municipalities should be asking more of developers, pressing them to create opportunity-rich, affordable communities like the one described above.

When political will, social responsibility, and financial resources work together, we can change our housing policy to foster greater residential integration across race and class to create more opportunities for low-income families. It requires the sustained investment of social and financial capital. A broad-based, concerted effort to end the zero-sum funding of the voucher program to allow both more families to be housed and more families with children to change their zip codes is one avenue that must be pursued. Continued advocacy to end the larger structural problems that limit opportunities for voucher holders and for all low-income families is another.

Outcomes matter. Costs and funding matter. Zip codes matter.

Children and Housing Vouchers: A Practitioner's Perspective

by Stephen Norman

There is little question that low-income children's futures can be significantly improved by access to housing in safe, healthy neighborhoods. Public housing authorities, organizations whose mission in significant part revolves around successful long-term outcomes for the 2.7 million low-income children they house, fully subscribe to this goal. From the practitioner's perspective, however, the challenges and the solutions to accomplishing this are more complex and nuanced than they may appear from the national policy and advocacy level.

The King County Housing Authority (KCHA) houses more than 15,000 federally assisted households annually (including more than 14,500 children) in the metropolitan region surrounding the city of Seattle. Ninety-five percent of these households have incomes below 50 percent of the area median income (AMI), and 81 percent have incomes below 30 percent of AMI.

As a regional housing authority, KCHA covers an expansive suburban landscape that includes thirty-nine local jurisdictions. Two-thirds of the region's population, and a majority of households living in poverty, reside outside Seattle. The region includes wide disparities in income-subsidized meal eligibility rates (one index of concentrations of child poverty), ranging from 3 percent to 70 percent of student population in local school districts.

For more than a decade, KCHA has pursued policies and program modifications intended to encourage and enable geographic choice. Our tools in opportunity areas have included a two-tiered payment standard that sets allowable rents at over 130 percent of fair market rent, mobility counseling, the commitment of project-based Section 8 subsidies to underwrite a pipeline of nonprofit development efforts, and the acquisition of existing multifamily housing, setting aside some share of units for project-based Section 8 subsidies or public housing and prioritizing tenant-based voucher applicants. Few of these approaches would have been possible absent KCHA's participation in the Department of Housing and Urban Development's (HUD's) Moving to Work (MTW) program, which enables a very limited number of housing authorities to develop their own strategies for addressing local housing challenges.

In 2012, to assess progress, KCHA began analyzing household distribution utilizing the Kirwan Institute's "opportunity mapping" approach, which identifies low-poverty neighborhoods that offer the advantages recognized in mobility research, such as high-performing schools and access to employment. How are we doing? In 2016, 31 percent of our federally assisted households with children resided in communities with poverty rates at or below 10 percent. This compares to Philip Tegeler and Barbara Sard's statistic that nationally only 15 percent of children in households receiving federal subsidies lived in low-poverty neighborhoods.

This ten-year effort has helped us identify valuable tools and significant challenges to success in encouraging mobility and retaining households in opportunity neighborhoods. The key challenge is funding. While Tegeler and Sard's paper posits that "even in the current fiscally constrained environment, we can make substantial progress toward these goals in the next few years, without . . . additional funding," this is not our experience on the ground. Higher-opportunity areas tend to be more expensive housing markets, and if housing subsidy levels cannot support payment of market rents, this is a very short conversation with landlords.

Consider our experience in the Seattle region, which like many around the country is seeing housing costs rise as the economy rebounds. KCHA is currently supporting rents on two-bedroom homes in opportunity neighborhoods that are roughly $750/month above our lower-tier payment standard. These standards have been frozen for almost five years as a result of federal budget cutbacks and the failure of HUD to provide annual inflation factors that accurately reflect local increases in rental costs. Existing Section 8 housing choice voucher households in these markets face growing shelter burdens, and an increasing number may be forced by financial necessity to move to lower-cost, lower-opportunity neighborhoods.

As a result of federal budget cuts, the housing choice voucher program is now serving 90,000 fewer households nationally than it was three years ago. Without additional funding, it will be increasingly difficult to support households currently living in lower-poverty neighborhoods, much less to significantly increase this number without further decreasing the overall number of households served.

The prospect of taking mobility to scale is also constrained by housing typologies and rental opportunities in lower-poverty neighborhoods, and by landlord reluctance to rent to housing choice voucher households. Apartment complexes are less common in many suburban low-poverty neighborhoods. Overall rental opportunities (as a percentage of stock) tend to be limited. Single-family home rentals, where available, entail additional costs, some of which are reflected in utility allowances (which further drives up the cost of the voucher), and some of which, such as yard maintenance, become the financial responsibility of the renter. Available single-family homes can also be "oversize" for smaller households, resulting in unsubsidized bedrooms and higher rental costs that have to be borne by the household.

"Source-of-income discrimination" is also a problem. There is no overarching federal fair housing statute protecting against source-of-income discrimination and historically in King County, local protections were enacted on a patchwork city by city basis. For jurisdictions lacking this statutory protection, periods of low market vacancy saw many apartment complexes implementing "no Section 8" policies promulgated in many cases at the national corporate level. Even with the 2017 passage of a statewide source of income discrimination statute, enforcement remains challenging. While blanket discrimination is no longer allowable, property management firms continue to raise the application bar in ways that promote source of income discrimination through less explicit language. This is an issue that must be addressed by federal policy and by national and local advocacy.

Finally, low-income households must have a voice in their locational choice. In King County, we serve a diverse community that includes a significant number of refugee or immigrant families. Relocation to high-opportunity neighborhoods, given local geography, does not necessarily mean moving just a few miles or a neighborhood away. In the low-density sprawl of suburbia, this may entail moving twenty to thirty miles from their current neighborhood. In focus groups, we have heard clearly from households that this type of geographic separation from support networks that include extended families, tightly knit ethnic communities, religious institutions, and culturally competent services and shopping (such as halal butchers) is not perceived as being in the family's best interest. Concerns also include the higher cost of living (everything from groceries to day care) in low-poverty neighborhoods, lack of access to public transportation, and the cultural competency of local institutions such as schools. "English-language learner" programs, for example, may be more easily available in school districts with extensive student diversity and greater experience around this issue.

All of this leads us to a somewhat different list of priorities for increasing housing choice and opportunity.

First, housing choice voucher funding must be increased. An expectation that housing authorities can support household moves to higher-cost neighborhoods at a time when funding cutbacks are forcing reductions in the number of households served is unrealistic. A partial offset for higher rents in opportunity neighborhoods can be provided by more flexible submarket payment standards. HUD needs to accelerate efforts to provide housing authorities with the flexibility to more finely structure subsidy approaches to local submarkets.

Administrative costs need to be adequately funded as well. Tegeler and Sard assert that the current administrative geography of the housing choice voucher program undermines the program's ability to promote access to high-opportunity neighborhoods. KCHA currently administers more than 2,600 "port-in" vouchers from other jurisdictions. Clearly, portability is not that great a barrier. While administrative consolidation on the regional level is an important long-term goal, the more immediate issue is administrative caseloads. Housing authorities are currently being funded at 79 percent of actual administrative costs, as estimated by HUD. Heavy caseloads erode the ability to efficiently administer this program, much less provide mobility counseling and deal with the portability process. KCHA has significantly reduced its administrative workload through use of its MTW flexibility, eliminating unnecessary HUD paperwork and procedures and freeing up staff time to more effectively serve our clients—including households porting into the region and those looking to move to opportunity areas. In the absence of full funding for administrative costs, lessons learned from the MTW program should be used to overhaul unnecessary and overly prescriptive HUD program rules.

Second, the mix of housing and administrative strategies KCHA employs is only possible through the Moving to Work program. The operational flexibility this program provides should be expanded to more housing authorities. There is no single answer as to what approaches work in any particular market. Rather than simply "requiring better outcomes," HUD should be paying attention to what is working, where, and why and should be aggressively disseminating these best practices, and the flexibility to utilize them, nationally.

Third, the discussion around increasing the number of federally subsidized households living in low-poverty neighborhoods has been focused almost entirely on the voucher mobility approach. Our experience has been that this ignores an equally powerful tool: the placement of "fixed" subsidies, in the form of housing-authority- or nonprofit-owned housing, in opportunity communities. Approximately 43 percent of KCHA's 1,450 subsidized households with children in high or very high opportunity areas live in fixed subsidy units. This approach can ultimately be more cost effective, as rents in these units reflect actual operating costs rather than market-driven pricing and can provide—particularly in jurisdictions without strong tenant protections—greater access and more stable tenancies.

Probably the strongest evidence we have on the academic benefits of moves to opportunity areas comes from Heather Schwartz's study of low-income students living in public housing units in Montgomery County, Maryland,[11] where inclusionary zoning policies created place-based subsidized housing with extended housing tenure. The successes in Montgomery County and our experience in King County argue for a greater emphasis on providing access to opportunity neighborhoods through stable fixed-subsidy units in these neighborhoods.

Increasing geographic choice and household opportunity is a critical goal. Regional governments, local jurisdictions, and housing authorities should all be incentivized to make it a reality. But new mandates and regulations at the federal level won't get us there; adequate federal resources, combined with fewer regulations and increased local flexibility, are needed. At the same time, it must be understood that mobility will only take us so far. Mobility must be coupled with a robust program to revitalize neighborhoods and provide strong schools and economic opportunity in the communities where many low-income households already live.

Notes

1. Craig Evan Pollack, Rachel L. Johnson Thornton, and Stefanie DeLuca, "Targeting Housing Mobility Vouchers to Help Families with Children," *JAMA Pediatrics* 168, no. 8 (2014): 695–696.
2. Barbara Sard and Douglas Rice, "Creating Opportunity for Children," Center on Budget and Policy Priorities, October 14, 2014, https://www.cbpp.org/research/creating-opportunity-for-children.
3. Ingrid Gould Ellen and Keren Mertens Horn, "Do Federally Assisted Households Have Access to High Performing Public Schools? Civil Rights Research," Poverty & Race Research Action Council (NJ1), 2012, https://eric.ed.gov/?id=Ed538399.

4. Stefanie DeLuca, Holly Wood, and Peter Rosenblatt. "Why Poor People Move (and Where They Go): Residential Mobility, Selection and Stratification." *City and Community* (forthcoming).

5. Stefanie DeLuca, Philip Garboden, and Peter Rosenblatt, "Segregating Shelter: How Housing Policies Shape the Residential Locations of Low Income Minority Families," *Annals of the American Academy of Political and Social Science* 647 (2013):268–299.

6. Peter Rosenblatt and Stefanie DeLuca, "'We Don't Live Outside, We Live in Here': Neighborhood and Residential Mobility Decisions Among Low-Income Families," *City & Community* 11, no. 3 (September 2012): 254–284, https://doi.org/10.1111/j.1540 -6040.2012.01413.x; Holly M. Wood, "When only a house makes a home: How home selection matters in the residential mobility decisions of lower-income, inner-city African American families," *Social Service Review* 88 (2014): 264–294.

7. Anna Rhodes and Stefanie DeLuca, "Residential Mobility and School Choice Among Poor Families," in *Choosing Homes, Choosing Schools: Residential Segregation and the Search for a Good School*, ed. Annette Lareau and Kimberly Goyette (New York: Russell Sage Foundation, 2014), 137–166.

8. Stefanie DeLuca and Peter Rosenblatt, "Increasing Access to High Performing Schools in an Assisted Housing Voucher Program," Poverty & Race Research Action Council, 2011, https://ecommons.luc.edu/cgi/viewcontent.cgi?referer=https://www.google.com /&httpsredir=1&article=1005&context=soc_facpubs.

9. Kathryn Edin, Stefanie DeLuca, and Ann Owens, "Constrained Compliance: Solving the Puzzle of MTO's Lease-Up Rates and Why Mobility Matters," *Cityscape* 14, no. 2 (2012): 181–194.

10. Jennifer Darrah and Stefanie DeLuca, "'Living Here Has Changed My Whole Perspective': How Escaping Inner-City Poverty Shapes Neighborhood and Housing Choice," *Journal of Policy Analysis and Management* 33, no. 2 (March 2014): 350–384, https:// doi.org/10.1002/pam.21758; Stefanie DeLuca and Peter Rosenblatt, "Walking Away from The Wire: Housing Mobility and Neighborhood Opportunity in Baltimore." *Housing Policy Debate* 27 (2017): 519–546.

11. Heather Schwartz, "Housing Policy Is School Policy: Economically Integrative Housing Promotes Academic Success in Montgomery County, Maryland," in *The Future of School Integration*, ed. Richard D. Kahlenberg (New York: Century Foundation Press, 2012).

MAKING VOUCHERS MORE MOBILE

Expanding Neighborhood Choices for Voucher Tenants Using Small Area Fair Market Rents

by Robert Collinson

Since the Housing Act of 1949 set out the goal of "a decent home and suitable living environment for every American family," federal low-income housing policy has targeted the dual aims of improving both the physical housing-unit quality and the neighborhood environment for low-income families. The housing choice voucher program is expressly designed to give low-income families the choice of a better neighborhood environment.

The disappointing fact is that, on average, the voucher program doesn't actually move families to less impoverished or substantially safer neighborhoods. There are a number of explanations for why this is the case: landlords discriminate against voucher holders; rental housing in safe, low-poverty neighborhoods can be scarce; voucher holders may lack information about units in these neighborhoods; or they may elect to stay close to family or friends in poor neighborhoods. Another important explanation is that vouchers simply don't pay enough to help most low-income tenants afford rental units in nicer neighborhoods. Tenants in the voucher program are required to pay 30 percent of their income as rent and the government pays the rest, up to a subsidy ceiling (a Fair Market Rent, or FMR) that is usually set at the 40th percentile of metro-area or countywide rent.[1] Thus, the amount the government supplements is the same for both relatively expensive and relatively cheap neighborhoods *within* a metro area. Vouchers cover the cost of rent for 68 percent of rentals in poorer neighborhoods, but just 15 percent of rentals in wealthier neighborhoods.

Recently, HUD has proposed expanding an exciting demonstration targeting this latter challenge. Known as Small Area Fair Market Rents (Small Area FMRs), the policy replaces a single voucher subsidy ceiling that applies across all neighborhoods in a metro area with a subsidy maximum tied to the typical rent within each zip code. This allows the voucher to be large enough to pay for more expensive rents in higher-rent zip codes while cutting the maximum subsidy in low-rent communities.

In a recent study with Peter Ganong, I examined the effects in Dallas of Small Area FMRs, which have been in effect since 2011, and found that voucher holders in Dallas moved to measurably better neighborhoods after the implementation of Small Area FMRs, relative to a control group of voucher holders in neighboring Fort Worth.[2] Tying the Fair Market Rent to zip-code rents led voucher families in Dallas to move to less impoverished neighborhoods with substantially lower violent crime levels.[3] Using an index of neighborhood quality that incorporates crime, poverty, single-parenting, school quality, and employment, we found that voucher holders moved to neighborhoods that were 0.23 standard deviations higher in quality—equal to about one-third the Hispanic-White gap in neighborhood quality and one-quarter of the Black-White gap in the Dallas metro area.

We contrast this with an existing policy of raising the FMR across all neighborhoods from the 40th to the 50th percentile of metro-area rents.[4] This policy fails to move voucher holders to high-quality units or neighborhoods. When the FMR is raised across all neighborhoods, voucher holders don't appear to take their vouchers to better neighborhoods. Instead, they search in the same neighborhoods, either to improve their odds of leasing-up at all (only about two-thirds of families issued vouchers successfully lease-up through the program) or to find units with more space or amenities. In contrast, Small Area FMRs level the odds of finding a unit in high- and low-quality neighborhoods, encouraging families to search for units in higher-quality areas where their voucher "goes further."

Identifying cost-effective strategies to improve the neighborhood environments for voucher families—particularly those with young children, who are likely to benefit most from low-poverty neighborhoods—is critically important for the voucher program. Some concerns remain about negative consequences of FMR reductions in low-rent neighborhoods: will voucher families simply occupy worse-quality units in low-rent neighborhoods, or will they occupy the same units but shoulder more of the rent (or will voucher tenants find acceptable units at all)? These are legitimate concerns that should be tracked closely. However, in many markets, voucher tenants already occupy units well below the FMR, so these tenants may be relatively unaffected by reductions in FMRs.[5] The effectiveness of Small Area Fair Market Rents may vary by housing market conditions and population groups (such as the disabled and the elderly); both are areas that warrant further research. But Small Area FMRs can be a critical tool to enable voucher families to find units in less impoverished neighborhoods where children and adults can realize the benefits of safer streets and better schools.

Housing Choice Shouldn't Be at the Expense of Other Low-Income Renters

by Rachel Fee

HUD wants to expand its successful pilot for Small Area Fair Market Rents (SAFMR) to New York City. With promising outcomes in a Dallas demonstration program, HUD proposes new rules for New York City and other regions with high levels of voucher concentration to both encourage and enable voucher holders to move to areas of higher opportunity and lower poverty. Instead of a citywide Fair Market Rent (FMR), rents will be set by zip code. This "cost-effective" proposal will raise allowable rents in some zip codes and lower them in others to more accurately reflect housing submarkets within a region. This proposal is full of promise and may work well in some localities, but in a high-cost, extremely-low-vacancy city like New York, it could have disastrous consequences.

In New York City, our housing agencies estimate that roughly one-third of our 120,000 voucher holders' rental assistance payments would go down. HUD's proposal is made without a Section 8 budget increase, so housing "opportunity" for some low-income families will come at the expense of others. Families who choose to stay in their current homes in high-poverty areas, or those who are unable to move, will literally pay the price of higher rents for families using their voucher in more expensive neighborhoods. Half of impacted households are elderly and/or disabled, with an average annual income of less than $15,000; paying higher rent will surely affect the quality of life for these households. In a red-hot real estate market that has driven homelessness to all-time heights and a vacancy rate of 3.4 percent, classified at emergency level by HUD, finding an apartment at all will be a challenge, even in an only marginally lower-poverty neighborhood.

Within thirteen to twenty-four months, 36,000 families would be expected to move to a higher-income neighborhood or remain in place by negotiating a lower rent or paying more. A higher rent burden is the likely outcome for families who stay. The premise underlying HUD's policy proposal is that landlords will accept lower rents in high-poverty, low-rent neighborhoods so that tenant payments won't rise much when subsidy amounts fall. This is an unrealistic and risky assumption when rents are rising and vacancy rates are low, even in high-poverty neighborhoods, some of which are rapidly gentrifying. For movers, the new vouchers, set at 40th percentile rents, may have insufficient purchasing power in a tight rental market to open up new neighborhood options to families. Another problem with SAFMRs is that zip codes fail to delineate meaningful boundaries for housing submarkets in New York. While HUD's proposal may offer some flexibility for housing authorities to combine zip codes upon application, the geography of zip codes offers no comfort to affordable-housing advocates concerned by the immensely complicated process of finding an apartment using a Section 8 voucher with 176 rent levels (our number of zip codes).

Section 8 is a mobility program. When only one in five families use their vouchers to rent in low-poverty areas nationally, it is clearly not providing the mobility intended. In New York, vouchers are primarily concentrated in poor neighborhoods in Brooklyn and the Bronx. That must change. Giving low-income families more housing options, especially in high-opportunity neighborhoods with better schools, lower crime, access to employment, and transit, is what the program should do. But program improvements should not be achieved on the backs of low-income families who choose not to or are unable to move. Only with a significant budget increase, should HUD consider offering higher rent levels in New York City—not by zip code, but perhaps in high-performing school districts or other more meaningful boundaries.

Small Area FMRs: A Jump-Start to Affirmatively Furthering Fair Housing

by Demetria McCain

Robert Collinson concludes from his quantitative analysis that Small Area Fair Market Rents (SAFMRs) help housing choice voucher (HCV) families to find units in less impoverished neighborhoods where they can realize the benefits of safer streets and better schools. The on-the-ground experience of the Inclusive Communities Project's (ICP's) Mobility Assistance Program (MAP) in the Dallas area suggests that nothing could be more true. While Collinson highlights important research showing that Dallas movers accessed lower-poverty areas with better schools and less crime when SAFMRs came to town, his essay doesn't sufficiently emphasize the power of zip-code-based subsidies to combat racial segregation and affirmatively further fair housing.

HUD's interest in expanding SAFMRs to other metros hinges, in part, on the expectation that they will enhance the ability of voucher holders to access housing in integrated neighborhoods in support of the agency's goal of affirmatively furthering fair housing.[6] Notably, Dallas Housing Authority's (DHA's) May 31, 2016 Resident Characteristics Report shows that 87 percent of its 15,749 voucher holders are Black, and a similar share existed in 2011, when SAFMRs came online. According to then DHA executive director Mary Ann Russ, more than five thousand DHA voucher holders moved to more integrated and opportunity-rich areas during the first three years the agency used zip-code-based subsidies.[7]

For many MAP families, if being called from the voucher waiting list was like winning the state lottery, accessing zip-code-based subsidies was like winning the Powerball. It was a ticket out of a high-poverty, racially concentrated neighborhood.

Despite outcries from landlords who worried they might lose their longtime above-market rents in high-poverty segregated areas, for families like Lamesa White's, the program change meant the world. Many MAP families regularly say they enjoy "the peace" after making the choice to move to lower-poverty locales; for Ms. White, it meant being able to leave an area where her child's classmate was shot the day her family moved.[8] The move led her to an environment that inspired her teenage daughter to attend college and provided a school with more one-on-one special education attention for her younger child.

While a small pool of families with DHA litigation-designated vouchers with enhanced rents (about 2,500) regularly reached low-poverty, moderate-income, high-opportunity communities before Dallas's SAFMR era, few regular HCV holders could access these neighborhoods. Some explain the concentration of regular voucher holders in high-poverty, segregated areas as the result of families' choices to live near what is familiar. However, when SAFMRs were introduced in Dallas, families showed strong interest in moving to different neighborhoods. About 82 percent of the approximately three thousand regular MAP relocation briefing attendees signed up in 2012 to hear more about MAP's counseling and housing search assistance for families interested in what would be beyond "the familiar." While all did not move that year to ICP-defined high-opportunity areas, in part because of some of the additional barriers that Collinson notes, the long sign-up sheets belie the notion that no one seeks integrative moves out of high-poverty segregated neighborhoods. For these families, zip-code-based FMRs mattered.

That said, implementation of SAFMRs acts as a floor, not a ceiling, for what housing program administrators should do to help families who wish to move out of racially segregated areas.

Comprehensive mobility counseling and policy improvements (within and outside the HCV program) can remove many barriers to fair-housing choice for voucher families. But these efforts go nowhere if the voucher's buying power remains strangled under a metro-area-wide FMR system. Collinson is correct. Expansion of SAFMRs is exciting. In fact, it could be the most important jump-start HUD and public housing authorities can take to meet their obligation to truly affirmatively further fair housing.

Supporting and Protecting Low-Income Residents Are Essential to Ensuring Successful SAFMR Implementation

by Diane Yentel

Almost 14 million people live in neighborhoods of concentrated poverty, and the number is growing, nearly doubling since the year 2000.[9] The impacts of this trend are felt most within communities of color. One in four poor black families and one in seven poor Latino families live in concentrated poverty, compared to one in thirteen poor white families.[10] The recent work by Raj Chetty and colleagues affirms the profound impact of place on the trajectory of our lives. On average, the years that a young child spends in a deeply poor neighborhood contribute to lifelong negative outcomes—lowering educational attainment, lifetime earnings, even life expectancy.[11] Given this knowledge, it is distressing that so many recipients of HUD-subsidized assistance live in neighborhoods of concentrated poverty.

Recent legal and policy developments may help to reverse this troubling pattern. In the summer of 2015, HUD published its long awaited Affirmatively Furthering Fair Housing rule, providing communities with tools, incentives, and an obligation to advance strategies that reduce disparities in access to opportunity. HUD's intent to expand the use of Small Area Fair Market Rents (SAFMRs) is another important and much needed step forward.

As Robert Collinson points out, SAFMRs are meant to make it easier for those in the housing choice voucher program to move out of areas of concentrated poverty. This change has the potential to provide voucher households easier access to lower-poverty neighborhoods with higher-quality schools, lower crime rates, and better access to jobs. His research indicates that they have accomplished this result in at least one area of the country.

Still, to ensure that SAFMRs achieve the intended outcome, other policy improvements are needed at the federal, state, and local levels to address remaining obstacles for underresourced families to live in higher-cost neighborhoods. Many voucher households that wish to move may be limited by very low rental vacancy rates. Others may face financial barriers to moving, such as an inability to afford a security deposit or moving costs. High-quality mobility counseling may be necessary for voucher holders to successfully locate and retain homes in new neighborhoods. Landlords may reject vouchers, particularly in high-demand locations, because of limited program knowledge, unwillingness to wait while the housing authority schedules inspections, or outright housing discrimination. Expansion of "source-of-income" protections is needed; only a handful of communities proposed to transition to SAFMRs offer such protections. And retrofitting more affordable units to be accessible for elderly or disabled tenants may be necessary for them to successfully move to another community.

At the same time, we must ensure that SAFMRs don't harm those voucher holders who choose to remain in their communities. Some may want to remain close to social and other networks. They may be better able to find housing units of the size or structure that best suits their families' needs in current neighborhoods. Others who are elderly or living in households without children may choose neighborhoods for qualities other than schools, transportation, or access to child care. For the residents who stay in low-rent/higher-poverty communities, the change to SAFMRs may mean reduced voucher subsidies, which can result in increases to their share of rent payments and increased housing instability (though HUD's rule provides protections for sitting tenants).[12] Lowered voucher subsidies may drive some landlords who currently accept vouchers to leave the program, resulting in displacement of current voucher households and a further reduction in homes affordable to people who need them the most. In these cases, strong tenant protections accompanying SAFMRs are necessary, including exempting current voucher holders from lowered payment standards for as long as they remain in the same unit and phasing in the changes over an extended period of time.

Ultimately, supporting and protecting voucher participants will be essential to ensuring successful SAFMR implementation and to truly creating new opportunities for low-income people.

Notes

1. The rent ceiling, known as the "payment standard," is determined locally by public housing authorities, but it must be between 90 and 110 percent of the Fair Market Rent, which is determined by HUD and is typically set at the 40th percentile of a metro rent distribution. Tenants may rent units above the payment standard, but must bear the cost of each additional dollar above the ceiling.
2. Robert Collinson and Peter Ganong, "How Do Changes In Housing Voucher Design Affect Rent and Neighborhood Quality?," *American Economic Journal: Economic Policy* 10, no. 2 (2018):62–89. Note that this paper uses a special tabulation of American Community Survey data to calculate the fraction of units below a metro 40th percentile rent within each census tract. Census tracts with median rents of 150 percent of the FMR or greater have only 15 percent of their rental stock renting below the 40th percentile of the metro distribution.

3. The median number of zip codes in a metro area is thirty-seven, and the average number across all core-based statistical areas (CBSAs) is greater than sixty.

4. This equivalent to an across-the-aboard increase of approximately 11 percent.

5. Using data from the mid-2000s, Collinson and Ganong estimate that 60 percent of voucher tenants rent units below FMR.

6. Fed. Reg. 39222 (2015).

7. Mary Ann Russ, presentation at the Dallas Fair Housing Symposium, April 30, 2014.

8. Binyamin Appelbaum, "Vouchers Help Families Move Far from Public Housing," *New York Times*, July 7, 2015, http://www.nytimes.com/2015/07/08/business/economy/housing-program-expansion-would-encourage-more-low-income-families-to-move-up.html.

9. Paul Jargowsky, "Architecture of Segregation," Century Foundation, August 9, 2015, http://apps.tcf.org/architecture-of-segregation.

10. Jargowsky, "Architecture of Segregation."

11. Raj Chetty, Nathaniel Hendren, and Lawrence F. Katz, "The Effects of Exposure to Better Neighborhoods on Children: New Evidence from the Moving to Opportunity Experiment," National Bureau of Economic Research Working Paper No. 21156, 2015, http://www.nber.org/papers/w21156.

12. Housing authorities have leeway to delay new payment standard for sitting tenants. Further, HUD will limit the decrease in SAFMR to no more than 10 percent from prior year. Housing authorities are also allowed to set different payment standards for disabled tenants, and HUD may approve exception payment standards for certain ZIP Codes.

GENTRIFICATION AND THE PROMISE OF INTEGRATION

Transforming Gentrification Into Integration

by Rachel D. Godsil

The demographics of the Bedford-Stuyvesant neighborhood of Brooklyn, New York, are changing. According to data from the Furman Center, the percentage of White non-Hispanic residents in Bedford-Stuyvesant grew from 2 percent to 16 percent between 2000 and 2011. The percentage of Black residents fell from 75 percent in 2000 to 61 percent in 2011. Latino (19 percent in 2000, 18 percent in 2011) and Asian (1 percent in 2000, 2 percent in 2011) residents' percentages remained more stable. During this same period, the crime rate decreased, and the percentage of children scoring at grade level in math more than doubled.[1] These outcomes seem positive from an integration perspective: the community is less racially isolated, crime is decreasing, and children's achievements are growing. But Bedford-Stuyvesant is described as "gentrifying" rather than "integrating." And it seems that activists are more likely to be protesting, and significant percentages of residents of the neighborhood worrying, rather than celebrating.

Gentrification is not equated with integration even if, in literal terms, a neighborhood's demographics have become more racially, ethnically, and economically diverse. The reasons are myriad, but generally people focus on two related but distinct phenomena: forced displacement and imposed culture shift.

These concerns are not illusory—as anyone who has recently spent time in Bedford-Stuyvesant or neighboring Crown Heights, Brooklyn, can attest.

According to one caricature, when gentrification occurs, "Housing prices balloon; boutiques and bistros blossom; and before you know it, some bearded dudes in vests have bought the local bodega and opened a saloon festooned with taxidermied animals."[2] While the image is ridiculous, the perceived loss to the longtime residents is not. This pain of loss of community and the harm of lost autonomy are well recognized from eminent-domain literature.

As a longtime civil rights lawyer and Brooklyn resident, I ardently support integration—but I worry deeply about gentrification. The distinction in my mind is choice: between scenarios in which people of all races and ethnicities choose to live in a racially and economically integrated neighborhood or town, and scenarios in which only the affluent (who are often White) have the means to make choices.

But I think we need to move beyond the familiar antigentrification and pro-development binary. Residential change in neighborhoods is inevitable, whether a neighborhood gentrifies or not. The forced exit of sizable numbers of community members is harmful both to them and to those who remain. The problem is that gentrification currently causes nonconsensual exit—and, as such, threatens the autonomy of the displaced in a way that is unlike a choice to move. The goal, I think, is to recognize a broad scope for those who have a stake in a neighborhood and to devise mechanisms for ensuring the autonomy of current residents.

The ideal response is a vehicle that allows current residents to remain but also allows them to choose whether to leave, rather than being involuntarily displaced. Such a vehicle would seem to blunt the criticism that gentrification is an illegitimate invasion by outsiders, and it would transform gentrification into a mechanism by which truly fair housing can be furthered.

Cities, with the help of the federal government, have the option of creating such a vehicle—and indeed they have, when using eminent-domain powers against owners. I argue that cities like New York, borrowing from eminent-domain remedies and federal government mobility programs operated by the Department of Housing and Urban Development (HUD), should use rental vouchers or low-interest loans to restore the autonomy of current residents, providing them with viable, self-determining options to remain or exit the neighborhood. Indeed, the Fair Housing Act legally obligates HUD and its grantees to "affirmatively further fair housing," and HUD has funds available to fulfill this mandate.[3] The absence of true autonomy and choice for current residents of gentrifying neighborhoods threatens the legitimacy of any integration that may occur as a result of the influx of new residents.

Why Should Gentrification Trigger Government Action?

Many will assume that the displacement and other outcomes that occur in the wake of gentrification are simply the result of people's choices expressed through the market—in which case, the argument goes, government intervention is not appropriate. Others will be of the view that government has a role to play whenever vulnerable populations are at risk of adverse consequences. People can fall on either side of this debate and still, I would argue, be persuaded that government has an obligation to act in the context of gentrification, because the evidence is overwhelming that the current harms of gentrification follow directly from government action.[4]

In the context of urban neighborhoods, the decline in property values that occurred following World War II was a direct consequence of decisions made by the federal government, bankers, and real estate brokers. The private hand of the market was consciously manipulated in ways that caused a decline in property values and in the quality of life in urban neighborhoods.

The role of government—federal, state, and local—in creating the conditions that now lend themselves to gentrification and reduced autonomy for current residents suggests that the government has an obligation to play a role in addressing gentrification and enhancing such autonomy.

Legal Mechanisms to Address Gentrification

The "upscaling" of reasonably stable urban neighborhoods alters the current aesthetic and use norms of a particular area. The existing land-use legal toolkit, however, is rarely at play to protect community interests. Two simple, but important, differences are scale and political power. Accordingly, when "gentrification" begins—when outsiders with more capital move into neighborhoods their ilk once abandoned—the current residents have to counter the political might of the extant middle and upper class of the city.

Gentrification often does not require zoning changes. This means that current residents of gentrifying neighborhoods lack many of the land-use controls that others utilize to protect their autonomy, and new devices are needed to afford that protection.

First, governments will need to decide what level of gentrification warrants intervention, and second, they will need metrics to determine which residents qualify for protection. To the extent that any intervention requires expenditures, in these budgetary times, governments will also need to identify sources of funds.

The Gentrification Trigger

The first issue in structuring protection for current residents is how to determine when gentrification is occurring. I would suggest three metrics for determining when gentrification may be at play: increased rents, higher home-purchase prices, and a shift in the income level of residents. For many concerned about gentrification, the most obvious signal is the growing number of high-income Whites moving into their neighborhood, but for constitutional and other reasons, linking the trigger for gentrification to the percentage of people of a particular race is a nonstarter.

New York City requires careful attention to the data because of the presence of rent-controlled, rent-stabilized, and public housing in neighborhoods that can artificially depress the median rents. So at first glance, it appeared that Bedford-Stuyvesant's rental rates actually decreased slightly (1.79 percent) between 2009 and 2011. Once we disaggregated market-rate housing, however, the picture changed dramatically: Bedford-Stuyvesant had a 48 percent increase in market-rate rents between 2002 and 2011, with 12.7 percent of the increase between 2008 and 2011.

Still, a single metric with an artificial cutoff is likely too crude. For example, including the percentage of high-income households moving to low-income neighborhoods is a more useful measure for the "culture shift" and power-dynamic change that underlies opposition to gentrification. Limiting the focus to neighborhoods with a median household income less than 40 percent of the median household income for the metropolitan area would limit the focus to lower-income neighborhoods while also taking into account the local cost of living. Further limiting the focus to neighborhoods where the median income of new homeowners is 50 percent or more above the neighborhood's median income targets efforts specifically at neighborhoods experiencing a more unequal power dynamic as the neighborhood changes.

However we define the gentrification trigger, the next question is what tools a city might employ to preserve the autonomy of renters. Obviously, one option is simply to reimpose rent control or stabilization more widely. I would suggest, however, that this move is flawed because it only preserves the renter's ability to stay.

An option that relies upon existing tools and a "market" model would be to issue a voucher to cover the increased rental costs to all renters able to establish that they had lived or operated a business in the neighborhood for a set number of years. Arguably, those entitled to the voucher would include the grown children of people who had lived in the neighborhood for the set number of years, since they would have inherited the home had their parents been homeowners rather than renters. The voucher would be available for a set number of years correlated to the number of years a person has lived in the neighborhood. Another option would be to offer these same residents a very low cost guaranteed loan with a minimal down payment to allow for purchase of a home.

The rental voucher or low-cost loan would directly address the displacement concerns. Any long-term residents (or their children) would have the option of remaining in the neighborhood. And while perhaps paradoxical, I argue that such a voucher or loan option should also be transferable out of the neighborhood, which would offer true choice and autonomy for current residents. When long-term residents or business owners and their children have choice and autonomy, the anger over any change to the culture of the neighborhood would seem to be quelled.

Once current residents have a choice of whether to stay or move, there is the potential for residents to organize and to persuade other residents and business owners to stay. If many current residents and business owners were to remain, the retail offerings and street life would likely not change in any meaningful way. Or if they did, the change would occur on the residents' own terms. If too few people stayed, those who remained might feel a sense of loss but not, presumably, a sense that outsiders had pushed out their neighbors.

If most voucher holders remain, one presumes the gentrification cycle would either slow down considerably or halt altogether. Gentrifiers tend to come in waves—artists and others seeking low rent and an "authentic" community, families seeking diverse neighborhoods, and then, as amenities follow, wealthier families whose capital drives the housing costs and retail demands even higher. If most current residents remain, however, a lack of supply would prevent the subsequent waves. Although this harms the economic interests of landlords, in gentrifying neighborhoods, rental properties were among those that were devalued by the disinvestment and abandonment, so landlords would have been able to buy very cheaply initially, which mitigates any equity concerns.

Affirmatively Furthering Fair Gentrification

Why should the federal government play a role in facilitating these vouchers? To respond to its legal obligations under the Fair Housing Act of 1968 Congress required HUD and its grantees to do more than combat private housing discrimination.[5] In recognition of HUD's own legacy of segregation, HUD has a mandate to actively promote integration.

Government played a significant role in creating the conditions that led to the harms of current residents; therefore, government at the city and federal levels ought to lead the effort to eliminate the aspects of gentrification that generate the most intense opposition. Given HUD's mandate, cities experiencing gentrification should have the option of seeking HUD funds to counter the current dynamic, which continues the cycle of denying autonomy to residents of urban neighborhoods.

Neighborhoods undergoing gentrification generally experience significant influxes of private wealth and political clout. This combination tends to generate increased commercial activity and governmental services and amenities. If current residents have the financial means to remain, they will ideally be able to benefit from the employment opportunities, educational opportunities, and other quality-of-life improvements that are precisely the qualities HUD seeks to incentivize in its pursuit of "mixed-income communities of opportunity." Accordingly, the federal government should be encouraged to expend funds to transform gentrification into a strategy for affirmatively furthering fair housing, rather than allow it to continue as yet another racialized dynamic that denies autonomy to the Black, Latino, and Asian American families that remained in neighborhoods hard hit by the policies of last century.

New York City is perfectly positioned to experiment with mobility vouchers or other mechanisms to recognize the interests of longtime residents of newly popular neighborhoods. Mayor DeBlasio is committed to affordable housing and to protecting those who have not prospered in the past two decades. I worry that if action is not taken soon, we will once again have trammeled the autonomy of longtime residents of Bedford-Stuyvesant, Crown Heights, and other "up-and-coming" neighborhoods. The residents of these neighborhoods experienced decades in which their neighborhoods were synonymous with urban crime and racial tension. The discovery of the beautiful homes and access to transit by affluent young families should not be at the expense of families who maintained the neighborhoods during those years.

Creating Integrated Communities Is More Than Preventing Displacement

by Lance Freeman

Rachel Godsil's essay takes up the challenge and opportunity posed by gentrification. Gentrification often entails the movement of higher-socioeconomic-status whites into relatively poor, predominantly minority communities. Rachel's observation of increased racial and socioeconomic diversity in Bedford-Stuyvesant is borne out by more systematic research that I have undertaken that shows that neighborhoods that experienced gentrification across the 1980s and 1990s were more diverse, both in racial and ethnic terms and in terms of socioeconomic status, than other central-city neighborhoods that did not experience gentrification.[6] Despite the increased diversity associated with gentrification, however, cynicism and despair are the hallmarks of this type of neighborhood change. Godsil's idea offers a starting point for addressing some of the fears associated with gentrification. For reasons I outline below, however, there is more that could and should be done to address the challenges posed by gentrification.

Long-term residents, particularly renters, often fear that if rents rise during gentrification, they will no longer be able to afford to remain in the neighborhood. Offering housing vouchers to residents of gentrifying neighborhoods would help allay one of the major fears of gentrification—that of displacement.

But offering vouchers only to those who currently reside in the gentrifying neighborhood might not be sufficient for maintaining racial/ethnic and socio-economic diversity in the long run. Several studies have shown that the major force of demographic change in gentrifying neighborhoods is the alteration in who is able to move into such neighborhoods, not how quickly the current residents move out.[7] If we remember that neighborhoods are dynamic entities, with people being born, dying, and moving away all the time, we realize that neighborhood stability is only apparent when the incomers look like those leaving. Voucher holders also die, retire, and move away. Under Godsil's plan, these voucher holders will be replaced by others who don't necessarily look like them, and the risk of resegregation will remain.

To maintain housing affordability and consequently racial and ethnic and socioeconomic diversity in gentrifying neighborhoods, we need affordable housing that is open to both current and future residents of the neighborhood. One way of doing this would be to fund a community-based organization (CBO) to help provide affordable housing in a gentrifying community. The CBO would help define its catchment area or zone. Financing could come from the increase in property values and consequently property taxes that, by definition, accompanies gentrification of the type that might cause displacement. This increase in property taxes in the gentrifying neighborhood could be set aside specifically to fund affordable housing in the very neighborhood undergoing gentrification. These funds could be used for vouchers or, if appropriate, to construct new affordable housing developments. Inclusionary zoning could also be adopted to cover new market-rate developments within the gentrifying zone. Funding affordable housing that is open to all is more equitable than limiting scarce subsidies to those who happen to live in a gentrifying neighborhood. After all, there are many other poor households who also need housing. Moreover, setting aside increased property taxes to fund affordable housing could help circumvent the politically difficult challenge of paying for more affordable housing. Given that the New York City Housing Authority (NYCHA) does not have sufficient funds to adequately maintain its existing stock and that NYCHA has not accepted applications for vouchers since 2009 for lack of funds, this is a challenge that should not be overlooked.

Finally, providing CBOs in gentrifying neighborhoods with the resources to fund affordable housing might also help sustain these organizations to undertake other activities such as community mobilizing. Such mobilization is required so that long-term residents feel that they have a say in what happens in their community, and so that they won't come to ask questions like the one posed by a long-term resident of one gentrifying Brooklyn neighborhood: "Why does it take an influx of white New Yorkers in the south Bronx, in Harlem, in Bed Stuy, in Crown Heights for the facilities to get better?"[8] Too often, residents of gentrifying neighborhood feel that the improvements taking place are for the benefit of newcomers. A mobilized community with the capacity to look after its own interests would be better positioned to effect change in the neighborhood and would likely be less cynical about the changes taking place.

Choice and Gentrification

by Olatunde Johnson

Discussions about gentrification are often puzzling. To start, we cannot seem to agree on the definition of the term. Commonly, it has a negative tint—newer, wealthier residents come into a community and make housing less affordable for existing residents. This is the concept of gentrification that dominates recent debates about tech-induced neighborhood change in San Francisco, as well as discourse about Brooklyn by cultural critic residents and filmmaking former residents of the borough. But listening to these discussions, one might begin to wonder who constitutes the gentry, and who one should blame for change. Artists and middle-class residents worry about an influx of wealthy residents and luxury condos. But these artists and middle-class residents could easily be recast as first-wave gentrifiers themselves—increasing housing prices and giving formerly lower-income neighborhoods cultural appeal (be it for hipsters or breeders). And then sometimes the term "gentrification" disappears from our discussion of neighborhood change. Blocks from Columbia University, the South Harlem neighborhood along Frederick Douglass Boulevard ("Eighth Avenue" to Harlem's old-timers) was utterly transformed in the space of a decade, with new condos, luxury rentals, beer gardens, and craft cocktail bars. This change was orchestrated by city planners who sought to remake the troubled corridor. Indeed, the very devastation of the neighborhood—its abandoned lots and brownfields—allowed for its dramatic, from-the-ground-up transformation. This change, though, is not faulted as gentrification, but celebrated as "revitalization."

In this confusion, Godsil invites us to consider the integrative benefits of "gentrification," and the role of law and social policy in offsetting potential harms to poorer residents as communities "upscale." As Godsil recognizes, neighborhood change is inevitable. Accordingly, Godsil appropriately places a large part of the onus on government planners and policy makers to identify and offset harms to low-income residents who will inevitably lack the clout to advocate against private interests. I particularly appreciate that Godsil recognizes the crucial role of federal policy and specifically the Fair Housing Act, which are often left out of discussions of how to constitute our urban spaces.

At the same time, I have questions about the "autonomy" framework. If change is truly inevitable, one might wonder who constitutes the "community." One might feel less confident in determining who is "old" and who is "new," or in identifying the point at which neighborhoods begin to change. Further, many of the urban neighborhoods whose character we wish to preserve are a construct of discriminatory public policy and private discrimination—revealing the complexity of disavowing that history yet honoring individual and family connections to place.

This all leads me to ask whether honoring "autonomy" is the best goal. Should it instead be ensuring participation and advancing inclusion? Participation and inclusion allow us to ask: What kinds of neighborhoods do we want to create? How do we preserve and expand affordable housing? Who should participate in planning and policy decisions? And how do we construct public policy to achieve these goals? We might then abandon our struggle with terminology—gentrification, displacement, integration—and instead construct a positive vision for communities, one that recognizes the constancy of change. If our goal is economically and culturally vibrant, mixed-income, racially and ethnically integrated, and democratically inclusive neighborhoods, we can stop talking now about who was there when and focus our efforts on how state, local, and federal policy might best be harnessed to achieve those goals.

It Will Take More Than a Voucher

by Brad Lander

As Rachel Godsil writes, it is intellectually tempting—but currently misguided—to think of gentrification as a solution to the segregation that divides New York City.

I have been grappling uneasily with this tension for the past twenty-five years, at the Fifth Avenue Committee (whose founding mission in 1977 was to confront displacement and preserve diversity in Park Slope), at the Pratt Center for Community Development, as a past board chair of the Association for Neighborhood and Housing Development (ANHD), and for the past decade representing much of "Brownstone Brooklyn" in the New York City Council.

We have built and preserved hundreds of units of affordable housing, helped thousands of people find good jobs in growing sectors, pioneered new "mandatory inclusionary housing" and 421-a tax incentive policies, and helped to preserve rent regulations.

But we certainly have not succeeded in preserving diversity. Rents and home prices are no longer affordable for young professionals, much less teachers or artists, much less old-timers or low-income families. Even in those places where there is a bit more diversity within a few blocks (e.g., near subsidized housing), the schools often remain more segregated than the neighborhood.

Don't get me wrong. I love my community—its great public schools, parks, livable streets, and locally owned businesses—and yes, its contradictory but very real commitment to social justice and fighting inequality. We remain keenly aware of the contradictions.

Even as gentrification and immigration have taken a bit off its rough edges, NYC remains firmly segregated. We have seen the smallest declines in segregation of any big city in the United States, and we are the second highest in racial segregation. Economic segregation is growing, with fewer mixed-income neighborhoods and more very wealthy and very poor ones.

New York's schools are the most racially segregated in the country. As Aaron Pallas writes, this is true even in gentrifying neighborhoods, where zone-based neighborhood schools resegregate rapidly and dramatically.

While a modest number of homeowners have benefited from the changes, renters (outside of subsidized housing) are likely to be displaced from their neighborhood just as the schools and services are improving. New Yorkers are mostly renters. Lower-income New Yorkers are overwhelmingly renters.

Godsil is also right that gentrification compels government action in order to make sure more residents benefit. While the more highly linked articles about gentrification are cultural, for me the policy issues are ones of class and opportunity. Our goal should not be to engineer neighborhood culture—but it should be to offer far more equality in life chances.

But confronting the problem of gentrification with a commitment to real equality of opportunity is far harder than Godsil acknowledges with her prescription for "gentrification vouchers."

For starters, it is not only too expensive, but even self-defeating to offer subsidies that would further fuel the speculative increases in land prices that are driving displacement.

A bizarre but horrible case in point was the mass eviction of more than one hundred seniors (in their eighties, nineties, and over one hundred, including a Holocaust survivor and a Tuskegee airman) from the Prospect Park Residence assisted living facility in Park Slope. These residents paid more than $5,000 per month (including a meal plan and some services in addition to rent), but they were pushed out by a landlord whose base greed simply knew no limits. The assisted living facility was making money, but as soon as his "J-51" tax abatement (for renovations done 15 years prior) expired, he realized he could make far more by evicting them and selling the building to the highest bidder, who would turn it into luxury condos.

Gentrification vouchers for the seniors at the Prospect Park Residence would have cost far more than we could justify subsidizing—and they still would not have abated the trauma of a 102-year-old great-grandmother forced to move many miles away and see her great-grandkids far less often. The right answer was stronger protections to keep the elderly residents in place, not very expensive public subsidies that would justify the mass eviction of seniors, and further fuel rental price increases in the neighborhood.

If we want to leverage the benefits of growth in a more equal way, if we want to create "neighborhoods of choice and opportunity," we have to be willing to do more to temper, regulate, and redistribute the speculative increases themselves. Toward that end, we should embrace stronger regulatory tools that might give values of decency and equality a fighting chance.

- *Stronger rent laws.* The Governor and State Legislature must close the loopholes in New York State's rent regulation laws (e.g. preferential rents, individual apartment increases, major capital increases, vacancy bonuses, and vacancy decontrol) that put hundreds of thousands of tenants at risk of harassment and displacement. Operating multifamily rental property in NYC is good business. We don't need to allow super-profits to owners looking to convert their buildings, out of some sense of obligation to the market. In gentrifying places outside of New York, policy makers might want to consider the intriguing contemporary model of selective rent regulation proposed by Arlo Chase.[9]
- *Mandatory inclusionary zoning,* to insist on affordable units in all new multifamily developments, regardless of whether they receive density bonuses or tax breaks, and with additional units required where there they do. Such requirements would not only create many new affordable housing units, they would also moderate spiraling land prices a little bit, as the affordability obligation gets built into the price of land.
- *Rezone neighborhoods of opportunity (not just low-income communities) for additional density.* So far, all of the neighborhood rezonings by the deBlasio Administration using "mandatory inclusionary housing" (MIH) have been in low-income communities of color. To realize the potential of MIH to increase overall housing opportunities citywide, and to achieve integration without displacement, the City must also rezone whiter, wealthier neighborhoods (like Gowanus, which we are currently working toward, and many others) to create affordable housing opportunities all across New York City.
- *Permanent and deep affordability of subsidized housing,* to better prevent families from being pushed out at the end of the regulatory period. We have seen too many cases in which families have been evicted and affordability lost, for a return that developers never imagined or relied on when they negotiated the deal thirty years earlier. On publicly owned land, municipalities should prioritize community land trusts, limited equity cooperatives, shared equity homeownership, and not-for-profit developers who are mission-driven to preserve affordability, and that remove speculative pressures to increase rents or sales prices over the long term.

- *More durable mixed use.* It is not only residents that get pushed out, but businesses too. We've got a real opportunity in Gowanus to preserve blue-collar jobs, some room for arts and industry, and a mixed-use neighborhood, even as we permit some new residential development—but only if we include far stronger zoning tools to protect manufacturing and mixed-use areas (and provide for the infrastructure needed to sustain smart growth), as we have aimed to do throughout our community planning efforts in Gowanus.
- *Confronting school segregation head-on.* As a result of advocacy from students, parents, educators, electeds and civil rights advocates, the City has finally begun to recognize the harms of school segregation, after decades of inaction. In 2017, New York City released a plan to increase diversity in New York City's schools, and for first time set (still too modest) numeric targets. A handful of districts and schools are doing even more—District 1 (elementary schools) on the Lower East Side and District 15 (middle schools) in Park Slope are taking bold action to integrate, including the elimination of academic and behavioral admissions screens, along with set-asides in every school for low-income students, at their percentage of the district overall. We are encouraged by the progress we have made, but now it's time for some heavy lifting. We need to see more of these community-driven district-wide plans, new approaches to elementary schools that can increase diversity even as residential segregation persists, a plan to desegregate the vast majority of our high schools, more ambitious citywide diversity targets to which we can hold ourselves accountable and more resources for culturally responsive education to ensure these schools can succeed.

I am not naïve. We are not going to hold back market forces. I support smart growth and development, even when many of my constituents resist it. And even as I am nostalgic, I like a lot of what is new—even the new "shuffleboard club" in Gowanus (okay, not quite as much as the old slot-car racing track in Kensington)—much of which has been driven by the "creative destruction" of market-led gentrification. I'm not aiming for some ideal society, and I am mindful of the messy consequences of regulation.

But it is not the market that has delivered us Prospect Park, or my kids' public schools, or a livable and walkable neighborhood, or our neighborhood libraries, or the affordable housing units that remain. And it will not be the market—even tempered with some vouchers—that confronts the crisis of inequality and allows our neighborhoods to be shared a little better.

Notes

1. Sean Capperis et al., "State of New York City's Housing & Neighborhoods—2014 Report," NYU Furman Center, 2014, http://furmancenter.org/research/sonychan/2014-report.

2. Adam Sternbergh, "What's Wrong with Gentrification?," *New York Magazine*, December 11, 2009, http://nymag.com/nymag/rss/people/62675/.
3. Fair Housing Act of 1968, 42 U.S. Code § 3608, accessed July 12, 2017, https://www.law.cornell.edu/uscode/text/42/3608.
4. For a recent thorough exploration of the role of federal, state, and local government in engineering residential segregation, see generally Richard Rothstein, *The Color of Law: A Forgotten History of How Our Government Segregated America* (New York: Liveright, 2017). Seminal works also include Dougalas S. Massey & Nancy A. Denton, *American Apartheid: Segregation and the Making of the Underclass* (Cambridge, MA: Harvard University Pres, 1993) and Kenneth T. Jackson, *Crabgrass Frontier: The Suburbanization of the United States* (New York: Oxford University Press, 1985).
5. Fair Housing Act of 1968, 42 U.S. Code § 3608.
6. Lance Freeman, "Neighbourhood Diversity, Metropolitan Segregation and Gentrification: What Are the Links in the US?," *Urban Studies* 46, no. 10 (September 2009): 2079–2101, https://doi.org/10.1177/0042098009339426.
7. Lance Freeman and Frank Braconi, "Gentrification and Displacement New York City in the 1990s," *Journal of the American Planning Association* 70, no. 1 (March 2004): 39–52, https://doi.org/10.1080/01944360408976337; Lance Freeman, "Displacement or Succession?: Residential Mobility in Gentrifying Neighborhoods," *Urban Affairs Review* 40, no. 4 (March 2005): 463–491, https://doi.org/10.1177/1078087404273341; Terra McKinnish, Randall Walsh, and T. Kirk White, "Who Gentrifies Low-Income Neighborhoods?," *Journal of Urban Economics* 67, no. 2 (March 2010): 180–193, https://doi.org/10.1016/j.jue.2009.08.003; Ingrid Gould Ellen and Katherine M. O'Regan, "How Low Income Neighborhoods Change: Entry, Exit, and Enhancement," *Regional Science and Urban Economics* 41, no. 2 (March 2011): 89–97, https://doi.org/10.1016/j.regsciurbeco.2010.12.005.
8. Spike Lee, "Spike Lee's Gentrification Rant—Transcript: 'Fort Greene Park Is like the Westminster Dog Show,' " *Guardian*, February 26, 2014, http://www.theguardian.com/cities/2014/feb/26/spike-lee-gentrification-rant-transcript.
9. Arlo Chase, "Rethinking the Homeownership Society: Rental Stability Alternative," *Journal of Law and Policy* 18 (2009): 61–119.

DISCUSSION 25

COMMUNITY PREFERENCES
AND FAIR HOUSING

An Inclusionary Tool Created by Low-Income
Communities for Low-Income Communities

by Rafael Cestero

When New York City helps finance the construction or renovation of affordable housing, it requires that in half of the affordable units the property developer give a preference to income-eligible residents of the community district where the property is built. Fair housing advocates recently filed a lawsuit against the city, arguing that this community-preference policy perpetuates segregation. Although I share the commitment to furthering fair housing, I believe the lawsuit is misguided and actually threatens an important policy tool in the city's efforts to maintain stable, diverse neighborhoods in the face of continuing gentrification and housing price increases.

In the 1980s, when the city was struggling to improve conditions in neighborhoods that had suffered from disinvestment, it created the community -preference policy in response to demands from low-income residents who insisted on their right to be able to stay put and to benefit from the redevelopment after years of watching the neighborhood's infrastructure and services deteriorate around them. Residents in neighborhoods across the city formed block associations and community organizations to participate in the redevelopment process and to try to ensure that as they worked to improve their neighborhood they wouldn't in turn be forced out by those very improvements.

The community-preference policy reflects a belief that redevelopment is not just about building affordable housing, but about building communities. To rebuild the fabric of a neighborhood, it is essential to start with the people who are there, to recognize the claims of those who want to stay and participate in that redevelopment. The policy was at its creation, and remains now, an important part of assuring community boards and community organizations in low-income neighborhoods that redevelopment is not aimed at removing current residents against their will through new investment but is designed instead to ensure that those residents who want to can stay, participate in redevelopment, and enjoy the benefits of new investment.

As the city's economic fortunes improved and the Department of Housing Preservation and Development (HPD) shifted from seeking to attract investment to creating mixed-income communities and preserving affordable housing in the face of rising market pressures, community preferences became an important tool to prevent displacement. Affordability is now an acute issue in every corner of New York City.

I understand where the fair housing advocates are coming from. Residency preferences have been and continue to be used to exclude lower-income households and black and Latino families from white, wealthy, suburban enclaves. But there are very few neighborhoods in New York City that are the exclusive bastions of the wealthy. And low-income residents of relatively high-income neighborhoods such as the Upper West Side or the Lower East Side are saying that to protect the fabric of the low-income community as rents continue to rise, those neighborhoods are even more in need of community preferences than neighborhoods such as the South Bronx.

New York City differs from most of the rest of the United States in that nearly two-thirds of the city's residents are renters. One factor that has historically made this predominantly rental market work so well in New York City is the stability of residency in the city's communities. In some other localities, people oppose rental housing because they associate it with transiency. Most renters in New York City, however, are not transient. Renters live in the same New York neighborhoods for forty or fifty years—they want to stay there. And that neighborhood stability is an important part of the argument for community preferences that is often overlooked. I may have the same income as another applicant, but if that applicant has lived in the neighborhood for thirty-five years and is facing displacement because of the loss of affordable units, it makes more sense for that long-term resident to be able to remain there and support the stability of the neighborhood's social fabric than it makes for me to be able to move in.

There are pressing concerns related to continuing high levels of metropolitan-area racial and economic segregation. Tearing up New York City's community-preference program, however, will make things worse, not better. Indeed, we should arguably be more focused on the fair housing implications of gentri-fication, on the large numbers of black and Latino households being displaced from neighborhoods with rising economic fortunes, such as Williamsburg or the Lower East Side, through the loss of rent-regulated housing units and other affordable housing. Community preferences play an important role in allowing the residents who have made up the fabric of many New York City neighbor-hoods to remain, and they enable New York City to continue to be the thriving, diverse city we love.

Community Preferences Discriminate

by Errol Louis

New York City is one of the most segregated urban areas in the United States. Indeed, the Civil Rights Project at UCLA recently called New York's schools the "most segregated in the country."[1] This is not surprising given the Uni-versity of Michigan analysis suggesting that the New York metropolitan area is second only to Milwaukee (among metros with a population greater than 500,000) in metro-area black-white residential segregation. As Craig Gurian, who filed the lawsuit that motivated Rafael Cestero's essay defending the city's community-preference policy, points out, "these patterns didn't drop from the sky. The city participated in the creation of segregation; it's obligated to now try to end that segregation."[2]

What Gurian's lawsuit should provoke New York City's progressives to pon-der is whether we are genuinely committed to integrating our city. A truly fair housing policy is one that allows all people access to all of our neighborhoods. The city's community-preference policy works against those values. Maintain-ing 50 percent of a community district's affordable housing for "insiders" is a politically convenient arrangement that ensures black, white, and Latino neigh-borhoods will stay as segregated as they currently are.

Cestero provides a thoughtful critique of Gurian's lawsuit, drawing from his decades of experience advocating for those who have borne the brunt of New York's segregated history, but he hardly takes into account the realities of the city's segregated present and the forces that maintain it. He mentions segre-gation a couple of times, but only in passing—merely to acknowledge that the problem exists. The hard truth is that, contrary to Cestero's arguments, if we are serious about dismantling segregation, we must take on the city's community -preferences policy.

What purpose does the community-preference policy serve? For Cestero, it is about maintaining the "fabric" of a neighborhood when more affordable housing is built there. This is the same sort of "there goes the neighborhood" logic that brought about white flight and has foiled integration for decades. If integration is to happen, neighborhood "fabrics" simply cannot be preserved whole cloth. Most New York City neighborhoods are either less than 10 percent white or less than 10 percent black. That is the fabric of our neighborhoods.

The city's community-preference policy is also patently unfair. Why should half or more of the affordable units in a new development—subsidized by everyone in the city—exclude people who don't happen to live nearby? There is no question that people who have worked to improve their neighborhoods after decades of disinvestment should not be once again forsaken by urban politicians as neighborhoods improve. But the community-preference policy does not touch on the true forces of displacement at work in our city. Cestero may be right to be worried about unchecked gentrification, but gentrification is driven by higher-income individuals, not the construction of more affordable housing. Community preference is a regulation that pertains only to the latter.

The community-preference policy serves to preserve the politically convenient status quo. It allows city officials to overcome anti-affordable-housing NIMBYism in rich white neighborhoods without desegregating them. Politicians of color can embrace the policy because it allows them to preserve their political bases and to win political points for opposing displacement. This status quo is precisely what we need to change if we are to achieve integration. Ending community preferences is no panacea, but it is an important step on the road to dismantling segregation.

The Community-Preference Policy: An Unnecessary Barrier to Minorities' Housing Rights

by Robert G. Schwemm

Housing restrictions that discriminate against "outsiders" in favor of local residents have, as Rafael Cestero recognizes, long been a concern of civil rights advocates. The first successful challenge based on the federal Fair Housing Act (FHA) to such a local-preference rule—imposed by an all-white suburb of Mobile, Alabama—dates back to 1980.[3]

Local preferences imposed by predominantly white communities in racially diverse areas may reflect intentional discrimination.[4] But even if they do not, such preferences invite FHA disparate-impact claims, a long-recognized method of establishing liability that was recently endorsed by the Supreme Court in *Texas Dept. of Housing and Community Affairs v. Inclusive Communities Project, Inc.* (2015). That decision establishes a three-step method of analyzing claims alleging that a policy violates the FHA because it has a disparate impact on a racial minority or other protected class: (1) the plaintiff must first prove that the defendant's challenged policy causes greater harm to the protected class than to others; (2) if the plaintiff meets this burden, the defendant must prove that its policy is necessary to achieve a valid interest; and (3) if the defendant satisfies this burden, the plaintiff can still win by showing that the defendant's interest could be served by an alternative policy with a less discriminatory effect. This is a fair system. It's not designed to displace valid governmental policies, but only, as the Court stated in *Inclusive Communities*, to remove "artificial, arbitrary, and unnecessary barriers" that "function unfairly to exclude minorities from certain neighborhoods without any sufficient justification."[5]

Satisfying the first step is usually easy for plaintiffs challenging a local-resident preference in a community that is less diverse than the surrounding area. As Judge Gertner wrote in an influential 2002 decision in *Langlois v. Abington Housing Authority*, ruling against local preferences by Boston-area suburbs, there is an "overarching intuitive principle" here: "where a community has a smaller proportion of minority residents than does the larger geographical area from which it draws applicants, a selection process that favors its residents cannot but work a disparate impact on minorities."[6]

Thus, a disparate-impact challenge to a local-preference policy generally centers on steps 2 and 3. New York's community-preference policy provides a classic example of how this analysis would work.

Justifications for Local-Preference Rules

The key to a defendant's proving that its challenged policy is necessary to achieve a valid interest is that its justification "must be supported by evidence and may not be hypothetical or speculative."[7] Cestero notes that the city's community-preference policy was originally adopted in the 1980s "in response to demands from low-income residents who insisted on their right to be able to stay put and to benefit from the redevelopment" in their neighborhoods. Today, the same policy is defended on different grounds—that is, as a way of helping to "maintain stable, diverse neighborhoods in the face of continuing gentrification and housing price increases." The policy, Cestero says, builds a sense of community in gentrifying neighborhoods. "To rebuild the fabric of a neighborhood, it is essential to start with the people who are there, to recognize the claims of those who want to stay and participate in that redevelopment."

Two interests are identified here: (1) to protect local residents from being forced out of their neighborhoods by gentrification; and (2) to maintain the stability and "fabric" of those neighborhoods, a process in which keeping local residents is allegedly essential. The first does not so much identify a legitimate interest as engage in circular reasoning; that is, the city's justification for wanting to give an advantage to a certain group is that it wants to help that group.

Again, the 2002 *Langlois* opinion is on point. Judge Gertner there concluded that the defendants could not simply cite the goal of wanting "to make it easier for their residents to keep living in their communities," because this basically just reflects "the very definition of residency preferences. If I accepted these as legitimate justifications, residency preferences in and of themselves would forever justify the disparate impacts that they cause." Rather, she held, "defendants must set forth the reasons why they want the preferences. And it is the reasons that must be legitimate. [Defendants] must offer a record of local conditions and needs that suggests why the residency preferences are necessary, [such as] a fire in the community has left an abnormally high number of residents homeless [or] economic factors have hit the community especially hard—a plant closing, for example."[8]

This brings us to New York's second justification—maintaining the stability of its neighborhoods. Stability is undeniably a legitimate interest. But can New York prove that this interest is "supported by evidence" and "not hypothetical or speculative," as the HUD regulation requires? There are two problems here. One is that the policy has been in place for decades, and its original justification has now changed.

Second and more important, the city has yet to produce any tangible evidence that favoring local residents is needed to maintain stable neighborhoods. (Self-serving statements by residents who've been given preferences over outsiders will hardly suffice.) This lack of evidence is particularly damning here, because New York, having used this policy for more than twenty-five years, should by now have studied it and developed methods for evaluating its effectiveness.

Even if the city could produce such evidence, the real question would be whether its policy is necessary for stable neighborhoods. And this question could only be answered by comparing the stability of New York's neighborhoods with that of other cities' neighborhoods where resident preferences are not used. In the absence of objective supporting evidence, the city's "stable neighborhood" defense is the very essence of a "hypothetical or speculative" justification.

Less Discriminatory Alternatives

Even if local housing authorities were to prevail at the justification stage, the plaintiff might prove that a less discriminatory alternative could serve their interests. Let's consider alternative policies that New York and other cities might adopt to foster neighborhood stability.

One alternative would be to narrow the "size" of the local preferences (e.g., by reducing the portion of locally favored applicants from, say, New York's current 50 percent to 25 percent; or by allowing the policy to continue in certain neighborhoods but not others that, say, have other stability-enhancing factors in place). Courts have looked favorably on such a "tempered approach [that] would still help support local residents in their efforts to maintain their residencies in the defendant communities, while at the same time keeping the strategy from running afoul of the fair housing requirement of no disparate impact."[9]

Another possibility would be to replace a total preference for current residents by giving them a "plus" and allowing outsiders to compete with other "pluses" that demonstrate their commitment to the target neighborhood. The analogy here would be to affirmative action cases where race may be counted as a "plus" but not as the totally determinative factor.

Finally, cities like New York might consider alternative policies that have proved successful in other municipalities with substantial experience in fostering stable and racially diverse neighborhoods. There are numerous examples, one of the most famous of which—Oak Park, Illinois—has been engaged in this process for decades. Cestero argues that "New York City differs from most of the rest of the United States" in certain ways. Perhaps so. But has the city actually studied other places with an eye toward what might be usable in New York? Or is it so parochial that it won't even consider trying to learn from anywhere outside New York?

Conclusion

The Fair Housing Act is legitimately concerned with local-resident preferences, particularly those whose justifications are old or not well considered. Unless proponents of such policies show a greater willingness than New York has yet done to confront the real difficulties posed by these policies, they must expect that their efforts to discriminate in favor of local residents over outsiders will be seen as the kind of "artificial, arbitrary, and unnecessary barrier" to minorities' housing rights that the FHA rightly condemns.

Local Preferences Require Local Analysis

by Sam Tepperman-Gelfant

When it comes to local preferences, local context makes all the difference. While prioritizing a percentage of affordable homes in a neighborhood for local residents could advance fair housing and community stabilization goals in gentrifying neighborhoods, a similar policy would perpetuate segregation and inequality in areas that are already wealthy and predominantly white.

Our fair housing laws are flexible enough to embrace this reality and permit local preferences in some places while prohibiting them in others.

Tectonic shifts are reshaping the geography of opportunity in regions and cities throughout the country. On the West Coast, in the Northeast, and in many other places, long-neglected urban neighborhoods are rapidly gentrifying, and suburban poverty is on the rise almost everywhere. At the same time, more traditional patterns of exclusionary privilege and concentrated poverty persist. These complex dynamics demand comprehensive and nuanced public policy intervention—driven by organizing and power building in low-income communities of color—to increase opportunity for those to whom it has been systematically denied for generations. We must analyze the legal and real-world implications of housing policies against this shifting terrain and embrace local solutions that respond to local challenges.

Not since the postwar period have metropolitan regions undergone structural transformation on this scale. Private tastes, profit seeking, and government policies are again embracing urban living, inundating long-neglected areas in many cities with new buildings, new money, and new residents. For decades, communities of color were effectively trapped in cities gutted by public and private policies such as redlining, white flight subsidized by the interstate highway network and home mortgage interest tax deduction, the dismantling of local transit infrastructure, and the decline in manufacturing and military jobs. Today, however, low-income people of color are being forced out of many of these previously "undesirable" neighborhoods by skyrocketing rents, evictions, foreclosures resulting from racially targeted predatory lending, and militarized police and "private security."

Gentrification and displacement are the new frontier of racial exclusion, and they are driving resegregation of cities and regions. As opportunity increases in urban neighborhoods, people of color are generally forced out to low-opportunity suburbs and exurbs. For example, between 1990 and 2010, San Francisco and Oakland lost 35 percent of their African American residents—84,000 people—while the overall population grew by 9 percent; in Silicon Valley, African Americans declined by 46 percent while the region grew by 16 percent. These refugees have largely landed in far-flung exurbs such as Antioch and Tracy that have limited access to jobs, transit, social services, and other resources. Similar patterns are occurring in many other regions nationwide. The white population increased in nearly half of the fifty largest cities between 2010 and 2014, and a majority of low-income people now live in suburbs. Equally important when considering local preferences is the realization that racialized displacement is also playing out at the neighborhood level, which can be masked by city-level data. San Francisco's Mission District, for example lost 27 percent of its Latino population between 2000 and 2013 even while the city's overall Latino population increased by 13 percent.

The individual and community costs of displacement are well documented. An involuntary move to a new town or even to a new corner of the same city can disconnect people from their families and support systems, make it difficult to get to work and worship, and disrupt the networks that ground community and political power.

To avoid these harms and secure affirmative benefits, many people want a safe, healthy, stable, and affordable home in their current community. A local housing preference can help to achieve this, along with other policies to promote healthier neighborhoods and the opportunity for low-income people to stay in them if they so choose: rent control and just-cause eviction, minimum wages and middle-wage job creation, training and career pathways for people with barriers to employment, local business preservation, restrictions on conversion of apartments into condominiums or hotels, community-directed infrastructure investments, and affordable-housing production strategies, to name just a few.

In this context, local housing preferences can be a powerful tool to help stabilize communities and promote fair housing and integration. Gentrification often brings new housing development, mostly for wealthier newcomers, and new jobs—highly paid white-collar jobs for those with advanced degrees and a larger set of low-wage retail, service, and support jobs for the rest. Given the persistent correlations between race, income, and education, these patterns often mean that white residents are flooding into neighborhoods that have previously been home to a mix of nonwhite populations. While the influx of white professionals into neighborhoods of color might appear to be creating integrated neighborhoods, this is likely to be true only for a short period of time before the process culminates in wholesale displacement and resegregation. In such cases, local housing preferences can help anchor communities of color that are at risk and promote stable integration over the long term.

Notably, neighborhood preference policies should, and do, include safeguards to balance community stabilization and open access. They universally apply to only a percentage of affordable homes in a neighborhood, helping ensure that they do not unduly restrict mobility or individual choice. Moreover, the number of people given priority access can be increased in ways that respond to real community needs and increase the size and diversity of the applicant pool. Local low-income workers, not just residents, should generally be given preference. And in places where some displacement has already taken place, it makes sense to include former residents as well as current ones.

We must also remember that local preferences can easily be misused in places with exclusionary histories and current practices to deny people of color equal access to opportunity. In affluent white neighborhoods and suburbs, local preferences are likely to perpetuate segregation; they should be examined closely and are likely to run afoul of the law.

A locally responsive approach to evaluating local preferences is fully consistent with fair housing laws, which are designed to promote integration and equal opportunity, not to mandate a one-size-fits-all set of housing policies. A sound neighborhood preference policy should take this into account, perhaps by permitting local preferences only in areas with below-median income and/ or only when a neighborhood currently meets some minimum threshold of racial diversity.

Given the shifting ground in metropolitan regions across the country and the very real danger that we are moving toward renewed segregation—only this time with low-income people of color relegated to the outskirts, as they already are in many regions globally—it is vital that all tools, including local housing preferences, be considered and deployed strategically to anticipate and head off such an outcome while we still have the chance.

Notes

1. John Kucsera and Gary Orfield, "New York State's Extreme School Segregation: Inequality, Inaction and a Damaged Future," Civil Rights Project, March 2014, https://files.eric
.ed.gov/fulltext/ED558739.pdf.
2. Errol Louis, "How NYC Perpetuates Segregation," *New York Daily News*, July 14, 2015, http://www.nydailynews.com/opinion/errol-louis-nyc-perpetuates-segregation-article
-1.2291024.
3. United States v. Housing Auth. of Chickasaw (S.D. Ala. 1980).
4. United States v. Town of Oyster Bay (E.D. N.Y. 2014).
5. Texas Dep't of Hous. & Cmty. Affairs v. Inclusive Communities Project, Inc., 135 S. Ct. 2507 (2015), 2522–2524.
6. Langlois v. Abington Hous. Auth., 234 F. Supp. 2d 33, 62 (D. Mass. 2002).
7. HUD's Discriminatory-Effect Regulation, 100.500 (b)(2) Title 24: Housing and Urban Development PART 100—DISCRIMINATORY CONDUCT UNDER THE FAIR HOUSING ACT Subpart G—Discriminatory Effect Electronic Code of Federal Regulations § (2016),—, http://www.ecfr.gov/cgi-bin/text-idx?SID= ab45e89458e9c2ea96667e90d8fe429a&mc=true&node=se24.1.100_1500&rgn=div8.
8. *Langlois*, 234 F. Supp. 2d at 70.
9. *Langlois*, 234 F. Supp. 2d at 70.

CONCLUSION

We hope that readers come away from these discussions learning as much as we have from their wide variety of perspectives. Collectively, they offer a number of insights and lessons. First, they highlight some important areas of consensus about racial and economic segregation. There is agreement that over the past few decades, black-white segregation has fallen in the United States, Latino-white and Asian-white segregation have remained relatively constant, and economic segregation has risen. Both poor and wealthy households are living in more economically homogenous communities than twenty or thirty years ago.

There is also consensus that rising income segregation is driven in part by the growth in income and wealth inequality that has occurred over the past few decades. As the gap between the poor and the rich has grown, their ability to pay for housing has widened as well, leading neighborhoods to become more stratified at both ends of the income distribution. A growing chorus also points to the significance of local land-use regulations in exacerbating rising income segregation. These restrictions, which localities can use to restrict both the amount and type of housing development, combined with the fact that local governments in the United States bear much of the responsibility for funding schools and other critical local services, both incentivize and facilitate economic segregation. There is generally more debate about the causes of racial segregation, but there is an emerging consensus that the residential choices of white households play a significant role in perpetuating the high levels of racial segregation that continue to characterize most U.S. metropolitan areas.

As for consequences, we have mounting evidence that neighborhood environments shape the life chances of children. Poor children who grow up in high-poverty neighborhoods fare less well educationally and economically as young adults than do poor children who grow up in more economically integrated neighborhoods.

Second, the discussions point to areas of continuing debate. For example, there is considerable disagreement about the nature of the residential preferences of white households, and to what extent those preferences are driven explicitly by a neighborhood's racial composition. There is also disagreement about the extent to which gentrification may contribute to racial and economic integration and how stable any such integration will be. As for consequences, while we have mounting evidence about the costs that poverty concentration imposes on the poor, there is less consensus about the harms of racial and ethnic segregation, though most of the contributors who address the issue conclude that segregation perpetuates racial inequality by often constraining children of color to live in neighborhoods with fewer resources. We also need to better understand the costs that segregation imposes on society as a whole by cutting off opportunities for economic and social interactions.

Perhaps the greatest disagreement surfaces when we consider policy responses. Most fundamentally, some contributors question whether governments should actively intervene in the market to encourage integration rather than simply policing antidiscrimination laws. But even those who agree that there are grounds for government intervention disagree about the appropriate goals. Should the aim be to equalize public resources across neighborhoods or to integrate neighborhoods themselves? Further, there is disagreement about the best means to achieve either of those ends.

There is much to learn from pinpointing where exactly people disagree. Some of these disagreements are rooted in normative judgments, while others concern facts and thus lay out an important agenda for future research. For example, we need more research to understand the pathways through which segregation may undermine the opportunities of children of color and children who are poor. Given limited resources, what types of neighborhood improvements should we prioritize? Should the focus be on public safety, schools, or access to transportation and jobs? Or should the focus be fostering a mixing of incomes? We also need more experimentation and research to understand the types of policy reforms that can break down barriers and afford households a broader array of residential choices.

Finally, and most fundamentally, these discussions highlight the value of debate itself. They show how much we can learn in conversation with people with different viewpoints. The contributors model the dialogue and disagreement that is essential to academic learning as well as civic discourse. There is still much to learn about segregation, but in the meantime, we need to continue not just to talk to each other, but to engage more deeply in reasoned debate about why people live where they do, what that means for people's lives, and what constitutes an appropriate and effective role for government action.

CONTRIBUTORS

Dolores Acevedo-Garcia is the Samuel F. and Rose B. Gingold Professor of Human Development and Social Policy at Brandeis University and director of the Institute for Child, Youth and Family Policy at the Heller School for Social Policy and Management, Brandeis University.

Scott W. Allard is a professor in the University of Washington's Evans School of Public Policy and Governance with expertise in the areas of social welfare policy and poverty.

Michael Allen is a partner at the civil rights law firm Relman, Dane & Colfax.

Roger Andersson is a professor in Social and Economic Geography in the Institute for Housing and Urban Research (IBF) at Uppsala University, Sweden. His research covers the dynamics and effects of residential segregation and policies aimed at reducing it.

Nancy O. Andrews is the former chief executive officer at the Low Income Investment Fund (LIIF).

Mariana C. Arcaya is an assistant professor of urban planning and public health at the Massachusetts Institute of Technology (MIT) School of Architecture and Planning.

Patrick Bayer is a professor of economics at Duke University and research associate at the National Bureau of Economic Research.

Ben Beach is the legal director at the Partnership for Working Families.

Monica Bell is an associate professor of law at Yale Law School.

Alan Berube is a senior fellow and deputy director at the Brookings Institution Metropolitan Policy Program and coauthor of *Confronting Suburban Poverty in America*.

Kendra Bischoff is an assistant professor of sociology at Cornell University.

Angela Glover Blackwell is founder and CEO of PolicyLink, a national organization advancing racial and economic equity.

Lawrence Bobo is the W. E. B. Du Bois Professor of the Social Sciences at Harvard University. He holds appointments in the Department of Sociology and the Department of African and African American Studies.

Michael Bodaken is the president of the National Housing Trust.

Erin Boggs, Esq. is the executive director of Open Communities Alliance, a Connecticut-based nonprofit that promotes access to opportunity in partnership with an urban-suburban interracial coalition.

Raphael Bostic is the president and CEO of the Federal Reserve Bank of Atlanta; he was previously the Bedrosian Chair on Governance and the Public Enterprise at the Price School of Public Policy at the University of Southern California.

Anthony A. Braga is a distinguished professor and director of the School of Criminology and Criminal Justice at Northeastern University's College of Social Sciences and Humanities.

Sheryll Cashin is the Carmack Waterhouse Professor of Law, Civil Rights and Social Justice at Georgetown University Law Center. Her contribution to this volume includes material excerpted from her previously published book, *Place Not Race: A New Vision of Opportunity in America* (Beacon Press, 2014).

Rafael Cestero is the president and chief executive officer of the Community Preservation Corporation (CPC) and its for-profit development subsidiary, CPC Resources, Inc.

Camille Zubrinsky Charles is the Walter H. and Leonore C. Annenberg Professor in the Social Sciences, Departments of Sociology and Africana Studies, and Graduate School of Education at the University of Pennsylvania.

Robert J. Chaskin is professor and deputy dean for strategic initiatives and holds the UNESCO Chair for Inclusive Urbanism at the University of Chicago School of Social Service Administration.

Ngina Chiteji is an associate professor at the NYU Gallatin School of Individualized Study.

Charles Clotfelter is the Z. Smith Reynolds Professor of Public Policy Studies and a professor of economics and law at Duke University.

Rob Collinson is a doctoral fellow at the NYU Furman Center and a third-year doctoral student at the NYU Robert F. Wagner Graduate School of Public Service.

Philip J. Cook is the Terry Sanford Professor Emeritus of Public Policy and a professor of economics and sociology at Duke University.

Stefanie DeLuca is an associate professor of sociology at the Johns Hopkins Krieger School of Arts and Sciences.

Richard A. Epstein is the Laurence A. Tisch Professor of Law at the New York University School of Law, the Peter and Kirsten Bedford Senior Fellow, the James Parker Hall Distinguished Service Professor of Law (Emeritus) and a senior lecturer at the University of Chicago, and the director of the Classical Liberal Institute at New York University.

Jacob Faber is an assistant professor of public service at the NYU Robert F. Wagner Graduate School of Public Service.

Jeffrey A. Fagan is an Isidor and Seville Sulzbacher Professor of Law at Columbia Law School and professor of epidemiology at the Mailman School of Public Health at Columbia University.

Rachel Fee is executive director of the New York Housing Conference.

Lee Fennell is the Max Pam Professor of Law at the University of Chicago Law School.

Patrice Alexander Ficklin is fair lending director at the Consumer Financial Protection Bureau.

Jose F. Figueroa is an instructor of medicine at Harvard Medical School and an associate physician at Brigham and Women's Hospital.

Richard Florida is university professor and director of the Martin Prosperity Institute at the University of Toronto's Rotman School of Management, global research professor at NYU, and senior editor at the *Atlantic*, where he is cofounder and editor at large of *CityLab*.

Richard Ford is the George E. Osborne Professor at Stanford Law School; previously, he was a Reginald F. Lewis Fellow at Harvard Law School, a housing policy consultant for the city of Cambridge, Massachusetts, and a commissioner of the San Francisco Housing Authority.

Lance Freeman is a professor in Urban Planning at Columbia University and is the author of *There Goes the Hood: Views of Gentrification from the Ground Up*.

George Galster is the Clarence Hilberry Professor of Urban Affairs, Emeritus, at the Department of Urban Studies and Planning, Wayne State University, and the author of *Driving Detroit*.

Edward Glaeser is the Fred and Eleanor Glimp Professor of Economics at Harvard University and former director of the Rappaport Institute for Greater Boston.

Sherry Glied is the dean of NYU Robert F. Wagner Graduate School of Public Service, where she is also a professor of public service.

Rachel D. Godsil is the Eleanor Bontecou Professor of Law at Seton Hall University School of Law and is a cofounder and research director for a national consortium of social scientists and law professors focusing on the role of implicit bias in law and policy.

Edward Goetz is a professor in the Humphrey School of Public Affairs and director of the Center for Urban and Regional Affairs at the University of Minnesota.

Adam Gordon is associate director and staff attorney at the Fair Share Housing Center and cofounder of *Next City* magazine.

Solomon J. Greene is a senior fellow in the Center on International Development and Governance and the Metropolitan Housing and Communities Policy Center at the Urban Institute.

Christina M. Greer is an associate professor of political science at Fordham University.

Rosanne Haggerty is the president and chief executive officer of Community Solutions.

Glenn Harris is president of the Center for Social Inclusion. He previously served as manager of the Race and Social Justice Initiative for the city of Seattle, Washington.

Thomas B. Harvey is the national director of strategic partnerships and advocacy for the Bail Project. He was previously the executive director of ArchCity Defenders, a nonprofit civil rights law firm in St. Louis, Missouri.

Nathaniel Hendren is an assistant professor of economics at Harvard University and a principal investigator of the Equality of Opportunity Project.

Sandra B. Henriquez is the chief operating officer of Rebuilding Together, Inc., the former assistant secretary for public and Indian housing at the U.S. Department of Housing and Urban Development, and former chief executive officer of the Boston Housing Authority.

Jennifer Hochschild is the Henry LaBarre Jayne Professor of Government and a professor of African and African American Studies at Harvard University.

Ellen Lurie Hoffman is the federal policy director of the National Housing Trust.

Robin Hughes is the president and CEO of Abode Communities.

Jackelyn Hwang is an assistant professor in the Department of Sociology at Stanford University and a faculty affiliate at the Center for Comparative Studies in Race and Ethnicity.

Sherrilyn Ifill is the president and director-counsel of the NAACP Legal Defense and Educational Defense Fund, Inc.

Paul A. Jargowsky is a professor of public policy at Rutgers University–Camden and director of the Center for Urban Research and Education.

Alan Jenkins is president and cofounder of the Opportunity Agenda.

Olatunde Johnson is a professor of law at Columbia Law School; her area of expertise lies at the intersection of housing, race, and poverty.

Rucker C. Johnson is an associate professor of public policy at the University of California, Berkeley, and a faculty research associate of the National Bureau of Economic Research. His work considers the role of poverty and inequality in affecting life chances, and he is author of the forthcoming book Children of the Dream: Why School Integration Works.

Mark L. Joseph is the Leona Bevis and Marguerite Haynam Associate Professor of Community Development at Case Western Reserve University and the director of the National Initiative on Mixed-Income Communities.

Robert Kaestner is a professor in the Institute of Government and Public Affairs of the University of Illinois and a professor in the Department of Economics at the University of Illinois at Chicago; he is also a research associate of the National Bureau of Economic Research. Dr. Kaestner's areas of research interest are the economic and social determinants of health, health demography, and health, labor, and social policy evaluation.

Richard D. Kahlenberg is a senior fellow at the Century Foundation.

Jerry Kang is the inaugural vice chancellor for equity, diversity, and inclusion at the University of California, Los Angeles (UCLA). He is also a professor of law, professor of Asian American Studies, and the inaugural Korea Times–Hankook Ilbo Chair in Korean Studies and Law.

Micere Keels is an associate professor in the Department of Comparative Human Development, a member of the Committee on Education, and a faculty affiliate with the Center for the Study of Race, Politics and Culture at the University of Chicago.

Nicholas F. Kelly is a PhD student in urban studies and planning at the Massachusetts Institute of Technology (MIT).

Desmond King is the Andrew W. Mellon Professor of American Government at the University of Oxford. His books include *Making Americans: Immigration, Race and the Origins of the Diverse Democracy* (2002), *Separate and Unequal: African Americans and the US Federal Government* (2007), and, with Rogers M. Smith, *Still a House Divided: Race and Politics in Obama's America* (2011).

Carol Lamberg is the former executive director of the Settlement Housing Fund.

Brad Lander is a New York City Council member representing Brooklyn's Thirty-Ninth District and the council's deputy leader for policy.

Michael Lens is an associate professor of urban planning and public policy and associate faculty director of the Lewis Center for Regional Policy Studies at the Luskin School of Public Affairs at the University of California, Los Angeles (UCLA).

Errol Louis is a CNN political commentator and the host of *Inside City Hall*, a nightly political show on NY1, a New York all-news channel.

Demetria McCain is president of the Inclusive Communities Project.

Chris McCrudden is Professor of Human Rights and Equality at Queen's University Belfast, and the William W. Cook Global Law Professor at the University of Michigan Law School.

John Mollenkopf is a Distinguished Professor of Political Science and Sociology at the CUNY Graduate Center and director of its Center for Urban Research.

Stephen Norman is the executive director of the King County Housing Authority, serving the suburban Seattle metropolitan region, and president of the Council of Large Public Housing Authorities (CLPHA).

Katherine O'Regan is a professor of public policy and planning at the NYU Robert F. Wagner Graduate School of Public Service and a faculty director of the NYU Furman Center for Real Estate and Urban Policy. She served as the assistant secretary for policy development and research at the U.S. Department of Housing and Urban Development from 2014 to 2017.

Dennis Parker is the director of the American Civil Liberties Union Racial Justice Program.

Mary Pattillo is the Harold Washington Professor of Sociology and African American Studies at Northwestern University. Her areas of interest include race and ethnicity (with an emphasis on class stratification), urban sociology, and qualitative methods.

Rolf Pendall is an Institute Fellow at the Urban Institute. His areas of expertise include metropolitan growth trends, land-use planning and regulation, racial residential segregation, and the concentration of poverty.

Georgette Chapman Phillips is the Kevin L. and Lisa A. Clayton Dean of the College of Business and Economics at Lehigh University and a professor in both the Perella Department of Finance in the College of Business and Economics and in the Africana Studies Program in the College of Arts and Sciences.

John A. Powell is a professor of law and African American and ethnic studies at the University of California, Berkeley. He is the director of the Haas Institute for a Fair and Inclusive Society.

Sean F. Reardon is the endowed Professor of Poverty and Inequality in Education at the Stanford Graduate School of Education.

Dan Rinzler is senior policy analyst at the California Housing Partnership Corporation.

Stephen. L. Ross is a professor of economics at the University of Connecticut.

Richard Rothstein is a research associate of the Economic Policy Institute and senior fellow of the Chief Justice Earl Warren Institute on Law and Social Policy at the University of California, Berkeley, School of Law.

James Ryan is dean and professor of education at the Harvard Graduate School of Education.

Robert J. Sampson is the Henry Ford II Professor of the Social Sciences at Harvard University and founding director of the Boston Area Research Initiative at the Radcliffe Institute for Advanced Study.

Richard Sander is an economist and professor of law at the University of California, Los Angeles (UCLA) School of Law and the coauthor of *Moving Toward Integration*.

Barbara Sard is the vice president for housing policy at the Center on Budget and Policy Priorities (CBPP).

Robert G. Schwemm is the Ashland-Spears Distinguished Professor at the University of Kentucky College of Law.

Patrick Sharkey is a professor of sociology at New York University. His research focuses on urban inequality and violence, and he is the author of *Uneasy Peace: The Great Crime Decline, the Renewal of City Life, and the Next War on Violence*.

Alina Schnake-Mahl is a scientific doctorate candidate at the Harvard T.H. Chan School of Public Health.

Denise Scott is the executive vice president for programs at Local Initiatives Support Corporation.

Susan Ann Silverstein is a senior attorney with the AARP Foundation Litigation.

Jeff Smith is an assistant professor of politics and advocacy at the New School for Public Engagement and a former Missouri state senator from St. Louis.

Robert Smith is an assistant professor of law at the University of North Carolina at Chapel Hill; he previously served as the legal and policy adviser to Harvard Law School's Charles Hamilton Houston Institute for Race and Justice (CHHIRJ).

Jorge Andres Soto is the director of public policy at the National Fair Housing Alliance.

Michael A. Stoll is a professor of public policy in the Luskin School of Public Affairs at the University of California, Los Angeles (UCLA).

Cheryl Staats has conducted research at the Kirwan Institute for the Study of Race and Ethnicity at the Ohio State University focusing on how unconscious associations can contribute to societal inequities.

Todd Swanstrom is the Des Lee Endowed Professor of Community Collaboration and Public Policy Administration at the University of Missouri–St. Louis.

Philip Tegeler is the executive director of the Poverty and Race Research Action Council (PRRAC).

Sam Tepperman-Gelfant is a senior staff attorney at Public Advocates Inc., a nonprofit law firm and advocacy organization.

J. Phillip Thompson is an associate professor of urban planning and politics at the Massachusetts Institute of Technology (MIT).

Christopher M. Tinson is director of the African American Studies program and associate professor of history at Saint Louis University.

Gerald Torres is the Jane M. G. Foster Professor of Law at Cornell University and is a leading figure in critical race theory, environmental law, and federal Indian law. He previously served as the president of the Association of American Law Schools and the Bryant Smith Chair in Law at the University of Texas School of Law.

Margery Austin Turner is senior vice president for program planning and management at the Urban Institute. Her areas of expertise include urban policy and neighborhood issues.

Lawrence J. Vale is the Ford Professor of Urban Design and Planning at the Massachusetts Institute of Technology (MIT).

Jon Vogel is vice president of development at AvalonBay Communities, a real estate investment trust (REIT) that develops, acquires, and manages apartment communities in select markets in the United States.

Sheryl Verlaine Whitney is a partner at Whitney Jennings. She was previously the deputy county executive of King County, Washington, and a consultant to HUD on its Affirmatively Furthering Fair Housing regulation review.

Diane Yentel is president and CEO of the National Low Income Housing Coalition.

INDEX

opportunities of, 81; African Americans and, 239; geography of, 342; high-opportunity areas, 233, 237, 265, 270, 272; high-opportunity neighborhoods, 250, 300, 306, 310; job opportunities, 283; lower-opportunity areas, 235; lower-opportunity neighborhoods, 304; low-poverty, high-opportunity areas, 301; neighborhood opportunity, 49; opportunity hoarding, 62; poverty and, 222; rental, 310; in U.S., 282. *See also* Moving to Opportunity
Opportunity Agenda, 213
O'Regan, Katherine M., 12, 13, 63, 205
Oregon Medicaid Experiment, 174
Orfield, Gary, 34, 73, 78
Orfield, Myron, 68
out-of-wedlock birth, 281

Pager, Devah, 122
parents, 81
Parents Involved in Community Schools v. Seattle School District No. 1, 78, 84, 260
Parker, Dennis, 202
Park Slope (Brooklyn), 331, 333
parochialism, 197, 341
partisan polarization, 259, 261
party politics, 44
paternalism, 278, 279, 288
patriarchy, 197
Pattillo, Mary, 23, 24, 32, 34, 40, 230, 244
PD&R. *See* Office of Policy Development and Research, HUD
Pendall, Rolf, 203
people of color, 249–250, 344; economic shocks and, 179; exclusion of, 110; implicit biases against, 125; in poverty, 68; subprime lending and, 212, 215; in suburban areas, 67
people-oriented strategies, 247
person-based interventions, 243, 251
Pettigrew, Thomas, 34
place-based interventions, 243, 244, 246, 251, 285n17; benefit from, 278; next generation of, 245
place-based investment, 109, 233
place-based subsidized housing, 209
Plaut, Victoria, 123
Plessy v. Ferguson, 3, 15n5

police, 84, 142, 147, 157; bias by, 156; brutality, 150, 158; implicit bias and, 122; militarized, 342; murders by, 136, 141, 243; new policing, 153–154, 157; NYPD, 159; policing practices, 136–137; problem-oriented policing, 158
policy intervention, 251
policy investments, 246
PolicyLink, 240
political clout, 326
political impoverishment, 151
political terrorism, 3
Pollack, Craig, 299
poor doors, 206, 287, 289, 292, 294
poor households, 63
poor housing quality, 303
populism, 262
postindustrial knowledge economy, 247
poverty, 24, 36; among African Americans, 71; antipoverty assistance, 69; children in, 282; compounded deprivation and, 251; concentration of, 22, 23, 25, 26, 46, 61, 236, 265, 276–277; concentration of, societal processes that create and sustain, 62, 64; deconcentration of, 58, 181, 280; differentiating experiences of, 250–251; extreme, 57, 111, 245, 300, 301; in Ferguson, Missouri, 142; gaps, 107; health and, 167, 172; high-poverty communities, 305; high-poverty neighborhoods, 63, 226, 270, 271, 277, 280, 299; high-poverty schools, 102, 103, 204; Latinos in areas of concentrated poverty, 112; low concentrations of, 307; lower-poverty neighborhoods, 281, 302; low-poverty, high-opportunity areas, 301; low-poverty areas, 207–208; low-poverty neighborhoods, 271, 278, 309, 310, 316; multigenerational, 82; national debate about, 272; opportunity and, 222; people of color in, 68; persistent, 248; poverty line, 81; poverty traps, 154; race and, 73, 81; racial segregation and, 38; schools and concentrations of, 79; spatial distribution of, 61; stigma of, 30; in suburban areas, 26, 68, 69, 342; urban poverty, 69, 279; voluntary poverty deconcentration, 237; War on Poverty, 233; zoning and concentration of, 73